In the City

In the City

Paul Du Noyer

Published by Virgin Books 2009

2 4 6 8 10 9 7 5 3 1

First published in Great Britain in 2009 by
Virgin Books
Random House, 20 Vauxhall Bridge Road,
London SW1V 2SA

www.virginbooks.com
www.rbooks.co.uk

Addresses for companies within The Random House Group Limited can be found at:
www.randomhouse.co.uk/offices.htm

The Random House Group Limited Reg. No. 954009

A CIP catalogue record for this book is available from the British Library

ISBN 9781905264605

The Random House Group Limited supports The Forest Stewardship Council (FSC), the leading international forest certification organisation. All our titles that are printed on Greenpeace-approved FSC-certified paper carry the FSC logo. Our paper procurement policy can be found at www.rbooks.co.uk/environment

Mixed Sources
Product group from well-managed
forests and other controlled sources
www.fsc.org Cert no. TT-COC-2139
© 1996 Forest Stewardship Council

FSC

Typeset by TW Typesetting, Plymouth, Devon
Printed and bound in Great Britain by CPI Mackays

To my two little Londoners

Contents

Preface   ix

1   **What Anarchy and Din**   1

2   **Ginger, You're Barmy!**   23

3   **There Were Angels Dining at the Ritz**   45

4   **More in Soho than in Ongar**   69

5   **Smashing Time**   93

6   **Male West One**   116

7   **Dartford, Alabama**   139

8   **Oh! You Pretty Things**   166

9   **Guttersnipes**   198

10   **Every Day is Like Friday**   227

11   **Innit?**   261

Afterword   281

London's Brilliant Parade: 140 Recommendations   283

Sources and Acknowledgements   307

Index   313

Preface

And so we commence our descent into London. Belts have been securely fastened and seat backs are in the upright position. A velvet blackness spreads below, strung with the orange dots of sodium lamps which trace the ancient trackways, the Roman roads and 1970s motorways. Their curves delineate forgotten river courses, medieval field patterns, royal hunting forests, Victorian parks and post-war council estates.

This is London, all right. But it's not London. Beyond the dull roar of the aeroplane's engine, it's entirely silent. That's not right. Down there the London we know is never silent.

A thousand years ago there were two kinds of music in London. There was the formal art created for church and palace. And there were the popular tunes of the streets, to be played at fairs and bawled in taverns. Marvellous music was made at both ends of the spectrum. But it's the everyday tradition that I'm celebrating here: the music of the people. Popular songs have been the perfect expression of London's character.

When I first came to this city many years ago, I had never met a Londoner. The train pulled out of my home town, Liverpool, past the welcoming slogan daubed for visiting football fans – 'Cockneys Die'. Would I find anything friendlier when I reached Euston?

In fact I found a real welcome in London, though it took a while to recognise. I was already won over by the Kinks, David Bowie and the Small Faces. Soon there would be Ian Dury, the Sex Pistols and the Clash. Over the years these artists, and many more besides, revealed to me the soul of a busy, outwardly indifferent city. In the twenty-first century I'm hearing new music as thrilling as anything that's gone before.

Every time I return to London – by train, or plane or automobile –I am excited to be back. Back in the city. And when I leave again, I take its fabulous music with me.

Paul Du Noyer

2009

Chapter One

What Anarchy and Din

Early street music. Ancient songs of drunkenness and cruelty. And the monk who invented swinging London.

Pity the peasant troubadour arriving in London with his heritage of village folk songs. The rustic newcomer, however musical, had picked a hell of a place to compete with. Even in the Middle Ages, five centuries before electricity and the combustion engine, London was extraordinarily noisy. Music could not be mellow if it hoped to flourish. A German observed of London in 1598 that the inhabitants were 'vastly fond of great noises that fill the ear, such as the firing of cannon, drums, and the ringing of bells'.

To those we can add the appeals of beggars and the diverse honking of livestock en route to market. There were horse-drawn butchers' wagons, rattling over cobblestones, and dung-carts and brewers' drays. From the menagerie of the Tower came the roaring of tigers and, at one period, the yapping of a two-legged dog. Early street-cleaning was the preserve of natural scavengers, of ravens and kites who swept down – shrieking – for scraps, while half-wild pigs, squealing and grunting, feasted on offal and filth.

Amid its magnificent forest of steeples, London possessed a clamour of church bells, commemorated by the town's most famous nursery rhyme ('Oranges and lemons, say the bells of St Clement's . . .'). When drunk, which was often, Londoners rushed up the towers and let loose the bell-ropes. The same bells summoned Dick Whittington to turn back from Highgate Hill, to meet his destiny as

Lord Mayor. The Great Bell of St Mary-le-Bow in Cheapside supplied the very definition of a cockney. Bells are so evocative of the city they have been employed by the Kinks ('The Big Black Smoke'), the Small Faces ('Lazy Sunday') and the Clash ('Clash City Rockers'). Broadcasters have long understood the power of Big Ben. Ding-dong ding-dong ... Bong. Bong. Bong.

London was for much of its history the largest city on earth. Through it poured more wealth, and blared a greater cacophony, than anyone had ever known. As if that were not enough, it seemed to be forever catching fire and burning itself to cinders.

Yet the wet River Thames, the so-called 'silent highway', was hardly a respite. Its sides were lined with forges and factories, often of the smelliest as well as the loudest sort, grinding forth by night and day. On the water were literally thousands of craft, pausing to load or unload their goods with a maximum of fuss. Its main crossing was London Bridge, whose twenty close-spaced arches sluiced the torrent into a colossal and frequently lethal tumult. The Thames' celebrated swans, protected by royal decree, proclaimed their status with ear-splitting pride.

The Thames watermen, ancestors of the London taxi-driver, shouted, 'Oars! Oars! Will you have any oars?' They had a famous custom of bellowing obscenities at one another. Every year about fifty of them perished in the murderous churn of London Bridge alone; they doubtless let off a few more oaths as they did so. When the Kinks sang of a 'dirty old river' at Waterloo, when blues bands alchemised the songs of slavery at Eel Pie Island or the Sex Pistols clashed with policemen on Jubilee evening, the Thames was only reprising its old role of dramatic arena.

Music had to be loud, or else get drowned out. Drunk or sober, Londoners sang lustily. From the fabric of their everyday lives came the songs of street traders and topical balladeers – purveying the sounds of commerce and observation. Instruments favoured in Shakespeare's time were the tabor drum, and the pipe or penny-whistle. There followed the concertina and the fiddle, though these were considered crude and best fitted for taverns. Later there were the inescapable organ grinders (often with chattering monkeys) hauling or wheeling their wheezing, handle-operated boxes. In time there were minstrel troupes and vagabond hollerers, 'Ethiopian serenaders' and German brass bands.

No wonder the sensitive writer de Quincey consoled himself by gazing at the tranquil farmland still visible from nineteenth-century Oxford Street. As recently as 1885, another writer was plagued by the relentless nature of all this mayhem: 'that blatant and horribly noisy instrument of dissonant, unchangeable chords, the German concertina,' he groaned. And 'the ringing of church bells in the grey of the morning'. And 'men and women who find their principal and unmolested amusement in the shouting of music hall songs'. By that time there were fewer itinerant street-traders (''Ere's yer toys for girls an' boys!'). But there were newer elements in the mixture, like the railway porters' calls of 'Train to Emma Smith!' (Hammersmith) or 'Change at Chairin' Krauss!' or 'This line for Monneym'nt!' The old broadside balladeers were gone but here instead were the cockney newsboys: 'Speshill 'dishun! 'Orrible railway haccident!'

Discouraging for the country troubadour, perhaps. But this city would produce an amazing abundance of song. With such a racket to overcome, London music could not afford to be dreamy. Commerce and observation were the great stock-in-trade of city song. Money and news, in other words, are where the story of London's popular music really begins. And, in some curious fashion, they've been central ever since. The racket of London was duly overcome. Money and news demand to be heard.

Brother Rahere: the First Swinging Vicar

Long before rock 'n' roll, there was St Bartholomew's Fair. If London's entertainment business has a formal beginning, it could be here. In 1133 one Brother Rahere, an Augustinian friar, was allowed by Henry I to stage a three-day fair in aid of the priory and hospital he had established in Smithfield. Rahere had once been a lively member of Henry's court, a minstrel and something of a jester. Now, in what remained of his life, he resolved to answer some higher calling. Yet he kept up his old skills, even juggling in his religious robe (which proved a crowd-pleaser), and Bartholomew's Fair grew as famous for its revels as for its merchandising.

Smithfield in those days was a massive open space on the fringe of the city. It was ideal for performances in front of large crowds and Rahere oversaw the rapid expansion of the phenomenon he had created. He died around 1143, but his tomb remains in the ancient Priory Church of St Bartholomew the Great (as used in *Four Weddings and a Funeral*), tucked between his other monument, Bart's Hospital, and the ancient Meat Market. In the nineteenth century his tomb was opened and the body found intact, but a parish official filched one of its sandals and Rahere is said to haunt the place as a result. It was no way to treat the founder of London's live music industry.

Smithfield prospered as a place where animals were butchered and criminals executed. And Bartholomew's Fair rolled on, every August, down the centuries. As well as traders and performers there were drunks, thieves, harlots in profusion, naive bumpkins and cunning urchins. Ballad singers were much in evidence – 'ballads' being story songs, not the softly romantic numbers of modern times – and some vocalists operated with pickpocket accomplices. As an old song records:

> Let not the ballad singer's shrilling strain
> Amid the swarm thy listening ear detain
> Guard well thy pocket, for these syrens stand
> To aid the labours of the diving hand.

Under Charles II the Fair was extended from three to fourteen days and the London theatres closed for that time while actors took to Smithfield's stages. In a manner characteristic of London, it co-mingled the highest and the lowest in the land. But it was not to everyone's taste:

What a hell
For eyes and ears! what anarchy and din
Barbarian and infernal . . .

So lamented William Wordsworth in 1805, recoiling from the 'grimacing, writhing, screaming', from the hurdy-gurdies, fiddles and kettle-drums, 'and him who at the trumpet puffs his cheeks'.

This was not a good review, it must be said. In fact, educated sentiment was now against the vulgar urban uproar of Bartholomew's Fair. It was finally suppressed in 1855. But it foreshadowed the 'variety' bills of the pleasure gardens, the music halls and post-war television. Hippies have dreamed of resurrecting its spirit in festivals and carnivals. Puritans detested it, of course, but the unruly part of London's soul may yet invent a successor.

Songs for the Stage, the Gallows and the Royal Fireworks

We know the music of the medieval churches and palaces because it was written down. But popular music was not. So we rely upon eyewitnesses, or look to literature, to get a general idea. Geoffrey Chaucer, the fourteenth-century sage, knew and relished the rough-and-tumble of London streets, but was also equally at home in elevated circles. He was above all a thorough Londoner, to whom nothing was alien and everything happened with musical accompaniment. The harp was his favourite. In *The Canterbury Tales* the brawny Miller plays bagpipes as the pilgrims exit town. Absalon, his parish clerk, danced and sang in taverns, playing his rebec (a kind of tiny violin) or that forerunner of the guitar, the gittern.

The point about taverns – which we will see are important to our story, from music hall to pub rock – is that they were linked, not only to drunkenness, but gambling, fighting and lechery. Thus does London's popular music, the music of the common people, begin to find its level in civic life. It is somewhere near the bottom. It is much less than respectable.

Theatre music would be important, too. It's impossible to miss the strain of sheer *showiness* in London song, whether it's *The Beggar's Opera*, Noël Coward or Adam Ant. (We find among the pop stars of London a huge proportion of stage school brats.) London's music is theatrical because its very streets are a sort of stage. The earliest performances were staged on the South Bank, or to the east, just outside the City's jurisdiction. (Theatre, like popular music, has had an uneasy relationship with authority.) Shakespeare, of course, had his Globe across the Thames in Southwark. And like the resourceful adopted Londoner he was, he stuffed his plays with borrowed music.

'Let the sky rain potatoes! Let it thunder to the tune of Greensleeves!' cried Falstaff in *The Merry Wives of Windsor*. Even in 1602 that song was already venerable. Shakespeare was not a composer. He did what other playwrights and the street balladeers did, adapting old tunes to his purpose, providing new words when he needed them. Thus, among many more: 'Where the Bee Sucks' (*The Tempest*), 'It Was a Lover and His Lass' (*As You Like it*) and 'Journeys End in Lovers Meeting' (*Twelfth Night*). His audience was raucous, not reverential, and good tunes were a prized aspect of the entertainment. He gave stage directions for oboes, drums and trumpets, and there was surely a tune being played as Duke Orsino spoke: 'If music be the food of love, play on . . .' Even a tragedy such as *Julius Caesar* was rounded off with a jig – the communal dance that brought an audience back into itself, perhaps with a welcome touch of life-affirming crudity.

Shakespeare's contemporary, the poet and dramatist Thomas Dekker, published a ballad in 1603 called 'Golden Slumbers', rediscovered by Paul McCartney in 1969 and set to music for the Beatles' *Abbey Road*. (That album has another Elizabethan echo – its finale 'Her Majesty' ends in a rhyming couplet, as McCartney's nod to Shakespearean practice.)

Many religious masterpieces were created in those days, too. They were not, perhaps, *of* the people, as ordinary hymns and carols were. But they entered the common consciousness. During the Reformation and its aftermath the composers of such pieces worked before a background of royal magnificence, courtly intrigue, persecution and terror. Perhaps the greatest was Thomas Tallis (1505–1585) whose forty-voice motet, 'Spem in Alium', still amazes. He was said to have written it for the fortieth birthday of Elizabeth I; what is certain is that he was a royal servant who understood the importance of pleasing your listeners. Music had to switch from 'Catholic' to 'Protestant' styles at the monarch's whim. William Byrd, a student of Tallis, rivalled him in genius, and navigated the treacherous waters of London's religious wars with some courage, as annoying the powerful was liable to get you killed. His fellow Catholic John Dowland, the melancholy creator of songs so enduring they've been covered by Sting (*Songs from the Labyrinth*) and Elvis Costello ('Can She Excuse My Wrongs'), had to rebut charges of treason.

Music to no one's ears, least of all its intended recipient, was the doleful song of the clerk of St Sepulchre's church. On the eve of executions he crossed the road to Newgate Gaol, and with a bell in his hand performed prayers and pleas for repentance under the windows of condemned cells. (The church still stands, despite the Blitz, but Newgate duly made way for the Old Bailey. Nearby are Smithfield and Rahere's ghost.) His serenade continued:

All you that in the condemned hole do lie,
Prepare you for tomorrow you shall die . . .
And when St Sepulchre's Bell in the morning tolls
The Lord above have mercy on your souls.

The wretches in question had one more role to play for London's entertainment. Their slow, three-mile procession to the place of death took them via Holborn and Oxford Street to Tyburn (now Marble Arch) where an expectant throng of thrill-seekers was waiting. Here, as we shall see, canny vendors sold souvenir ballads about the dying.

Being the seat of monarchy and the venue for state occasions, London learned the ways of grandeur and spectacle. Royal associations with music have been abiding. Centuries before the Beatles received their MBEs at Buckingham Palace, or Diana swooned to Duran Duran, the most musical of our rulers was Henry VIII. He was tutored in music for the church until the death of his brother Arthur made him heir to the throne. He played all the while and is known to have composed at least thirty-four pieces. It's thought unlikely that he really earned the credit for 'Greensleeves', perhaps the country's most enduring folk song. But who was to argue with him? It only foreshadows the tactic of a later king, Elvis Presley, who sometimes took a slice of his songwriters' copyrights. (Indeed the term 'royalties' began as shorthand for the sovereign's rights.) Henry does not disappear from our story entirely: he reappears in popular song in 'I'm Henry the Eighth I Am', a smash success in Victorian music halls and on 1960s jukeboxes.

Public entertainments were curtailed under Puritan rule (1642–1660), but blossomed again with the Restoration and Charles II, when London's theatres assumed the physical appearance we know today. One night in 1668, Samuel Pepys went to see *The Virgin Martyr* and was struck with feeling by the music (played on recorders) and the erotic vision of Charles's special friend, the actress Nell Gwynn: 'I could not believe,' he wrote, 'that ever any music hath that real command over the soul of a man as this did upon me.'

Momentous public events were scored by composers of genius. Henry Purcell wrote for the opera and for Westminster Abbey – he was born and died within its shadow – and excelled at state occasions. From 1689 to 1695 he wrote the annual birthday music for Queen Mary, which became keenly anticipated. Poignantly, a few months after 1695's offering, he sat down again to compose the music for her funeral, music of ineffable sadness, the chill of its mourning preserved with sinister iciness in Walter Carlos's movie theme to *A Clockwork Orange*.

A little later, for the really big day out in eighteenth-century London, Handel was your man. In 1717 he penned *The Water Music* for George I, performed upon a royal sailing from Lambeth to Chelsea. So enraptured was His Highness that the musicians were engaged to turn their barge around and play it again going back. The secular pageantry of coronations and regal firework parties were as much in Handel's line as devotional masterworks such as *The Messiah*. A German who became quite thoroughly English, he lived for nearly forty years in Brook Street, Mayfair. The house next door would one day be the home of another imported musical legend, Jimi Hendrix.

Who Will Buy? Songs of Commerce and Gore

As a newcomer to the capital I noticed how middle-class Londoners would turn slightly cockney when they spoke of (a) betting odds or (b) second-hand cars. There was something in those subjects – money, I suppose – that awoke their inner spiv.

'STAIN-DAD! STAIN-DAD!' was the first cry that I heard on arriving, issuing from a cloth-capped vendor of the evening newspaper. Nowadays we might encounter 'BIGISHOOO. Help the homeless. Gob-bless.' These are mere relics of what was formerly the city's mightiest symphony. Commerce is the soul of London and street sellers are the heartbeat of its musical history.

Particular trades, like shoemakers or tailors or barbers, had their own songs, and practitioners drummed up custom from their doorways. Cheapside, the city's oldest High Street, must have been a polyphonic spree. But the majority of merchants were itinerant, employing their distinctive calls in search of business. Doubtless some such cries were beautiful but a large number have gone down in history as being horrible. The traders' cries were much collected, anthologised and illustrated with varying degrees of hard realism and sentimental prettifying. (Apple-cheeked maids with lavender baskets have always made for popular prints.) Among innumerable books, *Old London Cries* is a diligent record, though careless of chronology. ('Dates, unless in the form of the luscious fruit of Smyrna, are generally dry,' its author sniffs.)

In an issue of the original *Spectator* brought out in 1711, the essayist Joseph Addison wrote his 'Proposal for the Control of Street Cries', an offer to curb the singers and instrumentalists who spread so much dismay. 'A freeman of London,' he wrote, 'has the privilege of disturbing a whole street for an hour together, with the twinkling of a brass-kettle or a frying pan.' Vocal styles were 'full of incongruities and barbarisms'. Milk was sold with a high, grating note. Chimney sweeps went erratically up and down the 'gamut', or musical scale. A friend, he reports, once bribed a match-seller to give his street a miss – only to be accosted by every other match-seller, demanding a similar tax. News stories were trumpeted with wild drama, regardless of their relative importance. And turnip-men from the shires bellowed with excessive zeal.

Surprisingly, the sow-gelder's horn was deemed pleasant (though the sow's opinion may have differed). The barrel-menders sang in a slow, harmonious way. The picklers of dill and cucumber were agreeable to hear, as was a pastry-man called Colly-Molly-Puff. Samuel Pepys noted these poetic cries: 'Here's your rare socks, four pairs a shilling!'; 'Dumplins! Dumplins! Diddle diddle, dumplins ho!'; and 'Buy my fat chickens!' But many vendors could not be understood by their words, only by their tunes. It's alleged that ignorant country boys ran out 'to buy apples of a bellows-mender, and gingerbread from a grinder of knives and scissors'.

The musicality of the traders was sometimes striking. There must have been a bittersweet pleasure in hearing this example:

Old chairs to mend, old chairs to mend,
If I'd as much money as I could spend
I'd leave off crying old chairs to mend.

The girls who sold the produce of hedgerows and market gardens were themselves hymned in song:

Here's fine rosemary, sage and thyme.
Come buy my ground ivy.
Here's fetherfew, gillyflowers and rue.
Come buy my knotted marjoram ho!
Let none despise the merry, merry wives
Of famous London town.

Yet the undisputed star of this daily production was a gingerbread salesman of Mayfair, named Tiddy Doll. He was quite the dandy and famous for his ditty, 'Mary, Mary, where are you now, Mary?' He ended with the old tune, 'Ti-Tiddy ti-ti, tidy tiddy doll.' In a Hogarth etching of 1747, Tiddy Doll is pictured among the crowds at Tyburn, selling his wares while the Idle Prentice is hanged. Nearby, a woman does brisk business with already-printed copies of the dying man's alleged speech. In fact, Tiddy's own demise was equally sensational – he plunged through the ice at a fair held on the frozen Thames.

Street markets survive in London that offer an echo of those times. They are a precious element of continuity. In the 1920s H. V. Morton observed pre-hippy Portobello Road, finding it without the sly cleverness of Petticoat Lane, but still rich in English qualities of Elizabethan ribaldry and frankness, with rough costermonger wit. (Of the 'costers' we will learn more shortly.) The style of Berwick Street in Soho, he thought, evoked the exotic Orient. The markets were essentially forms of outdoor theatre, where people went not merely to buy, but to enjoy the spectacle of being sold to. Like theatres, they were for years at their busiest on Saturday night, that being pay-day. Time and again we will see the influence of these markets on London's best-known performers.

Of all the multifarious trades sung upon London's streets, the most compelling was the trade in songs themselves. Street balladeers performed entire compositions, not mere advertising jingles. But they were not busking, as such. They sang to draw attention to their printed lyrics, their 'broadsides', available at competitive prices (if printed on more than one side they were called 'broadsheets'). Pepys, naturally, adored the ballads and organised them into a grand collection under sundry headings: 'History – True and Fabulous'; 'Drinking & Good Fellowshipp'; 'Marriage, Cuckoldry, &c'. All human life was there. Unsurprisingly the Puritans banned it (though their radical wing contained some hearty singers, forefathers of Billy Bragg) but business revived under the Restoration. Thereafter it would thrive until the nineteenth century, when mass literacy and cheap newspapers would usurp the broadsides' news function, while their entertainment role passed to the music halls.

Ballads told stories, and stories, true or imagined, need story-tellers. Yet the writers of ballads are mostly unknown to us. Singers normally worked for a publisher, the biggest being Jeremy Catnach in Seven Dials (Covent Garden's infamously vice-ridden slum), who set up there in 1813. He paid his writers one shilling per ballad, just for the words. As for music they simply recycled old folk tunes, familiar to everyone, and added topical verses. Thus the purchasers of 'Ann Wallen's Lamentation, for the Murthering of her Husband John Wallen' were told to sing it to the tune of 'Fortune My Foe'. It ends upon a moral note, as they often did: Ann begs her mother-in-law's forgiveness and concludes, 'In burning flames of fire I should fry/Receive my soule sweete Jesus now I die.'

The sheer quantity of ballads is staggering. They poured forth in their thousands. Many still exist, countless others have been lost to time. An 1861 report tells of one London firm having half a million ballads on its files. It goes on to give an interesting early use of the term 'hit': 'When a ballad makes a real hit, from 20,000 to 30,000 copies of it will go off in a very short time.' This was the foundation, of course, for the sheet music trade, which itself led to the modern music industry.

Ballads might be subversive and satirical, or pious and uplifting, or vulgar or twee or full of derring-do. For the most part they were telling you a yarn and keeping you up to date. To that extent, they set the pattern for London pop for centuries ahead, from Marie Lloyd to Madness, from Vera Lynn to Dizzee Rascal. Narrative and news value are great staples of the city's songwriting. Above all they are commodities. London is not in the business of not doing business.

Like the later music hall, and tabloid newspapers after that, ballads were a contradictory bundle of patriotism and nose-thumbing. One of the earliest surviving news-songs celebrates the downfall of politician Thomas Cromwell in 1540. In *King Lear*, Shakespeare quotes from William Birch's ballad 'A songe between the Quenes majesty and Englande', an imagined love duet between

Elizabeth ('Bessy') and her country. A foreign observer reported of Londoners in 1792: 'Love of their homeland and warlike valour are common themes of their ballads and folk songs, sung in the streets by women selling them for a few farthings ... Yet the scorn of the people for their King goes to astonishing lengths.'

Every event of the day, be it parliamentary proceedings or royal scandals and weddings, found its way into London ballads. A song of 1785 summarises and comments caustically on William Pitt's latest Budget. In the Napoleonic wars, recalled one writer, 'No battle was fought, no vessel sunken or taken, that the triumph was not published, proclaimed in the national gazette of our Ballad-singer.'

But the best sales were for murder ballads – the gorier the better. Execution reports were hardy perennials, presenting a mix of straight reporting, macabre sensationalism and moral lesson. 'A Warning to False Traitors' commemorates the extermination of six unfortunates at Tyburn on 30 August 1588. As typical was 'Jack the Chimney Sweep' who recalls his life and crimes, is told in Newgate that he'll drink no more brown ale, and finally takes that terminal ride down Holborn, pausing for refreshment at St Giles. Various versions exist, all drawn from Jack Hall's execution at Tyburn in 1707 for robbing a house at Stepney.

Death was a money-spinner. As one lyricist explained, 'I write most of the Newgate ballads for printers up in the Dials. I get a shilling for a "copy of verses written by the wretched culprit the night previous to his execution".' It was surely a blow to this honest trade when public hangings were abolished in 1865. The modern music industry would probably have campaigned in protest: 'Private executions are killing music.'

The wide-eyed countryman, new in town, was another much-loved theme. The singer of 'Bumpkin's Journey to London' finds himself in bed, undressed by an apparently friendly lady, but then 'the baggage hopp'd off with my money and cloaths'. In 'Dice, Wine and Women' (a forerunner, really, of Ian Dury's 'Sex and Drugs and Rock 'n' Roll') the luckless visitor from Cornwall is robbed in various districts, finally 'stript' and forced to go home. The story will find its echoes in everything from the calypsos of West Indian immigrants to the Jam's 'Strange Town' – not omitting George Formby Snr's 'Looking for Mugs in the Strand'. In 'The Humours of London', a singer of the 1790s declares:

> When I to London first came in
> How I began to gape and stare!
> The cries they kick'd up such a din
> Fresh lobsters, dust, and wooden ware.

Charles Dickens, in *Great Expectations*, has a character singing 'When I Went to Lunnon Town, Sirs', possibly modelled upon 'The Astonished Countryman, or, A Bustling Picture of London':

> When I first came to London Town
> How great was my surprise
> Thought I, the world's turned upside down
> Such wonders met my eyes.

Actual street performers were part of the scene from earliest times. Their 'minstrelsy' might be sung in a capella form or played upon instruments, where they could be afforded. There were 'chaunters' who sang and sometimes played fiddle. Popular tunes were 'Red Cross Knight' and 'Hail, Smiling Morn'. With the practical attitude of his profession, one chaunter confided: 'The very best sentimental song that I ever had in my life was Byron's "Isle of Beauty". I could get a meal off that quicker than with any other.'

Barrel-organs and wandering musicians of all sorts (not to mention church bells) were a special torment to Charles Dickens. And in the 1850s the great social chronicler Henry Mayhew found 'Italian organ boys, French singing women, the German brass bands, the Highland bagpipe players . . .' He divided musicians into those skilful enough to earn donations and those so bad they were paid to go away. Some were clearly no good but used the music to draw attention to their afflictions. Most could not read music and were thus unfit for theatre work, but some achieved a high standard. The wind-instrument players were said to have shorter lives than their string-playing counterparts, owing to their greater 'need' for liquid refreshment.

As recently as 1933 George Orwell, in his *Down and Out in Paris and London*, found street singers called 'chanters'. Less prestigious were the itinerant hymn singers whose craft, like the unskilled 'screevers' or pavement artists, was merely a way to dodge the anti-begging laws. As matters stood, complained Orwell, a beggar might be arrested for soliciting money – but if, instead, he assaulted our ears with a horrible howling, he could claim to be following his legitimate trade.

Organ-grinders, says Orwell, took up position outside cheap pubs (the grander ones chased them away). One such artist, Shorty, sent a one-legged man inside to collect the money. Having collected, it was a point of pride to give an 'encore', to assert they were not being paid to vanish. Organ-grinders faced less competition from German bands after the Great War, and a lot of them were in fact ex-servicemen. They 'rattle their boxes,' said a 1925 account, 'with a determination that the discordant Teuton never dared.'

Another class of street performers were the 'patterers', who lived off ingenuity and believed themselves 'the aristocracy of the street sellers'. Often educated men, who looked down upon lesser trades, they purveyed stationery, pamphlets and song sheets, but elaborated by improvising speeches – 'patter' was the London slang for talk – such as accounts of 'barbarous and horrible' murders, duels and deathbed confessions. The patterers had their private language or 'cant', of which 'crib' for home and 'toff' for gent are notable survivors. Their act was a blueprint for stage artists. The smart-alec 'patter man' became a staple of cockney variety shows – his descendants are, perhaps, in hip hop.

Mayhew made note of a further type, the Punch and Judy man, whose self-esteem was just as high. He too had his own 'good speech': *bona palare*. 'This is a broken Italian and much higher than the costers' lingo,' one insisted. 'We know what o'clock it is, besides.' Their *palare* would in time enter theatrical and camp circles while other terms, such as *donna* for woman, were adopted by the East End generally.

One musician told Henry Mayhew how street performers found the City a hard place to work, too preoccupied by business, but leisurely and 'low' parts of town offered richer pickings. Evenings in Oxford Street and Regent Street, St James's Park on Saturday nights, Whitechapel, Smithfield, Fitzroy Square and 'Carnaby-market' were all worth a punt. But 'Tottenham Court Road's no good at any time,' he added, mysteriously.

'See the Show, Sir?' Music Moves Indoors

'Proper' music was once reserved for the church and nobility. But there came a trend to attract the middle classes – and make a business of it into the bargain. In the 1670s a man named John Banister, one of Charles II's musicians, put on concerts in his house every day at four o'clock. This was not theatre, nor was it opera; it was just the simple presentation of music in its own right. Around the same time, a Clerkenwell coal dealer, Thomas Britton, used a loft above his premises to stage weekly recitals. The idea caught on fast. It meant that formal music could now be enjoyed by those not rich enough to employ their own musicians.

So London's popular music was becoming an organised form of indoor entertainment. Another production of that era, charging 'an English shilling the pitt', foreshadows the age of variety shows. Comprising opera, 'pleasant Dialogues and Commical Dances', its musical numbers ranged from patriotic ('Genius of England') to sombre ('O Land Me in Some Peaceful Gloom') to bright ('Let All Be Gay'). The dialogues sound affecting: 'Since Times are So Bad' and 'Oh! My Poor Husband'. In 1772 during the reign of George III, there opened at 58 Charlotte Street the King's Concert Rooms, later renamed the Scala (not to be confused with its namesake at King's Cross). Numerous re-buildings afterwards, and six years before its final demolition, it was the TV theatre in the Beatles' *A Hard Day's Night*.

Meanwhile, down at the White Horse on Fetter Lane, we witness something very like the Victorian music hall in embryo: spectators are allowed to smoke and drink (indeed their drinks are the only price of admission) while they enjoy 'posture makers and tumblers ... comical fancies ... One plays with a rolling-pin upon a salt-box, another grunts like a hog, and a third makes his teeth chatter like a monkey; and thus they each have something to make the Million laugh, and put common sense out of countenance.'

'Silence!' came the president's command. Rising importantly, he would strike the table three times with his hammer, proposing a toast before the entertainments could begin.

And there was panto ...

Pantomime survives all alterations in English life. Its blend of music, farce and fairy tale seems unstoppable. The formula was developed in London at the Lincoln's Inn Fields Theatre, where the actor-manager John Rich adapted an old Italian tale of Harlequin and Columbine. About a century later, in the 1806 panto *Harlequin & Mother Goose*, Joseph Grimaldi enjoyed immense fame for his song 'Hot Codlins' – concerning, as it does, a gin-soaked street seller, it was a quintessential London number. The nineteenth-century essayist Leigh Hunt saw the origins of panto's stock characters in Italian folklore, but found them now turned into distinct London stereotypes: 'The Clown is a London cockney, with a prodigious eye to his own comfort and muffins, a Lord Mayor's fool, who loved "everything that was good" and Columbine is the boarding-school girl, ripe for running away with, and making a dance of it all the way from Chelsea to Gretna Green.'

Vastly popular in the nineteenth century were the 'minstrel' acts – pseudo-black performers in burned-cork make-up. However deplorable to modern eyes, these 'Ethiopian serenaders' were a mainstay of the London streets (and soon its concert halls) from the 1820s onward. Their style emanated from the slave states of America, where companies such as that of Edward Christy took authentic Negro songs and gave them jolly, sentimental or comical twists for white audiences, normally to banjo accompaniment. 'Jim Crow' and

17

'Buffalo Gals' were great favourites, followed by 'Dandy Jim of Carolina', 'Black-eyed Susannah' and 'Going Ober de Mountain'. Far from dying out, the minstrel idea migrated to theatres, thence to Hollywood (reaching its apogee in Al Jolson) and even television – George Mitchell's *Black & White Minstrels* survived in England as mainstream viewing into the 1970s. Against their obvious naivety and degrading aspects, we should acknowledge that, for some Londoners, early minstrel songs were their first inkling of an unknown folk art, and led them to actively seek out the real thing. From such peculiar beginnings, London's appetite for genuine African-American music grew phenomenally, and would in time transform rock culture.

There had been for years a blending of 'high' with 'low' art. Composers and educated observers took an interest in folk songs and street music. William Playford, for instance, was clerk to the Temple church and vicar-choral at St Paul's; in 1651 he published *The Dancing Master* which used traditional themes. Yet when Addison praised the old song 'Chevy Chase', believing the common people drew from it a wisdom comparable to Virgil, he was mocked. The great poet William Blake would not have mocked. For all his vast, if idiosyncratic, learning he much preferred the popular music of the streets. He loved the tavern ballads of his time. His poem 'Jerusalem' was posthumously made into a song, but in Blake's mind it may have been a song already. Even on his deathbed he sang spontaneously of Heavenly visions. For William Blake, London itself was always a facade, in front of something mystic and eternal.

Mack the Knife in Newgate: *The Beggar's Opera*

The artful mixing of high and low art proved a smash hit in 1728. In that year John Rich, the great promoter of pantomime, backed a playwright called John Gay. The latter's latest work, *The Beggar's Opera*, was so stupendously successful that 'it made Gay rich and Rich gay'. More than that, they had probably invented the musical as we know it.

The Beggar's Opera is where the story of London's popular music becomes coherent. There were already musical dramas, or operas, to be had. But they were rather heavy weather and apt to be foreign; their core audience was well-to-do. The beauty of John Gay's brainchild was that it drew from well-known ballads for its score, and the real life of the city for its theme. Aristocrats, merchants and guttersnipes were all satirised within it, and Londoners of all types flocked to savour the experience. Unprecedented and vivid, this was popular art in the fullest sense – closer to Rich's pantomime than to the oratorios of Handel, but sharing the scabrous wit of the Restoration comedies that preceded it. This was an age of theatre as blood sport, when supporters of rival divas or *castrati* might fight tooth and claw. Gay wrote for an audience both raucous and participatory.

Money and news, the undying London interests, are central to *The Beggar's Opera*. Gay was a genial Devonian who conceived, perhaps abetted by his friends Jonathan Swift and Alexander Pope, of a satire against Robert Walpole's corrupt government, and the low-born scoundrels whose behaviour mirrored it. Of several scurrilous ladies, Jenny Diver was a pickpocket ('diver' being slang for that trade) based upon one Mary Young. In the highwayman Macheath, we have a classic cockney type, the villain as celebrity. Like Shakespeare, Gay took his music ready-made. There are sixty-nine airs in the play, of which forty-one were broadside ballads. His song of the gallows, 'Upon Tyburn Tree', was set to the tune of 'Greensleeves'; the famous 'Highwayman's Chorus' was lifted from Handel.

It's an especially London aspect of *The Beggar's Opera* that everything and everyone appears to be for sale. Perfumed nobs and grimy mobs are pressed together in moral squalor. Even as we enjoy the pageantry of wealth we are not taken in. The city is a huge game of deception, each against all, but there to be played. There is no romantic love or real friendship, virtue is negotiable: 'All men are thieves in love and like a woman the better for being another's property.' The wit seems cynical, but I would rather say sceptical and worldly – aware of humanity's imperfections and alive to their entertaining possibilities. The moral is to keep your wits about you. As befits a London parable, there is much upon the solace of 'strong waters' (that is, drink). And nothing is so popular as a good hanging.

The premiere was staged by John Rich at Lincoln's Inn Fields. Playing Polly Peachum, the robber's moll, the actress Lavinia Fenton so bewitched the Duke of Bolton that he made her his duchess. Gay's life was transformed by the play's success, but he lived for only four more years to enjoy it. Over time *The Beggar's Opera* outgrew its satiric purpose and became a story loved in its own right. Numerous revivals have included a film starring Laurence Olivier and Stanley Holloway and a TV version with Roger Daltrey of the Who and Bob Hoskins. In 1928, Bertolt Brecht and Kurt Weill rewrote it as *The Threepenny Opera*, from which we get the saloon bar classic 'Mack the Knife' – Mack being our old friend the highwayman Macheath. Of Gay's girls, Jenny Diver is still in there, along with Suky Tawdry and Lucy Brown. Strange to hear their eighteenth-century Smithfield names on the lips of Frank Sinatra at Las Vegas.

A feature of *The Beggar's Opera* is the way its story advances both in dialogue and song. Although there was nothing much like it in the decades that followed, it was certainly on the minds of Gilbert and Sullivan, 150 years later, whose own productions were the prototype of the modern musical. Broadway and Hollywood, therefore, owe their art to a tale of knaves and harlots in Newgate and Westminster.

Of Strong Drink and Pleasure Gardens

A folk song of unimaginable age, versions of 'London Bridge is Falling Down' have circulated for many centuries. In fact, Londoners themselves have been falling down for many centuries. From Chaucer's ale-house to Amy Winehouse, London music has frequently been tipsy – it's a traditional refuge from the hustling city's incessant concern with business.

Prior to the rise of music halls, commoners could always find entertainment in public houses. It was not necessarily welcome. In

1580 one Stephen Gosson complained: 'London is so full of unprofitable pipers and fiddlers, that a man can no sooner enter a tavern, than two or three of them hang at his heels, to give him a dance before he departs.' These were buskers, really, whose annoyance might be compared to piped Muzak or an inferior jukebox. Another customer, Sir John Hawkins, grimaced to hear 'half-a-dozen fiddlers' scraping interminably 'till themselves and their audience were tired; after which as many players on the hautboy would in the most harsh and discordant tones grate forth "Greensleeves", "Yellow Stockings", "Gillian of Croydon" or some such common dance tune.'

Just as London music was taken with a drink, it was very often *about* drink. In Shoreditch at the Curtain Theatre, in about 1610, we hear 'The Man in the Moon Drinks Claret' – praise for the grape by William Basse (whose other line was in topical ballads, like 'The Death of Prince Henry, 1613' and 'On Mr William Shakespeare, Who Died in April 1616'). 'Rich wine is good, it heats the blood,' William Basse declared. 'It makes an old man lusty, the young to brawl.' Having to sing so much of drink, we cannot blame the musicians who did a little research. In a 1628 survey of London's human types, 'The Trumpeter' and 'The Common Singing Men' were singled out for their drunkenness. Of the former it was written, 'The Sea of Drinke, and much wind make a storme perpetually in his Chekes, and his look is like his noyse, blustering and tempestuous.' As to the latter, they were 'a company of good Fellowes, that roare deep in the Quire, deeper in the Taverne . . .'

Londoners liked to enjoy their music outdoors sometimes, especially to the west along the river, where the air was sweeter than the muck you breathed elsewhere. On the opposite shore, where Waterloo Bridge now runs, there was Cuper's Gardens. From the 1630s until 1760 it supplied Londoners with arts and diversions, much as its South Bank successor does today. But disrepute befell Cuper's Gardens. By the time it lost its liquor licence it was informally known as Cupid's Gardens, a resort of low women and men no better. Popular music then, as now, had undertones of impropriety.

On the Thames itself, a big pleasure boat called *The Folly* was moored midstream near Cleopatra's Needle. Pepys, who enjoyed his wine, women and song, went there in 1688. Needless to say it acquired a reputation for vice.

Over at Vauxhall was the New Spring Garden. Until Westminster Bridge was built in 1750 you had to be rowed across. With the eclipse of Puritan prohibitions, Restoration types sailed over to frolic among its groves and lanterns. Re-named Vauxhall Gardens, it staged spectaculars such as a performance of Handel's *Music for the Royal Fireworks* before 12,000 people. Yet, rather like television, from high-brow aspirations it declined to cheap populism. It hung on until 1859. A little earlier, in 1836, Charles Dickens strolled about and heard the song of Mr Bedford – 'the first half-hour of which,' he drily noted, 'afforded the assembly the purest delight.' Everyone's a critic.

Ranelagh Pleasure Ground opened in 1742 on the present site of Chelsea's Royal Hospital Gardens (and the Flower Show). Offering food, drink and the usual entertainments, it was even bigger than Vauxhall. Cremorne Gardens was just upriver, where Lots Road Power Station came to be, and was entered from the King's Road. From the 1840s it featured music, fireworks and balloon ascents, as well as arbours, bowers, grottoes and fountains. By an 1869 account, regrettably, Cremorne was unsavoury after dusk, falling to those same low women and men no better. The Victorians shut it down eight years later.

But they could not shut down the taverns. The London pub matters a great deal to this story. From it there came the great leap forward that we shall now investigate, the wonderful popular art form of music hall. We hear the welcome sound of door-bolts sliding back. Opening-hour has arrived.

Chapter Two

Ginger, You're Barmy!

Who were the costers? The rise of the music halls. Gilbert, Sullivan and the girl who'd never had her ticket punched before.

Nineteenth-century London was spreading far beyond the sound of Bow Bells. New streets obliterated old farms and gasworks claimed the grounds of rich men's villas. Market gardens disappeared; railway trains rattled over drained marshes and grubbed-up woodlands; backyards and brick-fields lined the way. Formerly distant villages were swallowed whole, like rabbits in the belly of a python. The London we inherited from the Victorians has been called 'a horse-drawn Los Angeles'. It was diffuse where it was once compact. Almost nobody lived in the original City any more – the Roman nucleus was a business district now. Surprisingly, the term 'East End' is no older than the 1880s, born of a growing need to distinguish London's many parts.

The West End was the best end, and certainly more fashionable. The various suburbs aspired at least to respectability. But the East End was different. Here were the docks, the crowded hovels of the poor and the desperate refuge of immigrants. It was a foul, smoky place, worsened by the noxious industries of the Thames. The east was a place to stay upwind of, like the plague-prone City had been. As London winds are in general westerly, you therefore built your town house in Soho, or Marylebone, and then in Mayfair, Kensington or Belgravia. If you desired the country life, you might go further and try the artistic colony of rural Chelsea.

'Cockney' had been a name for anyone from old London, when the Bow Bells of Cheapside could be heard by all. Now it became reserved to the East End and similar districts across the river, like Bermondsey, Southwark and Lambeth. A new, industrial London was emerging, and the proletarian cockneys were its special urban tribe. These huddled, hard-working masses had to have something. And in time they did. The cockneys had their music hall.

The halls were not entirely new. The 1820s had their 'song and supper rooms', like the Coal Hole in the Strand and the Cyder Cellars in Maiden Lane. In the 1840s Charles Dickens and William Thackeray frequented Evans' Music & Supper Rooms in King Street, Covent Garden; formerly it was known as Evans Late Joys, meaning it used to be Joys' Hotel. Behind its fine facade they set about steaks and ales while the star turn, Sam Cowell, would tackle 'The Rat Catcher's Daughter'. (Like Dickens's streetwise Sam Weller, of *The Pickwick Papers*, Cowell had the common cockney way of confusing his 'v's and 'w's.) More than a century later the same walls sheltered the disc jockey John Peel and hippies of the Middle Earth Club. The frontage stands to this day, by the Piazza.

There had been for centuries (as we've seen) a type of street performer who worked the taverns. Landlords began to regularise this by setting aside a part of their premises. Some say the first true music hall was the Star, in Bolton, Lancashire, opened in 1832. It may be so, but London would dominate the genre by sheer force of numbers. By the 1850s the Canterbury Arms, in Lambeth's Westminster Bridge Road, had a purpose-built extension, a 'singing room', where men might take their wives. Legislation like the Theatres Act of 1843 led to a distinction between the 'legitimate' drama houses, where smoking and drinking were curbed and formal art performed, and the much freer, lightly supervised saloons.

Thus the Grapes Tavern in Southwark dubbed its new saloon the Surrey Music Hall. Further east, just beyond the Tower of London, stood the Prince of Denmark pub whose landlord, John Wilton, built a wonderful room behind it – on its opening in 1859 he claimed it was 'the handsomest hall in town'. Wonderfully, after many misadventures, Wilton's Music Hall survives to this day. So does the Eagle pub in City Road, so renowned that it featured in the rhyme 'Pop Goes the Weasel'. The new halls' bill of fare was often called 'variety'. (In America the preferred term was 'vaudeville'.) As well as singers there were comics, jugglers, illusionists, acrobats and memory men. But music was, as 'music hall' suggests, forever at the heart of it. The singer and the song trumped all else.

You ate and you drank, of course, and early halls were laid out like canteens, before the trend towards more formal theatres. A standard hall could take over a thousand spectators, whether at long wooden tables or standing at the bars or in the balconies. Running proceedings was an extroverted 'chairman' whose job it was to urge consumption as well as audience participation. An act would wait in the wings to hear his voluble introduction, and certain chairmen were not above being bribed to embolden their prose. The audiences at these drinking dens were mainly men and mostly very young, usually under twenty-five. Indeed there was an amount of generational warfare involved. Poor Charles Pooter, the Holloway clerk of the Grossmiths' *The Diary of a Nobody*, was daily pained and mystified by his son's swaggering quotations from music hall numbers of the day: 'What's the matter with Gladstone? He's all right!' and so on.

Most stars had humble origins. Harry Champion sang frankly of his salary: 'Now I'm getting eighty quid a week for doing this: *You can't help laughin', can yer?*' An act might perform three or four shows a night at different theatres. The sets need not vary much – crowds got cross if denied what they expected. Sentiment veered between Chartist dissent and hearty patriotism. Public moods are mercurial. 'The mob' is by definition fickle and London's mob was an age-old symbol of unpredictability. Music hall could be the satire of guttersnipes, funny and scurrilous. Or it might, especially in wartime, turn boisterously loyal. But it was nearly always scornful of pomposity.

Three 'artistes' (as acts now liked to style themselves) dominate the mid-Victorian music hall. Bessie Bellwood (1857–1896) was a rabbit-skinner from Bermondsey. That she became a formidable presence on the boards we have no doubt. Her response to a heckler, a coal-heaver with whom she'd had a six-minute slanging match, was reportedly so fierce and all-encompassing ('so sharp,' wrote an observer, 'with insight into his career and character, so heavy with prophetic curse') that the audience passed through shocked silence into a tumult of frenzied acclamation. On the unfortunate coal-heaver, history is silent.

Bessie's contemporary George Leybourne (1842–1884) was a handsome idol of the halls, and perhaps their first 'star' in the modern sense. Born Joe Saunders, he was a Birmingham labourer who came to sing at the Canterbury and around the East End, rising to a regular spot at the Holborn Empire and the spectacular salary of £120 a week (a worker might earn half of that per year). His career-defining moment arrived in 1868 when he sang 'Champagne Charlie', a hymn to that very beverage (sponsored in fact by champagne importers). Its theme reinforced his popular image as a 'swell': the high-living dandy with a mischievous eye. Working men and women loved a swell, otherwise known as a 'Lion Comique', he was a target of admiration and mockery combined.

Alfred Vance, alias 'The Great Vance' (1839–1888), was Leybourne's rival – in a sense they were the Blur and Oasis of their day – and a swell among swells. An immaculate dresser, he advertised his numbers as 'refined comic songs' and was friendly with the Prince of Wales. Yet, as he knew, the swell must have the common touch as well as an aristocratic swagger, hence such cockney crowd-pleasers as 'Costermonger Joe' and 'Going to the Derby'.

We have no recordings of Bellwood, Leybourne or Vance, but there is consolation in a lovely 1944 film, *Champagne Charlie*, which tells, in black-and-white, a colourful version of their story. Drink is really at the heart of this tale – hardly surprising, as music halls began in taverns. Playing Leybourne is the London comic Tommy Trinder, in real life a popular patter act (catchphrase, 'You lucky people!') who straddled variety, wireless and film. As the Great Vance stands Stanley Holloway, a veteran who lived to find fame in Hollywood. With its mixture of original and newly written songs, the movie portrays their musical feud, regally overseen by Betty Warren as the matriarchal Bessie.

George opens the bidding with 'Ale, Old Ale' to which Vance responds with 'Oh, I Do Like a Little Drop of Gin'. George hits back with 'Burgundy, Claret and Port' ('I'll moisten my throttle with many a bottle'), prompting Vance to sing of rum, then George of 'Brandy and Seltzer', then Vance of 'A Glass of Sherry Wine' ('Some say it rots the liver/But I'd gladly drink a river'). It is of course George who ultimately hits the jackpot, with 'Champagne Charlie' itself. Thus the alcoholic arms-race is concluded. Leybourne knew a good racket to be in, following on with songs such as 'Moët & Chandon' and 'Clicquot', again bankrolled by wine merchants.

It's a prejudice of later ages that the Victorians were always sour and strait-laced. In fact, their popular entertainments could be riotous, jolly and hugely gregarious affairs. For evidence we look to that elite cockney caste who were the living spirit of music hall: the costermongers.

Ghetto Fabulous: Pearly Kings and Costers

Costermongers were mostly street sellers of fruit and veg. (Their name derived from medieval 'costards' or large apples.) Trading on their wits, costers were the original wheeler-dealers. They became the emblematic cockney type – provincials still picture Londoners as 'barrow boys' of glib tongue and dubious probity. Costers formed the core of music hall's early audience and were endlessly celebrated in its art. In the 1850s there were thought to be about 30,000 of them in London, concentrated in the East End and south of the river. They took their produce from the markets of Covent Garden and Billingsgate, to sell from stalls or barrows, or on street rounds. Their natural enemies were the police and regular shopkeepers.

Outsiders were awed by the costers' solidarity; the business was hereditary and its practitioners had their own impenetrable slang. Honest enough among their own kind, they evolved district hierarchies, dispensing justice with a Kray-like lack of ceremony.

From the late nineteenth century, coster leaders adorned themselves in formal finery, hence the pearly king and his queen, or 'donna'. The pearlies were indeed an early instance of 'bling' – dressed in communal style but decked with ostentation. Their look was echoed a century later, in American hip hop and the characteristically Essex fashions – casual sportswear with lavish helpings of 'tom' ('foolery') or jewellery.

Costers did not stint on entertainment. They loved their jigs, fiddlers, hornpipes and polkas. As the music halls developed the costers stamped their taste upon them, calling for comic songs and dancing in preference to noble recitations and dramatic sketches. (A great favourite was 'Duck-legged Dick', the affecting tale of a donkey and its drunken owner.) The writer Mayhew describes a typically rowdy night at the Royal Coburg, a South Bank venue that is now the Old Vic, where 'hamsandwich men' and 'pigtrotter women' strolled about shouting for custom, and 'a man with a tin can, glittering in the gaslight', issued his cry of 'Port-a-a-a-r! Who's for port-a-a-a-r?' The orchestra was encouraged with calls of 'Now then, you catgut scrapers!' The crowd was aged between twelve and twenty-three.

'But the grand hit of the evening,' says Mayhew, 'is always when a song is sung to which the entire gallery can join in the chorus . . . the throats of the mob burst forth in all their strength . . . An "angcore" on such occasions is always demanded, and, despite a few murmurs of "change it to 'Duck-legged Dick'," invariably insisted on.'

It was natural that such a tribe would demand heroes in its own image. The first great stage-coster was Albert Chevalier (1861–1923) who treated his people to numbers in the vernacular, like 'Down at the Welsh 'Arp', 'The Future Mrs 'Awkins' and 'Knocked 'Em in the Old Kent Road'. Best-loved of all was 'My Old Dutch', which he wrote on a cigarette packet strolling one foggy night from Oxford Street to Islington: 'We've been together now for forty years,' sings the old husband, 'it don't seem a day too much.' (They are, alas, about to be sundered by the workhouse, with its pitiless segregation of the sexes.) It's clear Chevalier had the measure of cockney taste, in all its vulgar humour, pathos and occasional fatalism. 'What's the Good o' Hany-fink?' went another of his songs. 'Why, Nuffink!'

If a time machine dropped us off in London's past, the biggest surprise might not be top hats, horse-drawn milk carts or public gallows, but the mysterious catchphrases that could draw knowing grins all round. In the 1970s people said 'Nice one, Cyril!' several times an hour, heedless of its links to Tottenham Hotspur (whose player Cyril Knowles it lionised). At the height of Gilbert and Sullivan's fame, the line from *HMS Pinafore* 'What never? Hardly ever!' was inescapable. In the Swinging Sixties you would hear 'What's it all about, Alfie?' The music hall was naturally a fecund source of such flourishes, from George Robey's 'Archibald, certainly not!' to Harry Champion's 'Ginger, you're barmy!'

Harry Champion, whose name would generally have been pronounced ''Erry Chempion', was really William Henry Crump of Shoreditch, a great star of late nineteenth-century music hall, and one of that generation who lived long enough to encounter early recording technology. Thus we have fragmentary evidence of his genius, transferred from crackling wax cylinders to CD and MP3. Even so, Champion is distinctively of the pre-microphone era – hollering stoutly like the coster street vendor he purports to be in 'Any Old Iron'. It's to Champion that we owe 'I'm Henry the Eighth I Am' and 'Boiled Beef and Carrots'. His vast popularity was well deserved, for his wit and delivery were much subtler than you might guess from the many and cruder impersonations of his songs. 'Ginger, You're Barmy' is a peculiar thing to modern ears, a stricture on the folly of bare-headed men. It's some indication of London's dominance in music hall that Harry sings blithely of his 'cady' (archaic slang for a hat) and 'Derby Kell' (or belly), as if the whole world spoke cockney.

His contemporary Gus Elen, a fellow East Ender, was something else again – a wry, lugubrious chap who sang of a coster's tribulations. Elen was born in 1863 and began as a busker with barrel organ accompaniment. Once embarked upon the halls, he specialised in marvellous portraits of a plain chap's struggles with the twin blights of work and marriage. His Sam Weller accent ('Upon my word she's awful aggra-watin'!') adds extra pathos to these domestic confessions: 'Never Introduce Your Donah to a Pal', 'Don't Stop My 'Alf a Pint of Beer'. 'If it Wasn't for the 'Ouses in Between'. To a cockney audience that knew real poverty, Elen was a hero: downtrodden yet resilient, finding solace in his pipe, his ale and his 'Pretty Little Villa Down at Barking'. There was nothing of the flashy cad in Elen. You hear his workaday realism, perhaps, in the songs of Squeeze and Madness. He retired in 1914 and then did little else but fish until his death in 1940.

For the coster virtue of sheer, brassy defiance, however, we look to the Queen of the Music Halls, Marie Lloyd. In those days you could get away with a lot if you treated sex as a joke. (The British seaside postcard has always proved as much.) Lloyd, who lived from 1870 to 1922, was a Hoxton girl who built her reputation upon East End cheek and cleverly suggestive titles like 'A Little Bit of What You Fancy (Does You Good)', 'Every Little Movement (Has a Meaning of its Own)' and 'She'd Never Had Her Ticket Punched Before'. Like Gus Elen, 'Our Marie' was a figurehead for all the put-upon classes of London town – larky stories like 'The Coster Girl in Paris' were a tonic to anyone who endured the daily humiliations of domestic service or factory routine.

For a time she was married to Alec Hurley, himself a major entertainer in the coster genre. But then, given her dictum that a little of what you fancy is indeed desirable, she ran off with an Irish jockey eighteen years her junior.

Respectability was never Marie Lloyd's lot. At the height of her fame and power she supported a strike of the struggling music hall artistes. And legend says that when the censors summonsed her for vulgarity, Lloyd confounded them with a performance of Tennyson's 'Come into the Garden, Maud' replete with leers, winks and inappropriate emphases. This she contrasted with a prim rendition of her own songs – to show, in all innocence, that *anything* might be taken the wrong way. Perhaps she treated them to that model of propriety, 'She Sits Among the Cabbages and Peas'.

She popularised many of the music hall's most famous songs, including 'Oh Mister Porter' and 'My Old Man (Said Follow the Van)'. But her best-loved number was a very early success, 'The Boy I Love is Up in the Gallery', which made her a national sweetheart. 'Her slightest naughty wink,' wrote the sage observer Max Beerbohm, 'carried its meaning to the heart of the gallery and was received personally by every gullible male in the house.' In the matronly phase of her later life, she would delight the crowds by singing 'I'm One of the Ruins that Cromwell Knocked About a Bit'. And when she died more than 100,000 mourners followed her coffin to Hampstead.

In a 1967 documentary, *The London Nobody Knows*, we see the actor James Mason amid the crumbling glory of Marie's favourite music hall, the Bedford in Camden High Street. Built in 1861 as an extension to the Bedford Arms pub, in its heyday it attracted the impressionist painter Walter Sickert and others of the 'Camden Town Group'. While Mason meditates in solemn grandeur upon the Bedford's vanished splendour, we hear in the background a recording of 'The Boy I Love is Up in the Gallery' – and the effect is poignant. The derelict hall had been closed for eight years by this point, and would be torn down in 1969, rudely evicting the ghosts of George Leybourne, Charlie Chaplin and Marie Lloyd herself.

In a song by Lloyd's contemporary Ella Shields, we can hear the whole essence of London's geographical class divide. A specialist in male impressions, Shields's fame was guaranteed by a gift from her songwriter husband, 'I'm Burlington Bertie from Bow'. Mimicking an older Vesta Tilley hit (simply called 'Burlington Bertie'), this 1916 masterpiece depicts the typical swell 'up West', cutting *la bella figura* on Piccadilly, consorting with the quality and concealing his profound poverty. He's 'Burlington Bertie', all right, but he is 'from Bow' – an East Ender through and through. Thus we have a woman masquerading as a man, who is a cockney pretending to be posh. In London, at the dawn of the twentieth century, East was East, and West still West.

Charles Coborn, a dignified gent whose name was taken from Coborn Road in Bow, was another comical toff. It was the dream of every music hall singer to find a signature song and Coborn achieved it twice – as the preening *boulevardier*, 'The Man Who Broke the Bank at Monte Carlo', and again with 'Two Lovely Black Eyes'. He'd bought the latter for ten pounds and claimed to have sung it 250,000 times. In the days before television, when a popular 'turn' might perform three shows a night, six nights a week – without exhausting the nation's patience – this was entirely plausible.

Black-face minstrel acts, the former 'Ethiopians' of the streets, were a pillar of the music halls, typified by George H. Chirgwin ('The White-Eyed Kaffir') and Eugene Stratton. Over the decades, however, there were numbers of actual black performers arriving from the USA, who aroused a certain respectful curiosity (which, in turn, paved the way for English acceptance of ragtime and jazz). And in 1897 it was noted of the Bell on Ratcliff Highway, that 'contrary to precedent, the negro element preponderates among the audience instead of on the stage.'

On a rung below the music halls were 'Penny gaffs', a magnet for juvenile audiences, serving a diet of blood and crime, with piano accompaniment, and lots of cheap booze. They were sometimes attached to East End pubs, or held in warehouses or even old shops crudely converted by removing the first floor (exposing the wall-paper and fireplaces of upper rooms). As in music hall proper, comical songs were favoured, especially when obscene. One example was reported, 'the whole point of which consisted in the mere utterance of some filthy word at the end of each stanza'. The cockney children, clearly no innocents, whooped their approval of 'Pine-apple Rock' – it seemed to offer 'greater scope to the rhyming powers of the author ... Ingenuity had been exerted to its utmost lest an obscene thought should be passed by.' Elsewhere, a kind of Victorian karaoke option existed. At the Albert Saloon in Tothill Street, for example, members of the public stepped up to give their party pieces.

And there were always panto and theatre, the forms that had preceded music hall and would outlast it too. Melodramatic stage plays were an obsession ('Dead, dead, and never called me mother!'), especially those with astounding special effects. The taste for satire was rife as well, and *Uncle Tom's Cabin*, the period's most popular drama, spawned several parodies. As for Charles Dickens, his live readings were a universal passion, delivered with such force that they hastened his death. Costers were nearly as fond of theatres – concentrated, as in Shakespeare's day, on the South Bank – as of music hall. 'Love and murder suits us best, sir,' said one to Mayhew. 'We are fond of music,' he added, nominating patriotic, sailor and 'flash songs' for special approbation. London's dustmen, a tribe somewhat smaller than the costers, preferred their own pubs and theatres. But a street sweeper declared, 'It's werry fine and grand at the Wic [Victoria Theatre] ... both the pantomimers and t'other things is werry stunning.'

Music hall songs were often topical, but they were ideally built to last and appeal to all classes. The greatest variations were probably in the patter between numbers, the stream of chat that is now lost to posterity. Where they did address the issues of the day the tone was populist. 'The Greedy Landlord' and 'The Man Who Waters the Workers' Beer' were assured of a sympathetic reception. A song of Florrie Gallimore's was heart-rending: 'It's the poor wot 'elps the poor, when poverty knocks at the door/Those wot live in mansions grand, orften fail to understand ...'

'Angelina Was Always Fond of Soldiers' marked the visit of Allied troops to London in 1868; 'Would You be Surprised to Hear?' was a catchphrase from a celebrated 1871 court case, the trial of The Tichborne Claimant (an impostor who tried to take the identity of a deceased aristocrat). George Leybourne immortalised Monsieur Léotard, the acrobatic sensation of the day, as 'The Daring Young Man on the Flying Trapeze'. And The Great Vance tackled an 1880s fashion craze in 'Toothpick & Crutch', rhyming its title with 'How did you get those trousers on, and did they hurt you much?' ('Received with shouts of laughter,' beamed the *Birmingham Post*).

Wars, more than anything, spurred the music halls to social commentary. 'Jingoism', meaning a patriotism that descends to coarse belligerence, was taken from 'The Jingo Song', performed by G. H. Macdermott in 1878, as British and Russian forces squared up

33

in the Dardanelles: 'We don't want to fight, but by jingo if we do/We've got the ships, we've got the men, and we've got the money too.' In the First World War, Marie Lloyd led recruitment drives from music hall stages. And the cross-dressing Vesta Tilley – as beautiful in boy's drag as in her own clothing – stirred cockney hearts with 1915's 'Jolly Good Luck to the Girl Who Loves a Soldier'.

By the 1880s there were about five hundred music halls in London, heavily concentrated in the East End but now to be found in nearly every residential area. The South Bank of the Thames maintained its Shakespearean status as an entertainment hub, preserved through the years of Vauxhall Gardens; York Road by Waterloo was the music hall's High Street, a place for artistes and their agents to meet, drink and bargain. The quality of the 'turns' was not guaranteed – we tend to remember the greats like Marie Lloyd, and their high-spots especially, but in such a mass of nightly performances some dross was inescapable.

A report from 1891 describes a music hall chairman, still wielding his magisterial hammer. 'There is a melancholy dignity about him, however, which causes him to be approached with much deference and respect by the young clerks and shop boys who take their pleasure here, and who are proud to be distinguished by a shake of the hand from him, and flattered when he condescends to accept liquid refreshment.' The reporter, an American, was less enchanted by the music: 'dull songs, hoary jokes, stale sentiment, and clap-trap patriotism'. On a typical night there would be twenty or thirty numbers performed, of which two or three were liable to catch on, be played around the country on barrel organs, then vanish. 'No superannuated thing,' he says, 'is so utterly dead and forgotten as a once popular music hall song.'

Audience misbehaviour was an abiding worry. An 1878 Act curtailed the serving of liquor in the auditorium. The halls, in fact, were undergoing a sort of gentrification, nudging them towards a more wholesome tone to suit the clerical worker, his wife and children. (This ambition, it must be said, was not always achieved.) The newer venues were properly theatrical, with proscenium stages and ample seating, plush velvet and gilt. Suburban examples, like the Grand at Clapham, survive to this day. These were the 'Palaces of Variety' that represent the maturity of music hall. At their apex were the epic constructions of Leicester Square: the Alhambra, the Hippodrome, the Empire.

The last two have survived in various guises, but the Alhambra, on the east side of the Square, made way for the art deco Odeon Cinema. Morally speaking, this may be no great loss. While the Alhambra was a splendidly Moorish affair with room for almost 5,000 – it could even host the snugly costumed Monsieur Léotard and his flying trapeze – it was infamous for its 'no-knickers can-can'. It was lamented, in 1860, that a sixty-piece orchestra was 'almost drowned in the noise of the promenading patrons, male and female, who are more inclined to lounge about the many little bars and "liquor up".' Downstairs was the Canteen, a big refreshment room where dancing girls consorted with top-hatted customers. Family groups attended, but also men who hired private rooms to entertain female 'friends'.

For all their rowdiness and bawdy atmosphere, the old East End halls were less sordid than their gas-lit superiors up West. The promenade aisles, a feature of every venue from the Alhambra to Wilton's, were no longer a fit place for the innocent to saunter. 'Brazen-faced women,' declared an 1869 account from the Alhambra, were 'blazoned in tawdry finery, and curled and painted, openly and without disguise bestowing their blandishments on "spoony" young swells of the "commercial" and shopman type ... There is no mistaking these women. They make no more disguise of their profession than do cattle-drovers in the public markets.'

The grandiose palaces of Leicester Square were patronised by the gentry despite their unsavoury aspects. For the more self-consciously respectable market were establishments like the Pavilion by Piccadilly Circus. It's still a landmark, having survived conversion to a cinema (all four Beatle movies were premiered here) and a tourist mall called the Trocadero. The Oxford, at 14 Oxford Street, was opened by 'the Father of the Halls', Charles Morton, who had run the old Canterbury many years before. He built his new hall over the stable yards of the Boar & Castle Coaching Inn – in later life it became a Lyons Corner House and in recent times a Virgin Megastore.

The operas and legitimate theatres endured, haughtily oblivious to music hall. And there were new venues arising for a middle-class audience. The Gaiety, in the Aldwych, and Daly's of Leicester Square were stalwarts of Edwardian musical comedy, a form that brought immense vitality to London in the years ahead. The musical comedy itself was inspired by London's prime songwriting partnership – two moustachioed, mutton-chopped men who, amid the rain-grey grime, brought to the honking metropolis a heady infusion of musical colour . . .

There is Beauty in the Bellow of the Blast: Gilbert and Sullivan

In a strip of park between the Thames Embankment and the Savoy Hotel is a surprisingly sensual statue. It looks like an escapee from the Parc Monceau, quite unlike London's standard monuments to Victorian rectitude. A lady has draped herself adoringly about a bust of Arthur Sullivan – the musical half of a double-act who brought new joy and energy to London music. His partner William Gilbert has no memorial here. I cannot imagine he would be pleased.

Gilbert and Sullivan's medium was 'operetta', lighter than the classic European imports. At the same time their stories had a barbed edge of satire that echoes *The Beggar's Opera*. The men were both Londoners. Gilbert was born off the Strand, became a prosperous playwright living in South Kensington, and wrote humorous ballads like 'The Bishop of Rum-ti-Foo'. He watched the comic operas of the French and yearned for something fresher and more directly English. In 1871 he met a rising young composer, Arthur Sullivan. Affable and charming where Gilbert was cranky, Sullivan was a musical prodigy, raised in Lambeth and classically trained. He was befriended by the elderly Charles Dickens.

Gilbert and Sullivan became collaborators and their potential was spotted by Richard D'Oyly Carte, the shrewd manager of Soho's

Royalty Theatre. Under his wing they wrote a comic opera, *Trial by Jury* in 1875, and became a sensation three years later with *HMS Pinafore*. This musical play was really a cutting portrait of London's ruling establishment, from the politician Disraeli to the retail magnate W. H. Smith. Watching it, said one writer, 'the average Englishman laughed, applauded and whistled the delectable tunes: the important Englishman watched, smiled wryly and sometimes writhed inwardly.' They followed it with *The Pirates of Penzance*, a veiled attack on aristocracy and monarchy. In *Iolanthe*, Gilbert takes a shot at both Houses of Parliament – he was not a radical, as such, but an impatient iconoclast. Gilbert and Sullivan were themselves respectable figures, who strived to be 'innocent but not imbecile'. They avoided vulgarity. *Patience*, in 1881, mocked the super-sensitive young poets, who were stock figures of fun in the music halls too. Essentially, humbug was their target.

In 1881, D'Oyly Carte built a permanent home for his acclaimed protégés at the Savoy Theatre. Its original entrance faced the Embankment (very near that statue) and can just about be found, though almost hidden by the mighty Savoy Hotel, which D'Oyly Carte founded on the riches of his career as an impresario. (The theatre's entrance moved to the Strand side in 1901, and was rebuilt in its familiar art deco form in 1929. Around the corner is the alleyway where Bob Dylan filmed 'Subterranean Homesick Blues'.) Gilbert and Sullivan's 'Savoy Operas' became a cornerstone of London life. There is a story of Sullivan standing at the back of the auditorium, humming happily to his own tunes. A man turned around and hissed, 'Look here, sir, I paid my money to hear Sullivan's music, not yours!'

The partners' greatest hour came with *The Mikado*, in 1885. The play's Japanese setting gave Sullivan many opportunities for musical exotica, but Gilbert's lyric was, as usual, keeping its beady eye on London. G. K. Chesterton observed: 'I doubt if there is a single joke in the whole play that fits the Japanese. But all the jokes in the play fit the English.'

Arthur Sullivan's gnawing sorrow was that he wrote operetta and not High Art. Yet he produced more solemn work, including the tune to 'Onward, Christian Soldiers' and a beautifully plangent piece, 'The

Lost Chord', composed beside the deathbed of his brother. The Victorians clasped this song to their bosoms – so much so that in a typically London way, several parodies ensued, causing poor Sullivan further anguish. There is, incidentally, a phonograph of 'The Lost Chord' from 1888, claimed to be the first musical recording. Fascinated by Edison's new invention, Sullivan told him that he was 'astonished at the wonderful power you have developed, and terrified at the thought that so much hideous and bad music may be put on record for ever.' How horribly prophetic.

For all his artistic yearnings, Sullivan liked the high life. Where Gilbert was prickly, competitive and prone to gout, Sullivan was smoothly sociable. He could write his music in crowded rooms while entertaining friends and chain-smoking. He enjoyed the company of royalty, who admired him also. He loved gambling at Monte Carlo and going to the races. His biographer Hesketh Pearson said he would rather have owned a Derby winner than written *The Mikado*.

But he depended on Gilbert. In such a partnership the librettist is often subordinate to the composer, but Gilbert was indomitable. The words-man was studiously casual about music – he liked to say that he knew only two tunes, one was 'God Save the Queen' and the other wasn't. He also said, 'I know nothing about music. I can't tell the difference between "Rule Britannia" and "Pop Goes the Weasel".' More to the point, he once described himself and Sullivan as suffering from a 'Master and Master' relationship. Rather like Lennon and McCartney, their powers grew incompatible, yet they really needed one another, to fully realise their own strengths.

In 1889 the simmering tensions spilled over. Their newest production *The Gondoliers* was a smash, but the partners were falling out – it's thought that D'Oyly Carte was siding with Sullivan and planning grand opera with him (he built the future Palace Theatre, on Cambridge Circus, to stage it). A trivial dispute about the cost of a carpet at the Savoy Theatre got out of hand. But then, they were never soulmates in the first place. They reunited four years later and sent the Savoy crowd into raptures with a public handshake at the curtain call. But their best work was behind them now.

Sullivan died in 1900. He wanted to be buried at Brompton next to his mother and brother but was taken instead to St Paul's Cathedral. Strangely, his patron and ally Richard D'Oyly Carte was dying also and news of Sullivan's death was kept from him; for some reason he got up and saw from his window Sullivan's funeral procession. Three years later, a wistful Gilbert was heard to say, 'a Gilbert is of no use without a Sullivan, and I can't find one.' His own last years were quiet, though he maintained an interest in the fairer sex (he had a room in his house called the Flirtorium). He was a more pragmatic man than Sullivan, though he also pined for more serious work. 'I have been scribbling twaddle for thirty-five years to suit the public taste,' he complained. He died of a heart attack in 1911, after eating a hearty lunch at the Carlton Club followed by a swim with two pretty girls in the lake of his country home.

In the century since then their popularity has scarcely waned. Rodgers and Hart, the classic American songsmiths, were hailed as 'the modern Gilbert and Sullivan'. The twentieth-century musical owed everything to their example, and their London disciples included Lionel Bart. In 1965, the Beatles' manager Brian Epstein booked the D'Oyly Carte Company to perform Gilbert and Sullivan at his own new toy, the Saville Theatre. The highest art was not, in the end, their calling. Gilbert and Sullivan were, first and foremost, commercially minded Londoners. To our lasting benefit, they knew which side their bread was buttered.

The Twilight of the Halls

D'Oyly Carte designed a magnificent building on Shaftesbury Avenue, dominating Cambridge Circus, and named it the Royal English Opera House. Far from hosting *meisterwerks* by Arthur Sullivan, however, it closed within a year and in 1892 became a variety theatre called the Palace. Fortunately its new manager was Charles Morton, late of the Oxford and Alhambra, the very man who'd brought music hall to the Canterbury almost fifty years earlier. And the Palace still packs them in today. But the twentieth century was dawning and the music hall was to undergo dramatic changes.

Gaudy and luxurious, the new halls looked to flashier formats to bring in customers. They were not the neighbourhood gathering places they had once been – the age of audience involvement was giving way to something more passive. The early halls had been a human counterpoint to urbanisation and the worst effects of the Industrial Revolution. Music hall was essentially 'interactive', to use a term unknown then. Its public were ordinary folk who felt powerless in the city outside but were to be reckoned with in a hall. Here they literally had a voice and performers must compete with it, which in turn helped those artists to grow. As T. S. Eliot observed, working men at a Marie Lloyd performance might sing along and fairly consider themselves to be part of the show.

Every formula grows stale eventually, and new punters were tired of old turns. American vaudeville inspired some fast-moving sketch shows, full of music and laughs and dancing, with scenery and costumes changing at delirious speed. At the Oxford in 1909 and the Palladium in 1911, Percy Honri offered 'a wonderful admixture of bright and catchy airs, of sad music, of dainty girls, of graceful dancing, of wild hilarity, of scenes of brilliancy constituting a veritable feast of colour, and of a constant succession of weird happenings, surprising transformations, and quick changes.'

Its settings included a Hoxton street, with 'a Coster and his Caricaturing Cockneys', but also the West End, the Moon and Fairyland. The coming taste was for a blend of fantasia and topicality, and the solution was called 'revue'. 'More and more,' recalled another of the Honri family, 'revue was taking over from the turns. The tempo of life was changing: syncopation was part of everyone's world.' Come the First World War, 'Tommy-on-leave wanted above all else to see glamour – light and colour and girls.'

What finally did for the music halls, however, was the cinema. After that came the wireless, and then the cinema's stunted cousin, television. As far back as 1885, the Alhambra was showing a short film as its 'end turn'. The Tivoli in the Strand followed suit. These early reels, called 'topicals', claimed an ever-growing share of stage time. Thus a great popular art form would be replaced – or, at least, partially displaced – by another. Music halls began closing down as picture houses sprang up everywhere.

Community was fading and consumerism was coming in. These new media were not at all interactive. Even on the variety stages, where live entertainment fought a valiant rearguard action, the introduction of microphones took something away; the new technology gave audience involvement a battering. At the same time, it permitted more subtle performers, whether actors or musicians, whose natural home was the wireless. With its author John Osborne, Laurence Olivier researched the last variety halls for his role as Archie Rice, in the 1957 play *The Entertainer* (released as a film in 1960). He saw how TV and microphones had utterly altered matters. Up on stage, his Archie was lost, trying to bask in a communal warmth that was no more. Yet his elderly father, a retired music hall veteran, could still inspire a pub to fervent sing-songs.

(Similarly, in Patrick Hamilton's novel *The Slaves of Solitude*, it's another minor character, a washed-up music hall star, who emerges as the last custodian of failing communal values, of jollity and solidarity.)

The Entertainer's story was foreshadowed by Charlie Chaplin in *Limelight* (1952), a movie drawn from memories of his own beginnings in the music halls of Edwardian London. He was from Kennington and still sounds remarkably English here, after years in the States (though it's slightly odd to hear him talking at all). He performs some comic numbers and also, in a nod to pantomime's origins, a straight ballet – playing the clown Harlequin to his leading lady's Columbine. In his character's final decline he returns to the truest roots of music hall, by busking in pubs.

Before the chairman's hammer falls for the last time, however, let it be said that the London music hall never died. Two of the best of its final flowering were both called Max – the 'cheeky chappie' Miller and 'Professor Wallofsky' Wall.

41

Max Miller's career post-dates the halls but he was a classic turn who worked the variety circuit and survived to star in films and on TV. Though born in Brighton, where he also died, he seemed to the country an archetypal cockney chancer – mouthy and cracking wise, forever dressed in some outlandish suit, looking out for Number One. As the writer Jeff Nuttall described him, Miller was the typical post-war spiv, without the class solidarity of Northern comedians – a smart operator who had escaped the daily grind.

He won the nation's affections after a 1931 Royal Command Performance. A favourite persona, typified in his signature song 'Mary from the Dairy', was the *faux*-innocent: 'It's people like you that give me a bad name!' he would scold his audience after some saucy foray. (This conspiratorial touch, much employed by later comics, was a favourite of the music hall star George Robey. *He* was always proper and correct; anything improper was in the audience's own mind.) Miller often played the part of a commercial traveller, the lecherous opportunist who was a stock type of the day. His London shows were seen and studied by some important figures in our later story, including Ian Dury and Ray Davies.

Max Wall (1908–1990) is even more of a linking figure in this tale, born to an Edwardian music hall family in Brixton and surviving to record with Stiff Records during punk rock. He went from panto in the 1920s to musicals, variety and nightclubs, re-emerging on TV and in film as a cult figure. His strutting creation, Professor Wallofsky, became a comedy standard, influencing everyone from John Cleese to Fat Les. Like so many old-time turns, he was only in part a musical performer but some of his own songs, like 'Me and My Tune' are quite delightful. The late Ian Dury was a devoted fan, and gave him a fine song, 'England's Glory', that hymns Vera Lynn, Noël Coward and Oliver Twist. (Its B-side, 'Dream Tobacco', influenced Madness.) He brought Wall into his show at the Hammersmith Odeon in 1978, billing him to a sceptical crowd as 'one of the jewels in England's crown'.

And what of the buildings? Around the West End and elsewhere are some surviving marvels of the variety age, like the Coronet in

Notting Hill Gate (albeit as a cinema) and the Hackney Empire. Less fortunate were scores of others, including the Holborn Empire, the Putney Hippodrome and the Metropolitan, Edgware Road (where Leybourne sang 'Champagne Charlie'; his screen embodiment Tommy Trinder topped the bill on closing night, 1963). The wrecker's ball found them all. Collins's Music Hall stood on Islington Green, just across from the site of a famous Sex Pistols show. Its Irish founder, Sam Collins, built his hall in the standard way, extending back from an existing pub, the Landsdowne, which was duly swallowed up. Its frontage now adorns a book-store, but a new 600-seater Collins Theatre is taking shape next door.

After the Second World War there was almost nothing left of music hall, though the East End preserved its spirit in pubs like the Pride of the Isle and the Waterman's Arms, both on the Isle of Dogs, and the Boleyn on Barking Road. The working men's clubs, up North, and the seaside theatres kept a little of the old magic too, and there was some self-conscious revivalism in TV shows like *The Good Old Days*. As we'll see, a surprisingly strong element of music hall entered the bloodstream of rock 'n' roll, via Bermondsey's Tommy Steele and later acts like the Small Faces.

But the 'turns' had disappeared as surely as the horses who had once hauled Victorian Londoners from A to B. (Declining, too, were the actual cockney sparrows who fed upon the horse dung in the streets. Blame the motor car, of course: 'Smelly sparrow-starvers,' said an indignant Marie Lloyd.) Music hall had seen a transition from the folk art of street ballads to the commodified age of mass entertainment. From it arose both show business and the music industry. The singers bought sole rights to a song from its writer for a few pounds or guineas, and they shared the sheet music royalties. Boosted by the mass-ownership of parlour pianos, sheet music publishing grew into a major trade; its covers spawned a medium for visual flair that prefigured the album sleeve.

A fondly nostalgic note was struck by *The Times*' leader column of 18 March 1932. 'It was a natural world,' it said of the halls, 'an un-selfconscious world ... it was a world that did not see the need for any pretence. It did not pretend, because it was not afraid to be itself. It had its prejudices, its excesses, its stupidities, and its not unwholesome coarseness; but it was an honest, genial, and sturdily English world, which had not learned to apologise to the habitable world for being English.'

In fact music hall became, for all our later sophistication, the default setting of English pop. We shall hear its echoes throughout this book.

Chapter Three

There Were Angels Dining at the Ritz

The smooth sounds of Mayfair. Vera Lynn's agent starts the Second World War. Noël Coward wins it. And Mary Poppins takes America.

Something subtle occurs when you cross Piccadilly from St James's to Mayfair. I hadn't noticed this until my barber pointed it out to me. His little shop is hidden behind the aristocratic shirt shops of Jermyn Street, in a narrow yard where the Duke of Ormond once stabled his horses. In the next yard was London's most exclusive club, the Scotch of St James, where Beatles drank with Rolling Stones. Adjacent was the art gallery where John Lennon met Yoko Ono. Next to the barber a restaurant and nightclub is undergoing drastic refurbishment: 'It used to be a Turkish baths,' he explains, 'and steam had weakened the structure.' (Not only steam. I knew that nightclub and observed our rock nobility in there, behaving like Caligulas.)

Further back in time, St James's was a lonely building in the marshes, where lived 'fourteen leprous maidens', tended by the Church. They heard no sound except the Angelus bell or a Kyrie Eleison ('*Lord have mercy*'), drifting over from Westminster Abbey. But every May, from St James's Eve, a six-day fair was held outside to raise funds for them. Then the event grew so riotous it was moved north of Piccadilly, to what became 'May Fair'.

The barber does not like crossing to Piccadilly's north side, to Mayfair. 'The atmosphere is completely different. The people are more aggressive.' An echo of that unruly old Fair? Perhaps, yet Mayfair has a more cultivated legacy also. If the earliest part of our story belonged to the old City of London, and the spiritual heartland of music hall was the East End, then the dominant sounds of the inter-war years, from 1918 to 1939, belong somehow to the elegance west of Regent Street.

Jazz became the rage in London when the Great War ended. (Its predecessor, ragtime, had been known since the 1890s.) In 1919 the Original Dixieland Jazz Band made a pioneering visit to Hammersmith to inaugurate its Palais de Danse. They were a white five-piece from New Orleans who billed themselves 'The Creators of Jazz' though they weren't, exactly. Another boost was the visit of an American band-leader, Paul Whiteman. Though Whiteman was indeed white, and his style a model of sophisticated orchestration, there was no missing the African-American provenance of this music.

We are now in the London of P. G. Wodehouse's silly toffs and Evelyn Waugh's bright yet decadent young things. In the 1920s, the decade that F. Scott Fitzgerald christened The Jazz Age, 'hot music' confronted the English with something that was strange and challenging, yet almost irresistible.

True, it was not to everybody's taste. G. K. Chesterton, in his essay 'The Prison of Jazz', lamented both the unfamiliar noise and its newly fashionable partner the 'cocktail'. (Once more a London musical trend was defined by drink.) He did not hear in jazz the exuberant transcendence that its admirers heard; he saw only a surrender of man's spiritual dimension. Yet he also pined for the earthier pleasures of his youth, when beer and music halls held sway, and the latter rang to hearty choruses of 'Daisy, Daisy, give me your answer do' (a nostalgic choice he shared, surprisingly, with HAL, the computer in *2001: A Space Odyssey*.)

One can appreciate Chesterton's intention, defending the plain people of Victorian times from posthumous condescension. Music halls do more than anything to up-turn the nineteenth century's reputation for prudery and grimness. But his withering assessment of the unfolding scene was surely misplaced: 'The poetry inspired by cocktails,' he complained, 'is timid and tortuous and self-conscious and indirect.' Well, much of it probably was. But Noël Coward was better than that, and Noël Coward is the figure who will soon dominate this chapter.

If you had the means to enjoy them, the new pleasure palaces of London might be dancehalls, grand restaurants or hotel ballrooms. All served up the popular music of their day, while the nineteenth-century halls were falling dark and silent. Folk still sang the old songs in parlours and pubs, but new environments called for new forms. Performers would increasingly expect to use a microphone. Some had found that unimaginably vast, mysteriously invisible audience created by radio. And happily for posterity, more than ever before were being recorded in studios and on film. Trilling out across the decades, they flicker in black-and-white before our puzzled gaze, for ever.

Despite the shock of jazz, the music on offer was hardly strident – this was a time of unparalleled elegance in London after dark. Orchestras were mellifluous. Patrons at restaurant tables wished to converse at normal levels, while attentive waiters hopped back and forth. People dressed well, adhering to strict codes. The musicians themselves were sometimes highly paid, even if they took their meals in rather plain back rooms, dining (as Tiny Winters, of the Lew Stone and Ambrose bands has recalled) on food less splendid than their customers enjoyed. They worked punishingly long hours well into the night and often with a recording fixture the next morning. At least, in those days, they could park their sporty little cars on Piccadilly, right outside the hotel ballroom.

The prestige of the London stage was such that America's leading songwriters, Rodgers and Hart, longed to craft a hit musical here. In 1926 they sailed for Europe and holed up for five weeks at the Savoy while they did their research. They found the pace agreeably more relaxed than New York: 'Rehearsals are quite the most leisurely affairs in the world. They are halted each afternoon for tea.' The resulting work, *Lido Lady*, suggests their research was not excessively strenuous, featuring numbers such as 'A Tiny Flat Near Soho Square' and 'A Cup of Tea' ('the sun never sets on a cup of tea', etc.). But they returned often and did better things, especially 1934's *Evergreen*, immortalised by Jessie Matthews ('the Dancing Divinity') who, for 'Dancing on the Ceiling', was partnered by a giant inverted chandelier. The beautiful young Matthews had come far since a girlhood spent dancing to barrel organs in Soho streets; she would travel much further to become the heroine of our post-war radio soap *Mrs Dale's Diary*. (In 1964 she appeared on TV's *Jukebox Jury* and judged the King Bees' song 'Liza Jane' to be a 'miss', crushing the hopes of its youthful singer, the future David Bowie.)

The most dashing character in London was Ivor Novello. He was an actor and singer, but also a songsmith whose name still adorns the annual awards ceremony for British writers and composers. (If you can't have an Oscar, it's always nice to get an Ivor.) A Welsh boy by birth, he became the West End's sex god and played his loyal part in both world wars, penning 'Keep the Home Fires Burning' for the First and 'We'll Gather Lilacs' for sundered lovers in the Second. He lived in a flat above the Strand Theatre, accessible only by a nerve-racking lift. The parties he threw there were hugely glamorous and markedly camp (his female fans were not to know their carnal imaginings were wasted); in 2005 the Strand Theatre was renamed the Novello in his honour. He was admired, and knew it, for his finely chiselled profile – some of his love scenes suffered because he would not turn his head.

What sort of London was this, after the First World War? It was racially mixed, to a degree, but its mainstream culture was not. At the Embassy Club or the nearby May Fair Hotel you might encounter the Ambrose Orchestra (led by Londoner Bert Ambrose) performing 'Limehouse Blues' – a tinkling evocation of East End Chinatown – but this was light exotica, not musicology. No Little Englander, even so, Bert searched broadly for tuneful inspiration: for every 'Big Ben is Saying Goodnight' there was a frantically African 'B'wanga' or the transatlantic 'She's a Latin from Manhattan'; for each parochial 'Embassy Stomp' a soulful 'Selection of Hebrew Dances' or even a 'Message from Mars'.

Across Regent Street was Soho, a little outpost of Bohemia that sheltered French and Italian immigrants and attracted all who valued the continental ambience. North of Oxford Street, in the area now called Fitzrovia, were more of their compatriots, while the poorer class of Italians gathered about Leather Lane off Holborn and Saffron Hill on the vanished banks of the Fleet River. Less affluent Jews still plied their trades around Whitechapel; the better-off moved to Maida Vale or Bayswater and Hampstead. All of these and others besides would come to enrich the city's music. But, for the moment, our attention wanders to the south-western suburbs and a plain-looking child disguised in a red beard . . .

London Pride is a Flower that's Free

He had been born in Teddington in 1899. His parents had met and romanced (or 'spooned' as singers once put it, usually rhyming that utensil with moon and June) at amateur rehearsals of Gilbert and Sullivan. The family shifted to Sutton, Battersea, Victoria and eventually to 50 South Side, Clapham Common. The boy was a born performer who showed his early promise in the church choir, although he admitted later he found the lack of applause depressing. His comedy beard we'll come to in a moment. This was Noël Coward, the next pivotal figure in London music.

Black-and-white video clips of Coward reveal him in late middle-age, singing for TV specials and beaming with pleasure as the applause rolls over him – rolling, in fact, as splendidly as his letter 'r's, which take entire minutes to complete. He was an urbane, polished perfectionist. Though a cosmopolitan man to his manicured fingernails he wrote music that defined the Englishness of its day. Equally at home in New York or the south of France, he was the author of 'London Pride', perhaps the loveliest love song to the city ever created. Whether it was in the patriotic costermongers of that song, or the Piccadilly street-walkers of 'Mad About the Boy', the city of his childhood remained the primary palette for his art.

In his time Coward wrote hundreds of songs, many of them for his leading ladies ('I'll Follow My Secret Heart' for Yvonne Printemps in

Conversation Piece; 'I'll See You Again' for Peggy Wood in *Bitter Sweet*). He wrote plays, revue sketches, full-blown musicals and also classic films, which he sometimes directed. He was quite an accomplished author. The jack-of-all-trades tag (implying 'master of none') was sometimes used against him. Manon in *Bitter Sweet* concedes she has only 'a talent to amuse'. And of 'Someday I'll Find You', the Gertrude Lawrence song from *Private Lives*, a character remarks, 'Strange how potent cheap music is.' Both quotes have been applied to Coward himself, not always kindly.

But he was much greater than his detractors. To his heritage of London music hall and Gilbert and Sullivan he added the surging energy of America's Jazz Age. In so doing he laid the foundations of English pop, and taught the British to use their native wit in the new transatlantic idiom.

As a child Coward was precocious, or even 'streetwise'. He was always intimate with London, remembering that 'Long before I was twelve years old I was capable of buying tickets and counting change, of ordering buns and glasses of milk in teashops, and battling in and out of trams and buses and trains.' As a schoolboy truant he whiled away his days gazing at trains at Victoria and Clapham Junction. He treated the city as a theatre; sometimes he was its audience and at other times its secret leading man: on one occasion he blew some pocket money on a fake red beard in which he strolled along the Embankment.

A real London boy, then, and already a knowing customer. The first proper song Coward wrote, aged eighteen, was 'Forbidden Fruit', remarkable for its sheer worldliness. To our eyes he might represent a sort of aristocratic languor but he was in fact the very model of middle-class energy, coupled at first with youthful ambition. Among his early plays was *The Young Idea*, a phrase deployed decades later in Paul Weller's frantic Jam song 'In the City'. There is a more resounding punk rock echo, though, in *London Calling* – a 1923 revue, its title borrowed from the newly founded BBC.

'Revues' are rare beasts in recent times but they were a staple of the interwar age; the term indicates a multi-act show with comic and musical sketches, topical skits, and plentiful dancing girls in less than abundant costumes. *London Calling* opened at the Duke of York's Theatre in St Martin's Lane. Fred Astaire assisted in its staging. Coward's closest female friend Gertrude Lawrence sang 'Parisian Pierrot' (one of the numbers re-created by Julie Andrews in the over-long Lawrence bio-pic *Star!*); she also gave us 'Early Mourning', the sardonic tale of a suicide off Waterloo Bridge. And there was Maisie Gray as a fading entertainer protesting 'There's Life in the Old Girl Yet'. Coward himself sang some parts, though not to great acclaim – he was not of the same heart-throb calibre as his debonair friend Ivor Novello.

Still, its success propelled him into fashionable London, of which he became a principal ornament. Money was finally coming his way – he could dine at the Ivy and the Berkeley, and observe London through the windows of a Rolls-Royce. If there was a pea beneath his mattress at that moment it was *London Calling*'s billboard – it faced the unsavoury Seven Dials rather than imperial Trafalgar Square. Still, he consoled himself by gazing – again and again – at his name up there in pink lights.

Coward's standing as a dramatist was confirmed by *The Vortex*; he followed it with another revue, *On With the Dance*, which featured a song called 'Poor Little Rich Girl'. In the back-to-front way of many of one's musical discoveries, I first heard this in a spectral 1998 version by Suede; their reworking was in fact true to the anxiousness that permeates some of Coward's portraits of the Roaring Twenties. He had begun the decade a penniless intruder and was now lionised, but he had a shrewd eye for the period's inner doubts. *The Year of Grace* had more in that vein, notably 'Dance Little Lady', though a show that also included 'A Room With a View' and 'Lilac Time' was hardly guilty of wallowing.

But no sustained run of success, however brilliant, comes without its backlash and Noël Coward felt his in 1928. *Bitter Sweet* aimed for emotional fullness and its audience approved. The more austere breed of critic, by contrast, despised its supposed sentimentality. Max Beerbohm defended it: pointing to *Bitter Sweet*'s commercial success he said, 'Thus we see the things that are out of fashion do not cease to exist. Sentiment goes unaffrighted by the roarings of the young lions and lionesses of Bloomsbury.' And Coward reflected that it was his fate to be called superficial: he was hurt, he confessed, but would resolve to wear his 'light-weight crown' with philosophical serenity.

The comedy *Private Lives*, again played with Gertrude Lawrence (and also Laurence Olivier), was perhaps Coward's zenith. But his musical ambitions soared ever higher, culminating in 1931's extravaganza *Cavalcade*. 'Popular tunes probe the memory more swiftly than anything else,' he said, studding the action with favourites all the way from the Boer War in his birth-year of 1899, up to 1930. There were paper-sellers shouting, commotion on the London streets (the capital being, to his mind, the whole locus of national history) and memories of Victoria Station in wartime (hospital trains, chaplains, officers, tarts). There was, too, a great Coward original in 'Twentieth Century Blues' – not really a blues, musically, but another snapshot of the giddy age around him, queasily pale in a nightclub's bar lights.

Coward was a patriot and hoped that *Cavalcade* would embody that feeling – he was thrilled when Royals came to view his play. But critics found the flag-waving shrill: 'I had not intended *Cavalcade* to be so Jingoistic and True Blue Conservative in tone as many people imagined,' he confessed. Once again however the wider London public had no such misgivings. Their city, after all, always assumed itself to be the natural home of British national sentiment, and as much its visual symbol as the white cliffs, rolling downs and sun-dappled cottages of an idealised rural South.

Yet it was not until the Second World War that this symbiotic bonding of Noël Coward, London and British patriotism reached full fruition. His regard for the city that raised him was suddenly sharpened by its experience of attack. 'In 1941,' he wrote, 'the real lights of London shone through the blackout with a steady brilliance that I shall never forget.' In that same year he penned four songs specifically to stiffen the country's morale. One was a trifle entitled

'Could You Please Oblige Us With a Bren Gun?' Another, far more famous, was the song he was inspired to write one morning while he watched resilient Londoners cope with the carnage and destruction of last night's air raid. It was the practically perfect 'London Pride'.

As Coward remembered, he'd taken the tune from an old street song of the flower sellers, 'Won't You Buy My Sweet Blooming Lavender?' Others point to a folk song called 'Who'll Buy My Violets?' Either way, its origins are in the impeccably London heritage of everyday commerce. More intriguingly, Coward believed the old English tune to have been stolen by the Germans for their own anthem 'Deutschland über Alles' (and the melodic similarity is indeed evident); he felt there was no better time to reclaim it. A folk song with the cadence of a church hymn, 'London Pride' begins amid the 'coster barrows' and expands into a meditation on the city's collective memory, preserved by tradition, imprinted in the very streets.

His family having moved out of their latterday home in Ebury Street (he installed them at a grander residence in Kent), Coward moved deeper into Belgravia, to Gerald Road. Temporarily ejected by the Blitz, he stayed for a while in the Savoy, and when a bomb blew out a door of the Grill, he sprang to the stage to join Judy Campbell in her new hit song 'A Nightingale Sang in Berkeley Square'. Coward's eminence in the war years cannot be underestimated. There is the tale of Winston Churchill and America's leader Franklin D. Roosevelt, each insisting they knew every word of 'Mad Dogs and Englishmen' – they wagered and Churchill lost, over a minor discrepancy in one line. 'England can take it,' he reassured Coward later.

Post-1945 Britain was much changed, obviously, and Noël Coward was not – he was only older. He felt estranged from the new ways and was sometimes written off as a snobbish anachronism. Yet he continued working and was never without an appreciative audience. The life of Soho after dark (the time, paradoxically, when Soho is really at its brightest) still fascinated him. As a theatre worker and a homosexual, the district's after-hours traditions of tolerance and discretion were welcoming. He made it the setting for his 1950 musical *Ace of Clubs*, a story of gangsters and lovelorn sailors. At one stage its chorus girls perform something called 'Would You Like to Stick a Pin in My Balloon?' – at which, one feels, Marie Lloyd would have winked.

He acknowledged the end of the music halls in his short play *Red Peppers*, in which he and Gertie Lawrence take the roles of fading players in a dying trade (its bracingly rude number 'Has Anyone Seen Our Ship?' is also in the Julie Andrews film). But Coward need not mourn the halls, nor rue the West End theatres that no longer loved him, for he was a solid presence in the newer and far more powerful medium of cinema. *Bitter Sweet, Cavalcade, Private Lives, Blithe Spirit, In Which We Serve, This Happy Breed* and *Brief Encounter* all reached the screen and, while he sometimes disliked the results, they kept his name in lights. Indeed my own generation's first sight of Coward, rather later, was his venerable convict in 1969's *The Italian Job*.

Just as importantly, to him, he discovered cabaret. In 1951 he performed his first run at the Café de Paris in Coventry Street. The opening night was attended by Princess Margaret and, as a forty-five-minute reprise of his greatest hits, it set the essential pattern. Similar stints would follow in America. In private he was painfully aware that he was out of step in the democratic age of rock 'n' roll, but he was still loved by millions. The fruity English voice, the witty observations of town manners, the poignant songs of romance and regret, are embedded in popular culture's memory.

If Coward has no obvious successors it is because the vacancy has never really arisen. His music and drama are still ubiquitous. Bryan Ferry translated Coward's mooing insouciance quite brilliantly; Paul McCartney's occasional homages can be heard from 'Honey Pie' on the *White Album* to the cover of 'A Room With a View' in the 1998 tribute album (which also has Robbie Williams tackling 'There are Bad Times Just Around the Corner'). He was obsolete only for a short time, and his ghost now shimmies in the pantheon of London's immortals.

Al Bowlly's in Heaven: More Mayfair Tales

Pre-war London hotels with pretensions to importance, and many ambitious restaurants, retained their own dance orchestras. Middle-class patrons swarmed in from the suburbs to enjoy a more refined time than was offered by the local fleapit or variety hall. From 1935 to '38, a Londoner named Bram Martin led the Holborn Restaurant's resident band, where he probably played the kind of hot new tunes that spoiled G. K. Chesterton's dinner. Martin was a cello player himself, and enjoyed a long post-war career. It is delightful to note that on 27 September 1967, long after he had hung up his white tie and tails, he was engaged to play a session at EMI's Abbey Road studios, sawing mournfully through a bizarre new Beatles piece titled 'I Am the Walrus'.

At the Monseigneur Restaurant in Piccadilly during the 1930s, one might dine to the smooth strains of the Tipica Orchestra, fronted by an equally smooth Italian immigrant called Mantovani. (By the 1950s he was a prodigiously famous recording star; his arranger Ronald Bynge helped achieve an ethereally spacey thing called 'Charmaine', so imprinted on young minds of the time that David Bowie evokes it in 1977's 'Sound and Vision'.) Elsewhere, the Georgians were a jazz ensemble led by the trumpeter Nat Gonella, whose style was an education for British successors like Humphrey Lyttelton. I like Gonella most, though, for his uniquely London singing voice; the charming result of Louis Armstrong's influence on a cockney larynx.

And there was Ray Noble. His band was a showcase for the exquisite crooner Al Bowlly, who sang the leader's own tune 'Goodnight Sweetheart'. Bowlly brought out the best in Noble's writing: their finest collaboration would have to be 1932's 'Love is the Sweetest Thing'. One night in the war, Bowlly came home from a gig in High Wycombe to sleep at his flat in Jermyn Street – alas the Luftwaffe dropped in that same evening and the singer was killed outright. In 1985 Richard Thompson wrote a song in his memory called 'Al Bowlly's in Heaven'.

When Cole Porter's musical *Nymph Errant* arrived in London in 1933 its cast included Elisabeth Welch, one of many American musicians to make their home in London (more than few, like Welch herself, were black). She had already made her name by bringing the Charleston to Broadway and was eternally linked to Porter's song 'Love for Sale'. Soon she was singing in Ivor Novello's *Glamorous Night* and appearing at the exclusive Café de Paris. She had her own radio series, *Soft Lights and Sweet Music*, and acquired an art deco pad in a mews off Sloane Street. She endured remarkably: I first found her in 1980, on a vinyl single at the bottom of the *NME*'s reviews box, performing 'Stormy Weather' from Derek Jarman's film *The Tempest*. Even then she had another twenty-three years inside her and lived to be ninety-nine.

A fellow African-American in town was Turner Layton, from Washington DC. Already the co-author of songs like 'Way Down Yonder in New Orleans', he teamed with Clarence Johnstone and sailed to London where he became a regular at the Café de Paris. He charmed, among others, Charlie Chaplin, the Prince of Wales and Lady Diana Cooper. ('He was an incredibly attractive man. I assumed that every woman in the audience felt that Turner was singing only to them.') He chose to stay in Britain through the Blitz, which may be another reason that Winston Churchill liked him, and he remained here until he died in a North London nursing home in 1978.

There were other great vocalists plying their trade around the West End in those years. The Grenadian Leslie 'Hutch' Hutchinson, London's most renowned ladies' man, might be at Quaglino's in St James's, intoning 'Begin the Beguine'. He was also known to hear that Nightingale from Berkeley Square (though not, alas, literally – when the site for Buckingham Palace was leased in 1703 it was still 'a little wilderness full of blackbirds and nightingales', but the latter species was destined for rural exile). Londoner Sam Browne was also in earshot of the Square, entertaining the May Fair Hotel with Irving Berlin's 'Let's Face the Music and Dance'.

And, before the fiddlers have fled, let us return to Browne's mentor Bert Ambrose. Whatever their own merits, band-leaders may be more remembered for their protégés (something which recurs in the London blues scene of Cyril Davies, Alexis Korner and John Mayall). Two of the bigger names who emerged from beneath Bert's wing were a Wandsworth trombonist, Ted Heath, destined to become Britain's biggest band-leader in his own right (though never Prime Minister; that was someone else); and a girl vocalist from East Ham. She of course was Vera Lynn, the Forces' Sweetheart ...

It's a Lovely Day Tomorrow: London during Wartime

'The War,' they used to joke, 'was started by Vera Lynn's agent.' It was a fair point. Though by no means untalented, her career was transformed by a macabre whim of Fate. From being the presentable singer of undemanding songs ('Be Like the Kettle and Sing'), she became the living embodiment of Britain's resistance to Hitler and the Powers of Darkness. She has remained as much to this very day. We cannot hear her trilling 'We'll Meet Again' or 'The White Cliffs of Dover' without imagining, to ourselves, the dismaying wail of air-raid sirens – or sensing a flush of that London Pride that her music instilled in a city's battered population. In 2007, when Dame Vera was ninety, the Sex Pistols walked onstage to her recording of 'There'll Always be an England'. Against all odds, the tribute seemed sincere.

Though an East Ender, her roots were in the Mayfair dance bands of the inter-war years, rather than music hall. Her fame began to grow when she sang with the Joe Loss Orchestra on BBC wireless; at twenty she joined Bert Ambrose (where she fell for the band's saxophonist Harry Lewis, her future husband and manager). Her first solo record was called 'Up the Wooden Hills to Bedfordshire' – a funny old term for bed-time which supplied a title for some later urchins of her home streets, the Small Faces. And then the Second World War happened ...

At first the nation's radio diet was rationed to the Home Service, but in 1940 a second station, the Forces Programme, was added, with an emphasis on entertainment. It was a tonic for the troops and a solace for those they left behind. Here, Vera Lynn really began to shine. A year later she had her own series, *Sincerely Yours, Vera Lynn* – and if it sounds like a letter from home that was probably intentional. She really was the Forces' Sweetheart. Her image was pretty and engaging, but definitely wholesome. She was not a glamorous sex-bomb pandering to the lonesome soldiers' lower instincts. Instead she aroused a wistful yearning for the idealised fiancée. And the female audience could approve of her completely.

Her wartime material had two great themes: consolation in separation, and faith in the final outcome. 'Wish Me Luck as You Wave Me Goodbye', 'I'll Pray for You', 'It's a Lovely Day Tomorrow', 'When the Lights Go on Again', 'When They Sound the Last All-Clear' … The messages were uplifting and direct. Under war conditions, however, it was hard to assemble full orchestras. Sometimes she was accompanied by Mantovani with a scaled-down band, as on that classic dream of peace-time, 'The White Cliffs of Dover'. Occasionally her only partner was Arthur Young, who played a tremulous electric organ called the Novachord – their version of 'We'll Meet Again' ('don't know where, don't know when') has the desolate eeriness of a spiritualist's séance. One remembers that, for many listeners in 1939, the reunion they longed for would not be in this life.

Vera Lynn's cockney origins were not in evidence. The time of pantomime costers was passing and, like so many of her generation, she aspired to the crystalline diction of the BBC. But her homages to London lacked nothing in warmth. She popularised 'A Nightingale Sang in Berkeley Square', with its almost hallucinatory visions of Mayfair – 'angels dining at the Ritz', streets paved with stars. (It's interesting that nightingales, as a naturalist of the time noted, 'are well known for their indifference to gunfire'. So there was, perhaps, a sub-conscious note of 'London can take it'.) And from 1941 comes a quite sublime affair, 'The London I Love'. It's a rapturous stream of images – of street lamps, newsboys and pubs, of Mayfair hotels, 'Palladium nights', church bells and 'the River gleaming'. It's London as a dream, summoned in a time when its utter destruction looked as likely as anything else.

It has often seemed – as non-Londoners tend to notice – that the capital is taken to represent all of England, even all of Britain. In the Second World War this habit was at its height, particularly during the Blitz. London's struggle was held to be emblematic of the entire Empire's fight for survival. Noël Coward could write of his 'London Pride' without a nod to the Mersey, Clyde or Tyne. The great toe-tapping example of 1943 was 'I'm Going to Get Lit Up When the Lights Go Up in London', written by Hubert Gregg (who would also pen 'Maybe it's Because I'm a Londoner'). An earlier number on the same black-out theme was 'Till the Lights of London Shine Again'. Rather less celebrated songs of the time included 'Billy Brown of London Town' (who, we learn, 'stood up and saved the Town when London Bridge was falling down') and 'The King is Still in London' (''cos it's where he wants to be').

During the war the more formal dances tailed off – there were simply no evening dresses to be had, nor enough male partners. But local 'hops' might thrive if there were servicemen stationed nearby. And popular dancehalls did very well, especially the Lyceum, the Dorchester, and the Locarno in Streatham. Being below street level the Paramount, in Tottenham Court Road, was favoured when air raids were threatened. And there was still the jewel of West London, the Hammersmith Palais. 'How I loved those evenings,' one girl recalled. 'I travelled twenty-nine stations on the Underground to get there and twenty-nine to get home again. The girls always managed to look colourful and attractive, and the servicemen of all nationalities appeared suave and handsome in their varied uniforms. We danced the night away jiving, jitter-bugging, waltzing, with a rhumba and a tango thrown in.'

Yet death came even to dance floors. The elegant Café de Paris, between Piccadilly and Leicester Square, was an art deco palace built in 1924. It had been a popular haunt of Cole Porter and the Prince of Wales. Some, however, called it unlucky because it was built on the site of a Tudor bear-pit. Others held its ballroom was modelled on the *Titanic*. What is more certain is that on the night of 8 March 1941, a German bomb came smashing through the Rialto Cinema above, plunged down and killed around eighty people, including the evening's star attraction, Ken 'Snakehips' Johnson. The Nazi propagandist William Joyce had earlier made a sneering broadcast about 'the plutocrats and favoured lords of creation' who enjoyed 'drunken orgies and debaucheries in the saloons of Piccadilly and in the Café de Paris' while dockland cockneys took a hammering. Now it was the toffs' turn.

Still, the stricken venue rose again – eventually its post-war doors would open for Frank Sinatra, Marlene Dietrich and of course Noël Coward; and in recent times there have been parties for Prince, Puff Daddy and the Spice Girls. If I am ever invited there I shall raise a glass to 'Snakehips' Johnson.

A hero of the home front was the singing comic Bud Flanagan. In jarring times his sleepy croon would soothe a nerve-racked city. Born Reuben Weintrop and raised in a Polish-Jewish household off Brick Lane, he was a call boy in the music halls and worked up his own act with partner Chesney Allen. When hostilities commenced, the man who had beguiled audiences with 'Underneath the Arches' could now calm wartime jitters with 'We're Going to Hang Out the Washing on the Siegfried Line'. Almost the last thing he did, before his death in 1968, was to record the theme song to *Dad's Army*, 'Who Do You Think You Are Kidding, Mr Hitler?' – a nicely nostalgic confection that offered him the perfect exit.

Among Bud Flanagan's best-loved numbers was 'Run Rabbit Run' (which he occasionally changed to 'Run Adolf Run'). It was written by Noel Gay, the composer of a landmark London musical, *Me and My Girl*. From this 1937 show we have the hardy perennials 'The Sun Has Got His Hat On', 'Leaning On a Lamp-post' and of course its title song. But above them all stands 'The Lambeth Walk', *Me and My Girl*'s supreme contribution to the war effort. The play itself is a genial yarn of English class differences, of Lambeth versus Mayfair, of Hampshire gentry and pearly costermongers. The latter perform their tribal dance, a jaunty strut that became a national craze, with its cockney war whoop 'Oi!' A Third Reich pundit denounced the Lambeth Walk as 'Jewish mischief and animalistic hopping', an opinion that failed to dent its popularity. In 1942 the song was famously put to spliced-up news footage of Hitler and his goose-stepping troops, creating a masterpiece of humorous propaganda that remains a YouTube staple to this day.

For civilians hunkering in their Anderson shelters, wireless stars of the period included the band-leaders Mantovani, Geraldo, Joe Loss, Victor Sylvester, Jack Jackson and – their doyen – the BBC's own orchestral supremo, Henry Hall. (Of him it was said, 'He was the only man who could introduce "The Teddy Bears' Picnic" as if it were a classical symphony.') Also popular was the avuncular Billy Cotton, though he found real celebrity as a fixture of post-war TV, bawling 'Wakey wakey!' at an audience who never seemed to resent him for it.

Billy Cotton's life was more extraordinary than one might guess. Born in London in 1899, he played drums and bugle for the Army in the First World War, and then football for Brentford and Wimbledon FC. Thus he came to see action at both Gallipoli and Plough Lane, which may be enough for anyone's lifetime. He was a successful racing driver and also flew bi-planes. By day he drove a London bus before turning pro-musician. As a band-leader he dabbled in hot jazz and progressed to a kind of neo-music hall novelty style, favourites including 'I've Got a Lovely Bunch of Coconuts'. He died at Wembley watching a boxing match. He is a distant ancestor of the TV presenter Fearne Cotton.

Billy Cotton was not what we would call a looker. Rotund and bald, he resembled a large grapefruit in horn-rimmed spectacles. But he was a harbinger of the new age: the age of television. His weekly shows brought him a fame and ubiquity that no mere band-leader or music hall act could ever achieve. 'It wasn't like this before the war,' you heard people say in those days. They were largely correct. We were post-war now, the telly was in the corner and nothing would ever be the same.

Supercalifragilisticexpialidocious: the Musical Fights Back

The Mayfair ballrooms never did regain their pre-war panache. The rich were all elsewhere or simply no longer rich. Music hall was aped in TV studios full of lights and wires and men in headphones but its spirit, of course, could never revive in places like that. The radio would remain, for a few more years, a solemn mahogany cenotaph in the sitting room, and a school of very English 'Light Music' still flourished under its aegis. The composers Eric Coates, Albert Ketelbey and Richard Addinsell were among the masters of the genre, running up pastoral idylls, historical suites and exotic fantasias. Coates had written, in the 1930s, some musical portraits of the smarter London locations, and you could barely move for orchestral sketches of Merrie England, Nell Gwynn and Robin Hood. Ronald Binge's 'Elizabethan Serenade', Ketelbey's 'In a Monastery Garden', Coates's 'Sleepy Lagoon' . . . such tunes lulled the towns and shires until the wireless was replaced by transistor radios – tinny and cheap, with harsher wares to peddle.

There were still a few revues knocking around. You took a bus past bombsite hoardings to the re-awakening West End and there were Flanders and Swann, two droll chaps with a hint of the 1840s supper-and-glee clubs to them. They sang of gnus, armadillos and the gas man – wry amusements knocked together on long afternoons in Hampstead Garden Suburb. The songs-and-sketches formula was now reduced in scale from anything the Edwardians might have recognised, but the newly intimate revue gave rise to a London brand of cabaret satire that would find its way to TV. Then it more or less expired.

The big bands of the 1930s and 1940s would find the going harder, as well. The outstanding American graduate of that school was, of course, Frank Sinatra, who sang some very affecting London songs and liked to stay at the Savoy, or else in a modest flat in Grosvenor Square, where Marines from the US Embassy would guard his car. 'London by Night', from 1957's travelogue LP *Come Fly With Me*, is a polished evocation of the lovers' city that may emerge 'when the moon shines on Circus and Square'. Another number, George and Ira Gershwin's 'A Foggy Day', perhaps attracted Frank with its stock tourist allusions to the British Museum and pea-soupers. It appealed to many great interpreters, too, from Ella Fitzgerald to Billie Holiday. And we owe its existence, curiously, to P. G. Wodehouse; when his 1919 story *A Damsel in Distress* was to become a film, George Gershwin was approached to write the score, having already worked on a Wodehouse musical before. Its first presentation, then, was by the movie's male lead Fred Astaire.

Britain itself had a capable crooner, in the form of Marylebone's Dickie Valentine, who had formerly served in Ted Heath's band. Mellow and romantic, he looks now like the last of a line. But closer to the Sinatra mould was another Londoner, Matt Monro – so close, actually, that his employers the BBC Showband thought of calling him Hank Sonata. It was a narrow escape for the Putney boy who had grown up as Terry Parsons, and was almost dubbed 'the Singing Bus Driver' after an early stint with London Transport. Then he was fortuitously teamed with the up-and-coming producer George Martin at Parlophone, and writers like Lionel Bart ('From Russia With Love') and Don Black and John Barry ('Born Free'), who all serviced his superb voice. Black has ranked him with Sinatra, Tony Bennett and Perry Como: 'In this country, they regard him as a short, overweight guy who was a bus driver. They don't appreciate how great he was.'

The post-war years were heady ones for the American musical. Richard Rodgers and his new partner Oscar Hammerstein were at the fore, creating stories and characters of more vigour and moral complexity than was common in the genre. Premiered on Broadway in 1943, their *Oklahoma!* ushered in a golden age. It certainly captivated Londoners. Through a long run at bomb-damaged Drury Lane, audiences huddled with blankets and hot water bottles against a hole in the roof and fog that crept up the aisles. Princess Margaret is said to have attended twenty-seven times. One of the players recalled, 'London was incredibly exciting, because obviously the war had been such a strain on everyone that the British public just opened their arms to this fresh and exhilarating Rodgers and Hammerstein musical.'

In musicals, as in much else, Britain was now the poor relation to America. Yet several of the greatest shows were inspired by London. They were steeped in its historical character and – overlooking the accent of Mr Dick Van Dyke – true to the city they celebrated.

My Fair Lady vibrates with the sense of London as market-place. Developed from George Bernard Shaw's play *Pygmalion*, Lerner and Loewe's musical sets out its stall, so to speak, in the Covent Garden Piazza of 1912. A cockney flower-girl, Eliza, meets the grandly patrician Henry Higgins. As in *The Beggar's Opera* two centuries earlier, all relationships are predicated on trade. Higgins and the girl's rascally father will bargain for her. For the Professor and his circle, the girl is only a scientific curio, good for a wager. As any musical must, *My Fair Lady* offers romance: 'On the Street Where You Live' and so on. But still it is a tale tinged with urban cynicism. And we savour, once again, the clash of rich and poor whom London life has thrown together – to their mutual, if horrified, fascination.

The original male stars of *My Fair Lady* were Rex Harrison as Professor Higgins, and the variety turn Stanley Holloway as Eliza Doolittle's father. (Holloway brings a world of music hall heartiness to numbers such as 'Get Me to the Church on Time'.) Both were in the New York opening in 1956, and survived its transfer to Hollywood. But the stage Eliza, young Julie Andrews of Walton-on-Thames, was replaced on screen by the better-known Audrey Hepburn. The snub would, ironically, give the English Rose her all-important career break – because it left her free to make her film debut in quite another London musical, *Mary Poppins*. After which, the very hills would be alive with the sound of her music.

For the gala premiere of *Mary Poppins*, held at Grauman's Chinese Theater in Hollywood, in 1964, celebrity guests were greeted by white-gloved British bobbies – or actors in the approximate costumes – while a pearly coster band played beside the red carpet. These were Tinsel Town moments, but it was not a phoney sort of film. Its creator, Walt Disney, had taken pains to root his tale of a magical flying nanny in the solid clay of London. He had spent years coaxing Pamela Travers, the somewhat crusty English author of the 1934 book, into granting him film rights. He'd assigned the highly capable US team of Richard and Robert Sherman to write the songs. And the movie opens with a beautifully painted vista of the city sky-line in 1910, at the peak of its Edwardian self-assurance.

But it's the music of *Mary Poppins* that is truest to London. The Sherman brothers had been diligent in their research. They were already familiar with music hall's American cousin vaudeville. (Even the crisply spoken Julie Andrews had a family past in knockabout variety.) Pamela Travers, who did not easily surrender control, asked them to include 'Ta Ra Ra Boom De Ay' and 'Greensleeves' – tactfully, they consented to a short passage from the latter. At first called 'The Pearly Song', 'Supercalifragilisticexpialidocious' – which is indeed performed by a cartoon troupe of pearly kings and queens – was based upon a brace of old Harry Champion songs, 'Any Old Iron' and 'Boiled Beef and Carrots'. And a number invoking the City's financial solidity, 'Fidelity Fiduciary Bank', took for its model the mock-pomposity of Gilbert and Sullivan.

The chimney-potted history lesson does not stop there. Upon the rooftops, where the chimney sweeps swagger like sooty princes, and the city spreads out with its Wren spires like stalagmites, 'Step in Time' was *Mary Poppins*' dance spectacular. It came about when Walt Disney heard some British stage-hands doing 'Knees Up Mother Brown' and asked the Shermans to contrive something similar. Then, as befits a London film, the soundtrack finds its keynote in the song of a street trader – 'Feed the Birds (Tuppence a Bag)'. Sung by the old lady on St Paul's steps, it struck both Disney and the Shermans that this was their emotional crux. Here was humanity in a stony city's heart.

The male lead of *Mary Poppins* is of course Bert, a jack-of-all-trades – including busker and pavement artist – but it is Bert the chimney sweep that we remember. London is traditionally known as the Smoke. Its lung-punishing air was for centuries a defining characteristic. The tribe of sweeps who lived a secret existence in the city's blackest crevices are a natural source of wonder. But let us admit that we mainly think of Bert because, playing him, was the American Dick Van Dyke. The actor's wildly uncertain way with regional British speech was a common Hollywood defect. (For a rare exception see the splendid rock satire *This is Spinal Tap.*) On its release in 1964, the massive American popularity of *Mary Poppins* reinforced a quaintly dated image of England. Yet it coincided exactly with the Beatles' epic conquest of that country, conveying an image entirely new and different. The four Liverpudlians' voices were inescapable that year, which might further explain Van Dyke's confused cockney vowels.

Where *Mary Poppins* saw London as a place of magical transformations – where angels might indeed be dining at the Ritz, or a patch of wasteland could become the psychedelic 'Itchycoo Park' – another musical took a less benign view. The gruesome tale of *Sweeney Todd, the Demon Barber of Fleet Street* originated in the 'penny dreadful' horror comics of the 1840s. Through its adventures of the dastardly barber whose clients end up as the filling for meat pies, we are reminded of London's most pitiless aspect – a city where all humanity gets reduced to the level of commodity. A city that literally eats you up.

Sweeney Todd was regularly adapted for the movies and the stage, but its most haunting expression came in Stephen Sondheim's musical – a 1979 Broadway production that would, in turn, spawn the 2007 cinematic version by Tim Burton, with Johnny Depp starring. But on a humbler level the Demon Barber's name had already been enshrined as rhyming slang for the Flying Squad, inspiring the 1970s TV crime series *The Sweeney.* (Which prompts a memory of that show's successor, *Minder,* the home of another London immortal, Arthur Daley, ageing wheeler-dealer and car-trade coster.)

Fond as I am of America's 'London' musicals, they were surely surpassed by a very British production. Written by the East Ender Lionel Bart, inspired by London's greatest novelist Charles Dickens,

Oliver! stands in splendid isolation. Nobody, including Bart himself, could ever match the swarming energy of this exuberant tribute to London in story, song and dance. (Its latest revival hit the West End in 2009.) In fact, few lives were ever as emblematic of London's musical history as that of its creator, which is why we shall meet Lionel Bart again, several times, in the chapters ahead.

Bart (1930–1999) was born Lionel Begleiter to a family of East European refugees. It's said that he changed his name on impulse when the bus stopped outside Bart's Hospital, in Smithfield, where old Brother Rahere had once rollicked. Within his own lifetime, Bart connects the inter-war Jewish life of Stepney with the post-war Soho of Tin Pan Alley. He wrote some enormous hits of the early pop era, for Matt Monro, for Anthony Newley, Cliff Richard, Tommy Steele and others. He was recognised and nurtured by Noël Coward, yet he also managed (fleetingly) the Rolling Stones. He became a central player in London's 'Swinging Sixties', socialising with Princess Margaret and the Beatles. And then, somehow, he contrived to lose everything. He died penniless, an alcoholic, a major talent whose best years were a very distant memory.

Bart's early promise was evident in his songs for a 1959 show, *Fings Ain't Wot They Used to Be* (which laments, among other things, the replacement of the local Palais with a bowling alley). He was offering a shot of that streetwise edge, impudence and working-class realism that the London stage had not known since music hall. And he was a superb tunesmith, quite the best of his generation. These were the virtues he could bring to Dickens's *Oliver Twist*, itself a magisterial examination of London's lowest depths, its casual inhumanity and sudden flashes of grace. *Oliver!* opened at the New Theatre (now called the Noël Coward Theatre) in 1960, and became a hit movie in 1968. The story's most endearing character, the cockney guttersnipe Artful Dodger, has at different times been played by Anthony Newley, Steve Marriott of the Small Faces, Davy Jones of the Monkees, Phil Collins and Robbie Williams.

Dozens of latterday music hall performers were hired for the dazzling crowd scenes of the *Oliver!* film. In downtime on the set at

Shepperton studios they kept up the atmosphere with renditions of 'The Rat Catcher's Daughter'. The show's own tunes are full of the same rambunctious cheer. Then there is the capital's mercenary streak: 'Boy For Sale'; 'You've Got to Pick a Pocket or Two'. Dickens never forgot that life in London – for all but a fortunate few – was a desperate, hand-to-mouth affair.

Lionel Bart observed that *Oliver!* was really about the search for love, and the special kind of loneliness that cities like London inflict. Yet again, though, it's a song of commerce that is the musical's most poignant. Framed by an achingly beautiful sequence of choreographed street sellers, 'Who Will Buy?' is surely the ultimate London song. Even the 'wonderful morning' is up for sale. Thus are the oldest cries of its population re-imagined. In a city that starves the body and denies the soul, here – in a heart-rending tune – is the Londoner's struggle to keep both body and soul together.

Chapter Four

More in Soho than in Ongar

Jazz nights under neon. Skiffle and calypso. Tin Pan Alley and the absolute beginnings of English rock 'n' roll.

So far we've sojourned in the City, prowled the East End and sported in Mayfair. Now is the time to cross back east of Regent Street, to visit a district more important to post-war pop than any other. This is Soho. Louche London. Bohemia, W1. This is everything Suburbia could never be. Above all, this is the land of Tin Pan Alley.

The *business* of music – a shadowy world of cash and contracts, of sharkish cigar-chompers in camel-hair coats, issuing their ever-hopeful cries of 'Boy, have I got a song for *you*!' – all of this was long established in the area. Just across from Soho proper, along the Charing Cross Road and New Oxford Street were publishers' offices that dated back to music hall. And the greatest concentration was in Denmark Street, at Soho's north-east corner. Today this little thoroughfare is a last fragment of the old slum-warren of St Giles, most of which made way for the 1960s behemoth Centre Point. Many still know Denmark Street by the nickname it acquired before the war, 'Tin Pan Alley'.

The original alley was in New York, on West 28th Street, where it is said that rival publishers would clang their metallic pots to drown out rivals. This may well be untrue, but show business thrives on colourful lies. Others suggest Tin Pan Alley was simply a sardonic term for the clatter of pianos from a dozen open windows. It was adopted by the London trade, anyhow. In its time, Denmark Street has housed at least one legendary studio (Regent Sound, which later became the rock 'n' roll bookshop Helter Skelter), an equally legendary coffee bar (the Giaconda) and provided temporary lodgings to David Bowie, the Sex Pistols and the *New Musical Express*. The Noel Gay Organisation is still here, as well as several instrument shops and the estimable 12-Bar Club. By the 1950s Tin Pan Alley was shorthand for the music business in general, especially its sharper and less respectable end, where songwriters, agents and managers circled each other in a perpetual, desperate dance.

In effect, Tin Pan Alley was the whole of Soho and some adjoining streets. It was simply in the personality of the area to host ambivalent glamour and shady commerce. Before the pushers of pop moved in, these streets were the lair of dishevelled artists and writers, like Julian Maclaren-Ross, Dylan Thomas, Francis Bacon and Patrick Hamilton. Several of their set, like the celebrated Quentin Crisp, preferred the northern side of Oxford Street, the part known as Fitzrovia, where pubs would unlock their doors a crucial half-hour earlier. In later years the living symbol of Soho was the journalist Jeffrey Bernard, forever awaking in bleary-eyed squalor and consoling himself that it would soon be 'opening-time in Billingsgate'.

In Dean Street, down Wardour Street (where the film industry clustered) and around Soho Square, the post-war reprobate could saunter and be among friends, or at least like-minded enemies. Refugees and immigrants, traditionally French or Italian, had already stamped their cosmopolitan style here. And immigrants, being ambitious and hard-working, supplied the kind of all-night dives that professional English layabouts required. It was undeniably a criminal district, too, with a hard subterranean layer, though its viciousness was seldom inflicted on civilians; Soho remains a relatively safe place to be. For everyone else, for the man on the Clapham omnibus or Northerners in town for the FA Cup, Soho was sex. It was London's little Pigalle, Reeperbahn and 42nd Street.

As the city's red-light district and the West End's hindquarters, Soho attracted a species called the 'spiv' – small-time profiteers on the wartime black-market who found the neon blink of primitive coffee bars, Caribbean drinking dens and experimental jazz joints an agreeable sequel to the Blitz. The spivs, of course, reinforced the national view of Londoners: too flash, too mouthy, too quick to take your money and vanish with the change. The spiv was a living repudiation of self-sacrifice; he was now 'post-war' in a very insolent sense, without respect, gratitude or idealism. And because the spiv was not a true English gentleman, he had no use for Savile Row, dressing instead in brash clothes of dubious foreign origin.

Soho supplied the spivs' sartorial needs, and its fashion doyen was Cecil Gee, an East Ender moved up West. He took his style from the United States, wide-shouldered and gangsterish, before adopting the slimmer 'modernist' look of southern Europe. While the spivs had liked the former, it was the latter that attracted a new breed: jazz fans. It's to these people that the next decade belongs. The jazz clubs of Soho were a bridge from old bohemia to London pop. They offer a picturesque passage in central London's progress from post-war wasteland to global fleshpot.

Over the next twenty years Soho, the time-honoured sanctuary of refugees, aesthetic misfits and sexual outsiders, was adopted by another wave. It was colonised by the founders of modern youth culture and the middle-aged entrepreneurs who hovered around them. Simultaneously came an explosion of electronic media, offering more opportunities for fame than ever before. For the young post-war rebel there was no better place to be. From Bromley and Bermondsey they flocked. From Betjeman's Metro-land they fled. And in Soho they found a home.

We Blew Real Good, Man: Jazz Among the Ruins

How did it feel to be young in Soho in 1945? The mayhem of war was over. There were bombsites and shortages, but the sirens had fallen silent. The men, or at least the fortunate ones, were coming home. Laurie Morgan, the jazz musician, has spoken of his generation feeling shell-shocked, disconnected. But then came a new mood in music, and all was suddenly clear. They say war adds an edge to the appetite for life. For certain young survivors of the London Blitz, there was only one kind of music that really worked now, and that was jazz. All the old terror and the brand-new exhilaration they felt were captured in this frantic noise.

The jazz that excited Laurie Morgan was the 'modernist' variety, a harsh, unsettling New York import that could also seem austerely intellectual. But before the modernists took root in London there were the revivalists, players who followed the style of early New Orleans. British interest in jazz had dwindled from its 1920s peak, though its impact on the mainstream was clear enough in the swing style of the big bands. Underground, the purist flame was kept alive by isolated enthusiasts who emerged as a movement in the 1940s, their figureheads being Ken Colyer, Chris Barber and Humphrey Lyttelton. Between the revivalists and the modernists there was at first no common ground.

The revivalists hit their stride in 1950, when the Hammersmith Palais held a huge show to mark the thirtieth anniversary of the Original Dixieland Jazz Band's historic appearance there. There were now jazz clubs everywhere in London, including the dancehall on Eel Pie Island, a future rhythm-and-blues venue in the middle of the Thames at Twickenham. But Soho was the nerve centre – Cy Laurie's club in Ham Yard, near the Windmill Theatre, opened in 1951 and eventually became an HQ of the London mods. Ken Colyer's Studio 51, in Great Newport Street, opened in the same year. Humphrey Lyttelton took over Feldman's Swing Club at 100 Oxford Street to found what later became the temple of punk rock, the 100 Club. Much of what developed in London's popular music can be traced to those post-war jazz days.

Against the revivalists stood the modernist adherents of bebop and 'cool jazz', fans in particular of Charlie Parker and, later, of Miles Davis. They favoured a sort of existential moodiness (indicated, for example, by wearing shades in darkened nightclubs) over the beer-swilling, student heartiness of rival jazz scenes. In search of kindred souls they gathered at the Nucleus coffee house in Monmouth Street – like Colyer's Studio 51, it was in that western strip of Covent Garden that's just beyond the Charing Cross Road yet feels, spiritually, like part of Soho. Or else they went to Johnny Dankworth's Club Eleven in Carnaby Street – an obscure Soho conduit at this point, but destined for bigger things.

The fans of modernism were often themselves musicians, which was an advantage when it came to understanding the style's complexity. Many were alumni of 'Geraldo's Navy' – the band-leader Geraldo (actually a cockney, real name Gerald Bright) had recruited numerous musicians to play the transatlantic passenger ships. In so doing he reared a race of educated London jazzers, exposed to authentic American playing at a time when real US musicians were rarely heard in London. As well as adopting the snazziest Stateside fashions, they could earn a little on the side by bringing home prized American bottles of Old Spice aftershave.

Ronnie Scott (1927–1996) was precisely such a modernist, in whose life a rich seam of London's jazz history is evident. Born to a family of East European Jews, the Schatts, he grew up in the East End near Tower Bridge. His father, an alto player and band-leader in the 1920s, changed his own name to Scott and Ronnie followed suit. His mother once paid a surprise visit to Scott Senior while he was on tour in Glasgow – he was, unfortunately, in bed with a girl at that moment and divorce ensued. But the son was destined to follow in father's musical footsteps.

As a boy Ronnie Scott's favourite sound was the commotion of nearby Petticoat Lane, especially the sales spiel of his racing tipster uncle, whom he helped as a runner. In the standard pattern of Jewish social mobility, his mother took him away from the East End, northwards to Stoke Newington and Edgware, but as soon as he was old enough he struck out for Soho and his father's way of life. In those pre-war days every jobbing musician stood on Archer Street – a short stretch off Rupert Street, with a Red Lion at one end and a White Horse at the other – and here his dad's old pals found him a tenor sax. On Archer Street the players hung around in hope of work, each identified by his instrument case (or in the case of drummers by the sticks poking from their pockets). Showgirls from the

Windmill Theatre kept them company and there was the Harmony Inn café for sustenance. In the shady underworld from there to Old Compton Street was a network of gambling joints, for added recreation.

Under the spell of US players like Coleman Hawkins and Lester Young, Ronnie progressed from Jewish youth clubs to Soho joints like the Jamboree, the Bouillabaisse and the Nuthouse. When war broke out, an all-night Lyons Corner House by Piccadilly became the musicians' new refuge. Here the young London boys met US servicemen who brought jazz records and invitations to play at their parties. And at the Nuthouse or Feldman's there might be moonlighting players from the Glenn Miller Band, to see and be studied.

In 1946, aged nineteen, Scott secured a place in Ted Heath's band, playing Monday nights at the Hammersmith Palais. Yet, like a lot of the younger set, his heart was really in the Charlie Parker school of bebop, not the corny old swing he was being paid for. With fellow modernist Johnny Dankworth he took a dance-band gig aboard the *Queen Mary*, courtesy of Geraldo's Navy, and could at last experience the New York sound at first hand. By the 1950s Scott was the best tenor player in London, leading bands that included Benny Green and Tubby Hayes. In 1959 he opened his own club, on Gerrard Street (John Lennon came here on his birthday in 1963, to see Roland Kirk). In 1965 he moved the main premises to Frith Street – though he retained 'The Old Place' for a few more years – and there it remains, surviving Ronnie Scott himself.

Paul McCartney, the only long-term London Beatle, was a regular at Ronnie Scott's and hired the man himself to play on the jazz-inspired 'Lady Madonna' (copied off Humphrey Lyttelton's 1956 'Bad Penny Blues'). In 1990 I was the editor of *Q Magazine* and hosted its first annual awards. Ronnie Scott's seemed ideal for the hip, coolly intimate event we had in mind, and I invited McCartney along from his office at the top of the street. He arrived so early I had to fetch him a pint of bitter while he and Linda helped us lay the tables. Maybe I should have asked Spike Milligan as well, because for years he had his own table there. Once, in a conversation I'd conducted between him and Van Morrison, Spike gave us both a glimpse of how deeply jazz had touched his generation:

> I played trumpet and jazz guitar and piano. In about 1933 through to about 1947 . . . when you were very young, Van, I was keeping the pop scene going. I was playing the music of my day. Jazz was looked on as barbaric. My father would say, 'Why do you play that nigger music?' But I kept playing it. And now they have jazz critics in *The Times*, in the *Guardian*. I was blowing that music real good, man. One of the greatest feelings in the world is to play music, it's total freedom. When I was playing that trumpet I couldn't think about the rates, the rent. It was liberation, self-therapy. And you can induce that therapy in other people.

From our comfortable distance the jazzers' internecine disputes look almost comically theological, like the schisms that beset Christian sects and left-wing organisations. But at least they cared enough to squabble. Of the revivalists, the trumpeter and band-leader Ken Colyer was perhaps the sternest in his outlook, so committed to early New Orleans that every development – including the later work of Louis Armstrong himself – was dismissed as a betrayal. His trombonist Chris Barber had a more open attitude. In 1954 he walked out of Colyer's band and took their banjo-player, one Lonnie Donegan, along with him. An apparently minor tiff, it was to be the catalyst that sparked a revolution . . .

What Do You Want If You Don't Want Money? Tin Pan Alley Rock'n'Roll

It's not that Chris Barber was some showbiz opportunist. He was just as serious as any jazz fundamentalist, and sincere in his love for the folk-heritage of African-American music. (He would in due course become the great sponsor of visiting blues legends.) He, Colyer and Donegan used to vary their shows with a short 'skiffle' spot, a brisk acoustic set inspired by the informal 'rent parties' of Negro ghettoes. Played in back rooms on improvised instruments, the original skiffle was not an exact style (it went under various names, including 'jug', 'hamfat' and 'spasm') and took in bits of everything. But it was lively, infectious and fun. Now in London, there was even an element in the audience who preferred it to jazz. When Barber left to found his own band, he was careful to keep Donegan's skiffle spots.

The Barber/Donegan brand of skiffle was mainly based on rural folk-blues of the Deep South, and was shockingly successful. Their version of Leadbelly's 'Rock Island Line' was so popular it gave Donegan a spin-off hit in 1956 – even, amazingly, in America. He promptly went solo as a full-time skiffle star and thus began the British skiffle boom. Easy to play, needing only cheap guitars, broom-handle basses and scullery washboards, it became the nationwide phenomenon that gripped John Lennon, Paul McCartney and almost every UK star of the next decade. Skiffle was the entry-level music of an entire generation.

Donegan himself, though Glasgow-born, had grown up in the East End. Of his solo work, his old employer Chris Barber noted, 'Lonnie liked English comic songs, so Max Miller came into it as well.' Indeed, Donegan's passion for imported US blues was tempered by a love for good old London music hall, which led him to novelty blockbusters such as 'My Old Man's a Dustman' and 'Does Your Chewing Gum Lose its Flavour (on the Bedpost Over Night)?' He was of course in exile from the jazz fraternity now, and in time his own facetious ditties grew tiresome. As he reflected, ruefully, some years later, he was 'flogging a dead horse' and had, in effect, thrown away careers in both the jazz and pop worlds.

At the same time that skiffle was appearing, Britain made its first attempts to ape the rock 'n' roll records of Bill Haley, Little Richard and Elvis Presley. Skiffle was still played by enthusiastic amateurs, but London rock 'n' roll was a product of Tin Pan Alley – of businessmen who were not in this for love. That's why they hired reliable jazz professionals to play it. Probably the first British single in the new genre was 'Teach You to Rock', a 1956 effort by the

London jazz drummer Tony Crombie, a pal of Johnny Dankworth's. Unlike the USA, Britain had no pool of players who had grown up on rock's root styles – blues, gospel and country – and absorbed them organically. Instead we relied on reluctant jazzers, paid to play what they despised, and hopeful showbiz types like the singer Alma Cogan, who were simply willing to give it a bash. It seldom worked well.

Johnny Dankworth has confessed to disliking rock 'n' roll on first hearing it, and seeing it as a threat to his beloved jazz – though, as it turned out, rock's popularity had the effect of turning jazz followers into a more devoted tribe. Mick Jagger told me: 'Jazz people hated rock 'n' roll. I can't even start to tell you how much they hated it. I guess they saw it as a threat, and they didn't think that rock people had any technical ability, which a lot of the time was true, but it doesn't really matter.'

The pre-Beatles period of British rock 'n' roll, from 1956 to 1963, is fascinating and somehow rather neglected. It was both the most cynical of times and the most innocent. There was Tin Pan Alley's habitual greed and opportunism, but also a youthful energy and optimism that could, given the chance, infiltrate the recording studios and work magic.

And, for the first time in our tale, we have a London musical movement that was not fuelled on liquor. Soho's coffee bars were the cradle of native rock 'n' roll, where the Italians who had made the place their home imported the latest espresso machines and brought a late-night chromium glint to the scene. They were open after the pubs had shut, even if cappuccino, Coca-Cola and Capstan Full Strength were the only stimulants on offer. In April 1956, the 2i's coffee bar in Old Compton Street introduced live music in its tiny basement. Wally Whyton's skiffle band the Vipers were the first attraction, followed by Adam Faith's Worried Men, then by assorted line-ups who would in turn produce Cliff Richard and the Shadows. But most importantly, for our story, was the arrival of a Bermondsey boy with a toothy grin, the boy whom George Melly has called 'the first British pop event'. He was Tommy Steele.

Born in 1936, Thomas Hicks was steeped in cockney tradition. Among his early homes was the Dickensian-sounding Nickelby House – indeed he loved to read Dickens, and listened to the street traders calling 'Any old iron?' and 'Get your ripe tomatoes, hearty lettuce'. His wits were further sharpened by doing racecourse work for his father, who also worked as a minder in a Soho nightclub. During the Blitz his dockland home was a prime target, but Tommy was comforted by the wireless, Vera Lynn and *Variety Bandbox*. His dreams were of the London Palladium, up West, glamorously advertised by the billboard on a Tower Bridge bombsite. He devoured the diaries of Samuel Pepys, as well.

On leaving school he tried for a lowly post at the Savoy Hotel – London urchins can watch the high and mighty at close range – and here he reverently touched the theatre's wall in honour of Gilbert and Sullivan. But what he became was a merchant seaman, a Cunard cabin boy. On board he played the crew concerts, doing musical comedy. (Once, on a Canadian dockside, he had the rare privilege of seeing Leytonstone's Alfred Hitchcock at work, full of directorial importance yet speaking cockney – a curious anomaly that Tommy filed for future reference.) Like the 'Cunard Yanks' of Liverpool, he sailed to New York and heard American blues and country music, as yet a rarity in English life. He bought his first guitar there and headed home for London, where the instrument was so unusual that spare strings were almost impossible to buy.

Tommy hit the emerging skiffle scene, firstly at the Bread Basket café in Cleveland Street, which had a Gaggia coffee machine and a welcome clientele of young nurses from the Middlesex Hospital. He took himself down to the agents' recruiting ground at Archer Street, guitar case in hand, and touted for more engagements. And then, while on his final Stateside run, he witnessed Buddy Holly performing, heard Elvis on a jukebox, and knew that rock 'n' roll would be his calling. He was already more clued-in than most British boys, but his great good fortune, back in London, was to meet a cockney songwriter who had just sold a song to Billy Cotton. The song was entitled 'Oh for a Cuppa Tea Instead of a Cappacini'. The writer, more importantly, was Lionel Bart.

With Bart's help Tommy formed an embryonic rock band called the Cavemen, who won themselves a regular spot at the 2i's. Here in 1956 he met his manager-to-be, a publicist named John Kennedy, who taught the gawky boy a few show-business moves and gave him a more streamlined name: Tommy Steele. One evening, Kennedy took a businessman friend of his, Larry Parnes, to watch Steele in action. 'I like him,' Parnes decided. 'He's got honest eyes.' Under the tutelage of both men, Tommy was steered from skiffle cellars to proper nightclubs, like the Stork in Regent Street, where his engaging smile and freshness saw him through. It was just as well, for his material consisted of little more than a cute piece of Lionel Bart nonsense entitled 'Rock With the Cavemen'.

That song, though, was enough to get Tommy Steele signed to Decca Records. With a session band of jazz musicians including Ronnie Scott and Benny Green, he cut the disc at Decca's West Hampstead Studios (in the very room where the Beatles auditioned, unsuccessfully, six years later). In the manner of a modern fairy tale, the silly song made Tommy Steele an overnight star. He was the first home-grown British rocker and, suddenly, press attention and fan hysterics attended his every move. Lionel Bart was urgently required to write some more material in a variety of styles: 'He was born in Bermondsey so there had to be something cockney in there; he'd been in the merchant navy so we wanted a calypso, and so on . . . I was brought up in the rag trade so I was able to cut the cloth to the figure, as it were.'

With Larry Parnes by now in sole command, Tommy was sent on tour. His new band were called the Steelmen, most of whom, according to the sardonic observer George Melly, 'were disgruntled jazz modernists who wanted to eat'. There were no such things as rock venues in those days, and Steele went straight into traditional variety. He made his theatre-sized debut in Sunderland, topping a bill of showbiz troupers such as Mike and Bernie Winters, who taught him how to use stage make-up. The girls screamed and fainted, as intended. It was a shock, therefore, when Tommy's next record failed to chart, but Larry Parnes was not alarmed. 'We never looked at Tommy as a recording artiste,' he said. It was probably true. Nobody seemed to see rock as more than a fleeting teenage fancy.

Nevertheless, Steele the rocker was not finished yet. He hit big with a version of Guy Mitchell's US number 'Singing the Blues' and generally played the Elvis card for a few more years. But his heart was still set on the London Palladium and Parnes could not have agreed more. According to Steele, his potential to be an 'all-round entertainer' (in the phrase of the day) was spotted by Noël Coward, no less, who admired him through a season at the Café de Paris and murmured, 'The theatre is calling you, dear boy. You *will* come when you're ready, won't you?'

He was allowed to skip his National Service – a chore that still crippled the careers of would-be young idols – on account of his flat feet. (The press were told, however, that Tommy had a heart condition.) Soon he starred in his own bio-pic, *The Tommy Steele Story*, and in a Lionel Bart-penned musical film called *The Duke Wore Jeans*. Within a year he was enchanting the Queen Mother at the Royal Command Performance. As befits a working-class pop star he lost no time in moving his family out to Catford, to a house with a garden, a bathroom and an indoor toilet. But he never lost touch with his cockney roots, and in 1960 scored a big hit with Harry Champion's old music hall song 'What a Mouth (What a North and South)'.

Thus had Tommy Steele arrived at the Palladium, done panto, rocked-up music hall and everything. Lightweight movies like *Tommy the Toreador* and its attendant hit, 'Little White Bull', made him the epitome of all-round entertainment, just as Parnes had planned. Their partnership would last into the 1960s, when Steele found new success in *Half a Sixpence*, and showed that rock 'n' roll lives can indeed have second acts. Well into the twenty-first century I took my children to see him star in *Scrooge* – at the London Palladium, naturally – based upon his beloved Charles Dickens. In his lifetime he has incorporated almost every tradition of London song and spectacle. Brother Rahere would surely have approved.

Mister Parnes, Shillings and Pence

Tommy Steele was not Larry Parnes's only project. Having taken the boy, half-formed, from his first svengali John Kennedy, Parnes found other young dreamers to mould. He was the prototypical rock manager, a link between the days of Tin Pan Alley and a British pop industry that would change the world. With the Beatles came the idea of actual artists, who were more than merely puppets, and Parnes's style – paternal, slightly manipulative – began to look dated. But he remains a defining figure in London rock 'n' roll, revered by Malcolm McLaren, Andrew Loog Oldham and all who regard rock management as an art form of its own.

It was an unlikely career path. From Willesden, Parnes was a moderately prosperous shop manager in his family clothing business. Rather like Brian Epstein (another disciple of his) he'd nursed ambitions to work in theatre. And in Tommy Steele he quite correctly saw a singer who belonged in musicals, variety shows and movies. So far as Parnes was concerned, London rock 'n' roll was a form of theatre, pure and simple.

He began to build his famous 'stable' of singers, usually good-looking young boys, whom he stripped of their mundane identities. Thus did Ron Wycherley become Billy Fury, Reg Smith became Marty Wilde and Roy Taylor became Vince Eager. (Twenty years later this trick was ironically revived in the punk names of Johnny Rotten, Sid Vicious and others.) For musical material he looked to Lionel Bart or searched, as managers always had done, down the halls of Denmark Street. The media seized upon him as the shadowy mastermind of British pop and dubbed him 'Mr Parnes, Shillings and Pence'. He certainly had a sharp business brain, but to his 'boys' he was less a mercenary shark than a fond, fussy matron. He knew what he wanted, and declined Epstein's offer to co-manage the Beatles. He abandoned the rock game and dedicated his remaining years to West End theatre.

Another admirer of Parnes was Simon Napier-Bell, who would go on to manage Marc Bolan, the Yardbirds and Wham! He describes the Parnes-to-Epstein era this way:

Gay managers bridged the gap between record companies and
artists. The companies were run by ex-public schoolboys who
didn't know how to deal with this new generation of stroppy,
working-class artists. Then along came these managers who
were mostly also public school; they could talk beautifully to the
record companies, yet spent their evenings going to see rough,
stroppy kids. They got the trust of both sides, exemplified at first
by Larry Parnes. And exactly as he came along National Service
finished – prior to that there were no groups. Suddenly groups
could stay together, rehearse and become real groups, and they
wanted managers. Along came these gay entrepreneurs, and the
result, five years later, was that the biggest groups in the world
all had gay managers.

And the artists enjoyed it. They found the gay world more
interesting than having some middle-aged car salesman telling
you what to do. But also in those days the only outlet apart from
tiny clubs was variety bills, weekends on the pier, including a
juggler, a comedian, a Number 1 pop star. We had Val Doonican
on with the Yardbirds. And this taught the artists theatre,
professionalism, how to dress up. And as theatre is luvvy-luvvy
land, it gave the artists even more tolerance of gay culture. This
is why Robbie Williams is so good, he's a great theatre artist who
could have played the London Palladium straight after a
juggling act.

Larry Parnes was also a creator of music TV in Britain, through his
alliance with the hot-shot producer Jack Good, whose 6.5 *Special* and
Oh Boy! shows were vital in launching Tommy Steele, Marty Wilde
and the rest. Parnes and Good were the first to see the medium's
importance and they used it brilliantly. A splendid product of their
creative partnership was the career of Joe Brown.

Less biddable than the average Parnes signing, Brown insisted
upon his real name, in preference to Parnes's suggestion of Elmer
Twitch. He was born in Lincolnshire but lived in Plaistow from the
age of two and grew up as cockney as they come. A Parnes signing

since 1959, he was a skilled guitarist who became a staple of Jack Good's TV house bands, and backed visiting US stars like Eddie Cochran and Gene Vincent. This in itself was a sign of progress. Inside three years there had appeared a cadre of English rockers who were deemed worthy of such a role, and Brown was highly rated.

As in Tommy Steele's case, however, there was no faith in rock as a career, so Brown's appeal was broadened for the family market. With his bloke-ish band the Bruvvers (their very name tried to domesticate the alien concept of rock) he played the cheeky chappy with bog-brush hair and a chirpy grin. He went for cockney novelty songs like 'Layabout's Lament' and 'What a Crazy World We're Living In'. There was even a cover of Harry Champion's 'I'm Henry the Eighth I Am'. The folk memory of music hall had definitely not receded.

Parnes's plan bore its ultimate fruit in Brown's arrival on the West End stage, performing in the 1965 musical *Charlie Girl*. But it was all a distraction from his true distinction, as England's first guitar hero. Recent years have seen Joe Brown recover the credibility and respect of his earliest days. Nowadays he records with a rootsy depth that is a world away from 'Henry the Eighth'. As a player whom the teenage Beatles used to worship and study from the stalls, he was a fitting choice to end George Harrison's 2003 memorial show at the Royal Albert Hall – which he did, to heart-melting effect, with a version of the old vaudeville favourite 'I'll See You In My Dreams'.

One of Parnes's unhappier protégés was Terry Dene, formerly Terence Williams, from the Elephant and Castle. He was discovered in the 2i's by Jack Good, but proved too fragile for the rigour of stardom. When he failed to complete his National Service he was sent white feathers through the post; he was eventually seen on Soho street corners singing with the Salvation Army. His guitarist Brian Gregg said of him, 'Terry was brought up in London and he wasn't evacuated during the war. It made him very insecure and he ended up with emotional problems.' Yet Dene survived his bad press and nervous breakdown – he once wrote an autobiography called *I Thought Terry Dene Was Dead* – and plays the nostalgia circuit with his dignity intact. In this respect he was luckier than another 2i's nearly-man, Isleworth's Vince Taylor, whose own zigzag career was marred by mental problems until his death in 1991. Still, having spent a part of his childhood in America, he had a cultural edge over the London boys, and in 1958 cut one of the few classic tracks of British rock 'n' roll, 'Brand New Cadillac'.

There was also Johnny Kidd, who wore a buccaneer costume but was really Frederick Heath of Willesden. (The eye-patch apparently concealed a recurrent eye problem.) To Kidd we accord the glory of two great rock 'n' roll songs, 'Please Don't Touch' in 1959 and 'Shakin' All Over' a year later. Yet he also recorded 'If You Were the Only Girl In the World'. In fact the tremendous 'Shakin' All Over' was conceived, in a Berwick Street coffee bar, as merely a token B-side to the old standard 'Yes Sir That's My Baby' – it was the perceptive Jack Good who switched them around.

In an age of brief careers there was still some wisdom in Larry Parnes's belief that theatre – or panto, at least – should be the teenage rock star's next priority. The Acton boy Terry Nelhams, better known as Adam Faith, used pop to get famous, then used that fame to build a string of new careers. Originally he was one more of Jack Good's 2i's discoveries, but unlike the others he decided his name-change for himself. Faith was in fact a sharp London boy and his appearance on *Face to Face*, a serious TV interview show, gave him a reputation as Britain's first 'thinking pop star'. He even took elocution lessons. Yet his singing made effective use of cockney vowels. His 1959 hit, 'What Do You Want (If You Don't Want Money)?', would have seemed a mere Buddy Holly pastiche were it not for Faith's pronunciation of 'By-bee' – the hook that caught the country by its ear.

An early role in the movie *Beat Girl* launched him as an actor, and he survived the Beatles' wipe-out of solo acts. He got involved in management and production, playing a role in the careers of Sandie Shaw, Roger Daltrey and Leo Sayer. He became a TV fixture of the early 1970s through his starring role in *Budgie*, the misadventures of a Soho wide-boy. He played David Essex's manager in the outstanding rock movie *Stardust*, and emerged as something of a business guru. In the latter guise he had his ups and downs. By the time he died in 2003, the one-time singer of 'What Do You Want (If You Don't Want Money)?' had been both a financial columnist for the *Daily Mail* and a bankrupt.

Dig It, Daddio: the Resistible Rise of Bongo Herbert

As the 1950s ended, London streets teemed with teenage pop stars. As a young man's rite of passage, twelve months in the Hit Parade appeared to have taken the place of National Service. There were few girls on the scene, however. An exception was Helen Shapiro, just fourteen, from North London. In 1961 her surprisingly strong, deep voice was booming out of transistor radios with 'Don't Treat Me Like a Child' and 'Walkin' Back to Happiness'. Like the majority of her contemporaries, she would find the new decade precarious – below her on the bill of her 1963 tour were the Beatles, but their relative importance was to alter overnight.

It was a white-boy world, as well, which made the pop-soul singer Kenny Lynch a rarity. Though black he was a characteristic Stepney lad – his first public appearances were as an illicit street seller, or 'fly pitcher': 'I'd have a suitcase outside Woolworth's or somewhere and they call it "fly pitching" because every time the law comes along, you have to fly.' As a singer he popped up on the same Helen Shapiro tour as the Beatles. But whereas she declined the Fab Four's offer of a song called 'Misery', Lynch accepted, so becoming the first to cover a Lennon and McCartney composition. Like Adam Faith he was smart enough to diversify his act, and co-wrote the hit song 'Sha La La La Lee' for his fellow East Enders the Small Faces. In time he would be a permanent presence in TV light entertainment.

As this population of pop stars multiplied, so the London music industry acquired its cast of backroom boys as well. The domestic market was dominated by a few large companies, notably EMI and Decca, each with its subsidiary labels like Parlophone, Columbia and London. Their atmosphere, pre-Beatles, was formal and hierarchical;

their studios were run like government laboratories, staffed by technicians in white coats. While these companies employed their own producers, such as George Martin or Norrie Paramor, a clutch of extraordinary singles were the work of a true independent called Joe Meek. The Tornados' 'Telstar', John Leyton's 'Johnny Remember Me' and Heinz's 'Just Like Eddie' were only a few of the jewels to emerge from Meek's peculiar home studio, perched above a leather goods shop in Holloway Road. Trailing wires from bedroom to bathroom, improvising kit from anything he could and generally bewildering the musicians he was processing, the RAF-trained boffin pioneered a school of electronically modified sound. A maverick genius, perhaps, but also a difficult, tortured soul, he shot himself in 1967, having already used the same gun on his unfortunate landlady.

That Cliff Richard's real name was Harry Webb – as Tommy Steele's was Thomas Hicks – suggests that underneath their slick showbiz identities, most pop stars of the time were reassuringly ordinary. Like the others of his 1950s intake, Cliff passed straight through rock 'n' roll to wider family favour. He shrugged off the Beatle challenge, did panto and West End musicals, and for fifty years has remained an amazingly persistent visitor to the music charts. He was a sort of Londoner yet not, somehow, a London artist. He'd been born in India in 1940 to colonial parents who had never seen England; he arrived at Tilbury Dock when he was seven, and grew up in the borderlands of Outer London and the Home Counties. Nik Cohn suggests that Cliff's gift to British culture was the 'classless' accent, perfect for a rising generation of media people such as David Frost.

Cliff Richard was the crowning achievement of the 2i's coffee bar. Here in Old Compton Street he played the obligatory skiffle and met his future collaborators in the Shadows, Bruce Welch and Hank Marvin. He was signed to EMI after a show at the Shepherd's Bush Gaumont, and taken under the managerial wing of Tito Burns, an old-school Tin Pan Alley man. It should be acknowledged that Cliff began his recording career with a scorching piece of 1958 rock 'n' roll, 'Move It', perhaps the best British single of its kind. (Once more we have Jack Good to thank for its promotion to an A-side.) He followed that with a Lionel Bart toe-tapper, 'Livin' Doll', and the rest fell into place.

The *Daily Mirror* took note of his eyes: 'dark, luminous and slumberous', they said, and thousands of fans agreed. But his image was swiftly softened. Within a year he had made a film, *Serious Charge*, instantly followed by a period classic called *Expresso Bongo*. In the latter he is a would-be star whose predatory manager (played by Laurence Harvey) transforms him – without consultation, of course – from plain Herbert Rudge to the scarcely more resonant Bongo Herbert. The dialogue is jazz-beatnik, all 'Dig-it-Daddio', but the music is poor and Cliff is unexciting. What is thrilling, though, is the footage of Soho itself, glistening with neon seediness.

Yes! We Have No Bananas: Tony Newley and Lord Kitchener

No record or film, however, captures the first flush of rock 'n' roll London like Colin MacInnes's novel *Absolute Beginners*. Written in 1959, its themes include the Notting Hill race riots of a year earlier, the swagger of Britain's first teen consumers and the complex Soho night. MacInnes's great insight was the rising power and influence of the post-war generation, and to see (in the words of his friend Ray Gosling) 'that the future was multicoloured'. We see a smart young cockney songsmith, the Lionel Bart-ish Zesty Boy, peddling his numbers ('Nasty Newington Narcissus', 'Chicory With My Chick') to the 'boy slave' singers, whose managers have branded them with trashy new names (Strides Vandal, Rape Hunger). Poor, war-weakened England is reeling under the impact of a virile US pop culture, and its generations are dividing in the process. Touchingly, the boy narrator's last human feelings for his father are shared over Gilbert and Sullivan, themselves the final trumpet of Britain's imperial, pre-jazz insularity.

The same narrator, implacably self-possessed, surveys the coffee bar squabbles of modernist and traditional jazz fans. His own aesthetics align him with the pristine modernists against the shaggy, duffle-coated revivalists, while his contempt for the greasy, dull-witted teddy boys foreshadows the next decade's clash of mods against rockers. In the jazz world he finds his blessed escape from the prejudice of class, wealth and race. And by extension he loves Soho, a place where liberties can be taken. It's not for nothing that Old Compton Street, the spine of MacInnes's Soho and the cradle of English rock, would in time become the country's Gay High Street.

The point about the Larry Parnes era, London's first rock period, is that popular music was still a form of theatre – and now a stepping-stone to cinema. Its leading artistes were led towards stage and screen. Failing that there was always pantomime – for whatever may change in English entertainment, there is still our cawing, cackling translation of Italy's Commedia dell'Arte. Few were the acts who traded under the names they'd received at the baptismal font. This was a time of desperate youths from the car factories of Dagenham, eager to please the man from Denmark Street. 'Authenticity' in rock would have to wait for later, for denim-wearing Californian millionaires.

In 1960 the genuinely big acts on TV were middle-of-the-road trusties like Billy Cotton and Max Bygraves, and Larry Parnes's rockers were groomed to join that same freemasonry. At the same time, travelling in the other direction, comedians were gate-crashing the pop charts. Little Charlie Drake, from the Elephant and Castle, followed Spike Milligan and Peter Sellers in recording for EMI's George Martin. Stepney's Bernard Bresslaw, who played the amiable dope in TV's *The Army Game* ('I only arsked') weighed in with 'Mad Passionate Love'. Mike Sarne, from Paddington, teamed with Joe Meek and the future *EastEnders* star Wendy Richards, to cut a funny snippet of teenage cockney courtship, 'Come Outside'.

Ordinary Londoners were still presented in song as cockney clowns, scarcely changed since Shakespeare's 'rude mechanicals'. Truly subversive, therefore, was the sophisticated – and influential – Anthony Newley. Born in Hackney in 1931, he was just a little too early, and too accomplished in the old ways, to really catch the rock 'n' roll wave. He did some good impressions of rock without belonging to it. Instead he supplies a link between the worlds of Gus Elen and David Bowie, of Noël Coward and Johnny Rotten, and of Stanley Holloway and the Streets.

Newley began as an actor – he'd been the Artful Dodger in David Lean's 1949 film of *Oliver Twist* – and became a singer almost by accident. Hired to play a comedy rock 'n' roller in 1959's *Idle On Parade* he performed a song, 'I've Waited So Long', that launched him into the charts as a real-life pop star. He did it with a cockney accent, as the role required, and sang that way thereafter. Over the next decade he built an extraordinary catalogue: Lionel Bart gave him a Number 1 record with 'Do You Mind?'; he made a Top 20 hit of 'Pop Goes the Weasel', a song that dates back to the Pilgrim Fathers. He devised clever jazz twists on the ancient street-sellers' ditty 'Strawberry Fair' and the costermongering 'Yes! We Have No Bananas', and put them both in the hit parade.

All of these he delivered in a voice that was unapologetically London, yet smoothly international. He was of the 1960s jet-set, as suavely transatlantic as Matt Monro, but also as dark as a French *chanteur*. A brilliant words-man, his lyrics for the cinema and musicals included 'Goldfinger', *Willy Wonka & The Chocolate Factory* and Sammy Davis Jr's 'What Kind of Fool Am I?' Nina Simone would cover his 'Feeling Good'. He moved to Beverly Hills and went through a string of marriages, including one to Joan Collins. Just before his death in 1999 he was returning to his roots with a part in *EastEnders*. Newley's most obvious disciple was the young David Bowie, whose 1967 period mimics his sound with slavish fidelity.

More than that, though, Newley pioneered a new and specifically British take on modern pop, much as Noël Coward had done for a previous generation. The past few years had proven some Londoners were adept at US imitations, whether it was Cliff's 'Move It' or Vince Taylor's 'Brand New Cadillac'. Now, however, the London studios were breeding a class of players and producers who really *felt* the new music, as opposed to the old pros who merely turned up on the day. But the only English spin, so far, was to play it for music hall belly-laughs. You were either Elvis Presley or you were Harry Champion. With Anthony Newley we see the first stirrings of a special sensibility, ironic and literate, steeped in its place of birth but adventurous and quirky. Without him, one wonders, could the Beatles and the Kinks have gone so far, so quickly?

Before the 1960s could truly begin, however, the jazz revival had one final spasm of life. This time around they called it trad. In 1959 Chris Barber scored his one significant hit, a version of Sidney Bechet's 'Petite Fleur', though most trad discs were less elegant. For the next three years the country was swept by a zany fad for strangely dressed men in bowler hats and waistcoats, plucking banjos, blowing clarinets and generally wowing a self-consciously eccentric student audience. Its leading lights, apart from Barber, were Kenny Ball and Acker Bilk but there were numberless crews in college rehearsal halls, or upon the backs of lorries at CND marches and rag-week processions. When it all became a bit passé, some of them defected to the rival trend, which was called beat music. Others would delve into the addictive and almost mystical music of the blues. A small, scattered bunch of enthusiasts were amassing blues collections, and supporting the occasional low-key visits by US players. Funnily enough, the blues would make more than a few of these suburban devotees into millionaires.

In the meantime, this post-war period of Commonwealth immigration was not without its racial tensions, as Colin MacInnes had already documented in *Absolute Beginners*. As he noted, the London jazz scene offered a refuge from the prevailing bigotries. In time the blues and R&B clubs did the same. From the very beginning, though, London's newcomers were bringing something of their own.

There had been black settlers in London for many centuries. The parish of St Giles, where Tin Pan Alley arose, was renowned for exactly that. Across the city, black and pseudo-black music was not uncommon as early as the 1830s. But the arrival at Tilbury Dock of the SS *Empire Windrush*, in June 1948, marked the beginning of a new era. Its 492 West Indian workers had been sought, by London

Transport and others, to assist in post-war reconstruction. Like earlier incomers, from the Jews to the Irish, these new Londoners preserved the music of their homelands. But the Trinidadians' particular favourite, calypso, was uniquely adaptable. The calypso tradition was one of story songs, which are as observational as any Elizabethan broadside. The art of calypso was more than a wistful souvenir of the old country. Rather, it was deployed to record the experiences of people who found themselves strangers in a strange land, both hopeful and wary.

Among the passengers on board the *Windrush* was one Aldwyn Roberts, alias Lord Kitchener, the Trinidadian 'Grand Master' of calypso. In his number 'London is the Place for Me', he records that momentous journey, and how eagerly he was anticipating the new life in store. Later songs of his, like 1958's 'Piccadilly Folk' are more touched by the ambivalence of experience ('Walk very very cautiously, don't ever look around, no matter what you see'). But in the same year's 'Rock'n'Roll Calypso' he is delighting in the cultural crossover, bringing a Soho jazz swing to his ditty of wedding-night exertions. Kitchener was the great figurehead of calypso but by no means its only London exponent. Young Growler's 'V for Victory' was in Kitchener's tradition of celebrating a West Indian cricketing triumph. The Guyanese Bill Rogers's 'Sightseeing in the UK' recommends a tramride to Buckingham Palace, the Royal Albert Hall and of course Lord's cricket ground.

Young Tiger, formerly the Trinidadian George Browne, presents an awful warning in 1954's 'Chicken and Rice', of the perils of bill-avoidance in Chinese restaurants – from Westbourne Grove, to Harrow Road and Sussex Gardens he flees from axe-brandishing vengeance. On a more august note, the same singer's 'I Was There (at the Coronation)' was written for Queen Elizabeth's big day in 1953. Of course he wrote his report *before* the event, thus having it ready for immediate release. *Plus ça change* – at Newgate and Tyburn, balladeers sold 'dying speeches' to the crowds before the luckless malefactors had even left their cells.

Calypso was the tropical equivalent of London's oldest folk music. It's somehow fitting that it created a festival, the Notting Hill Carnival, that grew to become a London institution, as intrinsic to the city's fabric as the Boat Race or the Changing of the Guard. In fact, perhaps Bartholomew's Fair never died – it only travelled a few miles west, beyond the Tyburn tree.

Chapter Five

Smashing Time

The Beatles, the Rolling Stones and the virtual Versailles of swinging London.

The King's Road is pop's cerebral cortex. In the 1950s it was the site of Mary Quant's fashion shop, perhaps the first sign of a distinctively modern pop culture. In the sixties it was the meeting point of pop music and high society. And in the seventies it became the cradle of punk rock. Despite the onset of chain-store branches, all the way from Sloane Square to World's End, Chelsea's high street has never entirely lost its chic. Formerly a private royal road, its purpose was to connect the London palaces with the Thames crossing at Putney. After 1830 this 'King's road' was opened to the public but a sense of exclusivity lingers.

Swinging London – the newspapers' name for that frothy time in music, art and fashion from 1963 to 1967 – was a creation of the King's Road. The whole show was really a new spin on two old London themes, namely theatre and commerce. Swinging London was about selling things, but the selling was dressed up as spectacle. In later years it was common to see Chelsea Pensioners in their vivid historic uniforms pose for the tourists alongside violently attired punk rockers with crimson Mohicans (the Pensioners, who have been around since 1682, now appear to be out-living the punks). It was thoroughly self-conscious, like the leggy models who totter with their dogs from Peter Jones's store to Royal Avenue. But it was London street performance in action.

In the years after the Second World War the King's Road was a respectable if unexceptional local high street, with the normal complement of greengrocers, newsagents and hardware shops staffed by solid, middle-aged men in brown work-coats. But the district had a racier element, comprised of a rich young breed who would later be called the Chelsea Set. They were sufficiently upper-class to feature in the gossip and social columns of the press, which had not as yet discovered the working class at all. But they shared the mood of post-war impatience. The boys drove sports cars and though the girls were still debutantes (the well-bred young women who were ceremonially presented to the Queen), they were ready for a change. The formality of their mothers' time no longer seemed right. And then, in 1955, Mary Quant opened a shop, Bazaar, on the corner by Markham Square.

Quant's designs were simple, sexy and young – she would later popularise the miniskirt. The debs who flocked to buy her clothes were experimenting with a whole new aesthetic. The Chelsea Set themselves were moving in louche circles, sauntering over to Soho, where they'd mingle with East End adventurers coming up West. It always helped to be rich, but it was now fashionable to claim you were classless. When the Quant style was picked up by the chain stores and mass-manufactured, who could tell a cockney shop-girl from a King's Road dolly bird? With her husband and fellow Goldsmiths graduate, Alexander Plunkett Greene, and their business partner Archie McNair, Mary Quant was obviously on to something. (She embodied the look in her own person, especially after Vidal Sassoon supplied her iconic 'bob' hairstyle.) Soon she opened a second shop, this time in Knightsbridge. Her brand of accessible fashion was spreading outwards, and down the class system. At the same time, rock music was asserting itself as a force in Soho bars and Northern beat-clubs alike. The two movements seemed destined to meet.

Andrew Loog Oldham, the future manager of the Rolling Stones, had a prime view of this spectacular and far-reaching collision. London pop, he says, began with fashion not music:

I was very lucky because when I was sixteen, before there was a rock business in England, my first job was in fashion and fashion was the first British pop business. It was pop. It did everything that the music business did later. People like Mary Quant and Vidal Sassoon were exports: they had stores, Vidal cut hair in New York. So I was lucky that my first job was with Mary Quant. When the school I was at when I was sixteen said, 'You may do well, but not here,' I decided that I may do well in the fashion business, where carpets were thick and the teacups were thin. And life did not end up on the cutting room floor. These were wonderful entrepreneurs. Like an independent record company, where Mary Quant designed the dresses, her husband sold them, and they were fortunate enough to have, which I didn't, an old schoolfriend to make sure they got paid.

Like any fairy-tale kingdom Swinging London had its royalty. Primarily this meant the Beatles and the Rolling Stones, who became the competing and co-operating arbiters of sixties hipness. Around them were perhaps a couple of hundred others, including musicians, photographers and models, fashion designers and gallery owners, the royal court of a virtual Versailles. The two bands were both to some degree outsiders, and both bands' music was transformed by London – but in turn they transformed the city itself.

To the Toppermost of the Poppermost: the Beatles and the Stones

In their early years of Liverpudlian struggle the capital seemed unattainable to the Beatles. Paul McCartney recalled to me the melancholy afternoons they spent at Lime Street Station awaiting their manager Brian Epstein's return, normally with news of fresh rejections by the music business. But one day that all changed, and within a year the Beatles had London at their feet. All their important music was to be made here. They were ultimately as shaped by 1960s London as by their Northern origins, and this city conveyed them to the world.

Back home they'd gee themselves up with a little ritual: 'Where are we going, Johnny?' 'Where? To the toppermost of the poppermost!' The Beatles' 'poppermost' was a geographical concept, as well as a dream, and it meant London. They saw the King's Road early on, for Brian (a failed actor) loved stage connections and installed them by the Royal Court Theatre, in the hotel of that name on Sloane Square. Then, more practically, they stayed at the President on Russell Square, convenient for Euston Station. After that they took lodgings, and were steered by Brian's taste to Mayfair, sharing a flat at 57 Green Street. Paul was soon away, up the road to Wimpole Street to live with his girlfriend Jane Asher and her family. John Lennon took a flat at Emperor's Gate in South Kensington for his wife Cynthia and baby Julian. George and Ringo had brief sojourns in Belgravia and Marylebone before succumbing, like John, to the stockbroker belt.

Their first professional destinations were EMI's modern office block (now demolished) in Manchester Square and its recording studios at Abbey Road. The former was immortalised by the photo in its stairwell for the first LP; the latter supplied the title and artwork of the last LP they ever made. When Epstein transferred his NEMS management agency down from Liverpool he chose 13 Monmouth Street, an artery of theatreland even now; when NEMS outgrew it he moved to Argyll Street, next door to that high temple of British showbiz the London Palladium.

Wherever they lived in the early years of their success, the Beatles were still firmly identified with Liverpool. Thus the search was mounted for a London rival. The newspapers found a group called the Dave Clark Five and in opposition to 'Merseybeat' proclaimed them kings of 'the Tottenham Sound'. If this consisted of anything it was a beefy, thumping style, befitting a band led by its drummer. Clark himself was a shrewd London operator in the Adam Faith mould; essentially self-managed, he steered his act from skiffle sessions to pop jamborees at Tottenham's Royal Ballroom, to a key position in the musical 'British Invasion' of America. For a while they really were contenders. In January 1964 their galumphing 'Glad all Over' replaced 'I Want to Hold Your Hand' at Number 1 and the London media grew very excited. The DC Five had 'toppled' the Fab Four.

Of course the moment passed, but Clark stayed sharp and prospered. He certainly had a quicker grasp of copyright economics than his Scouse counterparts – among his acquisitions was the TV series *Ready Steady Go!*

The Beatles' serious Southern challengers, of course, were the Rolling Stones. Their ascent to stardom began one night at the Station Hotel, a pub across the road from Richmond's railway terminus, when they were seen by Mary Quant's ex-office boy Andrew Loog Oldham. At only nineteen, younger than the band themselves, he was already an old hand. Apart from his King's Road fashion stint, he had worked for Ronnie Scott and at the Gunnell brothers' Flamingo club, a black music hot-spot. He'd observed, at close range, the dons of Soho's scene like Lionel Bart and Larry Parnes, and formed a lifelong passion for Laurence Harvey's scheming character in *Expresso Bongo*. He did PR work for Joe Meek, Phil Spector and visiting US stars. Most importantly of all, in the Stones' eyes, he was touched by the magic of Beatledom, having helped Brian Epstein introduce his group to London's media.

Oldham was to prove an alchemist in the Stones' story, despite his pure indifference to blues authenticity. In his classic London style he believed – as naturally as Shakespeare had believed – that saleability mattered more than anything. 'I have to thank the journalist Peter Jones for the tip,' he says of his date with destiny, 28 April 1963:

> I also have to thank British Railways, because it was a very easy route from where I lived in Hampstead to Richmond. Had I actually had to go into town and take the train out of town, I might not have done it, because it was a Sunday, and Mother cooked. But I also went because Mother gave me manners and there was no way I could turn up and hustle this journalist next Tuesday at his pub on Shaftesbury Avenue [De Hems, near the *Record Mirror* office at number 116] where all business was done, because he would have said, 'Did you see this group?' I had to and I did.

My idea of R&B rarely went above forty-five in the singles charts so, me believing that the two words 'commercial art' were forever joined, didn't at that time have much interest in it. It was just as well, because I had no idea whether the Rolling Stones were playing blues well or badly. So what that allowed was that a total wave comes over you – and there is no doubt what the rest of your life is going to be about.

The Rollin' Stones (who had yet to acquire that letter 'g') were largely a product of London's blues and jazz scenes, but were not themselves a cockney gang. Their singer Mick Jagger and guitarist Keith Richards were raised in Dartford in Kent, just beyond the city's boundaries. Their initial leader, Brian Jones, was from faraway Cheltenham, in Gloucestershire. The rhythm section of Charlie Watts and Bill Wyman were respectively North and South London suburbanites. Jagger attended the London School of Economics for a while; travelling there one morning he famously met his old acquaintance Keith Richards, himself en route to Sidcup Art College, and discovered their mutual passion for R&B (the name, back then, for blues goosed-up, *à la* Chuck Berry, with amplification and rocking rhythms).

Becoming their manager, press agent and producer, Oldham signed the Stones to Decca Records, having stormed the company's Thameside bastion more successfully than Epstein – he knew, of course, how frightened they now were of missing the next big thing. A Chuck Berry number, 'Come On', was quickly recorded and the standard process of chart manipulation could get underway:

You get a list of the chart shops and you go and buy the records. Fortunately the Rolling Stones had at least 200 really devoted girls who didn't even ask to be paid the money back for having purchased the records. So they would go around and that's how the Rolling Stones got to 48 the first week and 37 the next week and then the record company has confidence in you and starts to put records in the rest of the shops. It was a simple cottage industry then . . .

Oldham's manipulative gifts, Soho-schooled, did not stop there. He took the band's mild beatnik surliness, in which they cloaked their essentially nice manners, inflating it into a brand of calculated outrage. Falling eagerly on a press comment about the un-wisdom of letting your daughter marry a Rolling Stone, he hyped it to the hilt, positioning his boys as the Beatles' evil twins. In actual fact the two groups enjoyed cordial relations, which Oldham was grateful to exploit when it came time for a new Stones single:

'I Wanna be Your Man' was a John and Paul song and is one of those wonderful moments to do with songwriting where the Rolling Stones were in a club off Leicester Square [Ken Colyer's Studio 51] trying to find something to record and it was very tough because the R&B song barrel was being eaten up. I always believe it's the job of producers to know when to leave the room. So I left, and fortunately I turned left when I walked out of the rehearsal place and I bumped into John and Paul on the corner, who fortunately were nicely tipsy having just had their first award from the Variety Club or something like that, and they were perceptive enough to see that something was wrong with Andy. And they promptly repaired what was wrong with Andy by telling me that 'I Wanna be Your Man' was a song that hadn't been recorded yet – which it had, by Ringo – and they came in and did the magic in front of the Stones, in that they actually pretended to finish writing it right in front of them. It had been recorded at Abbey Road ten days before . . .

As their success began to build, the Stones moved through various London locations. Several of them shared a rather scabby flat at 102 Edith Grove, just beyond World's End in Chelsea. Here the Beatles came to visit after watching them one evening at the Railway/ Crawdaddy. Mick and Keith then moved, with Oldham, to Mapesbury Road in Kilburn. In this flat the manager nagged them into becoming songwriters: 'It was an awful lino-ridden, awful smell-of-bacon kind of environment. Probably the same place would cost half a million pounds now. It wasn't that I locked them in a room. You can't lock people in a room. But you can *sulk*. You can be *difficult*.' The technique paid dividends, anyway, and the team came up with 'As Tears Go By', to be followed with 'Paint it Black', 'Satisfaction', 'Jumpin' Jack Flash' and all the rest. Significantly, both Mick and Keith would soon be leaving Kilburn for their own separate residences in chic Cheyne Walk by the Chelsea Embankment.

A Conquered World: Bacchanals at the Bag O'Nails

By 1965 the Beatles and the Stones enjoyed a scale of fame so vast it could scarcely be enjoyed at all. Their work rates required that they be on tour almost constantly, or else sequestered in recording studios when possible. Their available leisure time was spent, necessarily, in the rat-runs of London's most privileged, where press attention was informal and one to one, where hysterical fans were cordoned off and inquisitive civilians kept to a manageable minimum. As Derek Taylor, the Beatles' owlish press-man, put it, 'Daylight movement above ground had to be nimble in the white heat of Beatlemania.' Memorably, the journalist Maureen Cleave described meeting John Lennon in Brian Epstein's office, when news came in of a Beatle being sighted on Oxford Street. 'One of the others must be out,' said Lennon, brightening. He talked, thought Cleave, 'as though speaking of an escaped bear'.

As the hunted often will, they headed for higher ground, which in Swinging London meant the Ad Lib club. Managed by Tommy Steele's old mentor John Kennedy, it was perched five storeys up above Leicester Square and accessed via a private lift. The Ad Lib was the night-time court of pop's beautiful people, a feudal fiefdom ruled absolutely by the Beatles, and to an extent by the Stones, inhabited until dawn by their lieutenants and confidantes. Nik Cohn recalls it as a place where jaded swingers slumped with scotch and Cokes and hoped the Beatles might show up that night, just to validate the evening. Spread out below its west-facing windows lay the silent, twinkling city. To the presiding figures of the scene, thought George

Melly, the hip and rich, the young and beautiful, it must have seemed 'a conquered world'.

For the Beatles the Ad Lib was a sort of anti-Cavern, celestial not subterranean, elitist not democratic, the temple of recognition not a testing-ground of struggle. But in 1966 the club was temporarily closed down after a kitchen fire. And when it re-opened, the beautiful people had all found somewhere else.

The next place might be Sybilla's at nearby 9 Swallow Street. Part-owned by George Harrison, its address has housed a nightclub from 1915 to the present day. Or, even more fashionable among rock's in-crowd, there was the Scotch of St James, at 13 Masons Yard. The Scotch, in common with the Saddle Room, another Beatles haunt, was inspired by French discotheques and shared a French fondness for tartan-themed decor. There was a restaurant at ground level and a dance floor downstairs. The Beatles and the Stones had regular tables set aside for them. And being rich, they were not required to pay for anything.

The Scotch's location in St James's was a symbol of pop's new status, pushing westwards, penetrating the establishment's strong-holds – returning, in fact, towards Chelsea where so much of the new world had originated. But Soho had not been forgotten. In a basement at 9 Kingly Street was the Bag O'Nails (where Paul McCartney would meet his future wife Linda). According to one authority, Bag O'Nails was a traditional tavern name, derived from the Bacchanals, or wild revels of ancient times. The explanation looks dubious, but has a poetic aptness all the same. Swinging London's inner circle were rehearsing a permissive approach to sex and drugs that the rest of Britain would eventually start adopting.

Just across Oxford Circus, in Margaret Street, was a music industry refuge called the Speakeasy, conceived in US Prohibition style. Further west, lotus-eating hedonists alit upon the Revolution, in Mayfair's Bruton Place, or the Cromwellian in Kensington. In Jermyn Street, near the Scotch, was Dolly's Club, where the Beatles, Stones and Bob Dylan convened one evening in May 1966. (In a way this must have been the Yalta Conference of its age.)

Brian Epstein was more attuned to London's upper-class life than were his inexperienced charges, and took a flat by Lowndes Square in Knightsbridge, enjoying the aristocratically raffish ambience of casinos like Les Ambassadeurs (which was featured in the Beatles' film *A Hard Day's Night*). He traded up to a town house in Chapel Street, deeper inside Belgravia, where the back wall of Buckingham Palace was just up the road. Soon he acquired a weekend place in the country, befitting the grand self-image he had cultivated even when toiling as a provincial shop manager.

The refined Epstein was also Jewish and homosexual – drawbacks, perhaps, in the narrower walks of British life. In pop management and London show business, however, he was almost stereotypically normal. Among his earliest social connections were 'Li and Alma', namely Lionel Bart (Jewish and gay) and the singer Alma Cogan (Jewish). Her regular *soirées* in Kensington High Street helped induct the Beatles into London's entertainment world, and Brian even considered proposing marriage. (She was, ironically, conducting an affair with John Lennon.) Bart's flat, off Queensgate, and his larger place on Fulham Road were known for their decadent parties. Although homosexuality was still illegal, Epstein could socialise securely with record company magnates like EMI's Sir Joe Lockwood, or fellow managers like Larry Parnes, Robert Stigwood and Simon Napier-Bell.

For reasons that were never clarified, Epstein was prone to restlessness and depression. He indulged his passion for theatre by putting on groups at the Prince of Wales in Piccadilly, and then buying the Saville in Shaftesbury Avenue, previously owned by the reigning monarchs of light entertainment Lew Grade and Bernard Delfont. Here he featured modern acts like Jimi Hendrix and the Four Tops and serious dramas like James Baldwin's *The Amen Corner*. He also staged the shows closest to old-fashioned English hearts, the D'Oyly Carte Company performing Gilbert and Sullivan. But Lionel Bart reported a sighting of Brian on the King's Road, looking dazed ('It was the first time I'd ever seen him without a tie in the city'). In May 1967 Epstein checked into the Priory clinic in Roehampton, where his visitors included Larry Parnes. Two days later he was back at home in Chapel Street, hosting the launch party for *Sgt. Pepper's Lonely Hearts Club Band*. And here, on 27 August, he was found dead of an overdose.

Perhaps the final word should go to Epstein's counterpart, the manager of the Beatles' friends and greatest rivals, Andrew Loog Oldham:

I have nothing but admiration for Brian Epstein. We are in a business that is prone to exaggeration but we probably wouldn't be here if Brian Epstein hadn't managed to secure a recording contract for the Beatles. Before I was with the Rolling Stones, I did publicity for the Beatles for about four months in the beginning of '63 and I like heroes, man, I don't like people who fall over and misbehave in front of me. And they were a magnificent animal to watch together. It worked. It was a very odd combination. Brian was from the manor born with a spoon in his mouth – as opposed to his nose, which came later – and it was wonderful to be around.

Swinging – and Swingeing – London

Others did what Brian could not. They learned to go with the flow and catch whatever opportunities, commercial, chemical or sexual, came along. The pop manager Simon Napier-Bell is studiously off-hand in his memoir of the time: a typical day in Swinging London, he says, might start with dinner at nine in the evening. Around midnight you went to the Ad Lib, the Scotch or Cromwellian. Various encounters would follow. He summarises Swinging London as 'the combined total of everyone's indiscretions'.

The new television show *Ready Steady Go!* was crucial in spreading the London style. Filmed in a studio at the Aldwych end of Kingsway, its weekly package of bands and hand-picked dancers, fronted by the thoroughly modern Cathy McGowan, imposed the fashions of the King's Road and its cheaper Soho version, Carnaby Street, upon the whole nation. The brief pre-eminence of Liverpool, whose Beatle-led 'Merseybeat' acts had recently defined British pop music, was over. The capital was back in charge.

In the build-up to psychedelia and 1967's 'Summer of Love', when hippy ideals of peace and flower-power met the world of commerce, the King's Road aesthetic was changing. Mary Quant had popularised a crisp, cool modernism in the late fifties and early sixties. Now she'd diversified her business into make-up and had rather left the realm of youth fashion. New shops were appearing, often called boutiques (another French word, like discotheque, that was suddenly gaining currency), including Hung On You and Granny Takes A Trip. Here the trend was florid Victoriana, or mock-Edwardian militaria. Those dandified old soldiers, the Chelsea Pensioners, offered a perfect picture amid moustachioed boys with sideburns, tight trousers and scarlet tunics.

Over in Portobello Road, where the market already specialised in second-hand clothing, there was a shop called I Was Lord Kitchener's Valet. (The hit parade's riposte was a novelty instrumental, 'I Was Kaiser Bill's Batman' by Whistling Jack Smith, complete with a 'Lambeth Walk'-style 'Oi!' at the end.) It was not a look the Beatles invented, but their *Sgt. Pepper* album brought it to the masses. The Stones' *Their Satanic Majesties Request* was a hesitant imitation, musically and sartorially. The actor Terence Stamp, himself a dashing blade of Swinging London, gave the style big-screen glamour in the Thomas Hardy costume drama *Far from the Madding Crowd*.

So a high time was being had, at least by some. But Swinging London did not come into focus until it was discovered by the Americans. In April 1966 *Time* magazine ran a much-quoted cover story identifying London as the pace-setting creative hub and all-round party capital of the Western world. The slumbering, fusty, tradition-bound city had woken up, dramatically re-imagined as young, vibrant and cool. The US country singer Roger Miller celebrated with a hit called 'England Swings' – England and London being, as usual, interchangeable concepts – replete with 'bobbies on bicycles', Big Ben and 'dapper men with Derby hats and canes'. As a travelogue it was scarcely more contemporary than *Mary Poppins*. But the country of the Beatles, James Bond and miniskirts was irresistible copy – a sixties' reprise of fifties' Rome and *La Dolce Vita*.

There were some highly decorative figures to be seen. The handsome Terence Stamp had a lowly East End background, reinforcing the notion of a hip meritocracy where glamour and talent trumped class or breeding. He squired the gazelle-like model Jean Shrimpton, who'd previously been with another cockney upstart, the photographer David Bailey. Shrimpton's sister Chrissie was an early girlfriend of Mick Jagger, and perhaps the object of a few Rolling Stones lyrics. And Jagger's next girlfriend was even more spectacular. She was Marianne Faithfull.

This former convent schoolgirl was still only eighteen when Andrew Loog Oldham spotted her at a party given by Peter Asher, the brother of Paul McCartney's girlfriend Jane. Her beguiling blonde innocence, with its undertone of utter decadence, had Oldham smitten: 'In another century you'd have set sail for her,' he wrote. 'In 1964 you'd record her.' Wasting no time, he took Jagger and Richards's 'As Tears Go By', and for a B-side teamed it with the perennial 'Greensleeves'. With the astonishing velocity of the times, the girl became famous immediately. As Oldham himself was still too young to sign various legal documents, Lionel Bart stepped forward, and for a time was technically co-manager both of Marianne and the Stones. It's likely that Bart had some songwriting input as well, though uncredited.

Faithfull was soon to marry the gallery-owner John Dunbar (an important character in London's emerging 'underground' culture) but she would in time become the consort of Mick Jagger and an emblem of Swinging London – especially, alas, at the point where its druggy hedonism began to look self-destructive. We see her in footage of Bob Dylan at the Savoy, charming him so much he offers her poems typed on toilet paper, but also in the press photos that followed a police raid on the Rolling Stones. As a noted beauty but only a very minor pop star, and too bright to be a mere 'dolly bird', she found her second-hand celebrity unendurable. Having no talent for normality, she sank into the heroin trance of 'Sister Morphine', a later Stones song she helped to write. From the pinnacle of esteem she descended, in the early 1970s, to addiction on the Soho streets. Two decades of slow recovery would follow, as she rebuilt her musical career and nursed her health.

Like John Dunbar, Robert Fraser was another London gallery owner and a man so central to Swinging London's innermost clique that he's been described as its Typhoid Mary. He was unfortunately caught up in the same 1967 drug-bust that snared Marianne Faithfull and the Stones. Taken to trial with Jagger in Chichester, the pair were needlessly handcuffed together; a press photo of them in the back of a police car was turned into artwork by the painter Richard Hamilton. In a comment on the authorities' unseemly zeal, it was pointedly titled 'Swingeing London'.

High Times: Norwegian Wood and the Chelsea Drugstore

A little industry sprang up around the secret meanings of Beatle songs, or what were imagined to be secret meanings. On the release of their *Revolver* LP in 1966, there was speculation that 'Dr Robert' might in fact be Robert Fraser – a known Beatle intimate and a ready source of illicit substances. In fact the group had someone else in mind, an actual New York doctor. Still, the Beatles' middle-period music is implicitly *of* London, from the years when all four partook of the city. Their earlier songs were mostly guided by the formulae of teen romance, and by the time of their final albums only Paul McCartney was still based in the capital. But in between, say from *Rubber Soul* in 1965 to *Sgt. Pepper* in '67, there is a sense of the city outside the walls of Abbey Road, its present reality mingling with Liverpool nostalgia and stoned mysticism.

Rubber Soul's most intriguing lyric was 'Norwegian Wood'. John Lennon's biographer Philip Norman traces it to the Beatle's family apartment at Emperor's Gate. Here, in the wood-panelled flat below his own, Lennon pursued an affair with a photographer's wife, coding his account in lyrical disguise. The Beatles seldom dealt in straight narratives (the reportage of 1969's 'The Ballad of John and Yoko' was unusual) and the London glimpses are oblique. But once they gave up touring they finally had time to take stock of their surroundings. George Harrison's 'Taxman' roots them in the real world of politicians Harold Wilson and Edward Heath. In general, *Revolver* is the work of a Northern group now mixing with sophisticates and decadents, including the Bayswater dentist who one evening introduced them to LSD, prior to a night spent floating around the Ad Lib.

Their movies *A Hard Day's Night* and *Help!* made use of London locations – railway stations, casinos, Bond Street jewellers – while their creative home at EMI's studios at Abbey Road, in St John's Wood, became world-famous when they adopted it for an album title. (A less celebrated work-place was Trident Studio, in a little passage between Wardour and Dean Street, where their occasional sessions included 'Hey Jude'; the same building would host David Bowie, Lou Reed, Elton John and Queen). *Sgt. Pepper*'s 'Lovely Rita' describes the 'meter maids' now appearing on London's streets. 'A Day in the Life' alludes to the death of their Swinging London friend Tara Browne, an aristocratic regular at the Bag O'Nails and Sybilla's. Browne was killed in Kensington, while driving a Lotus Elan with his model girlfriend Suki Potier – a very sixties way to go. But death was not yet in the script for London's *jeunesse dorée* and the incident caused a ripple of shock around their set.

It's pleasing to hear a few bars of the inescapable 'Greensleeves' stitched inside of 'All You Need is Love'. The Martha of 'Martha My Dear' was McCartney's dog, whom he would walk over Primrose Hill, where a sight of the improving London weather inspired 'It's Getting Better' and a chance encounter with a mysterious stranger led to 'The Fool on the Hill'. John Lennon's 'Revolution', like Mick Jagger's 'Street Fighting Man', originates in the student demonstrations of 1968. But whereas Jagger actually attended the protests at the US Embassy in Grosvenor Square, Lennon preferred to watch on TV, safely holed-up in Surrey.

Becoming entangled with Yoko Ono brought John into contact with London's 'alternative' culture, but his daily existence was rarefied. The reference to 'bent-back tulips', in 'Glass Onion', was merely prompted by the flower arrangements in a Knightsbridge restaurant. Paul McCartney remained more actively sociable. In the Bag O'Nails one night he met the Nigerian conga player Jimmy Scott, who gave him a useful Yoruba phrase meaning 'Life goes on' – *obla-di, obla-da* . . .

The Rolling Stones lived on a lower plane of celebrity than the Beatles, and could investigate London more easily. Jagger was their most socially adept member, and his accent has retained a way of sliding up and down the class scale, as if to assert his membership at every level. 'Play With Fire' describes a rich man's daughter whose family orbit has ranged from Knightsbridge to Stepney, by way of St John's Wood. From a few years later, in 1969, 'You Can't Always Get What You Want' has another female protagonist, gliding from street demonstration to private reception, to the Chelsea Drugstore – a trendy King's Road bazaar that opened in 1968, boasting a home delivery squad of motorbike girls in purple catsuits. Despite such groovy associations, the song carries a pall of doubt, one more sign of an era that was winding down.

The Beatles' organisation, Apple, offered a physical instance of the decade's innocence foundering on the rocks of experience. After an ill-fated retail venture in Baker Street the company, partly conceived as a tax shelter and partly an idealistic hippy variant on capitalism, took up residence at 3 Savile Row. Incidentally, the Beatles were not its first Merseyside occupiers. Nearly two centuries before, Lord Nelson is said to have acquired it as a home for his mistress, the Wirral's own Lady Hamilton. From the building's roof, of course, the Beatles played their final performance in 1969, for the cameras filming *Let it Be* and the bewildered office workers milling below. Running a business was a trial to the band, and hastened their internal conflicts. Long after the Beatles broke up, Apple was still untangling their affairs, moving to other discreetly salubrious townhouses on the way. But the Fabs fared better than Lady Hamilton, who died a pauper.

In December of 1968, just a few weeks before the Beatles' rooftop show, the Rolling Stones filmed a TV special in Wembley. The *Rock and Roll Circus* had guest appearances by Lennon, the Who and others, but its anticipated air of music hall jollity never quite materialised, and the production was shelved for many years. 'You've 'eard of Oxford Circus! You've 'eard of Piccadilly Circus! And this is the Rolling Stones' *Rock and Roll Circus!*' shouts Mick Jagger, as the Ringmaster. But the capering clowns and acrobats could not conceal some awkwardness.

Even the Beatles' *Magical Mystery Tour* a year previously had struggled in its conceit of four down-to-earth psychedelic superstars. The Rolling Stones were even less of the music hall mould, being neither comic nor instinctively communal. Still, the *Rock and Roll Circus* ended with its whole cast and crowd in zany medieval costumes, cavorting like drunken time travellers from Bartholomew's Fair. Perhaps an ancestral trace of ancient London survived, after all. Yet it's hard to disagree with Martin Scorsese's assessment – for him, he said, the Stones had never seemed like a London band, but a New York one.

Jagger made a more authentically London movie around the same period, in *Performance*. His character, a regally self-indulgent but jaded rock star, is mentally and spiritually sundered from the city outside his Powis Square home (the interiors filmed, in fact, in Lowndes Square) but elsewhere there is a convincing feel of Swinging London's come-down, colliding with East End thuggery. In real life Jagger's colleague Brian Jones was about to take his leave of such an existence, drowning, under mysterious circumstances, in the pool of his country house. The Stones' famous 1969 show in Hyde Park was by way of an epitaph for the dead Stone, and perhaps for a whole decade. But not an epitaph for London. People die, London doesn't.

The Land Where Pop Stars Were Made

The Beatles and the Stones were not the only show in town. Among their mightiest contemporaries were London bands the Who and the

Kinks, guitar hero Eric Clapton and an extraordinary visitation from Seattle, Jimi Hendrix. These we shall meet in a little while. In 1965 the city was suddenly abundant with fresh faces and new voices. From distant Dagenham, where the cars were made, came Sandie Shaw. She was spotted by Adam Faith and soon her model-sharp cheekbones and trademark bare feet were seen everywhere. For her second single she picked a Burt Bacharach number, '(There's) Always Something There to Remind Me', and topped the charts. She was just seventeen, and she's been around in some way ever since.

My favourite London girl of that time, though, would be Dusty Springfield. Born as Mary O'Brien to an Irish family in West Hampstead, she also imported Bacharach songs and made them into white soul epics. She'd begun as one-third of her brother's folk-pop trio the Springfields, re-vamped her look with lashings of mascara and pushed her vocals into a new realm of drama. 'I Just Don't Know What to Do With Myself', 'Some of Your Lovin'' and 'You Don't Have to Say You Love Me' were as grand as palaces. She effectively produced them herself, down at Phillips's studios by Marble Arch, where her recording manager was Johnny Franz. 'He allowed me the freedom to follow my enthusiasm,' she told me. 'He'd sit in the control room while I'd go out and scowl at the musicians. Bless him, he'd sit in there and read *Popular Mechanics*. But he had good ears, he'd suddenly look up from *Popular Mechanics* and go, "E flat!"'

After a while in decline, her career revived through a Pet Shop Boys collaboration in 1987. (One of their songs, 'Nothing Has Been Proved', was for the film *Scandal* and wonderfully evokes the London of 1963's political crisis, the Profumo affair.) When I met her, she was fifty-five and diagnosed with cancer, but as blunt as ever. Like Norma Desmond of *Sunset Boulevard*, she was still big, it was just the records that were smaller. 'I'm not English,' she said. 'My name is O'Brien and I'm glad it is. I've got nothing against the English and I'm glad I was born here. But I'm glad my mother came from Kerry and I'm glad my name is Mary Isobel Catherine Bernadette O'Brien and I can weep at *Riverdance* on TV.' On the day she died in 1999, she'd been due to collect a medal from the Queen.

The genuinely amazing feature of the mid-1960s was that Britain – staid old tea-drinking Britain – was suddenly pre-eminent in pop culture. Rock 'n' roll was an American invention, just as Hollywood had been. With London's grand theatrical past it could produce fine actors and intelligent films, but its popular music was parochial like music hall or derivative like Tommy Steele. To the coursing energies of jazz, blues and soul, Britain had no equivalent at all. Yet the Beatles and the Stones changed everything. Once they had broken through in the USA itself, curious young travellers set sail for England. All of a sudden, this was the land where pop stars were made.

Among the first to fetch up here was a drawling Texan firebrand named P. J. Proby. He'd worked in the movies a little bit and had a taste for advanced melodrama. His self-image, thought Nik Cohn, combined Jesus Christ, Judy Garland and Errol Flynn. He had some hits, kept a big house in Chelsea and caused lots of trouble. His trousers *would* keep splitting on stage. Jack Good was a long-term supporter and Proby has survived, against the odds, to the present day. I am told he has a better tailor, too.

From the same school of massive, minor-key balladry – until he discovered Art – was Scott Walker. His Los Angeles three-piece the Walker Brothers, who were not brothers and weren't really called Walker, heard the siren call of Swinging London. The drummer, Gary, had even worked here for P. J. Proby. Far away from the Vietnam draft board they found a pad in Chelsea and went to Marble Arch to record with Dusty Springfield's mentor Johnny Franz. Here in Phillips's Studio 1, at Stanhope Place, they constructed Phil Spector-influenced epics like 'Make it Easy on Yourself' and 'My Ship is Coming In'. Scott's voice was magnificent, full of haunted gothic grandeur. The Walkers' biggest success came in March 1966, with a song called 'The Sun Ain't Gonna Shine Any More', which was Number 1 in the week that Ronnie Kray gunned down a rival gangster in the Blind Beggar pub in Whitechapel. According to one legend, the disc was on the jukebox when Ronnie fired the fatal shot: 'The sun,' he quipped, 'ain't gonna shine for *him* any more.'

Scott was really too sensitive for that sort of thing. His tousled light brown hair enlarged his head and made his body look even frailer. He wore beatnik casual clothes that seemed half careless and half exquisitely chosen: Wrangler jackets and needlecords, open-collar shirts and dangling medallions, suede shoes. There were usually sunglasses, too. Wherever the Walkers appeared, teenage pandemonium broke out. In Portsmouth a fourteen-year-old girl was knocked down by their getaway car. Regaining consciousness she asked the ambulance crew if Scott was OK.

He rather disliked pop stardom and preferred to watch gloomy European films or to read cultish foreign authors like Jean Genet. Once he was reported to have attempted suicide in a gas-filled flat – recovering, he went out to Ronnie Scott's club where a member of the Hollies offered him a shilling for the gas meter. For a while he stayed in a monastery on the Isle of Wight. His former press man Keith Altham recalls him looking forlorn in clubs like the Scotch of St James, or simply staying at home behind drawn curtains in his Chelsea flat. Apparently even the latter pleasure was marred by the noise of football fans en route to Stamford Bridge.

When the Walkers toured with another US expatriate, Jimi Hendrix, Scott could see the rules of pop were changing. He withdrew to make some deeply personal solo albums (which, intermittently, he continues to do), intoning mournfully of night and rain, plagues and wars, and playing chess with Death. They've seldom sold hugely but are rightly venerated. Given his reclusive image it was odd to see him popping up in a 1980s Britvic commercial – black-and-white, with a Swinging London theme, its other cameos including Sandie Shaw and Dusty Springfield.

An equally interesting survivor from the time is Eddy Grant, the leader of a multi-racial pop band – pointedly named the Equals – who offered a glimpse of the real London, the teeming, evolving city which lay outside the King's Road fantasy. At the age of eight Grant arrived with his family from Guyana; he is supposed to have looked at the Kentish Town terrace and asked his father, 'Why has our house got all those doors?' He showed unusual focus, making his own guitar in the school's woodwork room after hours. He played classical trumpet in the Camden Youth Orchestra. And when he was twenty he started writing superb singles in a sort of tough bubblegum style, like 'Baby Come Back', 'Viva Bobby Joe' and 'Black Skin Blue Eyed Boys'. He dyed his hair blond and challenged Enoch Powell to a debate about Commonwealth immigration. (Sadly, the offer was not accepted.)

There was always something driven about Grant. After the Equals he hawked a solo LP around the music business, finding no takers. An executive asked him what he would do with the tape. 'I dunno,' he replied. 'I'll just take it home and listen to it by myself.' Ultimately unstoppable, he went on to make records that often reflected the immigrant experience, such as 'Cockney Black' and the Brixton-hymning 'Electric Avenue'; his 'Police on My Back' was picked up by the Clash. In some ways he was a classic London shrewdie, with the Tin Pan Alley nous to control his own copyrights. By the time I met him he was living in Barbados, the owner of a world-class studio where the Rolling Stones came to record. 'From the very first day that I came to England,' he said. 'I didn't like the cold. But I had no choice, my mother and father took me there and I had to take it.'

We sat in the shade of his colonial house, beneath a tree from which slaves were hanged in an 1816 uprising. He was a model of quiet intensity:

I hope you don't ever feel, in having a discussion with me about anything, that it is something I take lightly . . . When my turn comes around I know I'll be ready because I have practised and I'll be sharp. That's the only thing that kept me going. This industry has given me all that I've got: money, a rough face, a pain in the stomach. It's given me everything good and bad. And when it was good it was very good. So I can't say that I was ever really bitter. I know, sociologically, where I stand as a man in this industry. But I have never let it hinder me. I realised that I am in the field in which I am strongest and I'll just have to battle on the terms of the game.

The rules of the game were that if I was black, maybe I would not sell as many records as if I was white. Well, all right. So let me sell the maximum amount of records that I can sell as a black man, and then we'll look at the rest once we've done that. And I'm getting there! If, when it's all over for me, and people look back over what I have done, they must see a catalogue that shows the loops and bumps of a man's life.

The World's End: What's it All About, Alfie?

As Eddy Grant and others understood, Swinging London was never a real place. In that 1967 film *The London Nobody Knows*, the presenter James Mason walks its unsung streets with a pensive expression – he finds a city of brawling, drink-maddened tramps, of buskers and shabby market stalls, of tired old buildings and the rumbling lorries of the demolition men. This was a London that Dickens would recognise.

Even landmark movies of the era, mistaken for celebrations of Swinging London, have a rueful quality. Julie Christie's *Darling*, Michael Caine's *Alfie*, David Hemmings's *Blowup*, share a queasiness beneath the surface. They bring to mind some of Noël Coward's songs of the Jazz Age, when he too looked at London's gaiety and described an existential emptiness. The best London songwriters of the time, like Jagger and Richards, Pete Townshend and Ray Davies, each relayed their doubts. George Melly wrote a film called *Smashing Time* that satirised a shallow, self-deluding world – a world which was all but over by 1968. The 'smashing time' devoured its own, as well; the two Brians, Epstein and Jones, were not its only casualties.

Less spectacular than Swinging London, but ultimately just as important, were the several underground scenes currently brewing. They included the soul clubs of the mods, the folk and blues cults and the hippy-political activists; we'll look at each of these in a while. But if you belonged to none of these, and the vast majority of young Londoners did not, there were only the great stand-bys of ordinary English life: the telly, the pub and the pictures. The radio was, for a long time, slow to catch on. The BBC enjoyed a near monopoly and took until 1967, when it founded Radio 1, to accept that popular music had really been revolutionised. Until then the main carriers of sixties pop were the remote station Radio Luxembourg, and a gaggle of 'pirate' broadcasters who had sprung up on de-commissioned trawlers and derelict wartime forts around the coastal waters of Britain. From these cheerfully illicit outfits came the next generation of famous DJs including Tony Blackburn, Kenny Everett, John Peel and Johnnie Walker. The biggest sound in the south-east was Radio London, transmitting from a converted minesweeper in the North Sea near Essex. Payola was rife – they were pirates, after all – but their spirit of musical adventure was infectious, and the stations were much missed after the Labour Government's Marine Offences Act of 1967 closed them down.

It was always observed of Swinging London that the scene was classless: East End came up West, broken-nosed villains could dance with plummy-voiced debs, Belgravian mansions welcomed Scouse minstrels and cockney snappers. But even this apparent revolution was not all it seemed. Fashion held a clue to the enduring class divide. In the stalls of Chelsea Antique Market, at the retro paradise I Was Lord Kitchener's Valet, and in the new shop Biba, there was the reflected taste of England's upper classes, who inherited and cherished old things: first editions, worn carpets, historic costumes. Along the King's Road they were importing sailor trousers and dyeing them to create the first fashion flares. Peacocks pored over Indian silks, wide old ties, de-mob suits and collarless shirts.

By contrast, the working-class consumers of the 1960s were only too familiar with decrepitude and they wanted a change. With their improved spending power they desired what was new and shiny, not antique and historically quaint. They valued plastic. Bohemian students might like vintage clothes, which after all were cheap and rather clever. But their counterparts from the council estates craved something smart and up-to-the-minute. Long before the American TV crews were filming the King's Road, a totally separate world had been created. This was the Land of a Thousand Dances. It was London's greatest pop creation. It was our next stop: mod.

Chapter Six

Male West One

Mods, rockers and psychedelic costermongers. The Kinks, the Who and the Small Faces. Carnaby Street and the man in frilly nylon panties.

Carnaby Street is the cut-price King's Road but occupies a noble place in London's pop story. It was always cheap and cheerful and not above flaunting a big sign saying 'Carnaby Street Welcomes the World'. The King's Road is too grand to do that – its commercialism has an air of stiff necessity, like a Lord opening his home to the public or a Duchess taking in washing. In pop mythology Carnaby Street stands for Britain's perennial street style, mod. Ironically, given the street's unabashed populism, mods were once a thoroughly elitist tribe. But the wider world needed something it could fasten on to. And Carnaby Street was it.

The Who and the Kinks became the public face of mod, though neither was quite the real McCoy. From the East End, the Small Faces were much more like it. In later times Paul Weller ('the Modfather') has been its prime embodiment. Mod is a very London cult, which has had several descendants including Britpop. It has its own roots in post-war jazz and, arguably, in a much older tradition of aspirational cockney dandies. People assume that mod was merely short for 'modern'. But a real devotee knows it is short for 'modernist' and that is a very different idea. It is a personal philosophy, and an attitude to life. Occasionally it may, in fact, despise what is modern and prefer the traditional. Many might feel they are called to be mods, but few can live up to its demands.

Once upon a time the press acclaimed John Stephen as the King of Carnaby Street. In the late 1950s when it was only a backwater on the Soho side of Regent Street, he was a young Glaswegian on the make. At first he worked in Vince's, a rather camp menswear shop around the corner. Its owner was Bill Green, a 'physique photographer' who sold bright, tight-fitting and homo-erotic styles in that austere time of post-war masculine dress. His customers were patrons of the Marshall Street Baths across the way, or flamboyant showbiz types. John Stephen saw potential in taking this trade to a wider young public.

In 1957 he set up on his own in Beak Street and soon expanded a few yards into Carnaby Street, at that time home to some old-established Jewish tailors and a couple of tobacconists. In almost no time John Stephen had nine shops there. As early as 1959 the mighty Austin Reed on Regent Street sniffed a change in the neighbourhood's air – instead of looking left, to Savile Row, they ventured a glance over to Carnaby Street, and responded with a big pop art mural. Teens and hipsters were already swarming (Old Compton Street was not far away, either), attracted by Stephen's affordable but sharply modern clothes, the loud music, huge mirrors and ever-changing window displays. By 1963 he had eighteen shops in town, trading under names like His Clothes and Male West One.

So that was Carnaby Street. Who were the mods?

If we return once more to *Absolute Beginners*, we glimpse those modernist jazz fans of the late 1950s. They liked Italian clothes that were lightweight and colourful; they approved of French films and Gitane cigarettes; they sought imported Miles Davis LPs. A few even took to existentialism. Most, at any rate, lived for bebop and bespoke. They disdained the scruffiness of trad jazz, just as they opposed their later enemies the greased-up rockers.

Around 1961 the mod look was spreading to certain suburbs: Shepherd's Bush in the west, Stamford Hill, places on the Essex side. Mark Feld of Stoke Newington, who would eventually become Marc Bolan, liked to visit the Bishopsgate tailor Bilgorri. In 1962, aged fourteen, he advised *Town* magazine, 'You got to be two steps ahead.

117

The stuff that half the haddocks you see around are wearing I was wearing two years ago.' From a purist point of view this was mod's zenith. The newer mods coming up were less intense. They were content with ready-made clothes, for one thing. And they found them at John Stephen's shops in Carnaby Street.

There was now violence in the air. Mods presented a strange appearance that others found downright creepy. They could be effeminate (it was a mainly male affair) and some even toyed with make-up; they could be touchy, especially when fuelled by speedy drugs. As their numbers grew the lumpen element took over. In 1964 a mod contingent clashed with rockers at Clacton-on-Sea in Essex, beginning a two-year spree of such affrays. The usual venues – Margate, Brighton, Hastings, Southend, all around the South-East – betray the day-trippers' city of origin. Mods were typically London boys (it was hard to maintain the mod life anywhere else), recent school-leavers in the burgeoning white-collar sector. Their foes were small-town locals who had never abandoned teddy boy times, or country boys on motor-bikes.

Earlier mods of the first wave would sniff at the cheaply dressed scooter boys who claimed the name of mod. But it was a mass movement now, and punch-ups on the promenade begat the media coverage that begat a nationwide tribe of amateurs. Carnaby Street lost all snob value when the tourists arrived. Once the term reached America, what was globally called 'mod' lost all connection to its origins. By the time of Ray Davies's song for the Kinks, 'Dedicated Follower of Fashion', his 'Carnabetian Army' was a parable of foppish self-delusion, down to its protagonist in his 'frilly nylon panties'.

Proper mod may have only lasted a year or two but its musical importance was huge. For one thing it was a major conduit for black American and West Indian discs, played in clubs like the Scene, the Flamingo and the Marquee. Many such records found their first overseas audience among London mods. For another, it was felt that mods should have some home-grown acts to reflect their world back at them. To a large extent, this was how three of England's greatest

Above: 'The Enraged Musician' of Hogarth's 1741 engraving, tormented by the anarchy and din of London.

BETTMANN/CORBIS

Left: An 1885 production of Gilbert & Sullivan's *Mikado*. London, not Japan, was the object of its satire.

BETTMANN/CORBIS

Above: 'Busmen holloaing, Wot cher, khaki!' Marie Lloyd strikes the right wartime note of patriotic populism.

Above: Noël Coward: 'Serene, content with my light-weight crown.'

Above: Vera Lynn, of East Ham: consolation in separation, faith in the final outcome.

Above: Julie Andrews and Rex Harrison in the original Broadway production of *My Fair Lady*, 1956.

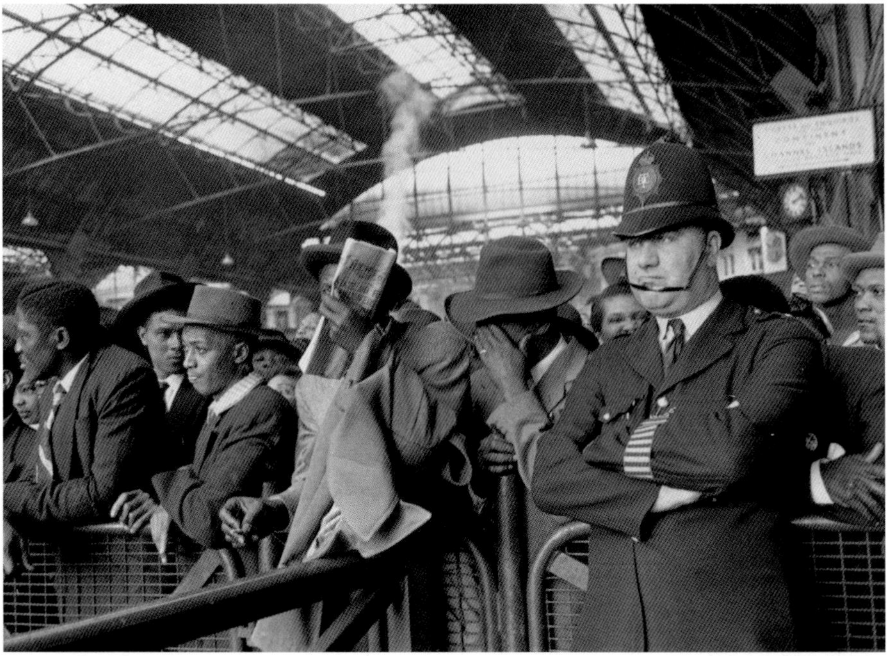

Above: 'London is the place for me': immigrants arrive at Victoria Station, 1956.

HULTON-DEUTSCH COLLECTION/CORBIS

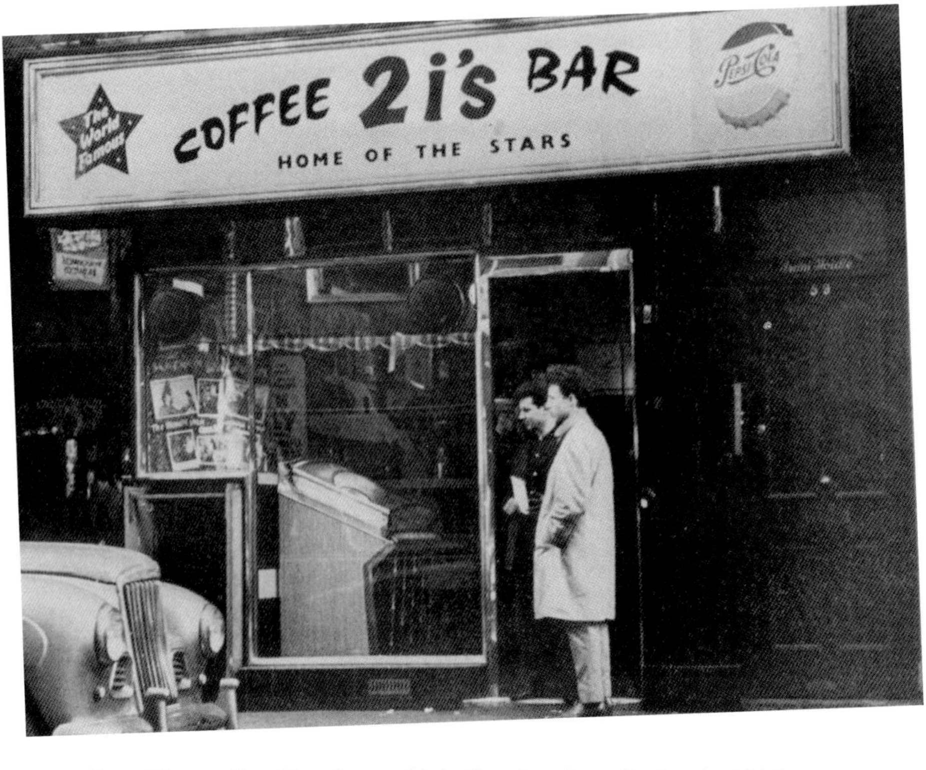

Above: The cradle of London rock'n'roll – the 2i's coffee bar in Old Compton Street, Soho.

Above: The Dominion in Tottenham Court Road, 1958, hosting a rock'n'roll parable of toffs and pearly kings. DEZO HOFFMANN/REX FEATURES

Above: 'It's a fine life':
Lionel Bart in his
prime, outside his
Kensington pad.

GEORGE KONIG/REX FEATURES

Right: Anthony
Newley in 1966:
smoothly
international yet
unapologetically
Cockney.

BETTMANN/CORBIS

rock bands came into being. The first of them was led by a gap-toothed boy from Muswell Hill.

I'm In with the Out-Crowd: Ray Davies and the Kinks

Commuters swarm through Waterloo Underground. Might there nowadays be a white-haired Terry and Julie among them? The Kinks' 1967 hit 'Waterloo Sunset', in which that courting couple appeared, and which is many people's favourite London song, drifts inescapably through my mind at this station. It was pleasing, anyway, that my rendezvous with Ray Davies should take me this way. When I re-emerged overground I was opposite the Archway Tavern, where the Kinks took a drink on the sleeve of their 1971 LP *Muswell Hillbillies*. Now I climbed Highgate Hill, passing a statue of Dick Whittington, and the capital sprawled below. Ray Davies did more than anyone to reveal the romance concealed in these everyday locations.

Another Kinks track, 'Big Black Smoke' from 1966, was made for views like this. Billowing chimneys, clamouring church bells, street cries of 'Oyez' – all in a tale of rustic innocence despoiled, like many an old folk song. The 'gate' of Highgate, Davies tells me, was the farmers' entrance on their route to the city markets, and the sudden sight of Christendom's biggest metropolis must have left them wonder struck. From here he points out to me the distant Surrey hills and, much closer, Arsenal's new home at the Emirates Stadium. I last spent time with Ray Davies at an Arsenal versus Liverpool game in the old Highbury ground, whose loss he predictably mourns. 'The new stadium is very comfortable,' he allows, 'but it's like an airport. I preferred the old place. I miss the smell. I miss the inconvenience.'

Bittersweet ambivalence is typical of him. Around Highgate Village and its very own Village Green, are various pubs that Davies knew as a teenager. But he himself grew up in Fortis Green, a little way up the road. Opposite the family's little Victorian house was another pub, the Clissold Arms, where he and his younger brother Dave would make their first public appearance. (Today the pub commemorates the Kinks with a corridor of framed photographs, leading to the Gents.) At the beginning of the 1960s he fell in with the R&B crowd who followed the gurus of that scene, band-leaders Alexis Korner and Cyril Davies, and began to play the same circuit as the Rolling Stones. He also studied at Hornsey College of Art, and all things considered, was very hip indeed. And yet, Ray Davies subverts the idea of hip. That bittersweet ambivalence intervenes.

The Kinks came to fame with the great, bone-crushing rock singles 'You Really Got Me' and 'All Day and All of the Night'. (It was often said they invented heavy metal.) But it was soon apparent that Ray, the resident songwriter, was a much subtler proposition. If the early records caught the roar and chaos of a big city, his newer songs were tinged with its complexity. The mixture of classes is a London perennial and the Kinks found themselves managed by a microcosm of that very system. On the one hand were a couple of posh chaps, Robert Wace and Grenville Collins, with an office in Knightsbridge. On the other was Larry Page, a working-class boy from Hayes whose Denmark Productions was named after his Tin Pan Alley base.

The financial complications were to haunt the band for years, but the social tensions gave Ray a rich seam of lyrical inspiration. As young Dave Davies marvelled: 'I think it was the first time I ever went to Chelsea. I never even knew what Chelsea was. Those Georgian houses – you'd be playing in one room with people ha-ha-ha-ing in the other.'

FOUR MODS SET TO MAKE THEIR MARK said the *Pop Beat* headline one week in 1964. And the Kinks were indeed taken down to Carnaby Street, or even to older theatrical costumiers, and decked out with houndstooth jackets or hunting pinks. Musically their repertoire took in some Motown covers along with London R&B and a sort of Muswell Hill Merseybeat. But they were never proper mods. They'd arrived at the point when the movement was so far overground that it was cut off from its roots. By now, anything young and colourful was labelled mod. The Kinks simply took advantage of the moment. And Ray Davies, being Ray Davies, sent the whole thing up. His 'Dedicated Follower of Fashion' was only one of many songs that established him as London's pop bard. From Bowie to Britpop via

Madness and Morrissey, there followed a whole school of observational English songwriters in his debt.

Soon there were perceptive storytelling songs like 'Well Respected Man' (which achieves the rhyming of 'regatta' with 'dying to get at her') and 'Sunny Afternoon'. There were mordant things like 'Dead End Street' and 'I'm Not Like Everybody Else' that confirmed Ray Davies's drift away from hip preoccupations. A diarist of all the lives that go unrecorded, he was in with the out-crowd. Through his gapped teeth came the voice of a voiceless country. When I suggest that he always seemed detached from Swinging London, he readily agrees.

> I still am. I guess everyone was going down Carnaby Street but I still had to go and see Arsenal play, and this was before it was cool. I wrote songs about where I grew up, and that was the source of my material. Even in the so-called groovy sixties I was writing songs about my neighbourhood. That's possibly why I seemed detached from the other things going on.

Even at the height of Swinging London, Davies's keynote was melancholy. Themes of regret, pessimism or homesickness are common in his songs of 1965 and '66. And one of the most affecting is called 'Where Have All the Good Times Gone?'

> I think David Bowie recorded that, on *Pin-Ups*. It was the B-side of 'Til the End of the Day'. A very strong record, I liked that song. I must have been around twenty-one when I wrote it and my tour manager said, 'You're too young to have written a song like that. You don't have the life experience.' And *now* when I sing it people think I'm embittered. You can't win. But when I wrote it I was referring to older people, to my mum and dad looking back on the things they used to do. I don't know, maybe I was anticipating that every generation thinks that at some point.

A misfit more than a rebel, Davies was not so much a social critic as an all-round sceptic, not only at odds with straight society, but with the new glitterati too. If there are defining themes in his sixties songs – written at a time of unparalleled optimism and enthusiasm for the new – they are nostalgia for Britain's flawed past, and unease about its golden tomorrows.

By the time of 1967's *Something Else*, the sleevenote writer could talk of 'Daviesland', as literary types talk of Graham Greene's 'Greeneland'. In the Summer of Love, our man's preferred season was autumn – 'Autumn Almanac', 'End of the Season'. The chosen time of day, of course, was sunset – the time when Terry and Julie make for that human hive at Waterloo.

Davies had several connections to this subject. In student days he would walk across the footbridge to Waterloo Station and catch a train to Croydon Art School (where he went after Hornsey). As a child he had stayed in a hospital ward at St Thomas's with a river view. And in 1951 his father took him to the Festival of Britain on the South Bank. Were Terry and Julie really Stamp and Christie? Stamp believed so but Davies says not. In fact he wasn't even thinking of London at first, beginning with an image of sunset over Liverpool in the decline of Merseybeat. He wrote it, he says, for an older generation who had lived through war and hoped to see Britain great again.

Does he understand why so many people choose 'Waterloo Sunset' for their favourite single?

> I think so. It's like people say they like *Casablanca*. I think, 'What is it they like?' I look at it time and time again and think, 'That's a good film.' 'Waterloo Sunset' is like that. It's just structured, I plotted it a bit. So it was my statement of what a single should be like and I think a lot of people liked the symmetry of it and the containment, the whole item being in that three-minute package and then it's over. And it was English, I think people liked that. It was our statement.

Through albums such as *Village Green Preservation Society* and *Arthur (Or the Decline and Fall of the British Empire)* the Kinks confirmed their position as Britain's most 'quintessentially English' band. The latter record, especially, was among the more fully realised 'concept' albums of the time. Its centrepiece, 'Shangri-La' is a miniature suburban symphony; 'She's Bought a Hat Like Princess Marina' has all the pathos and compassion that so many rock writers cannot summon. The red-brick villas, the faded terraces and the pebble-dashed mock-Tudor semis, hosting lives of quiet desperation, are rendered free of condescension.

Ironically, this 'quintessentially English' act were losing favour back home and found their salvation in America. Songs of the 1970s portray Davies as the rock star, abroad and disoriented. In 'Sitting in My Hotel' we find him with his 'chauffeur-driven jam jar' and 'two-tone daisy roots' – the rhyming slang is a last fragment of his inner self, to which he clings for fear of losing identity. He took to copying the camp old stage costumes of Max Miller. In the eighties I once followed the Kinks for a few dates in California, where Ray would ponce about the stages, fluttering and fey, impersonating Noël Coward to baffled, plaid-shirted rock fans. I asked him about this, backstage at the Hollywood Palladium. 'Oh God,' he groaned, 'you always see us at the worst gigs, you *NME* people. The best ones are when we're all pissed off and there's no one there. You should have come to see us in Dunstable.'

Does the Kinks' 'quintessentially English' label make sense to him?

Well, it would be silly to be called anything else. But when I sit down to play music I like blues and country, because I love the guitar. I'm just an English writer who happened to pick up the guitar, playing American-style music. I do my thinking through my narratives. In my RCA years, I was really struggling to stay English and putting rhyming slang in songs, things like that, enjoying the culture. I enjoyed working with the culture rather than fighting it and pretending, like some of my contemporaries, that they were in America or they grew up in Memphis. People say the Rolling Stones took Route 66 and the Kinks took the M1. I love American folk and blues but I drew on my English experiences. I had to write stuff but I didn't know what it was like living in the South or being on a chain gang. So I wrote about walking around Muswell Hill.

Back in England one cold winter night in 1981, Davies picks me up in a chauffeur-driven jam jar outside the Finsbury Park Rainbow. He of course wears a cloth cap. His new American girlfriend, Chrissie Hynde, is in the back with him. We are taken to the East Stand at Arsenal's old ground to watch them playing my team, Liverpool. A life-long Gunners fan, Ray points out the corner terrace where he stood as a boy. He claims he was known to cancel Kinks gigs if the dates clashed. But tonight's football is not top-notch. 'It's no wonder people are going mad in England,' he sighs. 'There's nothing to do. You go to a football match and it's *boring*. Actually, half of this Arsenal team look like pansies to me.' At half-time, while the Band of the Metropolitan Police play selections from *Fiddler on the Roof*, we go to the kiosk for hot drinks. Recognising him, a man grins inanely and says, in a voice of mock gentility, 'Harf-ter-noon teee?' Davies shrinks. Back in our seats, the game grinds towards its inevitable replay. 'It seemed like a good idea at the time,' he apologises. Chrissie Hynde is frozen. 'Boy,' she drawls, 'you really know how to show a girl a good time.'

Back on Highgate Hill, one sunny afternoon in the twenty-first century, the chief Kink stirs another cup of tea and stares across the city:

People associate me with the music hall side of it. In the William Blake sense, being a Londoner who lived round here, I feel an affinity to London. I have a problem with south-east London, I always get lost there. But North London – there's something I like about the light up here, where it's really high.

Ian Dury was a great writer, and under-recognised because he was almost like a novelty performer. And Madness – that's part of the storytelling of London people. For a long time, if you go back to the sixties and the kitchen-sink revolution, it was based on the Northern accent, those films by Keith Waterhouse and others. The London accent only re-emerged more recently, I suppose through Bob Hoskins in *The Long Good Friday*, and *EastEnders*. I was devising a show for the East End, *Come Dancing*, and at some of the workshops we were doing we got a lot of professional cockneys. But it's not all East Enders, there is a Londoner, there is a Londoner without music hall.

Having said that, Ian Dury and Madness, not so much Squeeze, there is a jack-the-lad type of delivery that you could do on a street corner or in a pub. But there is more depth to all those people than just the fun songs. Madness songs have a lot of humanity in them. But in the characterisation of the performers, they would maybe not be as emotional as I would be, even when they're singing something that's a love song. All their songs are well cast for that madcap humour.

My dad took me to see Max Miller play when I was really young, at the Finsbury Park Empire as it was – it's not there any more. He was a big fan of music hall. Originally my family came from Barnsbury, Islington, round there. Now I rehearse at John Henry's [the North London studio] which is near the pub where my grandmother used to drink in Copenhagen Street, and there's not a chance I would have written a lot of the stuff I've written without hearing her stories. It's true folk music when the family gets together.

Family tensions, however, have also played their part. An element of the Kinks' greatness lay in the combination of Dave Davies's hard rock guitar and brother Ray's theatrical fancies. The latter has never been content to stick at singles and albums; he has followed the London path to the stage. He's written several plays and musicals, the most recent being *Come Dancing* for Lionel Bart's alma mater the Theatre Royal, Stratford East. In his solo years, he's toured as a one-man show under the name that London artists wear like a badge of honour: *The Storyteller*.

We Can See For Miles: Pete Townshend and the Who

Where Ray Davies plays the wry observer, his great contemporary Pete Townshend is more of a theorist. The Kinks would gently mock the follies of English life and tenderly mourn the passing of its charm. The Who were more inclined to smash things up, and explain it as a revolutionary statement. Townshend's band were also latecomers to the mod party, but they adopted it much more seriously than the Kinks. Once Townshend had put his mind to it, mod became more than a youth fad or a flag of convenience. It became pop art.

As a quartet of personalities the Who were almost equally balanced, even if Townshend's vision has always steered their course. He was the son of a saxophonist in a dance band, the Squadronaires, and grew up in Ealing. He began by playing trad jazz on a banjo and then, in his Ealing Art School years, moved towards R&B and big, conceptual ideas. The Who's singer Roger Daltrey was altogether more bloke-ish, a Shepherd's Bush teddy boy who went to work on a building site and then in a sheet metal works. John Entwistle, the impassive bass player, went to school with Townshend in Acton where they played trad together. Keith Moon, the legendarily wild drummer, was from Wembley. As the Detours they joined the London beat group circuit. But one night, on 22 December 1963, at St Mary's church hall in Putney, they watched the evening's headliners, the Rolling Stones.

The effect upon the teenage Detours was electric. They raised their game overnight. Becoming the Who they were picked up by a teenage manager called Pete Meaden. An early sidekick of Andrew Loog Oldham, he was fascinated by the mods; he saw the band's potential to attract a scene that lacked acts of its own. The Who became the High Numbers, part of Meaden's obsession with mod's secret language – 'the face', 'third-class tickets' – some of which he probably invented himself. Pete Townshend, blossoming as a songwriter, saw opportunities to apply his art-school theories of pop to a living underground sub-culture. The High Numbers were to articulate the mods' message, in all its stuttering, pill-popping incoherence.

But soon the band were under new management. Meaden was, like Oldham, more of an image-maker than a businessman. His successors were Kit Lambert and Chris Stamp, two young film-makers in search of a subject. They offered an exquisite contrast in London backgrounds, this pairing of Toff and Tough. Lambert was born in Knightsbridge and educated at Lancing and Oxford. His father was the respected classical composer Constant Lambert. Stamp was from Plaistow, the son of a Thames tugboat man, and the brother of the actor Terence. The highly strung Kit was bisexual, the streetwise Chris was not, but they made a good team. Fully understanding the importance of 'front', their office address was in Eaton Place: 'It was the only slum in Belgravia,' Kit recalled, 'but it got us credit.'

There was now no stopping the Who. Having plastered fan-base bastions such as Shepherd's Bush with fly-posters, they played the prestigious Marquee. The Kinks' producer Shel Talmy auditioned them in the 2i's basement and they got busy making hits. Thus, one day in 1965, backed by scowling guitar chords, an elephantine bass line and the most volcanic drumming ever heard in pop, Roger Daltrey stepped up to the microphone to deliver a lyric that captured – in just a fraction over three minutes – the core text of all rock 'n' roll. The story goes that Pete Townshend had written 'My Generation' in Belgravia, angered by an order to remove his car – a hearse, of all things – for affronting the Queen Mother. One may or may not believe this tale, which was standard pop paper fodder. But nothing can subtract from the song's blast of passionate, stammering intensity. The Who were suddenly ranked right behind the Beatles and the Stones. They had even surpassed the Kinks. And not one of them was over twenty-one.

In America the Who's first LP depicted them by Big Ben, to underline their 'British Invasion' status. Elsewhere, the Union Jack joined other pop art graphics to suggest the band's mod intellectualism. Townshend wrote with furious energy, channelling his words through a singer who thought very little of them. Townshend understood the dynamics of sheer frustration and he fuelled the Who on its power. After a few more hits he moved from cheap digs in Wardour Street to premises above the Belgravia office, and then to nearby Chesham Place. As Brian Epstein had done for the Beatles, so the smooth Kit Lambert was showing his rough-hewn clients another side of life.

Sophisticated role models are the classic advantage of London musicians. Being the scion of a musical family, Lambert felt it right to coach Pete Townshend in new and more ambitious directions. He suggested, for example, a mini-operatic cycle, resulting in the 1966 opus 'A Quick One While He's Away' – nearly ten disjointed minutes of power-pop, music hall and country music. Another lesson introduced Pete to his classical London predecessor, Henry Purcell; this led to a cooing vocal backdrop in 'I'm a Boy' and the ominous guitar opening of 'Pinball Wizard'.

More curiously still, Townshend once told an interviewer he wrote a saucy 1967 hit, 'Pictures of Lily', on seeing a vintage postcard of 'an old vaudeville star, Lily Bayliss'. But did he? The song concerns a young boy's conversation with his father, regarding a sexy photo that he employs for self-stimulation. It's true there had been a distinguished pre-war lady named Lillian Bayliss, a producer and manager at both the Old Vic and Sadler's Wells. Without being unkind, no surviving photos of Bayliss seem plausible as pin-ups. Yet the real-life Bayliss was a close collaborator with Constant Lambert. Doubtless Kit would have known of her through his father and perhaps discussed her with him. So there is a link of sorts. Perhaps, however, Pete was thinking of one of the famously beautiful actresses Lilian Gish or Lillie Langtry (who, like the Lily of the song, died in 1929).

The operatic idea never went away. Kit encouraged Pete in the project that became *Tommy* – a 'rock opera', no less – followed by the grand mod-odyssey, *Quadrophenia*. Both albums led to movie versions and are undeniably stuffed with great Who songs. But neither was quite a *Beggar's Opera* for the twentieth century. Pushing against its boundaries, Townshend was among the first to discover rock's limitations – this was a music better at dumb intensity than narrative breadth.

It's possible that Lambert's deepest influence on the Who was through his self-destructive personality. He seemed hell-bent on emulating his famous father's alcoholic demise. His 'ultimate triumph', thought Simon Napier-Bell, would be 'to create a magnificent disaster'. Better than anyone, the Who captured a sort of fierce nihilism at the core of Swinging London – rather as the Stones caught its final decadence. Kit Lambert was one more to be smashed by that 'smashing time'. He died after a long and drugged decline in 1981. His predecessor Pete Meaden, who once coined a golden definition of mod as 'clean living under difficult circumstances', followed a similar trajectory. He died of an overdose three years earlier.

London is less explicitly present in the Who than in the Kinks. Townshend is possibly a more inward-looking writer than Davies. But there could never be much doubt where the band were born. 'Dogs' from 1968 is like rocked-up Harry Champion by way of Anthony Newley, celebrating beer and greyhound-racing at White City. The majestic 'I Can See For Miles' was inspired by a night on Primrose Hill. And, while *Quadrophenia* is more concerned with youth and disillusionment, the London–Brighton setting of songs like '5.15' is clear enough. Some of its characters were drawn from London mods that Townshend had known back in Shepherd's Bush or in their West End haven, the Scene club.

By 1970 he'd taken to wearing a pearly king costume on stage, as one sign of his antipathy towards the rootless and flaccid aspects of hippy culture. Of the supposedly magical Woodstock festival, he was scathing: 'I don't want to spend the rest of my life in fucking mud, smoking fucking marijuana. If that's the American Dream, let us have our fucking money and piss off back to Shepherd's Bush, where people are people.'

Like the Kinks, the Who would spend their later decades in a limbo of retirements and reunions, and were just as prone to inner conflict. After their 1982 show at Shea Stadium in New York, I joined the backstage party; I knew Pete slightly but had never met Roger, so I asked him where I might find the singer. 'Him? Don't bother. He'll have fucked off home to bed.' Their instability was made worse by casualties in the ranks. The first to go, not unexpectedly, was Keith

Moon in 1978. For a while Pete Townshend looked on course to join him. After one especially miserable business meeting in Poland Street, he and Chris Stamp repaired to the Speakeasy, across Oxford Street, where they met Paul Cook and Steve Jones from the Sex Pistols. The two punks, themselves Shepherd's Bush boys, were supportive. But Townshend drank so heavily he ended up in a Soho doorway and was moved on by a policeman, an episode he recounts in 'Who Are You?'

Himself no stranger to excess, the lugubrious John Entwistle passed away in 2002 in a Las Vegas hotel room, after a cocaine-induced heart attack. But the disciplined Roger Daltrey (who I finally found in New York, in the hotel gym), has retained the physique of a teenage sheet metal worker. He found a parallel career in acting. His finest role? The notorious highwayman Macheath, in *A Beggar's Opera*.

The Small Faces: the Darlings of Wapping Wharf Launderette

While the Who were essentially a West London act and the Kinks most definitely of North London, it was an East London band who represented mod in its purest form. More than that, the Small Faces stood for the whole cockney tradition in popular music. They were Swinging London's psychedelic costermongers.

The Small Faces had a private motto: 'Nuf, Nis and Reeb'. You have to spell it backwards to arrive at Beer, Sin and Fun – they were using a coster trick that was already old in the mid-nineteenth century, when Henry Mayhew described it. Inverting words and phrases was a way of entrenching tribal exclusivity. Thus, among those ancient market traders a 'top o'reeb' was a pot of beer; a barrow boy might want 'a yenep for a tib o'occabot', a penny for a bit of tobacco. 'Say' meant yes and 'on' meant no. To understand the banter you had to be in with the in-crowd – rather like a London mod, one hundred years later. Anything else and you were a third-class ticket.

The Small Faces were 'faces' in the mod sense, and 'small', simply because they were quite small. Their heights ranged from five-foot-four to a towering five-foot-five. It's somehow natural that their impish leader Steve Marriott should have played the Artful Dodger in Lionel Bart's *Oliver!* It was a role he never really grew out of. From Manor Park, where the old East End is giving way to the newer Essex suburbs, he went on to stage school after a year in *Oliver!*, scoring some minor film roles and TV parts in *Dixon of Dock Green* and *Mr Pastry*. Then he got briefly involved with Andrew Loog Oldham, still managing the Stones, and made his acquaintance with Tin Pan Alley.

As a result, Steve had done a bit of this (acting) and a bit of that (recording) by the time he met his fellow Small Faces. Working in an East London music shop he encountered his future songwriting partner Ronnie Lane of Plaistow, and his friend Kenney Jones, a drummer from Stepney. They found a keyboardist, Jimmy Winston, who was later replaced by Ian McLagan, a Hounslow boy who went to Twickenham Art School and therefore knew the south-west R&B scene. Ronnie Lane was utterly mod, one of the pure sort. Kenney Jones says: 'He used to wear a shirt and tie but he starched it so much that when his body moved his collars stayed facing the front. None of Ronnie's clothes moved at all, actually.'

The Small Faces were Dickensian as many mods were – somewhere on the cultural line from Sam Weller to Paul Weller. They were not hulking farm lads or toiling factory hands, but smart, crafty little urbanites. They were descended from generations of quick-witted errand boys, bookies' runners and wise-cracking junior clerks, nipping in between the city's thronging bodies and massive buildings. They settled on their name at the Giaconda coffee bar in Denmark Street, the home of other mod dreamers including Marc Bolan and David Bowie. This was a place, like Archer Street in Soho, where young musicians hung about in hopes of session work – hired on the spot, perhaps, for a publisher's demo disc. The Small Faces liked black American R&B and saw no reason why they shouldn't have a crack at it.

A hard-nosed manager called Don Arden signed them up and brought them to his office in Carnaby Street, over one of John

Stephen's shops. This was handy, because he would give them pocket money to spend on flashy clothes downstairs. For Decca they made a run of tough little R&B records, all smash hits, like 'What'cha Gonna Do About It?' and 'All Or Nothing'. They were, within their range, a perfect pop band. Marriott turned out to have a great voice – not so much soulful as bursting with brattish vitality. Just as importantly, now that British bands were running out of US songs to cover, he and Ronnie Lane revealed themselves – like John, Paul, Mick, Keith, Ray and Pete – to be exceptionally good songwriters. Kenney Jones remembers:

> This band was just meant to be. We didn't have to work at anything. In the studio everything came naturally, even learning an arrangement, because we were so locked into each other's telepathy. I don't remember any of us telling each other what to do or what to play, we just did it.

After Arden and Decca they signed to the ubiquitous Andrew Loog Oldham and his hip new label Immediate, whose slogan was 'Happy to be Part of the Industry of Human Happiness'. (It was the first of the independent companies, like Island, Virgin and Chrysalis, who would disrupt the conservative traditions of the established record companies.) Oldham had by now parted company with the Stones and was applying his mind to a roster of young acts including Fleetwood Mac and Rod Stewart. Rather like the Beatles in *Help!*, three of the Small Faces occupied a terraced house in Pimlico, just a notch below its neighbour Chelsea. For a while, Marriot was even going out with Chrissie Shrimpton. Brian Epstein was not far away, in grand Belgravia, but he liked to visit the boys and one night, all together, they took their first trip on LSD.

Thus the Small Faces stumbled out of 1966 and into the second phase of their career. They shared the Beatles' talent for pop-psychedelia (which the Stones did not). Oldham took them out of the formulaic studios where Decca had put them, and gave them a more adventurous setting at Olympic in Barnes, with the talented young producer Glyn Johns (both Olympic and Johns, like Immediate, were independents, another sign of the industry's cultural shift). Off the leash at last, the Small Faces made a blatant mods-and-pills anthem 'Here Comes the Nice'. Then came their masterpiece: 'Itchycoo Park'.

East End people had spoken of itchycoo parks for generations, usually a patch of land with stinging nettles, sometimes an open space where vagrants gathered (for example by Spitalfields Church) and often, since the war, an overgrown 'debris' or bombsite. It's usually said that Marriott and Lane were thinking of a particular piece of urban greenery in Ilford's Church Road. Quite possibly, but it's certainly true that the band already had a private slang word, 'ickyboo', meaning unpleasant. (Getting up early in the mornings, for example, was 'ickyboo'.) Filtered through the hallucinogenic prism of 1967, the Small Faces' 'Itchycoo Park' became something else again – a magical fantasia, a place to escape (like Lennon's Strawberry Fields), to get high. 'It's all too beautiful,' they sang. It was a really delightful vision of another kind of London, where there is always the possibility of something extraordinary around the next corner.

Amid the whimsy and trippiness the Small Faces also returned to their family roots in cockney music hall. 'For your delight!' cries Marriott in 'All Our Yesterdays', 'The darling of Wapping Wharf Launderette! Ronald "Leafy" Lane!' Another of their perfect pop singles, 'Lazy Sunday Afternoon' is pure coster nostalgia in modern hippy trappings; for its promo film they dance the old-time way, as their elderly relatives did around the old joanna, high on pale ales rather than reefers. A jokey neighbour voice enquires about 'your Bert's lumbago'. The working-class nostalgia and the Technicolor spaciness are oddly compatible.

They made a lovable semi-concept album called *Ogden's Nut Gone Flake* – it's memorably been called 'the cockney *Sgt. Pepper*' – that easily stands comparison with London's heavier rock operettas, like the Who's *Tommy*, the Kinks' *Arthur* or the Pretty Things' *SF Sorrow*. It has the London taste for storytelling – one song, of 'Rene, the docker's delight', positively relishes its salacious subject – though the album is partly a pastoral affair. There was a rustic side to these city boys. For much of the twentieth century even a Londoner might reach the countryside within a short bus ride, before the endless sprawl of later decades made this nearly impossible. Indeed Ronald 'Leafy' Lane would soon indulge those very yearnings.

Marriott and Lane now took a fashionable stab at 'getting it together in the country' by sharing a house in Buckinghamshire, by the Thames at Marlow (called Monk's Corner, it was the former home of *Three Men in a Boat*'s Jerome K. Jerome). Here, as the sixties dwindled to a close, the band's music grew smokier and hazier. In the back garden they recorded one of their last numbers, 'The Universal', sounding on the point of falling over.

In fact, under their feet a chasm was opening. In the late 1960s pop and rock became two different things. Pop was for teenyboppers, usually girls, and rock was for serious 'heads'. To turn 'heavy' was the goal of all ambitious pop bands: the Stones, the Who and the Kinks achieved it easily. Others announced their conversions in the weekly music papers and prayed for the best: the Move, the Marmalade, the Tremeloes. The Small Faces underwent the same heart-searching. Meanwhile, Andrew Loog Oldham's Immediate label was in chaos. 'Woody Allen once said that cocaine is God's way of telling you that you have too much money,' Oldham explains. 'In my case the cocaine came later and God's way was Immediate Records.' By the age of twenty-four he had done it all. He left the music industry in 1969, at the age of twenty-five. Drug addicted, he drifted for many years until, in 2000, he returned with two brilliant volumes of memoirs.

Unlike the other great London groups the Small Faces never made headway in America, which was now Steve Marriott's ambition. He left to form a new band, Humble Pie, who lumbered around the US stadiums playing very heavy rock. Rather at a loss, the remaining Small Faces turned to a bluesy North London singer called Rod ('the Mod') Stewart who had been to the same school as Ray Davies in Muswell Hill. They added the spindly, genial guitarist Ronnie Wood and abbreviated their name to the Faces – a band of shambolic, and abbreviated their name to the Faces – a band of shambolic, laddish charm who ultimately left a deeper impression than Humble Pie. After that, Kenney Jones's next gig would be as Keith Moon's replacement in the Who:

> I always describe the three major bands I've been in this way. The Small Faces was the most creative. The Faces was the funniest, most outrageous, party-going, happy-go-lucky time. Wonderful. And the Who was the most exciting – you had to be an athlete to play drums.

Posthumously the Small Faces have had a high degree of respect. The Sex Pistols covered them, Paul Weller has revered them throughout his career and Britpop bands would class them as a primary inspiration. 'I'm incredibly flattered,' says Jones, 'and I know Steve would be . . .'

> I'm proud of our achievements, given that we were only together for an incredibly short period of time. I always believed we were ahead of our time. We were a band that never minded experimenting and mucking around. The young bands are taking a leaf out of the Small Faces' attitude, the way we felt about music. It isn't to be taken seriously, but it's not to be abused.

A Mod World, My Masters: Two Unhappy Endings

Marriott, alas, saw little of this. When Humble Pie were finished he bought a cottage in the Essex countryside and settled down to playing ordinary pub gigs. (I saw him often at my local: an idol of my childhood, now a bit fat and bald, but in glorious voice and gruffly in love with his little London crowd. Pints of beer were ferried to the stage.) Finance and management were always a trial to the Small Faces and Marriott, the one-time Artful Dodger, could not scheme his way back into the limelight. Unhappily, in 1991, he came home one night after an evening's fun and was killed by fumes when his cottage caught fire.

His old partner Ronnie Lane had very mixed fortunes after the Small Faces. At first he became an actual rock star. He brought to the Faces' knockabout brouhaha his own more soulful touches like the poignant London love song 'Debris'. He was at all times a cheerful-looking foil to Rod Stewart's flash and swagger. Fag a-dangle, Lane would shuffle across the stage with a kind of tipsy toddle. When he left the group in 1973 it was the end of their great days.

With some of the cash he'd acquired, Lane embraced a new life, becoming a poet of the hedgerows. He bought a rambling farm on the Welsh Borders and reared sheep. For a while, he actually attended agricultural college. He also bought a mobile studio, enabling him to record at a safe distance from the temptations of the city. He named his new band Slim Chance. It was a typically wry choice: the self-deprecatory style of a plucky outsider. Unhappily, history would prove it apt. It should have been No Chance.

With Slim Chance he invented a fine, if slightly inebriated style of rustic English folk-rock. To launch their LP *Anymore for Anymore* they played at Chipperfield's Circus on Clapham Common. Their music was a merry squabble of mandolins, accordions and fiddles and Lane's new look took on a Pop Larkin aspect, with checked waistcoats and red neckerchiefs. He even bought a gypsy caravan. Instead of conventional touring they'd take a convoy of lorries, pitch a big tent somewhere and be regular vagabonds. But 'The Passing Show', as it was known, was a failure that left Lane penniless.

His music was acoustic pub rock with a trace of village sing-song and London music hall. Drink and mysticism, love of women and the struggle to keep cheerful – these were the great Ronnie Lane themes. His 1974 hit 'The Poacher' is an idyllic hymn to the pleasures of dawn angling. 'One for the Road' has a lovely, benevolent booziness. Perhaps the finest of his late songs is 'Kuschty Rye'; over a bouncing, McCartneyesque bass line, Ronnie declares devotion to a Romany girl. She mocks him wickedly in words that he doesn't understand, but he adores her for her simple optimism and trust in providence.

Although Lane's mobile studio had famous customers like Eric Clapton and the Who, his farm was not a money-spinner and he looked for a cash injection via collaborative albums with Pete Townshend and Ron Wood. He was even persuaded to try a Small Faces reunion but rehearsals proved abortive. Worst of all, he began to sense the early symptoms of multiple sclerosis, a disease that had afflicted his mother. He first noticed difficulties when he was playing the guitar.

The last chapters of Ronnie Lane's life make for sad reading. With the failure of his farm and a confirmed diagnosis of MS, he moved back to London, where his mobile studio was destroyed by vandals. It was around this time that I came across him one afternoon in a Twickenham pub. Star-stuck, I watched from across the room as he played pool with his cronies in a fug of cigarette smoke, with the swaying jollity of what I surmised had been a long session. It all looked wonderfully characteristic of the Ronnie Lane persona we fans used to admire. What I didn't know was how ill he was. It turns out he barely drank at all by this time.

In 1984 Lane moved to Texas, where he managed to play some final gigs before his strength gave out. Some of his medical bills were handled by Rod Stewart and Ron Wood. He'd lost all his money and then his health. But he had made the most emotionally generous music of his era. Eventually, on 4 June 1997, the Plaistow mod passed away at his new home in Colorado, deep in the Rocky Mountains.

Ready, Steady, Gone

The mods, and Carnaby Street itself, have had several revivals since the 1960s. Mainstream mod style became so flamboyant that it merged with hippy-dom. But in more obscure corners a stubborn few refused to grow their hair or get sloppy. Something of their style was passed down to the skinheads, and a lot of their ethos re-emerged in the Northern Soul scene of the 1970s. The Jam, one of the first punk bands, had mod leanings and inspired a neo-mod movement in 1978, its acts including Secret Affair and the Merton Parkas. North London's Madness, and their ska-loving peers on the 2-Tone label, were also heirs to the mod tradition. Mod motifs recurred in Oasis and Blur and a hundred others. If you sit on London Tube trains you may occasionally spot a well-presented man in late middle age and recognise him for an original.

Carnaby Street became un-mod and outmoded. By the 1980s my employer the *New Musical Express* (which had once lived on Denmark Street) had its office there, which almost seemed a post-modernist joke. Outside our third-floor windows the simultaneous noise of many bad pop records climbed up from the shops, where merchants sold their gimmicky tat, and punks, goths and neo-mods would pose for sightseers' cameras. Across the narrow street was the office of a new magazine, *Smash Hits*, too preoccupied by rising stars – Boy George, Kylie Minogue, Bros – to care about old legends. Behind our building was the birthplace of William Blake, that old custodian of Soho's soul. His ghost has overseen another upturn in Carnaby Street's prestige. Today it looks smarter and more expensive than ever before. But there is no place now for the one-room alteration tailors or Inderwick's, the eighteenth-century tobacconist's shop.

Chapter Seven

Dartford, Alabama

The blues boom. The folk frolic ... and some 'reggae in your jeggae'.

Beneath the brilliant and giddy distractions of mid-sixties Carnaby Street, there toiled many hundreds of musicians in defiance of commercial pop. To them occurred the novel idea that pop ought to be un-commercial. That was madness in Tin Pan Alley terms, but these were serious cats. Blues, soul and folk were their preferred sounds, all outside the mainstream, and they would now grow in strength and influence. By the end of the decade all three genres were feeding strongly into the emergent 'rock culture' – another expression that would have looked bizarre in 1959. In effect they became the new overground. The pop single gave way to the rock album. And the first sign of a shake-up was the London Blues Boom.

The arrival of blues music in London had a far-reaching effect on English life, a bit like the introduction of tea in 1657. It's always seemed strange that Swinging London should become the adopted home of the blues. Privileged young Londoners did not 'have' the blues – at least not as African-Americans of the former slave states had them. Nevertheless they 'got' the blues, in that they caught the universally human spirit of that music. It so happened that blues had fallen out of favour in the US, where urban blacks had moved on to the celebratory self-assertion of uptown soul. American whites, save for isolated scholars, were likewise uninterested – perhaps, for them, it carried too much cultural baggage.

White English boys, especially in London and its surrounding towns, could tackle this exotic import with a surprising lack of inhibition. They had fewer hang-ups about 'the Negro'. Here, he was not a social problem from just across the tracks, but a romantic and even noble figure from a world so distant it was unreal. If your impersonations of obscure black artists were poor, few in the audience would know it. Besides, it wasn't a question of authenticity. London took what it could of blues and transformed it. This was arguably the city's biggest gift to global pop in the twentieth century. Some pale, skinny art students made from blues the basis of a worldwide rock aesthetic.

This 'blues boom' proved the most fruitful of cross-pollinations. In London's art colleges and jazz clubs the movement hit critical mass, spawning the Rolling Stones, the Pretty Things, the Who, the Kinks and hundreds more. From Jimmy Page to Peter Green, Eric Clapton to Rod Stewart, London boys baptised themselves in imaginary Mississippi waters and were righteously reborn. Those were different times in England. We live amid such cultural saturation now that nothing affects anyone for very long. Back then there was cultural scarcity, and when young people discovered something exciting, they reorganised their whole beings around it.

Clapton's early band the Yardbirds once had to back the visiting blues star Sonny Boy Williamson, who was a big, mean, Delta-bred snarler, as real as real can be. His oft-quoted verdict on the young white hopefuls may be apocryphal but it's irresistible: 'Those English boys want to play the blues so bad,' he growled. 'And they do.'

The roots of the blues boom are partly in the trad jazz movement – from which, George Melly believed, it inherited a cliquey scholasticism. Mick Jagger told me that his circle of 'bluesologists' took their impetus from 'that middle-class knowledge, that sense of history, and the desire to know everything'. As trad jazzers were distinct from modernists, so the students of blues differed from working-class mods. While East End ravers were seeking freshly minted US soul, their college-boy counterparts were delving back into history. And sometimes to lucrative effect – pop's previous champions, the now-fading Merseybeat groups, slipped back into

Northern cabaret, while the London blues enthusiasts trained to become deities of stadium rock.

London offered, as always, valuable mentors to the young and untutored. Chief among the founding fathers of British blues were the jazzer Chris Barber (who had already nurtured skiffle) and two of his musicians, Cyril Davies and Alexis Korner, who in turn led bands of their own. Through their various ranks arose most of the first wave; a little later came the gaunt Northerner John Mayall, who sponsored many of the second. You might encounter their sect in the Marquee Club, initially a smoky dive below the Academy Picture House in Oxford Street; gradually, from 1962, its flavour changed from jazz to blues. There were, naturally, ideological rows between the factions, but once the Marquee had moved to 90 Wardour Street in 1964, R&B ruled.

Davies and Korner had been hosting skiffle and blues nights at the Roundhouse pub in Wardour Street since the early fifties, and performed guest spots for Barber. They formed their own band, Blues Incorporated, and made a home for themselves at the Ealing Rhythm & Blues Club ('Ealing Broadway Station,' explained its tickets, 'turn left, cross at zebra, go down steps between ABC teashop and jewellers'). Plump and balding, Davies was not star material but his acolytes included Mick Jagger and Brian Jones. Korner, meanwhile, was gravel-voiced and faintly exotic, having a Greek/Turkish mother and Austrian father; he was hugely knowledgeable too, and in his later incarnation as a radio DJ he spread the blues gospel to multitudes.

Between Blues Incorporated and Davies's next band the R&B All-Stars, graduates included Charlie Watts, Long John Baldry, Nicky Hopkins, Graham Bond, Jack Bruce and Ginger Baker. As the scene blossomed it spawned the Crawdaddy club in Richmond and Klook's Kleek at the Railway Hotel in West Hampstead. That venerable wooden ballroom at Eel Pie Island, on the Thames at Twickenham, made the inevitable switch from jazz to blues. Meanwhile from John Mayall's academy would emerge the future stars of Fleetwood Mac and Cream.

America's black musicians heard tell of the European market, a distant land where prejudice was less overt, where blues attracted serious attention and, more importantly, guaranteed wages. London was their landfall, rather as Paris had been for inter-war jazz players. There were various 'London Sessions' LPs arranged for visitors like Chicago's Muddy Waters. So enamoured was Sonny Boy Williamson, the Mississippi hard man, that he played the last dates of his long life in a Savile Row suit and Cheapside bowler hat. The razor-sharp R&B star Chuck Berry, whose career had been revived by British attention, mocked his pale disciples' piety: 'I don't mean "bleeeuws" . . . Ah means BLOOZE!'

The Pretty Things: 'That Bunch of Animals!'

When the Thames Delta went global its stars were the Rolling Stones. But there was another band, drawn from the same coterie of Kentish students, who were dirtier and more authentically dangerous. The Pretty Things have now slogged their way through more than four decades of adversity, and are a kind of shadow-side to the Stones (whose own story is not without darkness). One of their drummers, Viv Prince, was so uncontrolled that Keith Moon revered him. The last time anyone checked, the Pretty Things were pushing sixty and still banned from New Zealand. Their leaders, as always, are the singer Phil May and guitarist Dick Taylor.

Taylor remembers how hungrily blues imports were devoured, back in 1959, by his circle of teenage acquaintances, including Mick Jagger and Keith Richards: 'The building blocks were already there, with things like the good old trad jazz revival. Chris Barber brought Muddy Waters over to England very early on, so that's one strand. And I remember hearing *Skiffle Club* on the Home Service one Saturday morning when they played Bo Diddley. I just went "Oh! This is absolutely amazing" . . . I remember going up to London to get "I Think it's Gonna Work Out Fine", one of the early Tina Turner recordings on the Sue label. Other things were getting into the country, but few and far between. Mick

Jagger used to send off to a catalogue company which could do imports.'

As Phil May recalls, 'We had to send thirty quid to get a Sun import over here. So we'd have a little Thursday meet-up and eight people would bring a record and we'd make a tape, so you bought one record but you ended up with eight. I learned my licks out of Mick's notepad, cos he was a great one for getting words right. He gave me "Maybelline" and all the Chuck Berry stuff. The last time I met him, about four years ago, Bowie walked in and we were having a competition to see who could remember all the words. Jagger's the fucking king. He knows everything and he can even put the "Alabama-Dartford" on it.'

When Dick Taylor left an early line-up of the Stones – a move he never regretted – he and May used their lunchtimes at Sidcup Art College to fashion their influences into a startling noise. Phil May proved as good as Jagger in the Deep South-meets-Home Counties school of blueswailing, and even more committed. They were content to watch their old pals become recording stars. 'We still didn't see it as a possibility for us,' says May. 'It might sound naive but we thought the Stones had become entertainers, they'd taken the Queen's shilling and they wanted to be in showbiz. We were still playing the Ealing clubs and the Station Hotel in Dartford. Then suddenly we were in the charts and on telly, and I suppose without realising it we *were* in show business, we were entertainers.'

The Pretty Things were long-haired before anyone else, and life for pioneers is often dangerous. On the building site where May worked during college holidays, his co-workers turned him upside down and threatened to cut it all off. As well as looking wilder than the Stones, the Pretty Things took black American styles and played them harder, faster and dirtier. In so doing, this thoroughly London group became the blueprint for generations of white US garage bands. From their rough translations of the blues idiom arose a visceral tradition that has recurred constantly ever since, through the Velvet Underground and the MC5, in punk rock and the Ramones, to Nirvana and beyond.

Soon the young band was spotted by one Jimmy Duncan, a thirsty songwriter who haunted Denmark Street. He promised them stardom, joined their student friend Bryan Morrison as co-manager, and duly made contact with the Fontana label. Phil May remembers, 'Jimmy arranged this meeting, which we completely thought was not going to happen, because he was so pissed. But we turned up with Bryan at the café opposite the Central School of Art to find them all there, much to our surprise, a bunch of suits waving contracts. We thought it was a joke.' After an audition at Regent Sound, Fontana booked them into the studios of parent company Philips at Stanhope Place. At the Pretty Things' first album session, Fontana's label chief Jack Baverstock arrived to oversee the debut LP by his new signings. 'He walked out after half an hour with us,' says May. 'He went upstairs and said, "I'm not staying down there with that bunch of animals!"'

But here they made their amazing first single 'Rosalyn' and it came to pass: the Pretty Things really were pop stars, assisted not so much by glamour as by Phil May's brattish yelp, Dick Taylor's stinging riffs and the band's brutal collective wallop. Like the Stones and others they were largely reliant on outside songwriters to begin with. A tunesmith named Johnny Dee supplied the crucial follow-up, 'Don't Bring Me Down'. As May recalls, 'He turned up in a pink Cadillac in Denmark Street with a cowboy hat. He had an American accent, but I think he came from Darlington. He claimed Sioux Indian parentage, but the next time you met him he was Cherokee.' A Pretty Things original, though, was '13 Chester Street', named after the Belgravia address they shared with Brian Jones: 'It was the Duke of Westminster's property,' remembers Phil. 'Funnily enough it was where Princess Elizabeth and Philip of Greece used to go and have tea. We rented it but we got thrown out because they couldn't stand the lipstick-covered vehicles being parked next to the Rollers in the street. And also the parties and police raids . . .'

A measure of the Things' centrality in mid-sixties London is that 'Rosalyn' and 'Don't Bring Me Down' were each covered by Bowie on his tribute to the era, *Pin-Ups*, while it's claimed the band itself was name-checked in Dylan's 'Tombstone Blues'. 'There was an amazing amount of cross-fertilisation in those days,' recalls Phil May. 'Most bands were working nine days a week and there was a lot of interlinking. Any time off was spent with other musicians. I went out with the Beatles a lot, you went to the Scotch of St James; at the Speakeasy you'd be with Roger Daltrey all night, or Hendrix.'

Wherever the action was, there you would stumble upon the Pretty Things. Their favoured haunts, remembers May, 'were full of really odd people, like P. J. Proby and Diana Dors, or the scandal girl Mandy Rice-Davies, and then you'd have the Krays. It was a night-time set of people who didn't finish work until one or two, and ended up in these sort of places, and it would be extraordinary.' (On one occasion, which would be memorable if only anyone could clearly remember it, he and Nureyev, Brian Jones and Judy Garland enjoyed an evening to the fullest and wound up in bed. Now *that* was Swinging London.) 'There was a wonderful place called the Starlight Room – when we'd come back from Leeds or Manchester it was the only place where we could get a drink. So you'd end up with the most extraordinary cross section – a lot of CID, the Flying Squad, they used to be matey with the Krays – if you saw them all sitting at a table you couldn't tell them apart.

'And hookers. The people who worked the night shift and needed a watering hole somewhere. I remember there was another gig which was always full of celebrities which no one knew about – after the Ad Lib finished we all used to get into Rollers and drive down towards Heathrow Airport and go bowling. Out of your brain, along the M4, at Heston Services . . .'

In songs like 'London Town' they had moved on from R&B homages to the observational numbers so typical of the city. 'Basically,' says Phil, 'we were using personal incidents to make songs out of. Pretty Things songs have always been about things that have happened, about the people one has met. And that's not so far away from the blues stuff, where what they were singing about was just as important as the slide guitar and everything else. John Lee Hooker, "Poor People of Tupelo" and all those wonderful songs – it's a narrative. It's where we came from.'

Dick Taylor recalls songs that were 'like little movies', set to music. 'I can remember getting really stoned, wandering about in Fulham, and writing "Out in the Night" . . .' Their 'Death of a Socialite', like the Beatles' 'A Day in the Life', chronicled the 1966 car crash which killed Tara Browne, the young Guinness heir and hipster. 'It was in my road that his car fried,' Dick remembers. 'It was just down by Gunter Grove. There was this horrible mark on the road, which is probably why we wrote it.'

Now with EMI, the band were recording at Abbey Road at the time of *Sgt. Pepper* and Pink Floyd's *Piper at the Gates of Dawn*. In such stimulating company they made their most ambitious LP of all. Released in late 1968, *SF Sorrow* was a fully realised concept album, its narrative tracing the eponymous Mr Sorrow through his life's cycle as child, lover, soldier, worker and old man. *SF Sorrow* ranks alongside the other London rock operas of that period: it appeared in Britain five months before the Who's *Tommy*, though a US delay meant it was often viewed as a cash-in. Such was the ill-luck of the Pretty Things, who struggled on through many vicissitudes and line-up changes. Taylor and May endure to this day, when so many comrades have fallen on the field of combat. May insists he does not chafe at their lack of success. 'I think it stopped us killing ourselves,' he reasons.

How Much is that Hellhound in the Window?
Eric Clapton and Cream

The man that London's blues-boomers called 'God' was of humble earthly origins, growing up in Ripley, Surrey, surrounded by woods and weirs, farm labourers and village shops. From the wireless came his favourite sound, Handel's *Water Music*. Schooled in Surbiton, he picked up an acoustic guitar and at sixteen became a beret-sporting beatnik at Kingston College of Art, on the south-western outskirts of London. The young Clapton nursed a romantic admiration for self-destruction, spellbound by Robert Johnson, the haunted inter-war blues shaman with a hellhound on his trail. Stuck in pale suburbia, Eric's sense of cultural isolation was deep. In the blues he found at least second-hand roots, and passion in abundance.

He was soon to be found at Eel Pie Island; next he ventured into central London for the Soho folk and blues nights and to shop at Dobell's in the Charing Cross Road, pouncing on imported blues rarities. An encounter with Alexis Korner and Cyril Davies at the Marquee led him to the electric guitar (bought by a compassionate grandmother after the art school dropped him). He studied the Stones at the Crawdaddy and Ealing and Studio 51, and in time his own band the Yardbirds joined that same circuit.

In 1964 they backed the visiting legends Muddy Waters and Otis Spann, and Clapton was smitten by their 'extraordinary clothes: shiny, hand-spun silk suits with very baggy trousers and jackets that came almost to the knee. They were like angels.' By now the clothes-conscious Eric had ditched the beatnik look of his early teens for an austere mod style, still pre-Carnaby Street and conservatively hip. He would scorn the Stones for leaving their south-west London haunts, and say they 'went Chelsea'. (He would eventually go Chelsea in a big way himself.)

Disdainful of the Yardbirds' pop leanings he flounced out after the fourth single 'For Your Love'. It was a hot-headed decision, on the brink of stardom, but in 1965 he was thrown a lifeline by that tribal chieftain of the scene, John Mayall. To be hired by the venerated leader of the Bluesbreakers was all the credibility a twenty-year-old gunslinger could wish for, and Clapton was even given co-billing on the next album. Around this time the fabled 'Clapton is God' graffiti appeared on London walls.

Pop was being colonised by a more educated crowd, with aspirations to Art. Enter the cult of the musical virtuoso, borrowed from classical and jazz, which found its first rock avatar in Eric Clapton. To frame such talent to perfection he joined two alumni of Graham Bond's group, Jack Bruce and Ginger Baker, in a band christened – with deliberate *hauteur* – the Cream. Despite the perpetual warring of his new partners, Clapton and co enjoyed a rapid ascent. They had the hot-shot London manager Robert

Stigwood to assist and were signed to Atco in the States by music mogul Ahmet Ertegun, who'd already witnessed Eric jam with Wilson Pickett at the Scotch of St James. In Cream he lived out the Swinging London dream.

Newly adorned in psychedelic finery, Clapton joined his artist friend Martin Sharp in the Pheasantry, a rambling house on the King's Road where, in olden times, the royal pheasants were tended. From its windows Eric surveyed London's hippest high street. George Harrison was a regular caller. In the neighbouring room an Australian girl called Germaine Greer was writing *The Female Eunuch*. The ground floor housed a painter's studio, and the basement a club. An amusing new drug called LSD was making its appearance at parties. Clapton recalls taking his first acid trip to the strains of *Sgt. Pepper*, brought to the Speakeasy club on a pre-release tape by the Beatles themselves. The Monkees were in attendance, and John Lennon left with Lulu on his arm. It was 1967. It was that kind of year.

Clapton, the stern blues obsessive, had sufficiently unbent to front a most eclectic band. From Mississippi to Mayfair, Cream's range was phenomenal – they'd do hoary backwoods blues or pure Palais de Danse. There were numbers like 'I Feel Free' that could have set Fred Astaire spinning. But their real claim to greatness rests with the second album, *Disraeli Gears*. Its cover alone is a definitive psychedelic artefact: designed by the Pheasantry's Martin Sharp, the front and back present a baroque hippy collage, to be read as stained-glass windows were read by pre-literate peasants. *Disraeli Gears'* title came from a roadie's mis-pronunciation of the cycling term derailleur gears – this arch blend of groovy argot and mock-Victoriana captures the essence of Chelsea's Summer of Love.

The group's only real Londoner, the hyperactive jazz nut Ginger Baker, finished the record with a music hall joke, 'Mother's Lament', lurching from Victorian melodrama to broad cockney farce: 'Oh your by-bee has gone dahn the plug-'ole.' More characteristically, though, Cream's power-trio heaviness was a step forward from early British blues rock: with Hendrix, they paved the way for Led Zeppelin and heavy metal.

While Clapton took to changing his visual style with neurotic regularity, Ginger Baker was for a few years the most compelling sight in London. He'd stride about looking like a magnificently debauched Jacobean duke, then settle down to batter the hell out of his drum kit. All mad, panting, hollow-eyed, many-limbed ferocity, his was an artful blend of frenzy and dexterity. Jack Bruce, the bassist, was not so theatrical but no less intense – hunched over his instrument, fingers tugging urgently at its four fat strings, face screwed up in agonies of concentration. Then he would raise his head to the mike and let forth torrents of wounded jazz poetry in a Caledonian soul bellow.

Cream bowed out with two shows at the Royal Albert Hall in November 1968. An era was certainly ending – the Pheasantry was raided by the Stones' old nemesis Sergeant Pilcher (the 'semolina pilchard' of Lennon's 'I Am the Walrus'). Luckily, Clapton was not at home, but it was time to move anyway. Like many a fellow rock god he left London for the Home Counties, spending his wealth on a handsome residence in what was dubbed 'the Rockbroker Belt' of Surrey. George and Pattie Harrison were near neighbours; Eric, famously, fell in love with Pattie. And the Pheasantry became a branch of Pizza Express.

Through his years of romantic, alcoholic and narcotic turmoil Clapton played with Blind Faith and Derek & the Dominos, though the latter's country-rock saw the rustic Ripley boy of old displace the urban version. Married to Pattie he assumed the life of a traditional if dissolute squire. There were acoustic sessions with that other born-again bucolic Ronnie Lane, and extensive bouts of fly-fishing. But in the 1990s he took another place in Chelsea, just off the King's Road, and struck a new balance of town and country. He used his wealth to save the threatened clothes shop Cording's, a Piccadilly outpost of English dressing for the country gent. He became both a proper Londoner and a paid-up member of the Countryside Alliance.

'Mah Little Ground-hawgs': Foot-Soldiers of the Blues

God or not, Clapton had been but one of many gifted players and performers spawned by an extraordinarily fertile time. From the four corners of Britain, in 1964, the blue-eyed soul boys came to town. Van Morrison, of Them, forsook his native Belfast for a spell in London, where his first encounters with Tin Pan Alley left him permanently bruised. Yet he often wrote of London – 'You Just Can't Win', for instance, finds him prowling Camden Town, Park Lane and Tottenham Court Road – and he returned here to stay. His most revered album, *Astral Weeks*, ends with 'Slim Slow Slider', a nightmare vision of his girl walking to her death in Ladbroke Grove. In later years he was frequently to be seen in Holland Park, a brooding man who would be a kind of exile wherever he chose to live.

Peter Green suffered a sort of exile, too. He took over Eric Clapton's role in John Mayall's Bluesbreakers, before joining Mick Fleetwood and John McVie in Fleetwood Mac, whose first incarnation was synonymous with the London blues boom. A Bethnal Green boy raised in Putney, his guitar playing infused the most basic tracks with a startling grace, and his voice was softly soulful. He developed into a fine writer, his best-known contribution to Fleetwood Mac being the drifting instrumental 'Albatross'. But in the 1970s, when the band acquired some new members (including Christine Perfect, herself a star of London blues with Chicken Shack), poor Green walked away from it all. While Fleetwood Mac were becoming stadium superstars, their former guitarist was sleeping rough in West London doorways, the victim of mental illness. I'd always revered Peter Green and was stunned to discover him, no more than a tramp, keeping some wordless vigil on a street corner in Richmond. I heard of another occasion when children taunted him as he shambled by, oblivious. An onlooker turned, enraged: 'Do you know who that is? He's the greatest guitarist that ever lived.' In time Green recovered, and still plays occasionally.

Tony McPhee, of the Groundhogs, was a hard-working foot-soldier in the British blues wars since the early 1960s. From Tooting, he knew the teddy boy scene through his older brother, who was a regular at the famous Castle pub. He was drawn into the orbit of Alexis Korner, the Pretty Things and the rest, and formed his own band, the Groundhogs. (Knowing John Mayall's autocratic reputation, he refused an invitation to replace Eric Clapton in the Bluesbreakers.) Their break came with a chance to back the legendary Detroit bluesman John Lee Hooker on some European tours.

I meet McPhee one evening in the Pillars of Hercules on Greek Street, a venerable 'scene' pub; with casual pride, he tells me that his group impressed Hooker. They took his unusual guitar tunings in their stride; nor were they thrown by the great man's way with a so-called 'twelve-bar' blues, which he might play as eleven, or twelve-and-a-half. What also endeared McPhee to the elderly blues icon, it seems, was his agreeing to ring a girl on Hooker's behalf – the bluesman suffered from a stammer. Another southern Titan, the fearsome Howlin' Wolf, was equally fond, dubbing the shy McPhee 'mah little Ground-hawg'.

Then, when the blues boom faltered, Tony made a brief foray into psychedelia. But McPhee dislikes drugs and never felt right in clobber from Granny Takes A Trip. He re-formed the Groundhogs and they made some sterling hard-rock albums like *Thank Christ for the Bomb*, all dark, knotty parables and scything blues guitar. When glam rock happened, followed by punk, the Groundhogs were once more out of style. Yet McPhee endured, gigging where he could, watching his expenses. He never suited the star treatment, he says. And, so saying, he heads out into the cold Soho night for yet another show.

Soul Power

R&B or 'soul' music, as distinct from pure old-fashioned blues, was entering mainstream London taste in the mid-1960s. The Pretty Things' Phil May recalls the change: 'We played at places like the Inferno, at Harlow, with 1,200 mods in front of us. Overnight a lot of groups got three birds, a sax player and a Hammond in, doing all the Otis Redding and Solomon Burke.' Even the Beatles acknowledged the sound that swept through clubland, in their 1966 *Revolver* track 'Got to Get You into My Life'. For a long time, the definitive home of London soul was a joint called the Flamingo, on the stretch of Wardour Street below Shaftesbury Avenue. In a tiny basement (there was another club, the Whisky-A-Go-Go, upstairs), the Flamingo attracted a hip crowd of London West Indians, American GIs and the cooler class of mod. Live acts might include Georgie Fame (whose flashy name bespeaks his early stint as a protégé of Larry Parnes), Chris Farlowe or Zoot Money, pumping out Ray Charles numbers all through the Chinatown night.

The lanky blues apostle Long John Baldry was a star of this scene, to which Rod Stewart and Elton John were also apprenticed. Cliff Bennett & the Rebel Rousers, Brian Auger and Julie Driscoll would help take its style overground. A girl of eighteen, Billie Davis, lent a precociously powerful soul voice to hits like 'Tell Him' and 'I Want You to be My Baby'. For a dash of authentic black America there was the former GI Geno Washington and his Ram Jam band, named after the Brixton club where they played. Geno would become a fixture of London gigs for decades to come, his legend burnished by the 1980 hit song in his honour by Dexys Midnight Runners. Their great soul rivals were Marquee residents Jimmy James & The Vagabonds, led by a Jamaican whose own career – of similar longevity – took in the earliest UK reggae.

A strange, unhappy story was that of Graham Bond, the portly organist whose band, the Organisation, had been so important in London R&B. He'd always been a big, driven personality, but his jazz-man drug habits led him into psychedelic meltdown. When Bond discovered LSD the natty suits and skinny ties gave way to cloaks, robes and an unwise passion for the occult. He proclaimed himself the bastard child of Aleister Crowley. Where others only sang of hell-hounds on their trail, poor Bond really believed it. Finally, on a desperate day in 1974, he perished under a Tube train at Finsbury Park.

Among the best of the blue-eyed soul gang was the Spencer Davis

Group, whose star turn was a teenage vocalist named Steve Winwood. He had all the power of any down-home Memphis belter, but within a year he defected in the direction of hippy rock by forming Traffic, whose three-year sojourn at a farmhouse in Berkshire began the fashion for 'getting it together in the country'. When Winwood brought the fruits of his labour back to London for recording, he revealed himself as a sort of hip antiquarian, purveying the English pastoral folk of 'Forty Thousand Headmen' and 'John Barleycorn' – the latter an ancient song that countless country peasants must have carried in their heads as they arrived in London's seething streets.

In fact the folk impulse was to permeate London rock bands more and more. Even a monolithic band of blues-rockers like Led Zeppelin were not immune to the call. We must look next at this remarkable passage in the story of London pop – look to the young men and women who could hear, above the traffic's roar, the rustle and whisper of England's misted fields and immemorial forests . . .

Rus in Urbis: the Folk-Rockers of London Town

While their Celtic neighbours have seen folk music as bound up in national identity, the English have largely let it slide. When medieval peasants arrived in London they found their country songs were literally blown away in the urban uproar. London, which devours incomers from everywhere, crowds the mind with so many new sensations that the old ways get forgotten. New songs, new styles, arise in the city with irresistible force.

Still, there were those who ensured not everything would be lost. The great musicologist Cecil Sharp compiled an archive that future generations could cherish, and his heirs would gather alongside blues and jazz fans at the Marquee or Ken Colyer's Studio 51, where folk was accepted as part of the wider mix. More specialised centres of excellence might include the late, lamented Bunjies, off Charing Cross Road, or the tiny Troubadour (happily, still with us) in Old Brompton Road. The 1950s skiffle craze, which was by definition acoustic music, had at least one foot in folk traditions, British as well as American. In all these ways, something of old England survived into the nuclear age, and withstood the blasts of rock 'n' roll.

The dominant, even domineering, character on London's post-war scene was Ewan MacColl. Like a lot of folkies, down to Billy Bragg in our own day, he was strongly motivated by left-wing politics – which to Soho's sceptical bohemians seemed grating and dogmatic. There is probably a lot of MacColl in Colin MacInnes's *Absolute Beginners*, in the character of dour Marxist Ron Todd ('Mississippi jail songs are in praise of sputniks'). But MacColl's mission, by no means unworthy, was to prove that Britain's heritage of working-class song could rival any American material. And his dogged resistance to commercialism did not prevent him writing some beautiful music, stand-outs being 'Dirty Old Town' and (famously covered by the US soul artist Roberta Flack) 'The First Time Ever I Saw Your Face'. In the 1950s he founded his Ballads & Blues club, upstairs at the Princess Louise pub in Holborn, and in 1961 had the Singers' Club, with Peggy Seeger, Bert Lloyd and Dominic Behan. In hindsight, the Singers' Soho Square location is poignant – just across the railings is a memorial bench to his daughter, Kirsty MacColl, herself destined to become one of the great London songwriters.

But the club that shunted folk music into the popular consciousness was just around the corner from Soho Square at 49 Greek Street. Like its other near-neighbour the 2i's, it began life as a basement skiffle joint, but in 1965 re-opened as Les Cousins (like the hip French film of that name, though usually rendered as 'Lez Cuzzins'). For about the next five years, its importance was enormous. There was now a thriving network of folk clubs around the country, but only in central London was there a critical mass of media attention. 'The Cuzzins' was comfortably within a *Melody Maker* writer's ambit, fifty yards from Denmark Street and twenty from the Pillars of Hercules pub.

Out of its sweaty confines Les Cousins spawned a crossover generation of folk stars, its three wise men being Davy Graham, Bert Jansch and John Renbourn. In this intense little world, where novel guitar-tunings were matters of fevered discussion, the coolly scholastic Graham was already acclaimed for his era-defining instrumental 'Angi'. Jansch was a Glaswegian heavyweight with roots in the acoustic blues of Leadbelly and Big Bill Broonzy. Renbourn was yet another exemplary guitarist, from the same Kingston Art School background as Eric Clapton. Around them gathered a clique of players, the more famous alumni including the future pop stars Donovan and Cat Stevens, and folk stars Al Stewart, Michael Chapman, Roy Harper, Ralph McTell and Nick Drake.

For a while the Cousins crowd included a small, serious New Yorker called Paul Simon. With and without his musical partner Art Garfunkel he spent a couple of periods in London. From one such trip came a 1965 solo album, *The Paul Simon Songbook*, as well as several key Simon and Garfunkel tracks including 'Homeward Bound', the prettily pastoral 'April Come She Will' and 'Kathy's Song'. There was even a cover of Davy Graham's 'Angi'. More contentiously, however, many a Cousins customer has not forgiven his version of the English folk song 'Scarborough Fair'. Simon's arrangement of this traditional air strongly resembled Martin Carthy's version – Carthy being an admired figure in London folk circles – yet the eventual writing credit was taken by Simon alone. It's inarguable that Simon learned a great deal of his craft from the Soho folk players. London was really the first in a series of exotic places he would visit – the South Africa of *Graceland* was another – where he displayed his gift for absorbing a local style and turning it to commercial gold.

Actually, Paul Simon was not the first or even the biggest US folk star to serve a part of his apprenticeship in this city. As well as Ewan MacColl's musical and romantic partner Peggy Seeger (half-sister to America's folk figurehead Pete) there was the young Bob Dylan. He arrived in London in 1962, as yet obscure, to appear in a BBC TV play and performed in venues including the Troubadour and MacColl's folk club at the Pindar of Wakefield pub in Grays Inn Road. Back in the USA his next few albums carried mementoes of the London trip: 'Girl from the North Country' adapted 'Scarborough Fair' and 'Bob

Dylan's Dream' reworked the old tune 'Lord Franklin' (he may have heard both performed by Carthy); 'I Shall Be Free No 10' signs off with a cackled reference to his spell in England.

In these formative years of their careers both Dylan and Simon had more to learn than to offer when faced with a native culture that had been a thousand years in the making. If each man took from the tradition, no matter; it's what the tradition is there for. It's to the credit of London's folk activists that they preserved so much that might otherwise have disappeared into the oubliette of cultural history. The great irony would be that in Dylan's next few visits, including to the Royal Albert Hall, he'd be heckled by folk's hard-liners for betraying the true faith in favour of electric rock surrealism. As usual in folk circles there was a political dimension – this time it was the leftists who were the conservatives, and the pop audience that was open to experiment.

The central figures of that hip little scene in Les Cousins were more at ease with sixties life than the purists, and from their openness emerged a folk-rock crossover – and some ageless London songs. Bert Jansch and John Renbourn formed Pentangle out of their residency at the Horseshoe on Tottenham Court Road. Meanwhile a young Muswell Hill boy, Ashley Hutchings, teamed up with a local guitarist called Simon Nicol, whose parental home was Fairport, a stone's throw from Ray Davies's childhood home on Fortis Green Road. Duly christened Fairport Convention, the group included another guitarist, Richard Thompson, and, eventually, a suburban refugee from the other side of the city, Wimbledon's Sandy Denny. (Her own parental pile is on the front of Fairport's 1969 album *Unhalfbricking*). Thompson had formerly played in a school band with his fellow North Londoner Hugh Cornwell, the future scowling frontman of the Stranglers.

These young players, then, were scarcely the prisoners of an esoteric sub-culture. Fairport Convention, in fact, began with a leaning towards American West Coast rock until Hutchings pushed them down a more traditional English route. Before her tragically early death in 1978, Sandy Denny had helped put Led Zeppelin in touch with their inner minstrel, singing on their fourth album. Thompson of course developed into an original songwriter of startling force. And presiding over them was a visionary American manager/producer, Joe Boyd, whose London credentials began with studio work for the Pink Floyd. If one record alone would seal the movement's wider appeal, it was Ralph McTell's 'The Streets of London' – probably the most-covered song ever written about the city. (We should overlook, perhaps, that it was originally written about Paris. There again, we can be grateful that McTell did not name it after Croydon, where he came from.)

As decades go by there is one musician, above all, whose star shines ever more brightly. That would be the tall, hunched, charismatically shy figure of Nick Drake. He had been a Marlborough public schoolboy, from Tamworth-in-Arden in the West Midlands Shakespeare country, who made expeditions to the big city for R&B nights at the Flamingo and Marquee as well as the folk sessions of Les Cousins. By 1968 Drake was a student at Cambridge and already developing a prodigious if painfully introverted talent. He demoed the Renbourn/Jansch number 'Soho', with its 'streets of crime' and 'market cries'. A rare public performance, at the Roundhouse in Camden, was spotted by Ashley Hutchings, who alerted Joe Boyd, and so began a three-album career whose legacy grows.

Over those three albums we trace a poignant arc in Nick Drake's short, uneasy life. At Sound Techniques Studio, close to the Thames at Chelsea, he made his debut *Five Leaves Left*, still the self-exploratory sound of a boy whose thoughts are in Cambridge or at home in Tamworth. Its follow-up, 1970's *Bryter Later*, is always regarded as Drake's 'London album', written amid the gathering gloom of a gothic heap on Haverstock Hill, where he rented rooms and began to withdraw – London may not offer peace but like most cities it can nurture an existential loneliness. His last LP, *Pink Moon*, came out of grim months in a Muswell Hill bedsit, before the final retreat to Tamworth and the family home, where he died of an overdose of antidepressants in 1974.

It's interesting to look at the three albums' artwork. For the first,

Drake was photographed in a leafily derelict house by Wimbledon Common, and against the brick wall of a Battersea factory where a blurred commuter dashes past – he is the country dreamer who has strayed into the city but is not of its tempo. The next has him under sodium lights on the Westway at night, a Clash-like vision of urban alienation. The third, of course, has no image of Drake at all; he has already disappeared.

Let Us Break the Bonds Asunder: Handel and Hendrix in Mayfair

Nick Drake had begun with a recording called 'Soho' and among his posthumous releases was a delicate thing called 'Mayfair', written, according to one biographer, in gentle acknowledgment of his mother's taste for the sophisticated world of Noël Coward and Ivor Novello. Central London's most refined *arrondissement* would host a more surprising type of musical genius in the 1960s. To the early Georgian elegance of 23 Brook Street came, in 1967, the American guitarist Jimi Hendrix. It's entirely coincidental that the house next door, at number 25, had once been the home of George Frideric Handel. But it's a pleasing thing. Each, in their own way, were exiles. And being uniquely accepting of their talents, London fulfilled their genius.

Hendrix was discovered in New York and brought to London by his English manager Chas Chandler, who ensured high visibility for his boy immediately. Within hours of arrival he was jamming with Georgie Fame and amazing the jaded elite in the Scotch of St James. The Who's overseers Kit Lambert and Chris Stamp saw him too, and signed him to their label Track. A few days later, on 1 October 1966, he talked himself on stage at the Regent Street Polytechnic, as Jack Bruce recalls: 'The first time he played in public in London was with us, the Cream. I was in a pub in Charing Cross Road and this guy came up to me and said, "Hi, my name's Jimi Hendrix. I wanna sit in with your band." Which was practically unheard of. He played incredibly and blew us all away ...'

To Cream's guitarist, Eric Clapton, it was an unwelcome challenge to his London supremacy. Affectionate as these rather shy rivals later became, Clapton must have watched the American's triumph with the same inner dismay that led Bing Crosby to say of Frank Sinatra, 'A singer like Sinatra comes along once in a lifetime. But why did it have to be in mine?' Jimi had spent his whole life among the blues and soul music that Clapton and the others were learning like a foreign language. The striking thing was that Hendrix felt exactly the same curiosity about London, and fell upon the local psychedelia – both its sounds and its clothes – with eager energy. He acquired his band, the Experience, and in London studios from Kingsway to Denmark Street and all the way out to Barnes, he cut a series of explosive, insolently brilliant records. (Like the Stones, Clapton, and Led Zeppelin, he favoured Olympic Studios in Barnes, a converted Edwardian music hall.)

To his Afro-Dylan hairstyle, a traffic-stopping sight in those days, he added the silk scarves and peacock military jackets he picked up in Portobello Market, as if to symbolise the same, unprecedented fusion occurring in his music. He threw himself into the world of Ossie Clark and Granny Takes A Trip, quite the adopted Londoner, revelling in a freedom of self-invention he could not have known back in America. His wily PR, Keith Altham, contrived a story of old soldiers complaining about the uniforms (and receiving an assurance that Jimi wore only a 'non-combatant donkey-doctor's coat'). It was more fuss than the quiet, un-worldly Hendrix was up for. 'He was really the opposite of his stage persona,' says Jack Bruce. 'He was a very gentle person. He didn't go around setting fire to things a lot. Not like, say, Ginger Baker, who'd play paradiddles on everything, including your head.'

It was a tight-knit world that Hendrix had beguiled, leasing a flat from Ringo Starr in Montagu Square, socialising with Jagger, Townshend and McCartney at the Bag O'Nails. There was a valuable absence of musical segregation, too. He played in soul clubs from the Flamingo to the Ram Jam in Brixton, but also at Les Cousins. His admirers comprised the entire rock aristocracy. Yet it's almost more impressive that they included the revered folk guitarist Bert Jansch: 'I thought he was great,' says Jansch. 'It really opened my ears up to the electric guitar, which I'd never had any interest in until Jimi came along ... When I met him he was very nice, didn't say much, but that was his style. I shook his hand and I'm very proud that I did.'

Greedy as Hendrix was for every sensation that London could put his way, his lyrics were abstractions more than narratives (though it's believed he wrote 'Purple Haze' around a verbal riff, 'purple haze, Jesus saves', inspired by a visit to Speakers' Corner). In his gently stoned condition this welcoming but alien city seemed all the more bemusing. The pressures and attentions of sudden stardom were soon to undermine him. With his girlfriend Kathy Etchingham he took up residence next to Handel's ghost in Brook Street, and sought some kind of peace. 'He was essentially lonely,' she says of that time. 'He needed company but all he had were these hanger-on types. When we lived in Brook Street he was quite safe from these people because I controlled things. I wouldn't let them in. There was no bell on the door, we were three floors up and in a busy street like Brook Street you couldn't shout up because of the noise of the traffic. I used to take the phone off the hook. He was vulnerable because of his affability, he didn't know how to tell them to sod off.'

The final days of Jimi's brief life were played out in the Cumberland Hotel by Marble Arch (within the shadow of Tyburn's tree, indeed) and a flat in Notting Hill where, on 18 September 1970, he met his drug-hastened end. His last performance had been at Ronnie Scott's club two nights earlier. 'He gave me a couple of buckskin jackets,' recalls his one-time roadie Lemmy, 'but they didn't fit me exactly so I gave them away, like you do. I didn't know he was going to die, did I? He was the best, never seen anyone like him.'

Skinhead Moonstomps: London Reggae

The sterling efforts of calypsonians like Lord Kitchener aside, black recordings in 1960s Britain were mostly imported. A fledgling industry existed, through labels like Planetone and Melodisc, and shops such as Orbitone in Willesden, to service the capital's Afro-Caribbean market. But the trend among younger buyers was now moving away from calypso, towards Jamaican copies of US R&B. Around 1960 the style came to be called blue beat, which in turn led to reggae.

A DJ called Count Suckle, who had been attacked in the same Notting Hill riots described by MacInnes, opened his influential Cue Club in Paddington – where the sharpness of its dress code was noted, admiringly, by those fastidious white youths the modernists. (A similar mingling of mods and immigrants was of course occurring in town, at clubs like the Flamingo.) As normally happens in London, it was not long before an observant entrepreneur took notice and made his move. In the case of reggae, that man was Chris Blackwell.

Blackwell had been born in London but grew up, apart from his years at Harrow school, in Jamaica. His well-connected family were friends of another island regular, Ian Fleming, and young Christopher did a spot of location-scouting for the first James Bond film, *Dr No*. But music was his ruling passion, and in 1960 he set up Island Records to import American R&B into Jamaica, while producing a few local acts on the side. Soon he was enjoying healthy sales among the immigrant populations of Britain as well – not to mention the growing coterie of clued-up white consumers – and moved the Island operation to London. His first home-grown hit was the bouncy 'My Boy Lollipop' by the Jamaican girl Millie, and its success enabled Blackwell to diversify, signing white acts that included Traffic, Fairport Convention and Nick Drake. (Curiously, the perky Millie once did a cover of Drake's melancholic 'Mayfair'.)

Blue beat, in the meanwhile, had given way to a faster variant called ska, more distinctively Jamaican than its US-inspired predecessor. From around 1966, a slower Jamaican trend emerged, christened rock steady. Seized upon by young black Londoners, these imports were even finding favour with the hip elite – the Beatles' 'Ob-La-Di, Ob-La-Da' being one instance of McCartney's magpie disposition to pick up musical novelties. As Blackwell's Island repositioned itself in the emerging rock underground, reggae in

Britain was now dominated by the Island spin-off label, Trojan. By the decade's end reggae, as the sound was generally known, was a regular part of the nation's pop diet. And its biggest fans were a tribe of lairy-looking youths, the skinheads, descended from the mods.

Jamaican acts like Jimmy Cliff, the Pioneers and Dave and Ansell Collins would relocate to London in hope of better things. By the early 1970s London had a domestic reggae industry worthy of the name. It became a common practice to record the raw backing tracks in Jamaica's Kingston, where the 'feel' was deemed to be right, then send the tapes to London for commercial sweetening with strings and other overdubs. Figureheads of the circuit included the singer Laurel Aitken, the producer Dandy Livingstone (maker of the anatomically puzzling 'Reggae In Your Jeggae') and the sound system operator Lloyd Coxson. From a Fulham studio came Symarip's 'Skinhead Moonstomp', and from Chalk Farm came Greyhound's 'Black and White' and Bob and Marcia's 'Pied Piper'. Perhaps the most charming curio of this period was Boris Gardiner's 1970 hit 'Elizabethan Reggae', a jog-along homage to Ronald Bynge's staple of 1950s Light Programme wireless, 'Elizabethan Serenade'.

Chris Blackwell, meanwhile, had not lost interest in reggae. Through his stake in Trojan Records he'd released some singles by a Kingston group, the Wailers. In 1971 they paid a visit to his Island studios at Basing Street in Notting Hill, an encounter that led to a new deal with Island and the promotion of one Wailer, Bob Marley, to the forefront of the band. Subsequent albums were still recorded in Jamaica but sometimes overdubbed in London, at one point with some rock guitar. Blackwell's policy, which proved astute, was to present Marley as a cultural heavyweight – less akin to the breezy reggae of the pop charts than to the rising white rock bands that student audiences adored. The breakthrough would finally come with historic shows at the Lyceum in July 1975.

There were by now quite separate schools of reggae in London. Bob Marley came to embody its roots-and-Rasta aspect, opening a market for local acts like Aswad, Dennis Bovell's Matumbi and Misty In Roots. Not so heavy on the dread, and rather more feminine, was the sweeter and home-grown brand called lovers' rock, a trend launched by the 1975 hit 'Caught You In a Lie', a Lloyd Coxson production of the London teenager Louisa Marks. Reggae had, in fact, taken its place as one more current in the mainstream of London's own music. Within a year the rise of punk, and especially of the Clash, would bring another wave of white supporters on board. A reggae stall took up a commanding position in Petticoat Lane, where it seemed a natural if noisy addition to that ancient haunt of Huguenot, Jewish and Asian traders. And Portobello Road, of course, now reverberated like the markets of Kingston itself.

Can Blue Men Sing the Whites? Vivian Stanshall and the Bonzos

The Bonzo Dog Doo Dah Band were not commercial giants, yet they merit a pause for consideration. So many strands of London's music pass through the Bonzos' work that they are almost the Clapham Junction of this entire story. A motley rabble of art school conceptualists, they arose from the ashes of trad jazz and carried within their songs the legion spirits of music hall, Noël Coward, calypso, coffee bar rock 'n' roll, grinding white-boy blues, improvised avant garde, psychedelic prog-rock and pure, inspired nonsense. Each, it seemed, had to pass through the Bonzos before re-emerging for its onward journey. Even the Beatles regarded them with a wary fascination.

Their presiding genius was the lead singer Vivian Stanshall, whose humour mixed pop-culture pastiche with a buttoned-up British madness. Born in 1943 he'd been raised in Walthamstow and Southend, where his accent veered between street-cockney and his father's aspirational correctnesss. He managed to become both an Essex teddy boy and a student at the Central London School of Art. His great good fortune, in 1962, was to meet the musically gifted Neil Innes, from Goldsmiths College, with whom he formed the songwriting core of the Bonzo Dog Dada Band. Forming a gang of like-minded jazz band rejects they played camp parodies of pre-war records with a knowing modern air. Foxtrots vied with bebop. Stanshall liked to say that his influences were 'Ivor Novello, Noël Coward and Little Richard'.

In time their Dada turned to Doo Dah, before disappearing completely. Like the earlier Temperance Seven and the later New Vaudeville Band they tapped a market for stiff Dixieland whimsy and fruity-voiced crooning; there were gigs at pubs like the Tiger's Head in Catford and the Dueragon Arms in Hackney. The Bonzo Dog Band, though, were on another level, throwing in surrealism, fireworks and robotic props. By 1968 they were famous enough for a *Sunday Times* profile, wherein Stanshall announced himself 'a fan of decadence, de Sade and fish on the edge of evolution like the axolotl'. In the same piece he considers removing his appendix and playing it, pickled, onstage – 'the Jimi Appendix Experience', he explained.

In 1967, at Raymond's Revue Bar in Soho, the group performed with a resident stripper for cameras filming the Beatles' *Magical Mystery Tour*. Their 'Death Cab For Cutie' supplies one of the few really lovable sequences in a largely confused movie. The McCartney connection held firm, as he produced their only hit single, 'I'm the Urban Spaceman'. With hindsight it's possible to see the Bonzos as a link between the Beatles and Monty Python, for they were, at the same time, cavorting through a TV series called *Do Not Adjust Your Set*, starring several Pythons-to-be. (Neil Innes would indeed become a sort of auxiliary Python and, with Eric Idle, a creator of the Beatle-spoofing Rutles.)

In 'Can Blue Men Sing the Whites?' they nailed the debate that once animated smoke-filled Soho bars. In 'Jazz, Delicious Hot, Disgusting Cold' they fingered another insecurity and in 'My Pink Half of the Drainpipe' yet one more. Decades before Britpop and Tony Blair, they even had a song called 'Cool Britannia'.

In the 1970s, after the Bonzos had wound down, Stanshall partied hard with Keith Moon and recorded with Steve Winwood. When his first marriage ended he left the family home in East Finchley for a houseboat on the Thames at Chertsey. Called *Searchlight*, it had once seen action in the wartime evacuation of Dunkirk, but did not survive much longer, sinking in 1984. Meanwhile he enlisted the veteran actor Trevor Howard to star in a film of his radio and vinyl creation *Sir Henry at Rawlinson End*, which he called 'a Sur-Ealing comedy', though it left audiences baffled. Other projects attempted modern takes on music hall and Gilbert and Sullivan.

Sad to say, Vivian's last years were marred by anxiety attacks and depression. He retreated to a Muswell Hill bedsit, 'bingeing,' said a contemporary report, 'on whelks and curries and pills and vodka, rotting among the detritus of his rapidly collapsing world.' The robbery of his precious jumble of possessions – seemingly by some youths he had befriended – compounded the misery. At the magazine I was setting up, *Mojo*, we tried to involve him in writing a memoir, and I had several delightful phone calls from this remarkable if frustrating man. But of course it was not to be. In 1995 he died in a fire, the culmination of long years of calculated self-destruction – stage-managed, someone said, 'like a Viking funeral'. A unique London character was lost to us.

Old Gods, Young Dudes

Others, of course, left the London stage in less horrendous ways. The twilight of the 1960s, London's 'swinging' decade, saw a general exodus of rock stars to the country. Bob Dylan had done it in Woodstock, Van Morrison in California and now McCartney withdrew to the Mull of Kintyre. Eric Clapton was becalmed in Surrey. The Rolling Stones chose tax exile in France. The original fad for 'getting it together in the country' had been led by Steve Winwood and reflected a serious need to work in peace. Now it served the ageing rock gods' need for family privacy. Fair enough, but who would sing the songs of London?

Two young men stepped forward. One of them switched his hard mod swagger for ballet shoes and jet-black ringlets, lisping tales of fairy enchantment with a Hackney accent. The other had mismatched eyes, a strangely calculating manner and a prodigious talent for self-reinvention. Extraordinary specimens, both. Only England's capital city could have produced them ...

Chapter Eight

Oh! You Pretty Things

The glam years of Biba, Bolan and Bowie. And dark tales from London's other underground.

The strangest of London's many shrines may well be a dead tree by a humpback bridge, close to the tangled expanse of Barnes Common. Fans attach their messages of love, their trinkets and devotional photos, all for a man who was killed here in a car smash, just before dawn on 16 September 1977. For me, this eerie place always summons the line from his song 'Childe Star': gently, it chides the mourners who do not understand their lost one is still there in spirit, among the flowers and trees.

Marc Bolan, whose early songs were typically set in magical woodland groves, was nonetheless a London boy to his core. A self-invented legend, he was the epitome of his city: streetwise, flash and calculating. His career was one of astounding transformations: it's as if he discovered a golden Cadillac in Dingly Dell. He was called a traitor by the Notting Hill hippies but lionised by suburbia's glitter children. London, where he was born and lived and died, gave him what it took to become a star. But he lived to witness his own decline. In the final years he was the Last Cavalier in a new age of Roundheads.

Stoke Newington, N16, may be nobody's idea of Fairyland but in the imagination of little Mark Feld, that's more or less what it was. Here on the borders of East and North London lived his parents Sid and Phyllis Feld: Sid was a lorry driver of cockney Jewish stock, she was a Fulham girl who ran a stall in Berwick Street Market. Mark, their second son, was born at Hackney Hospital in 1947 and brought home to the family's flat on Stoke Newington Common.

Mark grew up small (he wore children's shoes all his life) but was given to grand dreams. At nine he found Elvis and Mrs Feld bought him a cheap guitar on hire purchase. An older schoolfriend was Helen Shapiro from neighbouring Clapton. They played together in a skiffle band, until Helen left for the big school. With his Mum's stall in Soho, Mark would slip around the corner to Old Compton Street and the 2i's coffee bar, right at the birth of English rock. It's possible that he worked in there (though his claims were sometimes self-mythologising). He used to say that he watched young stars in the making, like Tommy Steele. It's obvious that he grew up wise to the ways of show business. In that *Absolute Beginners* world of the 1950s, he was breathing the air of Tin Pan Alley as only a London kid could.

He got to know the rag trade, too, whether in Soho or the premises of Jewish tailors in Stamford Hill near his home. With a quick eye for style, young Feld observed the twilight of the teddy boys and the rise of the jazz-inspired 'modernists', the elite who would give way to the less exclusive mods. Obtaining his clothes money by fair means or foul, the fourteen-year-old Feld told *Town* magazine that he had 'ten suits, eight sports jackets, fifteen pairs of slacks, thirty or thirty-five good shirts, about twenty jumpers, three leather jackets, two suede jackets, five or six pairs of shoes and thirty exceptionally good ties.'

Cool as this kid was, what happened next must have floored him. Helen Shapiro, his old skiffle pal and youth club companion, became Britain's biggest pop star. Still in her mid-teens but with a booming voice, she was having proper hit singles and appearing on television. Her run of luck was interrupted by the arrival of the Beatles. But while it lasted, the effect on Mark Feld must have been tremendous. Here he saw a girl from his own gang becoming the country's top teen celebrity. It could be done! Maybe it was his turn next?

Then something else happened. The Feld family were suddenly rehoused, right over to South London. Summerstown has a pleasant,

Tolkien-ish name, but in 1962 it was a drab barracks of a place, some cheap public housing between Wimbledon and Tooting. Sundered from the mods of Stamford Hill, Mark Feld lost momentum. He soon left school and told the Labour Exchange he wanted to work as a poet. They sent him to wash dishes in the Wimpy Bar.

He lasted a week, followed by a week in a Tooting menswear shop. This was all very trying for a boy who felt the hand of destiny on his shoulder. He claimed that as a boy he'd carried Eddie Cochran's guitar for him into the Hackney Empire. So he now gave up 'straight' work as a bad idea, lolled around his parents' pre-fab and concentrated on the great project: himself. Morale restored, he ventured back up West, to the peacock-male shops that were just starting to appear in Carnaby Street. He may have done some modelling. He was certainly putting his pretty face about, getting to know the pop people. He took a flat-share in Earls Court and hung around TV studios. He landed a bit part in a series called *Orlando*. It's thought he became bisexual.

He started singing. It was a strange, quivering noise that sounded like Buddy Holly crash-landed in London; or like Adam Faith in pain. He wrote poetical lyrics. He posed in pictures with the works of William Shakespeare. He acknowledged some affinity with the spiritual bard of eighteenth-century London, William Blake. Those who knew him closely can't recall him as a disciplined reader, but he was a cockney kid, and as such, cheek was his birthright. Like the Larry Parnes boys before him, his identity was negotiable. In 1965 Mark Feld became Marc Bolan. He spun a myth of his adoption by a wizard in Paris. It's true that Bolan took a short trip to Paris, but nobody has ever taken this story seriously. His later manager, Simon Napier-Bell, believes the encounter with a mysterious older man was a basic gay pick-up.

Decca Records' first press release assured the world Marc had spent eighteenth months at the chateau of his Parisian shaman, followed by a solitary spell in the woods outside Rome. Furthermore, he now owned 'a magic cat', presented by a girl he had met 'at dead of night' in the King's Road. The enchanted young troubadour began hustling the London scene. Music journalists of that time recall a persistent boy, pestering them and prophesying a brilliant future. In the Brewmaster pub over Leicester Square station, or the front bar of the Marquee Club, lapels were grabbed and ears were bent.

Among Marc Bolan's fellow schemers in 1965 was one David Bowie, another Londoner, just a few months older than he. 'You know how we first met?' Bowie asked me. 'It's so funny. We both had this manager in the mid-sixties [Leslie Conn]. Marc and I were out of work and we were poured into the manager's office to whitewash the walls. So there's me and this mod whitewashing Les's office. And he goes, "Where d'you get those shoes, man?" [Bowie does a perfect impression of Bolan's fey but icily determined manner.] "Where d'you get your shirt?" We immediately started talking about clothes and sewing machines. "Oh, I'm gonna be a singer and I'm gonna be so big you're not gonna believe it, man." Oh, right! Well I'll probably write a musical for you one day then, cos I'm gonna be the greatest writer ever. "No, no, man, you've gotta hear my stuff cos I write great things. And I knew a wizard in Paris," and it was all this. Just whitewashing walls in our manager's office.'

Marc found his next manager in Simon Napier-Bell, the perceptive hedonist who has steered acts from the Yardbirds to Wham! Napier-Bell has described his young protégé as 'a wonderful, charming fraud'. He says that like many managers and musicians of the day, there was a strong sexual undercurrent to their relationship. They sometimes conducted business meetings in bed.

When Marc's new band John's Children collapsed, he retreated to his parents' home in South London and composed an advertisement: 'Freaky lead guitarist, bass guitarist and drummer wanted for Marc Bolan's new group. Also any other astral flyers like with cars, amplification and that which never grows in window boxes. Phone Wimbledon 0697. 9 a.m.–3 p.m.' What Bolan finally got was an acoustic two-piece, Tyrannosaurus Rex. And somehow, his speaking voice now softened from sharp-tongued barrow boy to lisping fairy prince. Cross-legged, he strummed rudimentary acoustic chords and voiced the unique Bolan bleat, sounding like a motherless baa-lamb lost on a wintry fellside. The bongos pattered like mice behind the skirting board.

In September 1967, Tony Visconti was a young New Yorker who had fetched up in Swinging London. He was now working for a production company:

> My boss told me to go find an act of my own to produce, so I opened up the *International Times* and around the corner from our offices was a club called UFO, the underground psychedelic club of the time. I walked in on the beginning of Marc's set and he was sitting cross-legged with Steve Peregrine Took. It was dark, but the impression I got was that he had some kind of a spell over the audience. There were about a hundred kids sitting cross-legged on the floor, and they were *swaying*. I was immediately taken in.

There were also hippy picnics and flower-child strum-alongs in Hyde Park.

At the Westbourne Park office of his new managers Bolan met his future wife, June Child. For a week they lived together in the back of her van, parked off Wimbledon Common, before finding a cheap flat in freak central, Ladbroke Grove. Even so, many doubted Bolan's hippy credentials. His co-manager of that period, Peter Jenner, told me: 'It was the era we used to call Buttercup Sandwiches, when everything was "very beautiful, man", and we'd sit cross-legged on the floor. We had no contracts because we were all "beautiful human beings, buttercup sandwiches". And I bought the line that he wasn't into being commercial. In fact, looking back, he was incredibly ambitious.'

As a child I heard Bolan on my radio and pictured him as a Pan-like child of nature. In fact he rarely left London, just as London never left him. He always had the city's instinct for commerce. According to Tony Visconti, 'Immediately from day one he was talking about hit singles. I knew this. And "Debora" was: "This is going to be a Number 1! We'll take England by storm!"' Through a friendship with Alice Ormsby-Gore, Marc met her boyfriend Eric Clapton and studied the maestro's electric guitar technique. As the 1970s loomed, Bolan sensed a generational sea-change. He moved to meet the new teen mood by returning to his own youth, remembering the neon vulgarity of 1950s rock 'n' roll. His first hit was 'Ride a White Swan', then there was 'Hot Love' and most dramatically of all, 'Get It On'. Bolan had truly taken his music to town.

Bolan's staunch ally, the underground DJ John Peel, was summarily dismissed – without explanation – from the court of T. Rex. (The band's name had taken some pruning, too.) This betrayal hurt Peel for the rest of his life. Marc's bongo-playing partner, Steve Peregrine Took, was likewise purged. Always more authentically underground than Bolan, he was pushed out in favour of a gypsy-handsome character called Mickey Finn. (In a world of implausible stage names, he really *was* called Michael Finn.) The new percussionist's existence was irrevocably altered by meeting Bolan: 'I remember he turned up in a long black cloak with a hood, and his hair, and his little ballet shoes with a gilded strap.'

What did you think of him?

'I thought he'd come to put a spell on me. He probably did. I still don't know.'

But the revamping of the band (who soon expanded to a four-piece) provoked a schism that tore the old fan-base apart. Had Marc Bolan 'sold out'? The underground press took an instant dislike to Bolan's new direction. Many of its central figures were still personal friends of the banished Peregrine Took. By 1970, London's hippies had fragmented in several ways, some into drugged oblivion and some to leftist politics, while others took the new-age lifestyle route, selling magic crystals and inedible carrot cakes. If one thing could unite them, it was contempt for their old comrade in the Portobello Road culture wars, Marc Bolan. He didn't even shop for clothes down their way any more: he preferred the flashy retro look developing in Kensington and Chelsea shops like Mr Freedom and Biba.

Kieron Murphy, one of Marc's regular photographers, remembers, 'I had lots of vague left-wing and hippy ideas, like "Property is Theft" and "Let's put LSD in the water supply". But he was far more hard-nosed about business and making money. We used to sit up all night arguing about capitalism versus socialism, and he was on the capitalist side.' Marc and June moved from their cold-water flat in Ladbroke Grove to the highly agreeable Little Venice district of Maida Vale. And all the frowning beardies in London were no match for the squealing teenies of Great Britain. Between 1971 and '73, T. Rex were the biggest thing since the Beatles.

A wild 1972 concert at Wembley's Empire Pool was dutifully filmed by Ringo Starr, no less, and released as *Born To Boogie*. But, from its opening moments, there were signs of some unravelling. It's said that triumphant Roman emperors employed slaves to stand in their chariots, whispering 'Remember, thou art mortal' – and here was Marc Bolan standing in a Cadillac, being driven by a Beatle who apparently worshipped him. Isn't it funny how there's never a slave in your chariot when you need one?

These were years when fame and praise were heaped at Marc's feet, and he took them as no more than his due. Admirers marvelled at his pop intelligence, his sheer cocky grace. Their acclaim, however, was but a shadow of Bolan's self-esteem. By 1974 he took no advice except his own, and could not understand why British fans were drifting away. The American audience chose to ignore him almost totally. He believed himself a modern-day magician who alchemised rusty blues riffs into platinum hooks. Then one day the magic didn't work any more and Bolan felt bewildered.

Worse, his old rival David Bowie – who had languished in the shadows while Bolan's star was zooming – was suddenly hipper and more successful than he. 'Bowie was doing so much better,' says Visconti, who had produced both. 'There was a point when David was looking to Marc for the lead, then all of a sudden it switched.' Not that he ever stopped strutting. Marc spent the last years of his career in much the same way that he'd spent the early ones, grafting, watching, looking for a way back in. From 1974 to 1976, he was a little pop Napoleon, plotting his return from exile.

June Child having departed from Bolan's orbit he took up with the US singer Gloria Jones, who had made the original version of

'Tainted Love'. His parents, meanwhile, relocated to a council estate near Putney Heath; Sid was now caretaker of the block, perhaps the only council caretaker who could drive to his local (the cosy Green Man) in a Rolls-Royce donated by his son. Phyllis retired from a job with London Transport. And when Marc and Gloria acquired a sizeable house nearby, on the road from Putney to Richmond, the elderly Felds could babysit the infant Rolan Bolan.

Still the singles stiffed. The cameras stopped loving him, too. Marc was putting on weight; his manner was hard and tired. He turned his mind to a grand musical idea called *The London Opera*. Had his career really blossomed, he might by this point have been in America: as matters stood, London was really all he had. Two new songs betrayed its nostalgic hold upon him: 'The London Boys', which pitches Petticoat Lane's street market at the heart of his memories, and the chugging 'Funky London Childhood'. But the projected masterwork fell by the wayside.

In his final year, 1977, Bolan gathered the punks around him, like a fond grandfather. He was only twenty-nine, but seemed a survivor of some bygone century. He invited the Damned to be his support act on the 1977 tour, and I caught the Finsbury Park Rainbow show, more for their sake than Bolan's. I found the T. Rex set an anticlimax. But he was now contracted for a short TV series, *Marc*, whose last show featured guest star David Bowie. There seemed little doubt as to who was doing whom a favour: by this time, Bowie and Tony Visconti were in the midst of that career-defining trilogy, *Low*, *"Heroes"* and *Lodger*. According to Visconti: 'He and Bowie wrote a couple of songs that might have been the precursor of a very interesting album. David always adored him. He wanted to be friends. He never saw him as a rival as much as Marc saw him as a rival.'

On 15 September 1977, Marc and Gloria hit the town. They spent the evening at the Speakeasy, and went on to Morton's restaurant in Berkeley Square. In the early hours, they climbed into Gloria's purple Mini. Their homeward route took them over Putney Bridge and through the tree-lined lanes that scythe across Barnes Common. On one of them, Queen's Ride, you drive up a humpback railway bridge with a bit of a twist, just where it joins Gypsy Lane.

And that's where this tale ends. Their car smashed into the tree. Marc, a non-driver who wrote love songs to Cadillacs, was in the passenger seat and died immediately. Gloria survived. The couple were only a few hundred yards from home. And Bolan was two weeks short of his thirtieth birthday. Mickey Finn told me: 'Failure was the worst thing for Marc. It was taboo. But the ironic thing is that he didn't fail. He's there in the records. He was a big part of many people's lives. He would have been in his glory today. He probably is.'

'That Revolution Stuff': the Other London Underground

Let's peer inside this 'underground' from which Marc Bolan was ceremonially expelled. The underground was a credo, founded on rejection of Western society. In its more hopeful moments it embraced the possibilities offered by youth culture. Mostly it was a tactical alliance of leftists in search of something groovier than Marxist discussion groups, and hippies trying to adapt their pastoral visions to the real conditions of city life. The counter-culture of 'alternative' London was only the local version of something happening worldwide. The city's scene had its counterparts in New York and San Francisco, in Amsterdam, Berlin and Paris.

London's underground can be traced back to those beatniks who rejected trad jazz, and hitched their wagons to Bob Dylan. Though the Beatles and the Stones were loved far and wide, only Dylan was seriously worshipped in these circles. Traditional socialism seemed too mundane to be inspiring – there was more stimulation to be had from oddball writers such as William Burroughs and Allen Ginsberg. There was stimulation to be had from certain other things as well.

Veterans commonly date the birth of London counter-culture to 11 June 1965, when 7,000 people turned up to the Royal Albert Hall for an event called Wholly Communion. Upon arrival they were handed flowers salvaged that day from Covent Garden Market. Pot was openly smoked. Ginsberg recited poems, as did many others. The writer Barry Miles observed a girl in a short white dress pioneering the sort of blissed-out dance that would soon become ubiquitous in hippy circles. Most of the crowd did not as yet dress especially strangely, but it was the first coming together of a tribe, an alternative society, finally seeing and recognising itself.

A year later, at Dylan's 1966 shows in Britain there were opposed factions of 'freaks' and 'folkies' – the former in favour of his new electric incarnation and the latter disapproving. The point is that, in London, the freaks now seemed to be a majority. This emergent community would soon have its own parish newsletter, the *International Times*. Mostly called *IT* for short, the paper was launched with a party at the Roundhouse in October of that year. On the bill were the underground's effective house band, the Pink Floyd, and the Canterbury free-jazzers Soft Machine, who were close friends of the organiser John 'Hoppy' Hopkins.

The underground had its overground champions. Both Paul McCartney and Mick Jagger attended the *IT* bash, which was tantamount to royal patronage. Posters around town had billed the night as costing five shillings in advance or ten shillings on the door: 'Bring your own poison' they advised. And there was a prize offered for 'the shortest/barest'. The paper's press release stated: '*IT* will appear fortnightly price one shilling on the streets of this portion of eternity named London ... *IT* will regard it as *IT*'s holy function to keep things swinging – for ever and ever ...'

And for a time it appeared they might. The UFO club opened, as if to perpetuate the *IT* party. Co-run by Hoppy and the American producer Joe Boyd, it was held on Friday nights in the premises of an Irish joint, the Blarney club, in Tottenham Court Road. (It was here that Visconti first found Bolan.) For about a year, in 1966 and '67, its polished dance floor filled with 600 freaks, marvelling at psychedelic music and light-shows. Hendrix, McCartney and Townshend were regulars. So were coppers from the police station up the road. Tensions between the underground and officialdom were beginning to surface, normally over drugs. There had been troublesome youth movements before, but this one came with its own ideology.

IT was in due course busted and a benefit show was organised by Hoppy. Held at the Alexandra Palace on 29 April 1967, The 14-Hour Technicolor Dream became the pivotal occasion of London's underground history: Soft Machine and Pink Floyd played, naturally; there were also the Pretty Things, Graham Bond, Alexis Korner and Mick Farren's band the Deviants. Both John Lennon and Yoko Ono were there, though separately. If Pink Floyd were the key band of the loosely aligned underground movement, John Peel was its DJ of choice, broadcasting on the pirate Radio London, in a ship moored off Felixstowe. His widow Sheila recalls him being at the Alexandra Palace event, endeavouring to impress young women by revealing himself as the voice of Radio London's *Perfumed Garden* show – without, it seems, much success.

Cleverly hidden in the bosom of Establishment London were the Indica Bookshop and Gallery, where John and Yoko met for the first time, next to the Scotch of St James in Mason's Yard. From here, Barry Miles and his partners Peter Asher and John Dunbar sold radical tracts, beat poetry and rare LPs. The Bookshop then moved across Bloomsbury to Southampton Row, and *IT* was published from its basement.

Strongholds of the freak community were Camden Town and Chalk Farm to the north, and Ladbroke Grove and Notting Hill Gate to the west. (The more sceptical East and South London did not figure so visibly.) Portobello Road's market was a kind of hippy high street, and a natural location for Richard Branson's fledgling enterprise Virgin Records. Living on a houseboat in Little Venice, Branson would embody what doubters came to call hippy capitalism, steadily expanding his small chain of freak shops (where customers could lounge on scatter cushions all day) and building the record label up on the strength of Mike Oldfield's *Tubular Bells*, until his interests embraced everything from railways to health insurance. (At the time of writing, Virgin Galactic space travel is on the way: a notion beyond the reach of satire in 1967.)

When Marc Bolan and Tyrannosaurus Rex were still fully paid-up members of the underground, they were often to be found at the

Tolkien-inspired Middle Earth club – housed, as earlier noted, in the Covent Garden building where Dickens had dined to music hall turns. Now John Peel spun the discs and all was loving. Of a less wholesome vibe was the smaller club Happening 44 in Gerrard Street, across in Soho. Here the children of the New Age mixed with a few criminals, strippers, street walkers and heroin addicts. Farren's Deviants were regulars, too: under the darker New York influence of the Velvet Underground, imbibing an ethos laced with junkie nihilism and sado-masochism, they foreshadowed less innocent, and perhaps less complacent, times ahead.

Politics was creeping into the underground. The student uprisings of 1968, especially their most glamorous example in Paris, could not be ignored. There were suddenly sit-ins everywhere, from the LSE to Lancaster, and resolute long-hairs faced down grumpy old security staff. The huge anti-Vietnam protest enveloped Grosvenor Square. As Farren noted, hostile policemen were a sign that young revolutionaries, like stoned hippies, could not expect the London working class to like them any better than did the ruling elites.

Then the UFO club began to be troubled by marauding skinheads. This new proletarian tribe, especially numerous in the East End, were the living embodiment of everything the hippies were not. They were the dispossessed children of the costers' pulverised communities, and were quick to express their discontent. They came up West in large numbers to cause discomfort at the Rolling Stones' Hyde Park show of 1969. *IT* magazine attempted to reach out to these lost brothers and sisters by adding a section called *Yell*: 'I took the girlfriend down to Margate last Bank Holiday Monday,' its skinhead columnist complained. 'We tried to get into Dreamland, the amusement park. A security bloke in a uniform and a helmet told me "No boots". So we went away and I bought a pair of four-bob rubber sandals to wear. Next time the same bloke says "No Levi's".'

In a later article he tackled the problem of violence at the Hyde Park concerts: 'I think a lot of the trouble is because quite a lot of the hairy music gets boring to listen to after a bit and people get restless and then there's trouble.'

The climate grew colder somehow, and the colours more sombre. London's brief Summer of Love was followed by a long sullen autumn. An Australian long-hair, Richard Neville, and some friends began a new magazine called *Oz*, with a more pronounced political agenda; soon there were also *Frendz* (which evolved from a short-lived UK version of *Rolling Stone* magazine) and *Gay News* and *Time Out*. 'Agit-prop' (agitation/propaganda) was the order of the day. All around, race relations and industrial disputes were poisonous. The tensions from a newly revived Northern Irish conflict spilled over as well. Nothing was just for fun by 1970. The underground was on a sort of war footing. *Oz* was put on trial for obscenity. A faction named The Angry Brigade took to setting off bombs around the capital.

On the aesthetic front a glam reaction arose to this post-hippy drabness. A sort of retro-decadence became the new chic. Prim maidens in flowery smocks reappeared in vampish Hollywood drag. Though diehards such as Hawkwind and the Pink Fairies still played benefit gigs wherever 'heads' assembled to fight the good fight, hippiness was nearly extinct. Grim bearded men sold cigarette papers and cheesecloth shirts in Camden Lock, and a new tourist business developed. But nobody pretended this was 'where it's at'. The underground press withered away as its star writers moved across to the music papers: the *NME* transformed itself from a Tin Pan Alley mouthpiece into the journal of hip young Britain.

The underground did not die entirely: much of it simply went overground. Some of its most cherished causes – especially in areas of sexual licence and ecological awareness – found mainstream acceptance. But for now its formative role in popular culture was over. If the underground could live without Marc Bolan, it could not compete with his successor David Bowie. Bolan's old London comrade would finally abolish the 1960s, to make a new world for the Young Dudes – for the rising generation who had never been much impressed by 'that revolution stuff'.

David Bowie: Now You're with the London Boys

'I didn't know if I was Max Miller or Elvis Presley,' Bowie admitted to me once. I had asked him about the period in the late 1960s, when he fashioned a curious body of songs that included 'The Laughing Gnome'. It wasn't a very successful time for him and he has seemed embarrassed by it ever since. Though I never loved 'The Laughing Gnome', I disagree that it was a wasted time. Around 1967 he wrote the most London-rooted music of his life, some of it exceptional, all of it fascinating.

Of course David Bowie is not the kind of figure we associate with 'roots': he is notoriously the triumph of artifice over authenticity. At the height of his early stardom he was not even considered an Earthling. But he has roots, all the same, in suburbia and Soho. It's true that he outgrew those influences (except in terms of his accent and, as we'll see, his haircut): yet they helped to make him the artist he became. And his influence, in turn, is incalculable. What a grey old place the London Borough of Rock'n'Roll had been before he skipped into view. It's to Bowie that pop culture owes its dominant post-modern characteristic, namely of self-awareness – and Bowie owes that, almost entirely, to the city that shaped him. He owes it to London.

His special status came home to me with startling force on the day in the 1990s when I had to chaperone him around a magazine awards ceremony in Piccadilly. Just from escorting him and his wife Iman through a packed hotel lobby and bar to his allocated table I realised how odd our response to celebrity can be. The conversational babble, hitherto deafening, dropped to near silence when he entered. And while nobody wanted to give the impression of rubbernecking, every eye flickered across him, then back, and back once more. The crowd, without prompting, reassembled itself in the style of the Red Sea meeting Moses. Most made some attempt not to gawp too obviously. Not the paparazzi, though: the snappers enacted the feeding frenzy of seagulls around a whelk-stall.

'In London it's peculiar,' he told me. 'It's impossible on the streets during the day, it really is. Forget it. It's easy going over to dinner at friends' houses, but anything public in London is just a circus.' In conversation he can slip between a cosmopolitan classlessness and a matey, colloquial South London.

In fact, he spent his first six years in Brixton, which was not yet the vibrant Afro-Caribbean district of later years, but a post-war white suburb quietly running to seed. Then his family moved to Outer London, to Bromley, where the majority of his growing-up was done. In his teens his older half-brother Terry would take him around the coffee bars and jazz clubs of Soho, in its *Absolute Beginners* phase. And I think its style has stayed in his heart ever since. As a boy he took his autograph book backstage for Tommy Steele to sign. The archetypal male hairstyle of that Larry Parnes time – the greased or lacquered perpendicular quiff – has been Bowie's default choice ever since.

He was a spiritual son of Parnes in his taste for showbiz contrivance, too. As early as 1962, playing sax and singing in the Kon-rads, he amended his real name of David Jones to Dave Jay. Like Marc Bolan and Malcolm McLaren he remained a product of London's Tin Pan Alley. None of those three really belonged to the 1960s: they were all obliged to sit out a fashion cycle, to wait for the seventies before re-fashioning the 1950s of their youth. Ziggy Stardust was essentially a Parnes boy put through some Rocky Horror-style Frankenstein experiment. In the 1984 film of *Absolute Beginners*, an older Bowie returned to the early style of Old Compton Street, back in that familiar haircut with a nice suit and sharp pre-hippy line in patter.

Even at fifteen he was hip to the schism that was splitting London jazz between trad and modernism. Taking saxophone lessons he adopted Charlie Parker, icon of the latter school, for his hero. Which is not to say that he was one for commitment. Through the 1960s we see Bowie glide, musically and sartorially, between neo-rocker, pristine mod, psychedelic flower child, cabaret chanteur and folk singer. He didn't actually go to art college (he left school at sixteen with one O-level, that being Art) but he's of a type with that wave of 1960s art school boys in his taste for the conceptual. His only proper job was office junior in a Bond Street advertising agency – perhaps the quintessential post in media-savvy Swinging London.

Along his path to the Spiders From Mars he had the King Bees, the Manish Boys, the Lower Third, the Buzz and others. He swam in every current; he could play the wide-eyed ingénue, eager to absorb, or a calculating city boy, looking for his chance. Like Marc Bolan he hung about the Giaconda café in Denmark Street; he played at the Marquee. He had the London boy's faster access to experienced mentors: of his early managers, Leslie Conn was a veteran plugger with extensive contacts (Max Bygraves called Conn 'the only man who could set fire to a bucket of sand'); another, Ken Pitt, had worked in press relations for Louis Armstrong and Frank Sinatra.

In 1966 and newly renamed 'Bowie' he told an interviewer: 'I've lived in London and been brought up here and find it's a great subject to write songs about . . . At the moment I write nearly all my songs round London. No, I should say the people who live in London – and the lack of real life they have.'

These London songs dominate Bowie's early catalogue: so many R&B favourites had been covered to death by older acts such as the Rolling Stones and the Yardbirds; by now he had to be an original writer or he was nothing. 'I Dig Everything' was breezy on the surface (he feeds the lions in Trafalgar Square, at one point) yet mindful that his fellow citizens were not always so groovy. 'Did You Ever Have a Dream' ponders psychic travel to New York while sleeping in Penge. The highly Who-ish 'Can't Help Thinking About Me' is nervous of grown-up life, looking back to childhood for reassurance. (When Bowie's band supported the Who, Pete Townshend commented tersely on the similarity of writing style.)

Once he was properly a solo act, signed to Decca, Bowie's writing began to diversify, almost bewilderingly so. But London remained his focus. 'Maid of Bond Street' portrays some 1967 dolly bird trapped in a deadening city nexus: amid the unseeing commuters of Oxford Circus, she is 'made of loneliness'; it's a Swinging London ditty in fairground waltz-time, but with a hurting heart. His first unarguably great song, 'The London Boys', took a similar theme of quiet desperation under neon Soho lights: its pilled-up mod protagonist has exchanged suburban drabness for something yet more desolate. Then there was the number dredged up some years later, to cash in on his stardom: 'The Laughing Gnome', with its chirpy lines about the 'London School of Eco-gnomics' and so on.

He was emerging as an individual voice, but easily overlooked: whimsical oompah-oompah songs like 'Rubber Band', 'Little Bombardier' and 'She's Got Medals' were out-ranked by the Beatles' cod-Edwardian *Sgt. Pepper*. Again it's the London writer in Bowie that shows most promise: 'Please Mr Gravedigger' was a macabre sketch, set in a Lambeth boneyard. 'Join the Gang' offered mordant observations of trendy specimens on the scene, from Johnny the existentialist sitar player to Molly the model on acid. (Only the price of a night-club Coke, at 'fifteen bob' a bottle, seemed to unsettle young Bowie entirely.) There was even a stab at the calls of an old-time street-seller in 'Come and Buy My Toys' purveying his gingerbread monkeys and sugar horses.

For a long time this was known as Bowie's 'Anthony Newley phase': it certainly struck his contemporaries that he was echoing the first modern pop voice to have a definite cockney twang. Outside of comedy records and stage musicals, English accents were almost unknown in popular song in 1967. The Beatles sang with a neutral, transatlantic tone, while Mick Jagger and most R&B acts were still in thrall to black America. Bolan was vaguely London, though the effect was so mannered as to be un-placeable. Syd Barrett and a few others were abandoning the holler of the cotton-fields for the measured cadences of Cambridge and Canterbury. But Bowie's approach was still a rare one and it sounds unusual even now.

I have never found him eager to talk about that portion of his output. 'Aarrggh, that Tony Newley stuff,' he said to me. 'How cringey. No, I haven't got much to say about that in its favour. There's a naivety there that's not disenchanting, but I'm not very comfortable with it. Lyrically I guess it was striving to be something, the short-storyteller. Musically it's quite bizarre. I don't know where I was at. It seemed to have its roots all over the place, in rock and vaudeville and music hall and I don't know what.'

It was indeed difficult to classify Bowie in the 1960s: 'Marc [Bolan] was very much the mod and I was sort of neo-beat-hippy, though I hated the idea of hippy because my brother had told me about beatniks and they seemed far sexier.' In late 1969 he was interviewed by a gay magazine in which he cites the following array of influences: Anthony Newley, four Northern variety acts (George Formby, Gracie Fields, Nat Jackley and Albert Modley), Bob Dylan, John Lennon and the gritty Belgian act Jacques Brel. Even if his own songs seemed lightweight he was engaged with more serious work. Recently he told me he was going back to his old vinyl and alighting on 'Daevid Allen, who was in Gong and Soft Machine. I think all the strands of glam rock are in that. He preceded us by about two years. And so did Kevin Ayers. Soft Machine, especially with Robert Wyatt, were great London favourites. They were like "our heavy band, man".'

Maybe so, but there was too much of the actor in Bowie to join the hairy throng whole-heartedly. Encouraged by his manager Ken Pitt, a cultured man of traditional tastes, he ran with a theatrical crowd. 'Little guys,' he recalled for me, 'running around London with cigar boxes full of make-up under their arm: "Working?" "No, just moving apartments!"' He was taken to see *Oliver!* and its creator Lionel Bart became a friend. (It's worth noting that Bowie's old band the Lower Third were known to encore with *Mary Poppins*' 'Chim Chim Cheree'.) He auditioned constantly for small parts, appeared in an ice-cream advert, made some short films of his own. But for a twist of fate, you feel, his future might not have been in rock at all. The Larry Parnes notion of an 'all-round entertainer' was certainly there.

As vital as Pitt in this theatrical respect was another mentor, Lindsay Kemp, in whose Covent Garden dance school Bowie enrolled. Here he studied mime and body movement, make-up and costume. He performed a short tour in Kemp's troupe. Where his musical peers were learning only minor variations on boogie riffing and how long a tie-dye T-shirt might survive without washing, David was absorbing centuries of performers' lore. When it came to underground idealism he could talk the talk where necessary, but ambition ruled his heart. Before the solo career took off he was briefly in a band called Hype, its very name a sardonic riposte to hippy sincerity.

When he stopped living at Pitt's place in Manchester Street, Bowie had a flat in Clareville Grove, South Kensington, with his girlfriend Hermione Farthingale. But in 1969 he returned to the suburbs, near his parents' Bromley base, this time to Beckenham. At the Three Tuns pub on the High Street he set up an Arts Lab, such places being a counter-culture staple ever since the first was founded two years earlier in Drury Lane. Bowie's Lab was not much more than a folk club and a showcase for himself, though Lionel Bart came down to read some poetry, and the future Cockney Rebel, Steve Harley, made an appearance too.

Soon he moved to a bigger pad in Beckenham, a rambling Victorian pile in Southend Road named Haddon Hall. Here he lived with his new American wife Angie; here he posed in a male dress, designed by Mr Fish, for the cover of his album *The Man Who Sold the World*. (An alternative cover was also issued, this one a cartoon of a gunman with a disintegrating head. The grim background building is Cane Hill Mental Hospital, near Croydon, the final home of Bowie's sadly afflicted brother Terry, who committed suicide in 1985.) The newlyweds went up West at nights, to a nightclub in Kensington High Street called the Sombrero. Angie believes its largely gay, fashion-world clientele provided David with his first real community. These people were rehearsing the 1970s aesthetic, its glamour and decadence, before anyone else. They were all the young dudes. They were to Bowie's next few records, she suggests, what the West London mods had been to Pete Townshend.

His solitary hit single for a long while was 'Space Oddity', and a paradox was already evident. He croons it with a definite cockney style, yet the lyric dispatches him across the cosmos. This was Bowie at that time, a man whose head is in the stars but whose feet have hardly left Bromley. He made a few brief visits to America and they galvanised him. He'd admired the Velvet Underground for ages, and noticed Iggy Pop: once he met Andy Warhol and the gang there was no turning back. The London themes begin to wither away: a casual single called 'London Bye Ta Ta' seems quite prophetic.

Side 1 of *The Man Who Sold the World* ended in a chilling way, fading in a ghostly music hall chorus of 'Oh by jingo'. Forlorn, too, was 'The Bewlay Brothers', the creepy finale of his next album *Hunky Dory*; the track seems to have been David's response to brother Terry's slow psychological demise – yet I've always guessed its title came from a large tobacconist's sign on the corner of Wardour and Oxford Streets, a minute away from Trident Studios (in St Anne's Court) where Bowie worked. The London touches, in short, have an elegiac quality, as of something left behind. He still lived in Beckenham, but New York was claiming him.

Then came *The Rise and Fall of Ziggy Stardust and the Spiders from Mars*. We tend to think of *Ziggy* as a London album because its cover images were so conspicuously of the city. During my first week living in London, I bought an *A–Z* and looked up 'K West' in the phone book – every Bowie fan knew it as the illuminated sign on *Ziggy's* cover. Looking for Heddon Street and its red telephone box was this writer's introduction to central London and my mental map of the city has grown up around it. Off Regent Street, it's full of smart restaurants now but in those days was a dusty alleyway of the rag trade. Strange to recall, I was so obsessed with finding Heddon Street that I didn't bother looking for a building that stands almost directly behind it – the old Apple HQ in Savile Row, where the Beatles had played their last gig a couple of years before.

Yet *Ziggy Stardust* is scarcely a London record in the true sense. Its slang is nearly all American, its themes either personal or universal, its protagonist an extraterrestrial. In creating Ziggy, the transgender space boy who becomes a rock 'n' roll star, Bowie spawned a self-fulfilling prophecy, and the location was a mere incidental. By the time of his breakthrough, he'd been labouring in London for eight years without much luck. 'It took me a long time to get it right,' he told me. 'I didn't know how to write a song, I had no natural talents whatsoever. I made a job of work at getting good. And the only way I could learn was see how other people did it. I wasn't one of those guys who came out of the womb like Marc.' (He refers to Bolan's T. Rex song, 'Cosmic Dancer', in which he dances 'right out the womb'.)

'I wasn't dancing, I was stumbling around.'

Bolan was the nearest thing to a role model for Bowie as he sketched out *Ziggy Stardust*: in the year the album was conceived, 1971, T. Rex were nearing their peak. Bowie's old friend was Britain's first sensation of the new era: a boy who had dreamed a whole persona for himself, who seemed to become an overnight rock 'n' roll star by sheer force of willpower: 'Oh yeah! Boley struck it big, and we were all green with envy. It was terrible: we fell out for about six months. It was [sulky mutter] "He's doing *much* better than I am." And he got all sniffy about us who were still down in the basement. But we got over that.'

Bolan was not *Ziggy*'s only true begetter. There is a hint of Hendrix in there, and Iggy Pop, and a few more besides. Prominent among the inspirations for the 'leper Messiah' was the fleeting 1950s star Vince Taylor. 'He looked like a tall, gangly Gene Vincent in his black leather,' Bowie says:

> He thought he was Presley-esque but he was much rougher looking than Presley. He was very messed up, both psychologically and with drugs. At his last performance, in France, he dismissed the band, then went on stage in white robes as Jesus Christ and said, 'I am the Resurrection, I am Jesus Christ'. They nearly lynched him there and then. But he did in his own mind become the Messiah.
>
> And he came over to London, so we got him. He used to hang out on Tottenham Court Road. He had these strange plans showing where there was money buried, that he was going to get together; he was going to create a new Atlantis. And he dragged out this map of the world, just outside Tottenham Court Road Tube station – I'll never forget this – and he laid it on the pavement. We were both down here [gets on hands and

knees] and he was showing me. I'm the kind of person who never says 'No', so I'm going, 'OK, mmm, oh yes . . .' He always stayed in my mind as an example of what can happen in rock 'n' roll. And so he re-emerged in this Ziggy Stardust character.

The last name, Stardust, came from another of my favourites, The Legendary Stardust Cowboy, who was on Mercury Records with me in the 'Space Oddity' days. And the Ziggy bit came from a tailor's that I passed on the train one day. It had that Iggy connotation but it was a tailor's shop and I thought, Well this whole thing is gonna be about clothes. So it was my own little joke.

Like most of his London predecessors, Bowie the singer cannot be separated from theatrical tradition. *Ziggy Stardust* would become a turning point in musical history, but it was nearly something else entirely: a West End family favourite:

I really wanted to write musicals more than anything else. At the time I thought that was probably what I was going to end up doing. Some kind of new approach to the rock musical, that was at the back of my mind. The initial framework in '71, when I first started thinking about *Ziggy*, was as a musical-theatrical piece. And it kind of became something other than that . . .

In the end, *Ziggy Stardust* was abandoned as a musical: its story-line is probably too fragmented to qualify even as a concept album. 'There was a *bit* of a narrative,' Bowie contends, 'a slight arc, and my intention was to fill it in more later. And I never got round to it because before I knew where I was we'd recorded the damn thing. There was no time to wait. I couldn't afford to sit around for six months and write up a proper stage piece, I was too impatient.' No matter. *Ziggy* would seize psychic control of the new decade. His 'up' hair and unrepentant flashiness revived the 1950s, while the stage shows' adoption of *A Clockwork Orange* clothes and soundtrack music were a dark nod toward the future. (Stanley Kubrick's film was not explicitly set in London but its locations, especially the brutally modernist estate of Thameside, were unambiguously of the city.)

After that, Bowie commanded a global stage. The next LP, *Aladdin Sane*, he has described as 'Ziggy goes to America'. It represents his elevation to superstar levels of self-indulgence and rootless neurosis. Hereafter his palette would range from Japanese Kabuki to Weimar German cabaret. From Haddon Hall in Beckenham, he and Angie moved to a Maida Vale apartment sub-let from the *Avengers* star Diana Rigg (though Angie was, by this time, spending many nights away with T. Rex's Mickey Finn). In 1974 the Bowies leased a five-storey house at 89 Oakley Street, SW3: Chelsea was, in Angie's view, the place to find precisely the right people. Around the corner were Mick and Bianca Jagger in Cheyne Walk; close to hand were the Speakeasy, Tramp's nightclub or the San Lorenzo restaurant in Beauchamp Place, Knightsbridge. Even so, David's new management had de-camped to Manhattan and his psyche took the same westward shift.

It's sometimes seen as a stop-gap album, but *Pin Ups* was symbolic – a great London rock star bids farewell to London. A set of cover versions, it was Bowie's nostalgic homage to the 1960s city of his musical education, to nights at the Marquee and Eel Pie Island, to a young man's life sound-tracked by the Who, the Pretty Things and the Yardbirds. For the LP's inner sleeve he chose to reproduce just one lyric: the Kinks' regretful enquiry, 'Where Have all the Good Times Gone?'

After that we are anywhere and everywhere. There ensued the apocalyptic New York dystopia of *Diamond Dogs* (rescued from another aborted musical project, this one based upon George Orwell's *1984*). There were the 'plastic soul' shudderings of *Young Americans*. As we'll shortly see, Bowie's influence on his home town never waned. In *Station to Station*, he wove between brittle white boy funk and fruitily warbled melodrama. Little did he know it, but he'd just invented Spandau Ballet.

By 1977 and *Low*, made during his stay in Berlin, he was the cosmopolitan nomad, not so much a man of the world as an eternal migrant, looking for 'A New Career in a New Town'. *Low* is uniquely bleak, sung in a zombie trance of emotional wipe-out over synthetic drones and crashes. One of its songs, 'Be My Wife', is vocally his most cockney, yet bereft of all community spirit. By side two the songs have died away completely and we're in some mournful soundscape where the sun hasn't shone for a thousand years. Little did he know it, but this time he'd just invented Gary Numan.

The movie version of *Absolute Beginners* returned Bowie to Britain; the video for its stirring title song returned him to the Thames Embankment. Then he made a video for his title song to Hanif Kureishei's *Buddha of Suburbia* – a fictional coming-of-age story that drew on punk's 'Bromley contingent', notably Billy Idol. That took Bowie back to Bromley itself. Here he was filmed in a street more other-worldly than anything in his sci-fi movie *The Man Who Fell to Earth*.

Talking to Bowie in America I asked him: Does New York feel like it's your home nowadays?

Yes, it really does. It's like being on holiday in a place I've always wanted to go to, that doesn't come to an end. So 'home' is not quite right, is it? I always feel a stranger here. I am an outsider. I really am still a Brit, there's no avoiding it. But I probably know this town better than I know the new London. London has changed beyond belief since I've been coming to America. I can walk around here and find my way far better than I can in Chelsea. I've forgotten all the streets. [He mimes befuddlement.] Where did Clareville Grove used to be?

He also mentions a novel he would like to write:

It needs about a hundred years of research, and it'll never be completed in my lifetime, but I'm having a ball. I start with the first female trade unionists in the 1890s in the East End of London and I'm coming right through to Indonesia and the political problems of the South China Seas . . . Maybe the notes will emerge after I'm dead. There's an awful lot of 'Did you know?' [He puts on a suburban pub-bore voice.] 'Did you know that in the 1700s the population of London was twenty per cent black?' They all lived in the St Giles area. There were black pubs.

You should read Peter Ackroyd, I say to him.

'Oh, I *love* Ackroyd. I've read everything he's ever written. That disquieting underbelly that he sees in London, that's how I perceive it too.'

From the Eye to the Brain: Glam London

On the revolutionary feast of May Day, 1971, a small bomb exploded in the Kensington fashion shop, Biba. A message was found from the Angry Brigade. In what they termed their Communique Number 8, the radical sect explained their latest outrage with a parody of a Bob Dylan line: 'If you're not busy being born you're busy buying.'

The letter went on:

All the sales girls in the flash boutiques are made to dress the same and have the same make-up, representing the 1940s. In fashion as in everything else, capitalism can only go backwards ... Brothers and Sisters, what are your real desires? Sit in the drugstore, look distant, empty, bored, drinking some tasteless coffee? Or perhaps BLOW IT UP OR BURN IT DOWN. The only thing you can do with modern slave-houses – called boutiques – IS WRECK THEM.

Whatever the merits of their analysis, the Angry Brigade had chosen their target astutely. Biba was the quintessential fashion statement of early 1970s London, and it styled the music scene that was succeeding the hippy underground. The shop had moved through various locations, and at the time of the attack was in 124–126 Kensington High Street. Such was Biba's growing prestige, however, that by 1973 they acquired huge new premises at the top end of the street in the 1933 art deco palace that was formerly Derry & Tom's department store. Here, rather as the radicals suspected, Biba gave the rising ideology of hip consumerism – of shopping as self-expression and 'retail therapy' – its most seductive guise.

Biba's style had evolved in tandem with fashionable London's tastes, from hippy through high Victoriana and art nouveau. Now the marbled halls of its art deco home would perfectly echo the retro sounds of glam-rock London. Lou Reed of the Velvet Underground, like the still-unknown Freddie Mercury, came shopping for make-up and to rummage through the plum, mulberry and mahogany artefacts on every floor. The future Siouxsie of the Banshees travelled in from distant Bromley and discovered a rust colour for her eyes. The pretty things of David Bowie's mental landscape came to look and be looked at. Though a lot of the stock was far too expensive there were always, as in Harrods or Tiffanys, inexpensive trinkets you could buy to prove you'd been there.

On the top there were the re-opened Roof Gardens, nearly invisible to the world below, with horticultural sculptures by the future Sex Pistols patron Andrew Logan, and penguins and flamingos. (The Gardens would eventually be owned by Richard Branson's Virgin.) But the jewel in Biba's crown was its fifth-floor Rainbow Room, perfectly restored to pre-war splendour. Here appeared Ian Dury's Kilburn & the High Roads, Manhattan Transfer and Cockney Rebel. Bryan Ferry filmed his video for 'Let's Stick Together'; Liberace threw a party for his fans; David Bowie came to see the artist Guy Peellaert exhibit his *Rock Dreams* paintings and commissioned the *Diamond Dogs* sleeve from him. And the New York Dolls played a London showcase ('price including meal £2.50') which so enchanted the young Chelsea shopkeeper Malcolm McLaren that he became their manager.

The Biba Restaurant promised 'foraging parties buying up the best that Smithfield, Billingsgate and Covent Garden have to offer'. But it was never destined for the longevity of those ancient London markets. Financial difficulties mounted and by degrees, floor by floor, Biba closed down. It was gone by September 1975, at the moment when retro-glamour was fading and punk rock was ready to replace it. Glam would find a sturdier monument, though, in the defining band of Biba's era: Roxy Music.

'I moved to London to seek my fortune, and myself,' said the Durham-born art student Bryan Ferry. Once he was in the capital, the band that he formed were a vehicle for him in that quest, encouraging him (and many a Ferry fan) to jettison aspects of himself and perfect a new persona. With his colleague Andy Mackay he picked the name Roxy from a list of period cinema titles: Essoldo, Odeon, Gaumont and so on. Roxy Music evoked escapism and art deco elegance. It was simultaneously just as backward-looking as the underground critics said it was, yet also futuristic. It was really not hippy or wholesome. Nor was it trying to be authentic. Nature, the new creed seemed to say, is what we're put here to rise above.

'In order to become a pop star,' wrote the Roxy biographer David Buckley, 'Bryan Ferry became a Londoner.' The singer possessed a knack for making the best connections. After the London-raised Mackay there came Brian Eno, an electronics enthusiast from Suffolk. (Mackay found him through a chance encounter on the Northern Line.) As the band took shape it moved away from anything resembling rock orthodoxy, whether sonic or visual. At a party in 1971 Bryan met the designer and stylist Antony Price who would have such an influence on Roxy aesthetics. When the band played an early show at the 100 Club their embryonic audience was drawn from this milieu; the crowd were dressed more vividly than the musicians.

They made their first LP in old BBC premises on Piccadilly, the spiritual home of pre-war cocktail music. Hypnotically dissonant, among the record's collages was 'The Bob (Medley)', vaguely about the Battle of Britain (its bomb sounds made by a VCS3 synthesiser) with an added touch of *Swan Lake*. Also invoked was Humphrey Bogart (in '2HB') who was, with Marlene Dietrich, a prime nostalgic icon for the Biba world. Bryan's vocal style was neither an American pastiche nor the arch cockney of Bowie but rather a foggy warble, as English as anything since Noël Coward. The lavishly gorgeous LP bore a sleevenote that was, in its way, an equally perfect summation of London style at that moment: 'Piccadilly, 1972: taking a turn off mainstreet ... Is this a recording session or a cocktail party? ... a mannerist canvas of hard-edged black-leather glintings, red-satin slashes . . .'

Roxy made one more album with Brian Eno in the line-up: 'Do the Strand' inaugurates *For Your Pleasure* on the most exhilarating note and became their best-loved number. The London street of its title was for centuries regarded as the city's most characteristic thoroughfare, and appears regularly in older songs. All human life passed through it, and minor dramas were daily enacted there. In the words of Ferry's PR man, his 'Strand' was 'the buzz, the action, the centre, the quintessence, the energy'. By 1973 the Strand was in reality a rather more anonymous route, despite the Savoy and a few theatres. It scarcely deserved the stupendous compliment this song appeared to represent.

After Eno left for a new career, which would take in collaborations with David Bowie, among others, Roxy Music cruised to a new plane: less adventurous but assuredly more commercial. Ferry was able to move from his shared flat in Battersea to grander accommodation in Kensington's Redcliffe Square. Many would say that he never stopped trading upwards thereafter. In his parallel solo records he addressed a wide variety of influences, from US teen pop to inter-war popular song. In the white tuxedo that he sports on 1974's *Another Time, Another Place*, he achieved his true Noël Coward moment: the look is no longer a Chelsea take on Hollywood, but solid Mayfair. As Peter York observed, 'Ferry is the only popular music star to have mastered the visual grammar of Jermyn Street.'

Of the band's failure to crack America, their later member Eddie Jobson said: 'Roxy spoke for a purely Euro culture: Paris in the thirties, Berlin in the forties or King's Road in the seventies. Americans could never put Humphrey Bogart and rock music in the same sentence, let alone the same theatre.' London's theatre influence, in other words, came to the fore in Ferry's band, where provincial art school met aristocratic glamour and celebrity chic. As for Ferry's detractors in the underground-leaning music press, Jobson spoke disdainfully of 'socialist grubs: scruffy idiots with black leather pants, living in Camden.'

The London retro-chic espoused by Roxy Music and their set was too attractive for the mainstream to ignore, and it found expression in several lesser acts. Sailor were one such: with a visual line in cabaret matelots, they were led by a continental aesthete called Georg Kajanus and made the likeable hits 'A Glass of Champagne' (pronounced 'cham-*pine*') and 'Girls Girls Girls'. Equally thespian was Steve Harley of Cockney Rebel: a Millwall supporter from Deptford he'd come up through folk gigs at the Troubadour and Les Cousins. Hitting glam at the height of his own ambition and prettiness, he transmuted his cockney vowels into precious little melodramas like 'Judy Teen', 'Mr Soft' and '(Make Me Smile) Come Up and See Me'. It was like sci-fi music hall.

Another was the young cockney actor David Essex, whose story is wonderfully emblematic. Born in West Ham to a lady called Dolly and her docker husband Albert, he was cut from the old coster cloth. His grandfather was a tinker; David's earliest memories were of bombsite stalls at Rathbone Street Market, where he sold ex-Army clothes for 'a man who doubled as Fagin'; he also helped a street corner paper seller, whose trademark cry was audible across Canning Town, though entirely incomprehensible. Summer months meant hop-picking in Kent; and there was a spell in West Ham United Boys. In his teens he was heading up West for Dobell's shop, the Flamingo, the 100 Club and blues-wailing Eel Pie Island.

By now his family had made the familiar East End move from Canning Town to Chadwell Heath in Essex, and David was playing in a semi-pro band at the Bell in Ilford. His group had all the benefit of London connections: their manager Derek Bowman was a show-business writer who brought Lionel Bart and Mary Quant along to see them play. They tried, for a while, some rhyming slang for street credibility and became the China Plates. David took the stage name Essex, and was given drama lessons and new clothes from Carnaby Street. Going solo, he was up against other London youngbloods such as Bowie, Bolan and Rod Stewart, all of them unknown. He had a song about miniskirts called 'Thigh High'. It flopped.

He plugged away. He sang in a Kray twins nightclub and did some repertory theatre. He understudied Tommy Steele in *Dick Whittington* at the London Palladium and got to perform 'Little White Bull' and 'Flash Bang Wallop'. The biggest break was playing Jesus in a rock musical, *Godspell*, at the Roundhouse (it then moved to Wyndham's in the West End, where Noël Coward hated it). There followed two leading roles, as the aspiring rock star of *That'll be the Day* (1973) and the same star in decline in *Stardust* (1974). In the former he lined up alongside Ringo Starr and Keith Moon; the soundtrack employed many notables including Pete Townshend, Billy Fury and Dick Heckstall-Smith, while Vivian Stanshall wrote a wonderful cockney tribute to his own Essex teens called 'Real Leather Jacket'. In a parallel career David took the 1950s revivalism of *That'll be the Day* into the charts with 'Rock On', a spacey hit single made with the expatriate New Yorker Jeff Wayne.

'Rock On' put Essex in the glam firmament, a real teen heart-throb. He followed up with a nicely Biba-ish piece of 1930s retro, 'Lamplight', and gradually took his place in the nation's heart. He moved with his wife and daughter to the Essex countryside. If it was momentarily puzzling to see him on stage as Che Guevara in the Rice/Lloyd Webber musical *Evita*, subsequent roles have seemed more comfortable. He tours the old hits, from time to time, for grateful matrons and plays cricket in Eric Clapton's team, quite the respected cockney squire.

The Los Angelean brothers Ron and Russell Mael, as Sparks, were not so much imitators of London glam as talented mavericks in need of an understanding audience. Thus they joined the lineage of American acts, like Scott Walker and Jimi Hendrix, whose one-way tickets to Heathrow were acts of personal reinvention. Their Anglophile rock act Halfnelson having struggled at home, they tried England in 1973 and found themselves more attuned to the King's Road than to Sunset Strip. One of them was androgynous and camp, while the other looked sinister with fascist undertones. (This worked pretty well in a sub-culture whose filmic reference points were *A Clockwork Orange* and *Cabaret*.)

Signed to Island and produced by Steve's brother Muff Winwood, Sparks scored straight away with 'This Town Ain't Big Enough for Both of Us', from their splendidly wry album *Kimono My House*. They were showy and ironic; they managed the rare trick of being both funny and cool. Their next record was produced by Bolan-and-Bowie's man Tony Visconti (a fellow American exile) and it brought them more success. A year or two later, by luck or good judgement, they slipped away just before punk rock; they've survived, under the radar, ever since. Sparks' finest encapsulation of glam London was a pastiche of 1940s jive, entitled 'Looks Looks Looks': in its key observation, that the eye and the brain are merely inches apart, it probably spoke for the whole Biba generation.

The mainstream of popular music sucked what it could of this London sub-culture, and spawned a monster. That was Freddie Mercury's band, Queen. Freddie was really something different in those days, an Indian Parsee, born in Zanzibar, with intuitive stage presence and not the slightest interest in blues authenticity. He'd grown up in Bombay but studied at Ealing Art College, like Pete Townshend. He was very camp, and a girlfriend who worked in Biba taught him all about make-up. He and a boy named Roger Taylor, a science student at Imperial, had a second-hand clothes stall next door to Biba, in Kensington Market. With two more science students they became Queen and in November 1972 played a showcase at the Pheasantry, the former boho hang-out and future Pizza Express. In a sense they embodied that same transition. They took elements of the capital's subterranean decadence and made them universally explicable. They were artful and heartless. They were heavy, like Led Zeppelin, but somehow rootless. Like Pink Floyd, they came together in London but were ultimately from nowhere. And like the Floyd, they ended up everywhere.

Meanwhile, amid the preening and the fuss, a young New Zealander wrote a new musical, *The Rocky Horror Show*. Richard O'Brien's kinky homage to sci-fi B-movies and current London styles opened in Sloane Square, at the Royal Court's Upstairs theatre, on 16 June 1973. A year later it moved to a new home along the King's Road (where it remained throughout the 1970s) and within two years it was made into a movie. You could view *The Rocky Horror Show* as either an epitaph for glam or as the harbinger of something new. In its theatrical and cinematic forms it carried enormous weight along the King's Road, especially at the far end, where Malcolm McLaren and Vivienne Westwood were now trading. Punk style, which of course claimed to come from nothing, owed a lot to *The Rocky Horror Show* – and to glam London.

Marc Bolan and David Bowie had between them taken English pop culture beyond the Beatles and Rolling Stones. From faraway south-east London, the future Boy George reflected that their combined effect on a 'little queer peacock' like himself was nothing less than life-changing.

The London music business had changed too. The paternal domination of EMI and Decca had been disrupted by the arrival of American companies keen to stake their claim. Around the old Tin Pan Alley were CBS in Soho Square and RCA, just off New Oxford Street. The mighty Warners encamped in Broadwick Street and A&M were in the New King's Road. The hippest of the smaller British companies, Island, Virgin, Rough Trade and Stiff, were dotted around West London. With so many eyes and ears alert to the Next Big Thing, nothing in London could go ignored for long. The Sex Pistols, sold as rock's greatest outrage, were at different times signed to no less than three of these companies. And the left-wing Clash were snapped up by the Yankee capitalists at CBS. But just before the punk storm broke, another movement paved the way. Outside a pub once more, we hear those door-bolts sliding open . . .

Chapter Nine

Guttersnipes

Pub rock, punk rock and a little bit of Wembley up your Ponders End.

Even as glam rock decked the streets in tinsel, London was inventing the antidote. Once again, the new trend had alcoholic overtones. It was rock, it was played in pubs, and so they called it 'pub rock'. This was a return to core values in more ways than one, a reaction to pop that looked too much like show business, and to rock that seemed too brainy, too 'progressive'. London's pub rock followed the timeless tavern code of fun, simplicity and vigour. But it nurtured incisive talents like Ian Dury and Elvis Costello. Historians of music have honoured pub rock as the bulldozer that cleared the ground for its successor, namely punk. But it should be celebrated in its own right.

In 1971 a US act, Eggs Over Easy, began a residency at the Tally Ho, a former jazz haunt in Kentish Town. In January of the next year, the Americans' slot was taken by a good-time British act, Brinsley Schwarz, who were themselves partial to rootsy US styles like funk and country, as popularised by Dylan's associates the Band. Soon there was a coherent scene, promoted both by *Time Out* magazine and Charlie Gillett of Radio London, starring bands such as Ducks Deluxe and Bees Make Honey. Its circuit included pubs like the Kensington in Shepherd's Bush, the Cock Tavern in Kilburn and the Lord Nelson in Holloway Road.

Pub rock was not much to look at. Nobody wore their finest array in a crowded back room, bristling with cigarettes, where the carpet

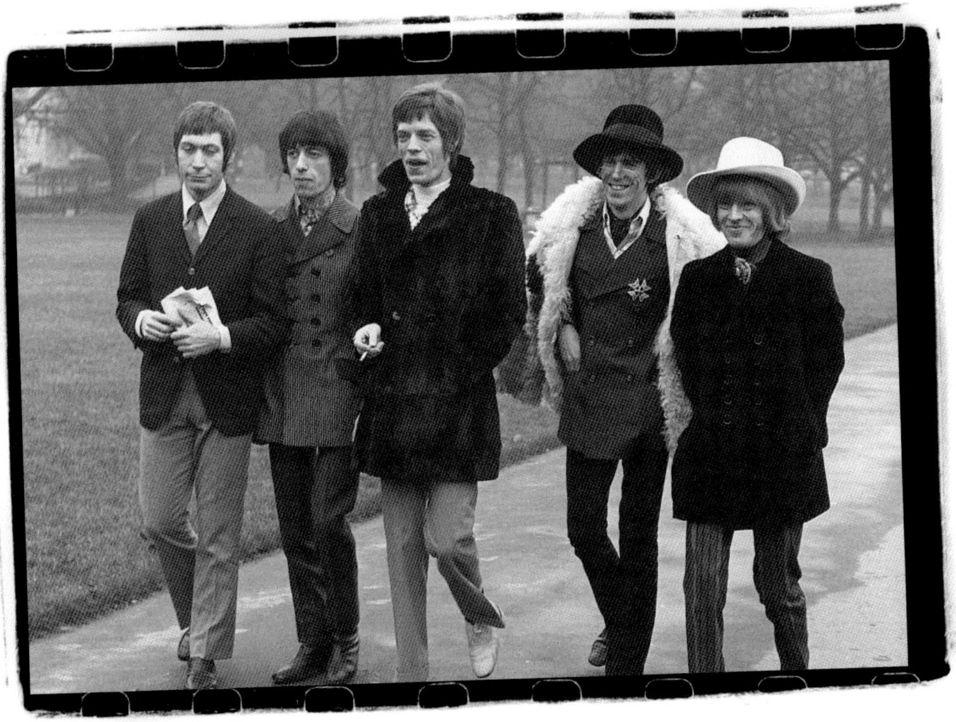

Above: Their Satanic Majesties: the Rolling Stones in Green Park, January 1967.

HULTON-DEUTSCH COLLECTION/CORBIS

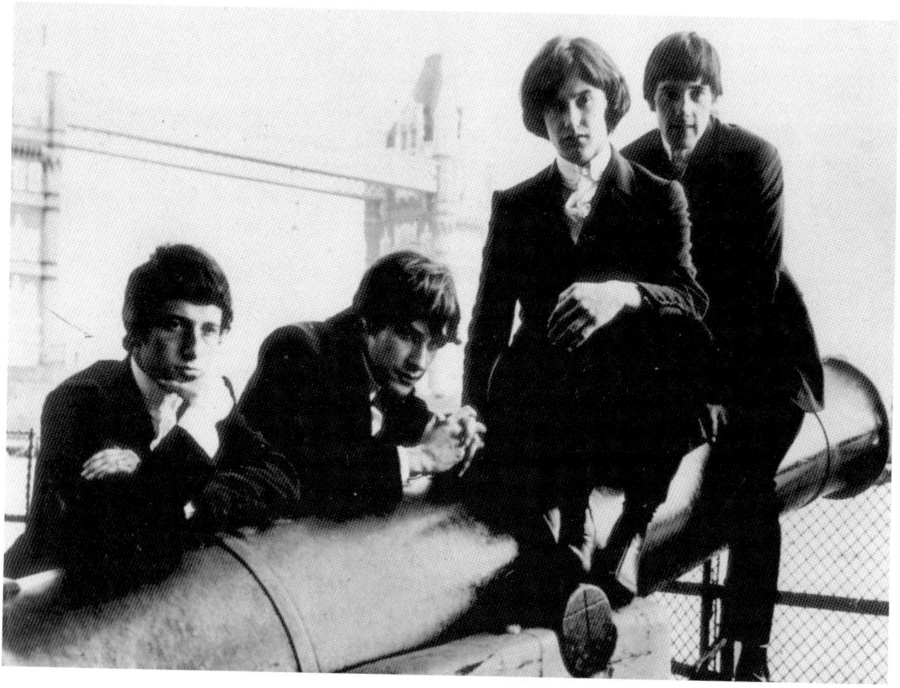

Above: Ray Davies (second from left) and the Kinks, by the Tower of London in September 1964.

Above: The Small
Faces visit Belgravia,
1966. From left:
Jones, Marriott, Lane
and McLagan.

Right: Self-invented,
shrewd and flash,
the epitome of his
city: Marc Bolan
in 1973.

Above: London's 'last great music hall act': the Sex Pistols appal Carnaby Street, 1976. RAY STEVENSON/REX FEATURES

Above: 'My heart's in the city': Paul Weller (left) with the Jam in 1977.

Above: New boots and panto: Ian Dury, in the costume of coster aristocracy.

Right: The last gang in town, The Clash. From left: Jones, Simonon, Headon, Strummer.

ANDRE CSILLAG/REX FEATURES

Left: Damon Albarn of Blur and Gorillaz, who turned from Britpop-bloke to London's psychogeographer.

REDFERNS/GETTY IMAGES.

Right: The new soul diva toasts her public. Amy Winehouse in Camden Town, 2007.

ANGELA LUBRANO

Below: Lily Allen ('a post-punk Marie Lloyd') at the Astoria in November 2006.

ANGELA LUBRANO

Above: Like Burlington Bertie, he is from Bow: Dizzee Rascal at the Forum, Kentish Town, in 2008. ANGELA LUBRANO

squelched with spilled beer. But there was bonhomie and good, hearty playing. Gigs were cheap or even free. Some acts, especially a seedy-looking gang from Canvey Island called Dr Feelgood, operated on the cusp of punk; others, like Joe Strummer's 101ers and Elvis Costello, needed punk to help them reach the wider audience. The unlikeliest star of them all, though, was music hall to his bones . . .

Ian Dury: New Boots and Panto

His body always looked at war with itself. Violence was packed tight inside his stocky frame as he hobbled across a stage, hollering 'Oi Oi!' in a gruff, unlovely voice. Born in 1942, Ian Dury was left partly crippled after contracting polio at the age of seven. He was not exactly the cockney-Essex geezer he seemed, coming originally from Harrow. Though his father was a bus driver, his mother was middle class and she set the tone. He did spend time in tough institutions for disabled children, but there were also trips to the Palladium to enjoy Max Miller and Max Wall.

Dury was not a simple product of the English class system; he was of the hybrid sort that often brings interesting results. He actually spent a period of his childhood in a Swiss villa that was later taken by Noël Coward. ('He probably found some of my old notes,' said Dury, 'and knocked out a couple of musicals on the strength of it, the old bastard!') Perhaps that's why Coward received an elegant tribute in Dury's 'There Ain't Half Been Some Clever Bastards', a song which rhymes 'charmer' with 'Brahma' and 'pyjamas'.

In his teens he mooched about the Essex suburbs, a period that's wonderfully evoked in songs like 'Upminster Kid'. It was the 1950s, a time of Cokes and Woodbines in the Regent Café, and Bill Haley on the jukebox. Teddy boys descended on rock 'n' roll movies at the Gaumont, or amassed in strength at the Mason's Arms. Upminster itself, he remembered, was a sleepy sort of town between the council estates of Dagenham and Ockenden. Inspired by skiffle and Eddie Cochran in *The Girl Can't Help It*, he bought a drum kit in Aylesbury for ten shillings. In 1957, at the Romford Ritz to see *Disc Jockey*

Jamboree, he found the Ted tribes gathering from Canning Town, Ilford and Barking. Seats were slashed, cigarettes were flicked and a girl had her ponytail cut off with a flick-knife. When the fire hoses were turned on, police with dogs arrived to clear the sodden aisles. 'It only made the *Romford Recorder*,' he later sighed.

At sixteen he left school to study art in Walthamstow, where his visiting teachers included the painter Peter Blake. Moving on to the Royal College of Art he found his niche in Soho jazz dives like Ronnie Scott's Old Place. Next, teaching at Canterbury College of Art, he dreamed up a band to be called Kilburn & the High Roads – who remained no more than a concept for two more years. (He had no particular link to Kilburn, either.) As a result he was already thirty when he finally emerged as the Kilburns' frontman. Visually he was not your standard rock material, but he had sharpened his verbal talents to perfection. A great cockney rhymester was in the making.

In 1973 Kilburn & the High Roads hit the pub rock circuit, playing the Tally Ho and everywhere else. I saw them a while later and was amazed. Such a motley crew, two of them disabled, one black, another perhaps psychotic, in all shapes and sizes, dressed like an explosion at a jumble sale. Their songs owed nothing to pub rock's favoured Americana, but were a blend of 1950s jive and pure London music hall. At the Hope & Anchor in Islington they were admired by some local urchins: 'The Kilburns and Ian Dury were a huge influence on Madness,' the singer Suggs has said. 'The sound that they made was almost exotic and their lyrics were very London.'

Their only album, *Handsome*, has a cover painting of them by Tower Bridge, looking confused. They split in the very week it was released. And there the tale could easily have ended, except that in 1976 Dury found a musical partner in Chaz Jankel. By now thirty-four, Dury's sense of time running out was given fresh urgency – he saw his young disciples the Sex Pistols start the revolution without him. Luckily, Chaz Jankel made a superb co-writer and musical director, adding the craftsmanship that Dury lacked. They signed their band, the Blockheads, to the up-and-coming Stiff Records and Ian Dury became the unlikeliest-looking pop star of the new wave.

The Blockheads' first single was 'Sex and Drugs and Rock 'n' Roll' – a triad destined for the *Oxford Book of Quotations* and a modern echo of the classic formulation 'wine, women and song'. (Or more poetically, Omar Khayyam's 'a flask of wine, a book of verse and thou'. Or less poetically, the Royal Navy's 'rum, bum and concertina'.) On its B-side was a cautionary tale of teenage shoplifting in Romford, '*Razzle* in My Pocket'. And the debut album, *New Boots and Panties*, remains a pinnacle of London's popular music.

There is a splendid, invincible vulgarity about this record, a fist-fight of tight, stroppy funk and stupendous verbal dexterity. In a manner both critical and compassionate, Dury gave voice to Essex's plebeian tribes. 'Billericay Dickie' lists all the stops on a low-end Lothario's progress from Shoeburyness to Burnham-on-Crouch. 'Plaistow Patricia' is savagely bleak and so is 'Blackmail Man', whose cascading cockney rhymes ('Hampton Wick', 'Berkshire Hunt') are far from jovial. More tenderly altogether, 'My Old Man' pays tribute to his father, driving a Number 18 bus to Euston, before spending his last years as a chauffeur.

Dury never regained those heights, though there were brilliant moments like 'Reasons to be Cheerful' (the reasons including 'seeing Piccadilly' and 'Hammersmith Palais'). A TV commercial voice-over, ''Ello Tosh, gotta Toshiba?', placed him in the ancient lineage of cockney street traders, updated for the modern age. And the final music of his life, on 1998's *Mr Love Pants*, was among his best work – 'Mash it Up Harry' is almost the further adventures of Billericay Dickie, older and more wistful: 'He wants a bit of Wembley up his Ponders End.' As in the Blockhead songs, what began as mockery became a bohemian's affectionate portrait of lives more ordinary.

I interviewed Dury in late 1999, when we knew that he was dying of cancer. Frail as he was, he still seemed faintly menacing. And he passed comment on each good-looking woman that passed. He spoke as openly of his illness, as wittily and free of bitterness, as he'd done of his disability. A month before his death in February 2000, he played a farewell show at the Palladium, billed as *New Boots and Panto*. Dury was a London original, steeped in its traditions. His head was a treasure house, a repository of language and popular culture. He was a walking archive – walking with a limp, perhaps, but an archive all the same. His old teacher Peter Blake remembered Dury as an educated man, not an authentic cockney but inquisitive and open – and surrounded by dictionaries. 'He was a great poet, wasn't he? In the same vein as Betjeman.'

'The Last Great Music Hall Act': the Sex Pistols

Life began to ebb from London's pub rock scene in 1975. Some of its leading bands split up that year, as if dimly aware of an impending change. The Hope & Anchor abandoned its studio business and sold the equipment to Eddy Grant, then between his two pop careers as an Equal and a solo star. The year before, Joe Strummer's pub rock band, the 101ers, made their debut at a Brixton pub called the Telegraph (its name indicates a staging post on the capital's communications line to the western naval ports: 'London calling to the faraway towns'). But Strummer had only to see the Sex Pistols to realise a new order was at hand.

Curiously the most vital acts of this transitional time were from the distant cockney fleshpot of Southend, in Essex, and its unglamorous neighbour Canvey. They were like Charles Darwin's Galapagos Islands, sundered from London's evolutionary mainstream; here the old values of 1960s R&B survived, and bands played fast, hard and loud. Mickey Jupp came out of this scene, as did Eddie & the Hot Rods. The latter, in fact, looked to many eyes like the next big thing, full of youth and energy and free of either foppishness or musical pretensions. In those respects they marked a break with the early 1970s. More importantly, though, there was a quartet called Dr Feelgood.

While Eddie & the Hot Rods were soon to be eclipsed by the Sex Pistols, Dr Feelgood were not in competition. They were older and quite ungainly, resembling an unsuccessful gang of petty criminals, with a manic guitarist, Wilko Johnson, who would ricochet around pub stages like a broken Dalek. Their singer, Lee Brilleaux, wore the clothes of a shabby office worker and sweated feverishly. They made the tightest, most ferocious noise that anyone could remember. Among the young fans who were irrevocably changed by seeing them was Paul Weller. Their influence even reached across to the New York punks, notably the Ramones, who in turn would galvanise British punks.

Lee Brilleaux was also a financial backer of Stiff Records, a company at the crossroads of pub and punk rock. Among Stiff's early signings were Ian Dury and Elvis Costello, while its in-house producer, the Brinsleys' Nick Lowe, was at the controls of Britain's first punk single, the Damned's frenetic 'New Rose'. Another label, Chiswick Records, with its Rock On stall in Soho, provided one more focus for a slowly coalescing scene of rock 'n' roll fundamentalists. The next requirement, really, was for a Grand Theorist, an *agent provocateur* or, in true London style, an amalgam of the wide boy and the storyteller. He, of course, was Malcolm McLaren.

A carrot-topped motor-mouth, McLaren was a North Londoner who gave the constant impression of brilliant ideas exploding behind his eyeballs. He studied art at Harrow, Croydon and Goldsmiths, and haunted Soho's chic joints: Les Enfants Terribles in Dean Street, La Macabre in Meard St, La Bastille on Wardour Street. While at Harrow he met a designer, Vivienne Westwood, with whom he had a son in 1969. At Croydon he teamed up with an artist named Jamie Reid, and together they made a film about Oxford Street: it ranged from the eighteenth-century Gordon Riots to the consumerist temple of twentieth-century Selfridges. It was already clear that McLaren loved London for its ancient anarchy and its ceaseless commerce. Perhaps he might, in time, combine the two?

He and Westwood set up shop at 430 King's Road, a long way west of Sloane Square, in the stretch between a crooked turning and the World's End pub. The address had already served as an outpost of hippy fashions in this cheaper district of the Royal Borough of Kensington & Chelsea. Under its new owners it was called Let It Rock, later becoming Too Fast To Live, Too Young To Die, catering both to diehard teddy boys and art school fans of vintage fifties flash. Among its visitors in 1973 were the New York Dolls, an American band of glam-rockers, whom McLaren promptly offered to manage. Back in their homeland he applied his twin persona of glib-tongued barrow boy and high-level conceptualist, even kitting them out in fantasy communist regalia. It was almost a wonder he came out alive.

Back in London the shop underwent another transformation. Now called Sex, it carried Vivienne Westwood's new designs, on themes of sexual and political extremism. There were bondage trousers, Marxist and Third Reich insignia, homo-erotic T-shirts and assorted items in violent pink. McLaren plotted a new band, combining his assistant Glen Matlock with two youths from Shepherd's Bush, Steve Jones and Paul Cook. It was the wide boy Jones, in particular, who fitted Malcolm's notion of a London band who owed more to Charles Dickens than to Elvis Presley. He understood the New York scene through his adventures with the Dolls, and saw that its musical primitivism would chime with London's current mood. The city of Dr Feelgood and Ian Dury's Kilburns was about to spawn a monster.

Matlock, from Kensal Green, was an art student at Central St Martins and a fan of the sixties pop virtues embodied by the Small Faces. Cook and Jones, drummer and guitarist respectively, were former skinheads and given to mooching around the King's Road. Into their orbit came a Finsbury Park boy of Irish family, one John Lydon, who auditioned for them at the jukebox in the shop. He sang with an urgent, imploring whine that was impossible to forget. If his vocals were untutored his brain was well stocked – he grew up devouring everything from the Irish jigs and West Indian reggae of his neighbourhood, to the adventurous 'Krautrock' on offer in Richard Branson's early Virgin stores. The arch-destroyer was, in fact, a young man of wide and accepting tastes.

With McLaren and Westwood behind them, the four Sex Pistols were a perfect London co-mingling of well-connected bohemians and proletarian rawness. To the manager's mind, their cultivated snottiness evoked a street mob of the Gordon Riots – a time of tumult described brilliantly in Dickens's *Barnaby Rudge*. And the taste for blatantly fake new names was very Larry Parnes; John Lydon became Johnny Rotten. They duly went to rehearse in Denmark Street itself, where a couple of the band actually lived. They made a home of that old jazz shrine the 100 Club on Oxford Street, beneath the old straight track that led to Tyburn's gallows. Here I came to see them in the summer of 1976, as the sun set bloodily in the west.

For the first few weeks there were plenty of tourists in the crowd, without the least idea of what was on offer. Beyond a small clique of art students and hardline gig goers, nobody had heard of the Sex Pistols. From the stage, Johnny Rotten smiled at everyone with equal malice. He passed sneering comment upon established rock idols: 'Deep Purple. They're real *heavy*, man ... Melanie. Oh, we *love* Melanie.' It was the hippy tourists one felt sorry for: they would stroke their beards uneasily. The sixties generation, which had defined itself through youth and rebellion, was facing its first internal mutiny. Obsolescence beckoned. Their long hair, clogs and denim flares – which had all survived the glam-rock years – were suddenly of another time.

That is not to say the Pistols audience dressed as 'punks', for the style had not yet been defined. There were some Roxy Music and David Bowie types, and I remember girls with a decadent *Cabaret* look, some with little swastikas on their cheeks. Most, though, were average rock boys, in cap-sleeved T-shirts and wide jeans, drinking lager from plastic beakers. Only the Pistols, onstage, were conspicuously dressed by Westwood and McLaren. And when they began to play, their noise roared out the same spirit of violent dislocation.

Rotten sang the old Small Faces hit, 'What'cha Gonna Do About It?' changing its lyric from 'I love you' to 'I hate you'. Another song was something to do with anarchy; it name-checked paramilitary groups from Ulster and Angola. The sound was chaotic but thrilling. It bristled with references to life outside the complacent rock world. It seemed desperate, pinging between extremes of euphoria and anxiety. If the tunes were crude, they were stirringly melodic. And between numbers, Rotten hung limply from the mike-stand, dazed and panting. He was always staring, but at nothing. He kept blowing his nose: I'd never seen anyone do that onstage. It was extraordinarily hot in that basement. Now stupendously bored, he stood upright and looked around for Malcolm: 'Mow-currmmm! Mow-currmmm! Can. I. Have. A fakkin' drink. Pleeeeeze . . .'

Then he slumped, suddenly, like a firing squad victim. 'Rastafaaarrrr-iiiiii,' he groaned, weakly. The truth is that nobody in the whole room understood what they were watching. Some laughed, some fled. Most of us just stood there, transfixed. More than once, on Tube trains home, I saw him in the same carriage, travelling up to his squat in Hampstead High Street. He sat by himself, drained and vulnerable. Punk and Rotten were not public knowledge. To everyone else in the carriage, I think, he looked disagreeable and strange. Even his hair was a sort of provocation – short and spiky instead of long and placid. The narrow collar, the skinny tie, the second-hand trousers, were all at odds with everyone else. There was tension across the country in that year, and the Sex Pistols' singer – that runty, vaguely disturbing boy – would become a sort of lightning rod in the storms that lay ahead.

The cat was out of the bag before the year was over. A calamitous national tour and brutally anthemic records – 'Anarchy in the UK', *Never Mind the Bollocks* (their stark artwork by McLaren's ally Jamie Reid) – made the Pistols infamous and punk notorious. Distraught citizens were said to punch their televisions when the group appeared. Rotten was physically attacked. The King's Road saw fights between rival tribes of punks and teddy boys. Above all, this was 1977, Queen Elizabeth's Jubilee Year. At the height of loyalist celebrations in June, the Sex Pistols took a boat trip on the Thames to publicise their new single 'God Save the Queen'. From the top deck of a craft called the *Queen Elizabeth*, the band played their establishment-baiting songs as they cruised past Parliament. The police were alerted; scuffles, arrests and national scandal followed. It was only a brief episode in the life of London's river, which has witnessed everything and flows indifferently on. But it was a marvellous spectacle.

As a turning point of popular music, punk rock was a dramatic rupture with the past. It suddenly made yesterday seem like years ago. But there was plenty of London's past already inside the Sex Pistols. In fact, like the Beatles before them, an element in their impact was their very Englishness. They owed so little to the US rock aesthetic, which in the mid-1970s ruled Britain as surely as it had in the 1950s. Both the Clash and the Stones were each more willing to adopt Americana. When the Sex Pistols appeared to be denouncing the monarchy, it was something far more interesting than conventional rock posturing. This came from within the soul of London itself. That made it look like treason.

They were not, as things turned out, quite the four-headed Anti-Christ – just a group of naughty London boys. Their short career was over in no time. Thirty years later they reconvened to perform some shows in Brixton and what everyone noticed, this time around, was what a music hall act the Sex Pistols really are. 'Maybe it's because we're all Londoners,' Rotten told *NME* readers beforehand, 'but there would be no Sex Pistols without dear old London town . . . See you all at Brixton with proper feelings and proper people all around. From London Bridge to the Rose and Crown, all of Britain is welcome so come on down.' They loped onstage to the backing of Vera Lynn's 'There'll Always be an England'. Around that time, Rotten took a filmed tour of London aboard an open-topped bus. Anarchy, he reveals, was really another way of saying 'Knees Up Mother Brown'. Now a wistful expatriate, living in America, he echoes the architectural values of Prince Charles, if not the vocabulary. 'Is there a London any more?' he howls. 'They've murdered the town. Where's my England? I want it fucking back!' He pines for the Georgian terraces, deplores the vast, inhuman towers of corporate power now obliterating the City ('history's important, warts and all'), despairs of all the non-smoking pubs and police enforcement cameras, and shares Ray Davies's distaste for Arsenal's blandly modern stadium.

In the same documentary, by Julien Temple, Paul Cook reflects on how much of the Sex Pistols' story took place around Soho, from the Cambridge pub where they used to gather, to their old offices in Dryden Chambers, a quaint alley off Oxford Street, now of course demolished. Meanwhile, Steve Jones strolls down Denmark Street and remarks that two of London's plagues began here – one from the churchyard of St Giles and the other from Number 6, the Sex Pistols' old rehearsal room.

The Clash and London: a Punk Romance

The Westway has been called, by J. G. Ballard, 'a stone dream that will never awake'. He saw in this elevated road a fragmentary vision of the futuristic London that we failed to build. But its promise of speed and freedom is apparent only to the motorists. To the earthlings in its shadows it wears a more depressing aspect. To the Clash it became a symbol of oppression, of urban dread, riot and confrontation.

But then, to the Clash, so were most things.

Mick Jones, their guitarist, grew up in a tower block by the Westway, off Harrow Road. (Tower blocks, too, loomed large in the Clash's iconography.) He had a band called London SS, with his friend Tony James, and they rehearsed in a place off Praed Street in Paddington. This was when the Sex Pistols were first making waves. It was quite a punk clique they all belonged to – in the same West London set were future members of the Damned, Generation X and the Slits. Contact was quickly made with the Chelsea punks, including John Lydon's friend (soon to be Glen Matlock's replacement in the Pistols) Sid Vicious. All line-ups were fluid. A good-looking local boy called Paul Simonon was next to join Mick Jones's band.

Moving to a squat-cum-rehearsal space in Davis Road, in Shepherd's Bush, Jones and Simonon saw and admired Joe Strummer performing at gigs such as the Nashville in West Kensington and the Red Cow in Hammersmith. An approach was duly made and so the Clash came into being.

Second only to the Sex Pistols in London's punk rock hierarchy, the Clash were destined to outlast and surpass them. They played every song like it might be their last stab at immortality. They were ideologically committed people but musically open-minded. Having started with a no-frills policy that bordered on the puritanical, they expanded into reggae, rockabilly and even funk. They loved reaching out to other styles, and the more their clenched fist loosened, the better their grasp became. But their first songs were solidly of London. '1977' served up typically apocalyptic warnings, of armed insurrection in Knightsbridge and vengeance on the rich. 'London's Burning', premiered at their Islington Screen on the Green show in September 1976, was written by Strummer in a fury of boredom. 'White Man in Hammersmith Palais', naming that venerable home of the foxtrot and tea dance, was born of a disappointing reggae gig. And 'White Riot' records their experiences at the 1976 Notting Hill Carnival, a tempestuous affair that saw the Clash attempt to set fire to a car.

The Carnival's ascent from neighbourhood party to national fiesta has been spectacular. But its progress in the 1970s was far from certain. Back in the 1960s when Notting Hill was still host to first-generation West Indian immigrants and to white hippies of the underground movement, common cause was found. Notting Hill's event was a home-grown version of the great Caribbean Carnivals and offered a healthy alternative to racial conflict. Here, it was hoped, London's ethnic divisions could be surmounted in a communal celebration of music, food and masquerade. When Mick Farren, the seasoned observer of such affairs, came along in 1975 he noticed a new and unwelcome tension.

He saw the reggae sound systems that boomed beneath the Westway, while the 'freak' bands Hawkwind and the Pink Fairies played for free in the open air. Some Brixton youths had come up north for the day. Red Stripe beer and ganja smoke both worked their magic. There was some thieving and a growing readiness to square up to the Metropolitan Police. But the trouble that year was as nothing compared to 1976, when the Clash witnessed full-scale street battles between the police and black youths. The group's emotional response was to wish for a 'riot of my own' – a similar surge of anti-Establishment militancy from the white youths of

Britain. It was the classic Clash mix of rock 'n' roll attitude with agit-prop theory.

Questions of race were inescapable at that point in London's history. Like the Sex Pistols the Clash proclaimed themselves the children of a ghettoised city, but children who had crossed the tracks. For the Clash especially, the love of reggae was emblematic of opposition to racism – they performed a stirring version of Junior Murvin's 'Police and Thieves', for instance – and the punk rockers inherited the Ladbroke Grove hippies' affinity with immigrant sub-cultures. The alliance was recognised by Bob Marley, no less, in his 'Punky Reggae Party' of 1977, which name-checks Dr Feelgood, the Jam, the Clash and the Damned, as well as the Maytals and the Wailers, and weaves in the freshly coined put-down 'boring old farts'. In a song by the Jamaican band Culture, 1977 was foretold to be a watershed year, when 'Two Sevens Clash'. Few of the punk bands had the rhythmic flexibility of true reggae players, and crossover was ideological rather than musical, but the Rastafarian taste for blood-curdling Biblical prophecy was nicely suited to the punks' dramatic world-view.

There was authentic drama to be had. Punk had arrived in a period of discord. There was violence on the streets, where the far right and the broad left competed for young support. Intolerance and menace were certainly in the air. On London Underground trains we wore out our thumbnails trying to scrape away the little stickers the National Front put everywhere. (They used good glue.) There were always strikes, and picket lines, which turned into pitched battles. There was inflation, unemployment and, it seemed, a perpetual sterling crisis. The Labour government appeared old and confused. Talk of a fascist coup was taken quite seriously. And the communists were always presumed to be plotting something. There was a general sense that something drastic was about to happen. For the first few months it was unclear which way punk might go.

The movement had its decadent elements, for whom Nazi fashions had a certain subversive chic. The ruling party of the day, the natural target of rebel sentiment, was nominally socialist. Punk, which had as yet no public manifesto, suggested a boot-boy thuggishness, or at least a nihilistic scorn for youthful idealism. Culturally, punk was attracting a mini-generation – the later contingent of the baby boom – whose outlook was shaped by the darker mood of the early 1970s (*A Clockwork Orange*, football hooliganism, economic pessimism) as opposed to the Aquarian optimism of their sixties hippy elders. Yet, when the National Front marched in strength through London it tended to concentrate the mind. Flirting with swastikas for the sake of style no longer looked clever. In 1977 the politics of race was crystallised by two new organisations, the Anti-Nazi League and Rock Against Racism. With the support of bands like the Clash, they proved decisive in swinging the punk vote leftwards.

The Clash's most perfect statement came, perhaps, in their 1979 album *London Calling*, whose title track (borrowed, you may recall, from both the early BBC and from Noël Coward) is like a William Blake vision – the city as celestial battleground. Vibed up by the legendarily loopy producer Guy Stevens, a near-mythical figure in Soho's mod/soul underground, the band were at last matching energy with eloquence. Their first LP to go Top 10 in Britain and the first to win acclaim in the USA, it transformed them from parochial pogo material into an international rock band. Being the Clash, however, triumph brought them more confusion than pleasure.

Soon after *London Calling* I was sent by the *NME* to interview Joe Strummer – or, rather, he called to our Carnaby Street office to collect me. The encounter lasted two days. We sat and gabbled in Italian coffee bars where the hiss of cappuccino machines drowned out my tape recordings. We stopped off at every pub between the Sun & 13 Cantons in Beak Street and the King of Corsica by Berwick Street Market. In the latter he could not relax until he was sitting with his back to the wall, facing the door – 'That was how they got Wild Bill Hickok,' he explained. (A likeably self-mythologising streak was typical of Strummer.) We stumbled unsurely past the Marquee, the 2i's and Ronnie Scott's. On the corner of Old Compton Street a terribly disfigured man was braying through the hole in his face. 'The Krays did that,' said Joe, darkly. 'He upset them, once.'

Due to my own inexperience the sessions produced nearly nothing of journalistic value, except to show me Strummer's romantic infatuation with the city. The place that gave him lyrical meat and drink was a daily source of fascination. In fact there were no limits to his enthusiasms that year, as became evident when the Clash produced their sprawling *Sandinista!*, a triple album of audacious indiscipline. (Its best track, incidentally, is an Eddy Grant cover, 'Police on My Back'.) When I next met him it was backstage at Shea Stadium in New York, where the Clash were supporting the Who. It was supposedly the latter band's 'farewell', though they would in fact outlast the Clash by many years. Both bands, in their respective dressing rooms, lived in a sort of London bubble.

For reasons of punk integrity the Clash refused to appear on *Top of the Pops*, the BBC's weekly celebration of corporate sales-power. So, when their single 'Bankrobber' became a hit, bemused viewers had to watch the resident dance troupe, Pan's People, cavorting to the song in saucy burglar-girl costumes. That was the Clash's career, really – a tragi-comic affair of high-minded idealism with occasional touches of farce. Cries of 'betrayal' attended their every move, and in truth the Clash could never learn to live with their own success. Were they a rock 'n' roll Red Brigade or posturing lackeys of the capitalist entertainment industry?

In the Middle Eastern desert, during the first Gulf War, their 'Rock the Casbah' was broadcast over forces' radio to boost the troops' morale. They earned their biggest paycheque when 'Should I Stay or Should I Go' was chosen by Levi jeans for a TV ad. And their catalogue became a valued asset of the multinational corporation who came to own everything about the Clash except their souls. These ironies of life were never lost on Strummer. But the great thing about the Clash is that they were always for their audience, more than they were against anything else. 'The truth,' they would sing, 'is only known by guttersnipes.' As their name implied, the Clash stood at the point where opposite forces collide. They never looked for an easy way out and they never found one.

The Clash were a thoroughly London band in some ways – their songs gave the Westway a place in British rock mythology that no one would have expected – but they were not confined by it. Towards the end of his too-brief life, Strummer said, 'We weren't parochial, we weren't narrow-minded, we weren't Little Englanders. At least we had the suss to embrace what we were presented with, which was the world in all its weird variety.'

Self-Mutilating Happiness: Punk in its Prime

Much debate arose as to whether punk's password was 'Destroy' or 'Create'. The punk impulse had its invigorating, and liberating, effects upon music – until it declined into a template for the less imaginative. Of the old guard who were supposedly under threat, the so-called 'dinosaur' acts like Pink Floyd and Rod Stewart, most survived and even grew more successful. Scarcely any punk act enjoyed much by way of long-term commercial appeal. But a few, at least, seized their moment and used it well. More importantly, punk not only lowered the barriers to entry, it dramatically widened the criteria of acceptability.

The Damned were of the same West London network as the Clash; they circulated members, used the same rehearsal rooms, signed on at the same Employment Exchanges. After the epoch-making 'New Rose' they thundered along with many more instalments of dumb but exciting London rock. They were, at heart, old-fashioned entertainers. Lacking the distinctiveness of the Pistols or the charisma of the Clash they concentrated on all-out swagger and – especially in the person of lead singer Dave Vanian – on horror movie looks that inspired the punk offshoot called goth.

In that respect they rank alongside Siouxsie & the Banshees, whose origins lay outside in the city, in the Sex Pistols' 'Bromley contingent' of original followers. The striking Siouxsie, alias Susan Ballion from Chiselhurst, had an intuitive gift for self-styling, which in her case drew on Louise Brooks and *Cabaret* by way of Sex-shop fetishism. With her guitarist Steve Severin she created a band that owed nothing to musical virtuosity; but nor did they mimic the chiming, primal rock of the Sex Pistols. Frequenters of a lesbian club in Poland Street (for gay venues were often the early punks' only safe haven), they had absorbed the Velvet Underground's New York heaviness and Biba London's decadence, to arrive at an image of icy, black detachment. Goth, once more, was just around the corner.

From the same posse of early-adopters came one William Broad – soon to be re-christened, in a most Larry Parnes-like way, as Billy Idol. Even his blond shock of upright hair signalled a return to the late 1950s and its values of showbiz artifice over denim-wearing sincerity. In his band, Generation X, he teamed with Tony James who had come from Mick Jones's London SS, via a band called Chelsea. (James and Jones are nowadays reunited, under the name Carbon/Silicon.) Of all the punks, Billy Idol looked the best bet for mainstream stardom and duly moved from tabloid rebel to pop pin-up to transatlantic rocker.

The pub rock venues had given punk a place to start; private parties, student halls and the 100 Club were also on hand. The Marquee was at first wary of the new noise and would not host punk until well into 1977; 'Business wise it's brilliant but at home I prefer the Eagles,' admitted its manager. The first club to be defined by punk was the Roxy, at 41–43 Neal Street in Covent Garden, where a dreadlocked DJ called Don Letts would deepen the new scene's love of reggae – as yet, there were hardly any punk records to play. Letts was also a film-maker and documented those innocent days when punk fashions were genuinely home-made – safety-pins and bin-liners were hit upon as cheaper alternatives to Vivienne Westwood. Gawky teens flocked to the one room in London where they could feel at home, tumbling on top of one another in self-mutilating happiness.

Through 1976 and '77, punk spread outwards from London to the towns and hamlets. From Manchester to Londonderry it struck root and produced local variants. Boys and girls adopted the look as best they could – the first mail-order bondage trousers were beginning to appear – and some of them formed groups. Then there were existing bands, like the Jam in Woking or XTC in Swindon, who seized the moment to redefine themselves. These were among the great bands to come out of punk, because they were not just imitations of the Pistols. Too many others took punk to mean a template, instead of a licence to create your own ideas. Grim it was, in those times, to hear Northern boys singing in a cockney whine, as if Johnny Rotten's Finsbury Park pleading was the only choice allowable.

Punk, like music hall before it, had a healthy national presence but has always borne a stamp of the capital. As XTC's Andy Partridge recalls, 'To our managers at the time, our not coming from London filled them with horror. They knew that I could hide my Swindon accent better than the others, so they said, "Right, you do the interviews." We were told not to say we were from Swindon. But I actually liked coming from a non-place. It kept us out of the rabble.' From Birmingham a boy called Kevin Rowland, not yet a Dexys Midnight Runner, spoke glumly of his band the Killjoys: 'London is the centre of punk. Birmingham people just do what London tells them to do.'

By accent alone the punks aligned themselves with London, and cockney London at that. Recently Poly Styrene, the singer in the charmingly odd punk band X-Ray Spex, confessed: 'I put on my London accent more. My mother was always telling me to say my "h"s and "t"s and you kind of rebel against that.' The public schoolboy Joe Strummer took up where Mick Jagger left off, inserting his glottal stops as carefully as a 1950s debutante would have done the opposite.

By 1978 the London punk bands were all signed to record companies and only mingling, if at all, in the hospitality rooms of TV studios. For a while it was necessary to pretend you were a punk band despite all evidence to the contrary. Hugh Cornwell, from North London, got his group the Stranglers on board in the nick of time: 'There was the Jam, the Police, Blondie, none of them were really punk bands but nobody was complaining, it was just a case of go with the flow. Elvis Costello wasn't a punk. But none of us were going to go, "Oh sorry, we shouldn't be here cos we're not really punks." It was "Yeah, get us on here!" It was an audience, a way to get noticed, to get a record contract. It was another step up the ladder and everyone used the tag for their own ends.' The Stranglers built a following away from London, where the in-crowd were more suspicious. But their protectors were a group of fans called the Finchley Boys; another loyalist in those fractious times was Dagenham Dave – a devotee whose private unhappiness led him to suicide off Tower Bridge.

They might have had their slightly artificial aspects, but acts like Poly Styrene and the Stranglers had much to offer and, had punk not given them a route to fame, we'd be the poorer for it. Whatever one thinks of punk rock's musical legacy – of its best bands, the Pistols recorded very little, and few of the Clash's CDs recapture their fierce glamour – it was a time of real opportunity. We've already spoken of Ian Dury. There were others who might never have escaped obscurity had punk not momentarily scrambled the rules. To take a few examples . . .

'My Heart's in the City': Paul Weller and the Jam

Paul Weller grew up in post-war Woking, a Surrey town then losing its rural self-containment thanks to the influx of displaced Londoners. (Weller's own mother and father were from Chingford and Lewisham respectively.) Twenty-six miles and half-an-hour from Waterloo, the place that raised Weller was a mixture of locals and the cockney diaspora, and this boy's loyalties were to the city. 'London was where it was really happening. London was a special day out, you'd only go a couple of times a year, which made it even more magical.'

He hungered for London. He tuned in to the Kinks and the Small Faces, and made Sunday pilgrimages to the 'suedehead' stalls of Petticoat Lane, where the clothes were a dandified variant on the skinheads. With the patience of an antiquarian he learned about the early Who and the first mods and has never lost his love for that secretive tribe. He talked in his teens of going up to London with a tape recorder, just to capture the raw sounds of the metropolis. How many actual Londoners would dream of such a thing?

In the early 1970s the weekly music papers were London's bulletin to the provinces:

When I was a kid the *NME* was the Bible. In Woking you got it on a Thursday and I'd rush out and read it cover to cover, even the articles about bands I didn't like. I'd read the whole fucking thing, scan the charts so I knew what was in the Top 20. And classic photos, I'd cut them out, Pennie Smith's pictures. A Nick Kent article about Syd Barrett. David Bowie was on the front cover. I've still got them.

The first band I ever saw was Status Quo, at the Guildford Civic, and I thought they were amazing. We were sat up in the furthest back row but I'd never heard music that loud before. And then the Feelgoods. Fucking brilliant, man. Wilko. Amazing. When you're young you need some signs, like Wilko, to tell you it's definitely the right track. I went to see the Feelgoods at the Guildford Civic and the first number goes 1-2-3-4 and Wilko did this fucking jump up in the air, did the splits.

When Weller's band the Jam began to get gigs in town, it was real progress. They would play the Fulham Greyhound or Upstairs at Ronnie Scott's, or outdoors at the Rock On stall in a temporary clearing by Chinatown. Their reverence for British pop history – evidenced by pop art Union Jacks and sharp dark suits – sat awkwardly with punk's pretend-iconoclasm, but their energy and youth were undeniable.

Later on I came up to see the Pistols at the 100 Club, that two-day festival with the Clash, and then the Lyceum all-nighter. That was it for me: 'I've got to be part of this.' It was happening, after a hick town like Woking. People have a chance to be themselves in London. In Woking if you had the wrong cut of trousers you'd get your head kicked in . . . I liked the attitude of punk but I also thought a lot of it was fake. We all saved up about twenty quid to go to McLaren's shop – was it called Sex at the time? – and we went in to buy some mohair jumpers and found we couldn't afford anything. We thought, 'This is bullshit.'

We were never accepted because we were always a little outside of the whole punk circle which was quite elitist, cliquey and art school. They were mostly middle-class kids with rich parents and they'd run away to join the circus. We weren't hip at all. We came from Woking, for a start. We saw things differently. I couldn't understand that trendy side of it all, that college crowd.

Weller wrote many London songs and most show this ambivalence. He is the outsider looking in, half in love and half excluded. From the Jam's earliest sessions, 'In the City' finds him bursting with the sheer possibilities of it all, with 'a thousand things' he is desperate to express, but also, in 'Sounds from the Street', sensing a barrier to be crossed: he is a Woking boy and knows the insiders find him suspect. But his heart, he insists, is in the city. For their second LP the group were photographed under the Westway (by Gered Mankowitz, who'd done similar service for the Rolling Stones on Primrose Hill). Weller's 'London Girl' was an echo of Bowie's 'London Boys' ten years before – the teenage escapee, acquiring her city survival skills. The Jam's bassist Bruce Foxton seemed less fascinated by the whole parade, grumbling of 'London Traffic' or grimly noting that 'Carnaby Street' was not the place it was.

The city of Weller's songs mirrored the tension of his music. 'Down in the Tube Station at Midnight' and 'A-Bomb in Wardour Street' are bruised and bloodied, puddled in beer, the latter set in a Soho venue called the Vortex. Even the daylight brings scant relief. In 'Strange Town' he is once again the defeated out-of-towner, tramping Oxford Street with his guidebook, rebuffed by Londoners' busy indifference. In real life, Weller was deeply disillusioned by some aspects of London, the place he had pined for all his life. The dilution of punk rock offended his sense of mod purity, especially when he saw the Roxy club overrun by what he called 'all those ageing, middle-class wankers in their £30 bondage trousers'.

It was natural that Weller would find his way to Colin MacInnes's *Absolute Beginners* and the book inspired a 1981 single of that name. A restless self-improver, he was always looking to widen his terms of reference. Investigations into mod had taken him back, past the 1960s to the roots of Soho modernism, whether in cool US jazz or chic Euro fashions. The outcome for a while was Weller's post-Jam band the Style Council, whose taste for Gauloise cigarettes and cappuccinos coincided with the 1980s renaissance of Soho's café society. Meanwhile he was consolidating his roots in the city – he took a lease on that historic Phillips Studio, in Stanhope Place, where Dusty Springfield and the Walker Brothers had once created splendour.

There followed some years of artistic dislocation for Weller, though he felt reinvigorated by London's acid-jazz scene of 1988. His ultimate salvation came as a solo artist in the 1990s – no longer a total city boy, but a writer exploring his own semi-rusticated Surrey childhood, and wider folk-rock influences like Traffic and Nick Drake. 'It's funny to look at those places,' he says of his childhood. 'Everywhere looks tiny and run down. It's all the reasons I wanted to get the fuck out of there. I've still got family there but my main link with Woking is the area where I used to play as a kid, the woods around there, the rural side. The actual town's a dump, like most satellite towns. They've got a big shopping mall but no one's got any bread and the shops are empty . . .'

Elvis Costello: London's Brilliant Parade

Another awkward customer whose talent might have gone unrecognised were it not for punk was Elvis Costello. The former Declan MacManus was born to Merseyside-Irish parents and spent his earliest years in Olympia, the rather uncertain district of Kensington that is bisected by arterial roads and lies in the impersonal shadows of vast exhibition halls. The family then moved to the south-western suburbs, before the boy was taken by his mother to complete his schooling in Liverpool. It was here that he began his performing life, around the folk clubs of a town still drowsy with its post-Beatle hangover. But his life in music had really begun much earlier. Declan's father, Ross MacManus, was for many years the singer in Joe Loss's hugely popular orchestra. Among other things, they had a residency at the Hammersmith Palais, where MacManus Junior could watch in privileged proximity.

He was back in London by the age of nineteen and soon trading on the pub rock circuit, in hallowed halls like the Hope & Anchor in Islington and the Half Moon in Putney. Like the majority of pub-rockers he was vaguely drawn to US country-rock, but he was nurturing a voice of his own, with a hard urban edge that owed nothing to hippies in cowboy boots. He had already connected with Nick Lowe of Brinsley Schwarz, who was helping two other pub rock stalwarts, Dave Robinson and Jake Riviera, to set up Stiff Records. And it was here, reborn as Elvis Costello, that the bespectacled singer-songwriter was launched upon the world. Given that the year was 1977, and Costello's spit-and-vinegar style was a world away from the mellower singer-songwriters of the time, it wasn't too much of a stretch to lump him in with punk. But even a casual inspection showed he was something else.

His background being what it was, the London-born Costello is sometimes called a Liverpool artist. In conversation his accent tends to slide between the two great ports. Football is always a key indicator – I've been to West London with him to watch Chelsea playing Liverpool and there is not the slightest doubt of his red allegiance. All the same, I would call him a great *London* writer. He himself is agnostic on the matter, wryly joking that each side claims him when he's in favour and disowns him when he's not. From the early days of his recording career, '(I Don't Want to Go to) Chelsea' is sardonic and bristling – all 'capital punishment' and scorn for the stale memory of London's Swinging Sixties. There are the sneers at washed-up groovers and the 'miniskirt waddle', while the artwork of his album, *Last Year's Model*, parodies David Hemmings's pose for *Blowup*. This, in 1978, was a necessary gesture, a clearing of the generational decks.

An exquisite little song, 'New Amsterdam', refers to both of his home cities, but declares that he's basically an exile. (The Irish element in his background has further blurred Costello's sense of national identity.) Rather more tender, but equally perfect, is 'Hoover Factory' – his unlikely homage to a vacuum cleaner HQ in Perivale. Five miles from the city, along Western Avenue, the factory is indeed an art deco delight, one of several built in the 1930s along a route that starts life as the Clash's fabled Westway. When it was clear that 'punk' could not define a protean act like Elvis, he was usually called 'new wave' – the somewhat looser category that also took in Squeeze, Dury and others of relative sophistication. Even that was soon found insufficient, however: his capacious tastes and abilities have moved on to encompass jazz, country and especially classical. Essentially, Costello is a whole city of his own.

But his best tribute to the capital, perhaps, is 'London's Brilliant Parade'. From the 1994 CD *Brutal Youth*, whose artwork shows young Declan with his boyhood friends on the backstreets of Olympia, it is a beautiful piece of work. There are filmic glimpses of sports cars and Routemaster buses, of Fulham Broadway and the Hammersmith Palais, the tigers of Regent's Park and the girders of Hungerford railway bridge. So it's the picturesque backdrop to London's eternal street theatre, of course, but it's also a song of *internal* life. In this parade, we are both public and private actors. We watch it by day and dream of it by night.

Cockneys, Rockneys, Anarcho-Vegetarians

Dury, Weller and Costello were among the idiosyncratic talents that punk had opened a space for. But it didn't stop there. For all its negative rhetoric, punk inspired a certain strand of idealism that often resembled the hippies it supposedly despised. Above all, it prompted some debate about the real nature of anarchy . . .

Beautiful Epping Forest is the relic of royal hunting lands. Here, Henry VIII rode to hear the cannons fired from the Tower of London, signalling that Anne Boleyn had been beheaded. Here as well began the journey of Barnaby Rudge, Dickens's sweet simpleton, to the urban conflagration of the Gordon Riots. In the 1920s H. V. Morton wrote of meeting a cockney factory hand, a veteran of the First World War. When asked what image of England he thought he had been fighting for, the man said it was not his own London street, but Epping Forest – the rustic refuge where he had spent his Bank Holidays.

Oak, birch, beech and hornbeam: in Epping's arboreal darkness, highwaymen once abounded. It has a history of lawlessness but also of liberty. The forest survived at all because of a nineteenth-century villager, Thomas Willingale, who fought for the ancient right, granted by Henry and Anne's child Elizabeth I, to gather firewood from its branches.

It was still a strange place, though, to find the nerve centre of punk anarchism. In the 1980s I would travel out to the eastern end of the Central Line (and how odd to see a London Underground sign surrounded by farmland) to visit a rambling cottage by Epping and Ongar. I spent long hours enjoying the hospitality of its residents, a loose collective who went by the name of Crass. Their musical arm was a fiercely noisy but pacifist punk band. Although they shunned all media exposure, were never on the covers of magazines or Radio 1 or *Top of the Pops*, Crass were massively popular from 1980 to 1985. Their name and logo were to be seen, alongside the anarchist symbol of an 'A' inside a circle, stencilled on leather jackets around the world.

Crass were the first punk band who really took anarchy seriously. To Johnny Rotten it was 'Knees Up Mother Brown'; to Malcolm McLaren it was a headline-grabbing conceptual prank. To everyone else it was kinda-like rock 'n' roll, right? But to Crass it was a creed, a philosophy to live by in the face of daunting odds. Their enemies, who were many, sneered that Crass were really hippies in disguise, which in punk times was a mortal insult. And it was partly true. The farmhouse had opened as a commune in the Summer of Love, 1967. A decade later its remaining original member, the (male) drummer Penny Rimbaud, met a young Clash fan named Steve Ignorant and

Crass were suddenly in business. Well, not in business, actually – their doggedly anti-commercial principles kept them outside the music industry. Tin Pan Alley was not their style at all.

The Crass community, whose line-up was never quite fixed, offered a sort of monastic peace to anyone who came in good faith. They aimed to be self-sufficient, baking bread and growing cabbages. They drank astonishing quantities of tea and smoked endless roll-ups. But they had a most un-hippy-like aversion to drugs – every year, the neighbourhood bobby would cycle around, sniff along the herb-rack, accept a cup of tea and wander off. There were cats and dogs and caged birds everywhere; and here, near the outlaw sanctuary of Epping Forest, Crass plotted the downfall of society. They were in a tradition of London radicalism that goes back a thousand years.

Their records were nasty, brutal and short, with titles like 'Nagasaki Nightmare', 'I Ain't Thick' and 'Banned from the Roxy'. But then, as Rimbaud liked to say, 'The nature of your oppression is the aesthetic of my anarchy.' It was not an easy life, promoting your anarcho-vegetarian ideas to rural halls of right-wing skinheads, or to media salons of tittering sophisticates. Crass persevered, buoyed up by huge record sales, but they were not in it for the money. In time the band expired, while Rimbaud and a female singer, Eve Libertine, explored other dimensions of their world-view with a tenderly disjointed record called 'Acts of Love'. It was Penny who introduced me to the work of Thomas Tallis. Pleasingly, he and his friends, and the farmhouse, all survived to fight another day.

From another remote outpost – Hersham in Surrey – came a rousing punk populist called Jimmy Pursey. With his band Sham 69 he made a Weller-like play on his outsider status. The heroes of his 'Hersham Boys' (alias the 'cockney cowboys') all speak 'country slang with a Bow Bell voice'. In fact Sham became more London than the London bands themselves, working up a style of music hall singalong – 'Hurry Up Harry ("We're going down the pub")' – that appealed to punks and boot-boys alike. The latter were a problem, however, especially the skinheads who had fallen under neo-Nazi influence. The hapless Pursey was a born entertainer who loved to fill a room with his heartfelt anthems, like 'The Cockney Kids Are United', but the demons he unleashed were impossible to control.

He tried his best. In February 1978 Sham 69 played a Rock Against Racism show with the Southall reggae band Misty In Roots. It seemed to work: 'I said it was the last time I'd play London if there was any trouble,' said Pursey. 'A lot hung on me, you know. We was the ones who was sacrificing ourselves by making that statement and we proved a point.' But a few months later I watched a chaotic gig at Middlesex Polytechnic, where the goon squad stormed the stage and Sham's ambitions foundered. These were tough times. Another Southall band, the Ruts, blended punk with reggae touches and achieved a dynamic subtlety that Sham 69's stomping style could not. The Ruts singer, Malcolm Owen, was a passionate character with the charisma to bring these burning issues of race and prejudice to the very youths who needed to hear them. I went out to Hayes to see him and his mum, who nurtured him through his withdrawal from heroin, and all appeared to be progressing. She would come in, beaming, bearing a tray of tea and biscuits. But a few weeks later she discovered him dead, the victim of a relapse and an overdose.

Punk proper had been a very West London show – Chelsea, Shepherd's Bush and Paddington account for most of its first wave. In the shadow of Sham 69, though, an East London variant arose. The Cockney Rejects were West Ham supporters with none of those King's Road affectations. For their musical template they took the steam-rollering guitar chords of the Pistols and the amphetamine rush of the Clash, with a boisterous overlay of football terrace hollering. One of their most characteristic titles, 'Oi Oi Oi', would give its name to a whole sub-genre of skinhead-punk.

Oi!, as the style was known, flourished for a couple of years in the early 1980s, though its unlovely roughness was never destined for mainstream acceptance. At its jolliest there was a raucous, *Carry On* vulgarity in there – but also an undercurrent of violence. Oi! never quite lost the stigma of its hijacking by far-right opportunists, looking to match the left's success in the anti-racist and anti-nuclear movements. All the same, on a cold night down at the Bridge House in Canning Town, Oi! was a hearty thrash-along successor to the cockney coster music that had now passed into history. Its own future, in fact, was in the hard-core punk styles that followed, in Europe and America, favoured by those who found the Clash's later records, and post-punk in general, too arty and self-conscious.

According to a sleeve-note by the Oi! movement's journalistic champion Garry Bushell, they were against bedsit radicals, Crass, the Tory Press, Russian tanks, Thatcher's dole queues and 'the "trendy" socialism of Gay Vegetarians against Whatever's Going'. What it favoured, wrote the Oi! poet Gary Johnson, was 'fighting back and having pride in your background . . . pie and mash, pints of lager, the spirit of the Blitz . . . having a laugh and having a say.'

So far as Britain was concerned, however, the real face of cockney music was not Oi! but Chas & Dave. A couple of seasoned session players, Chas Hodges and Dave Peacock developed a good-time piano act, with a touch of blues rock, that was naturally called 'Rockney'. In 1979 they upheld the link between London music and strong drink when their song 'Gertcha' was used in a national beer campaign. (Champagne Charlie would have approved.) They once recorded a live LP at Abbey Road by turning Studio 1 into a pub and inviting their friends along. Among their numbers was 'Ponders End Allotments Club' and 'Rabbit' (short for 'rabbit and pork', rhyming slang for 'talk'). The DJ Danny Baker suggests their lyrics are to London what Chuck Berry's were to America. In 1995 they released a record to commemorate the fifty years since VE Day, just as Vera Lynn was singing outside Buckingham Palace. Among their twenty-first-century fans were the Libertines, whom Chas & Dave have supported at the Brixton Academy.

Meanwhile, on the streets of London, some traditions survived. Buskers defied the weather and police, the indifference of cinema queues and the unwelcome attentions of shady men who offered to 'protect' their pitch for fifty pence. Among the mundane strummers attacking Simon and Garfunkel and, indeed, 'The Streets of London', were well-bred classical music students, supplementing their grants. Better yet, though, were stalwarts of the old school. There were, for example, Johnny Magoo OMB ('one man band') and his three ukuleles; Don Crown, his guitar and 'promiscuous budgerigars'; not omitting Ronnie Ross the Egyptian Sand Dancer, or the Earl of Mustard with his death-defying leaps over matchboxes. The itinerant performer's lot was still a difficult one. Too often their next engagement was Bow Street Magistrates, nursing their artistic dignity in the morning's procession of drunks, pickpockets and pimps.

By 1980, the time of the guttersnipes drew to a close. Oi! had been a last spasm of protest, but popular music was putting on its glad rags once again. Londoners will not dress down for very long. From the ranks of the punks came Adam & the Ants, Adam being a former protégé of Malcolm McLaren who reinvented himself as a 'dandy highwayman'. Partly at Malcolm's bidding he contrived a mixture of Johnny Kidd & the Pirates and American Indian, done with a street panache that London youths are often very good at. McLaren and Vivienne Westwood never stopped innovating and the King's Road shop – now called Seditionaries and later World's End – pursued a line of urban fantasy which might run to Napoleonic hats, ruffles and roller skates. Malcolm found a new outlet for his musical ideas in Bow Wow Wow, a band comprising Adam's former Ants and a young teenager named Annabella Lwin, whom he had spotted in a Kilburn dry cleaner's.

Adam Ant, a former Hornsey art student named Stuart Goddard, was already known for his role in Derek Jarman's 1977 film *Jubilee*. The setting of this strange and bleak work was a dystopian future London, time-warped to its Elizabethan past, where Toyah Wilcox and the Slits portray a feral gang of punk girls, accompanied by the Lindsay Kemp Company and Little Nell of the *Rocky Horror Show*. It was hardly escapist entertainment, but nor was it gritty realism. It pointed, somehow, to a changing mood in London after punk. A sort of twisted romanticism was in the air. The next thing you knew, there was David Bowie again, dressed as a post-nuclear Pierrot. His young disciples took careful note – with quite the strangest results.

Chapter Ten

Every Day is Like Friday

Nutty boys, New Romantics and Britpop.

The cockney inherits a cultural tradition, a certain ready-made identity. In rock mythology he has 'street credibility'. But the children of further-flung districts begin with a blank slate. Satellite towns lack the rebel authenticity of city life. And the suburbs are routinely denounced, especially by their own children. As the crucible of conformity, their influence must be defied. To escape from their embrace is to claim victory over deadened sensibilities.

From London's distant fringes came unearthly apparitions like David Bowie and (from Pinner) Elton John. Later there were George Michael, Siouxsie Sioux, Boy George, Kate Bush and Gary Numan. They all represented extraordinary acts of personal reinvention. That seems to be what suburban pop is all about. From further afield came Paul Weller, Jimmy Pursey, Brett Anderson and Damon Albarn. Each took pains to link himself to London, perhaps because they had all grown up in its gravitational pull, but could not take their membership for granted. So the geographical story broadens out. Two of the biggest acts after punk, the Cure from Crawley and Depeche Mode of Basildon, translated their very quality of isolation into something globally understood. If their style was broadly Thames Estuary, it was not especially of London.

The music of Kate Bush, for instance, dramatically transcends her London suburban background. She was from Welling, which is just inside the standard London A–Z but feels more remote, especially as it is not on the Underground system. Her childhood home in Wickham Street was surrounded by English poetry – Blake, Milton, Shelley and Wordsworth were just a few of the neighbouring roads, as was Chaucer: indeed that corner of the London sprawl still evokes the route of the Canterbury pilgrimage. Gathered to the bosom of EMI and the music industry in her teens, she built her career in central London. But the city never really entered her soul. Others from the area, like Bowie, looked towards the Smoke for their inspiration. But Kate looked the other way – to Kent, to the country, to a wider idea of England. She became, to my mind, one of the finest songwriters of the age. But London cannot claim her.

So, before we roam too far from Charles I's statue at Charing Cross – that traditional marker of distances from London Town – let's begin with acts like Squeeze, Madness and Spandau Ballet. They are Londoners first, last and always.

Sunlight on the Lino: Squeeze and South London

The original *Up the Junction* was a 1963 collection of stories by Nell Dunn, a Chelsea girl who crossed to Battersea and wrote of its white working-class life. (Her book was famously adapted for TV by the director Ken Loach.) Dunn writes with a quiet economy of this now-vanished world, whose inhabitants have since abandoned their terraced homes to bourgeois gentrifiers. These were the last years before the Beatles and pop culture would change Britain completely. The men's oily hair would soon be falling down across their foreheads, shampooed clean, and their girls discovered the Pill.

But in *Up the Junction*, Battersea is still a place of council flats and proletarian parties: of ham sandwiches, brown ale and Babycham. The boys are mostly bikers – manual workers, grease monkeys – and not the smart little mods of Pete Townshend's vision. Dunn's tales are punctuated by snippets of hit parade doggerel: Joe Brown's 'A Picture of You' is on the wireless in the corner. There is the leering banter of ton-up boys in transport caffs, where blank-eyed factory girls plan back-street abortions. It was all a dispatch from another planet, so far as Dunn's sophisticated friends across the River were concerned.

'Transpontine' was the dismissive word that George Melly's band used for a colleague from over the bridges – 'not one of us', somehow. The great barrier of water cuts this half of the city adrift. In former times the south was used to dump London's prisons and asylums, its smelliest manufactures and its power stations, as well as those endless clerical dormitories. It is above all a workaday place, beyond the pale of fashion.

And yet, as we've seen, the South Bank has harboured Shakespearean theatres, music hall impresarios and modern concrete culture bunkers. In Tudor times, whether your tastes ran to brothels or bear-baiting, there was something here for you, and then there came the mighty pleasure gardens of Vauxhall. Maybe the old ways resurfaced in the late 1980s, at Danny Rampling's cradle of rave in Shoom, by Southwark Bridge. Or, a little later, at the Ministry of Sound in Elephant and Castle. Either way, Lambeth resident William Blake was not the last to enjoy ecstatic visions from the 'wrong' side of the Thames.

It's somehow apt that Status Quo are a South London band. They were always on the outside, no matter how massively popular. Like South London they are never quite *à la mode*, but they are bracingly straightforward. They began in Beckenham in the early 1960s and were called Traffic Jam. It speaks for their innocence that they nearly called themselves the Queers – how different the culture of British heavy metal might have been. In the end, they settled on Status Quo and were marched up to Carnaby Street for the frilly and colourful clothes of the hour. They wrote for a while in a dreamy, psychedelic style, before perfecting the reliable boogie stomp that has served them ever since.

In 1970 they were playing at the legendary Castle pub, Tooting's former teddy boy fortress. Here the Quo evolved a grimy kind of look that reflected their audience. The singer Francis Rossi realised that if he shaved at bedtime, he would have a prized dusting of stubble by the next evening. From the hairy Tooting crowd, who liked to sit cross-legged and nod vigorously, the band took its trademark heads-down stance; and, with legs well apart, they were democratically closer to floor-level. South Londoners do not get above themselves.

Equally unpretentious, and even more successful, were Quo's fellow journeymen Dire Straits. They formed in Deptford and wrote their breakthrough hit, 'Sultans of Swing', about a lowly jazz band ('way on down south'), not in New Orleans but Greenwich High Street. The song is a model of South London's dogged unconcern with hipness. The Dixieland musicians play for love in the teeth of indifference; punters drift in out of the rain. From down the road, a little later, came the Alabama 3 – authors of that rasping, addictive theme to *The Sopranos*. Again we hear a mix of grit and scepticism, the sound of squat and bedsit, a sense of separation from the febrile glamour of life across the River.

The great Transpontine Troubadours, though, were Squeeze, led by their core song-writing partnership of Chris Difford and Glenn Tilbrook. The former was a Small Faces fanatic from a Blackheath council estate, whose early work varied from solicitor's clerk to something involving oil drums at Charlton docks. Tilbrook came from a similar Blackheath background but with more bohemian connections. They met through an advert Difford had placed, stating 'Recording contract, imminent tour' (both claims fictitious), 'influences Kinks, Lou Reed, Glenn Miller'. Their rendezvous was Blackheath's Three Tuns pub, where it was arranged that Difford would carry an *Evening Standard*. That he also wore a multicoloured Lurex coat was not mentioned. ('That still makes me laugh,' says Tilbrook, laughing.)

Tilbrook had a pianist friend named Julian 'Jools' Holland, with whom he had gained experience by playing in pubs. 'Which,' says Holland, 'confirmed that it was a good idea. Music was interesting and enjoyable to do. Girls wanted to be our friends, we got free drinks, there was a party everywhere we went and we didn't have to get up early in the morning.' As Squeeze, the new group played venues like the Bricklayers Arms in Greenwich and the Oxford

Arms in Deptford. Through Glenn's friendship with Peter Perrett of the Only Ones, they signed to a bright, energetic American manager called Miles Copeland. (Even South London boys could find vital contacts just up the road. Provincial groups were stuck with, say, the manager of a local carpet store, the owner of a telephone and van.)

Copeland, who also managed his brother's band the Police, was impressed by Squeeze but saw their somewhat homely image as being at odds with London's new sensation: punk rock. As Copeland recalls, the punk insider Tony James of Generation X was scathing: '"How can you be dealing with Squeeze? They're irrelevant! They're singing *love songs!*" And he spat the words out with venom. And I said, "Well, you know what, I see a lot of punks with girlfriends. Punks love too, buddy. And love ain't goin' away, no matter how big the punk thing gets."'

Still, these boys could use an overhaul. It was 1977 now, and flare-wearing pub bands were furtively queuing for the alteration tailors of Berwick Street. Chris Difford remembers, 'Miles did give us some spending money to go and buy some clothes. We went down Oxford Street and bought red and blue pairs of suede shoes and we swapped the left and right together, so we had one red shoe and one blue shoe each. Then we bought some cheesecloth shirts in an Indian shop. Miles hit the roof.'

The first Squeeze records were a little too cheeky-chappie to be hip. But the partners were finding their path as vernacular songwriters, while mingling with some of South London's 'dodgy geezers' in pubs after closing time. Tilbrook emerged as the band's star vocalist and supreme melodicist, but Difford's ear for a local lyric had all the London flair of Ian Dury. By their second album, *Cool for Cats*, the local argot was everywhere, from 'Slap and Tickle' to 'It's Not Cricket'. The title track involved the Sweeney, Wandsworth nick and 'villains in a shed up at Heathrow'. Chris Difford looks back:

We were local heroes. The pubs stayed open for us, we were swanning around from pub to pub making the most of it. Outside of Deptford and Greenwich, though, I don't know what it really meant. We were big in the baker's shop . . . I used to go out and test-drive cars that I knew I couldn't afford. I remember going up to Bristol Motors in Kennington and the guy who owned it personally took me out in his car. We were going along the Westway, fucking enormous leather seats, we're driving along and I asked him, 'How much is this, then?' He said, '£120,000.' Gulp! Er, I'll be back next week for this one . . .

With success there came a wedge between the group and their old manor. Tilbrook felt a little awkward in the Prince of Wales in Blackheath when he was on TV. Yet they were not exactly proper pop stars either, as Jools Holland recalls:

We never managed to be in the right place at the right time . . . We used to tour America a great deal. But it was always when we were having hits in Britain. We could never be there to get into clubs and be photographed with Bunny Girls, or drive sports cars down to the coast at five o'clock in the morning.

Story songs, and observational pieces, were the Squeeze speciality – all in a classic London manner. Their material was more exterior than interior, and delight was in the details. The emotional churn of 'Tempted', for example, is anchored by the line that puts the narrator by the church and its steeple, coming up to a 'laundry on the hill'; 'Goodbye Girl' has 'sunlight on the lino'. 'Pulling Mussels from a Shell' was Difford's memoir of childhood trips to the seaside, filtered through the Small Faces. 'Piccadilly' on their Elvis Costello-produced third album was a West End romance and 'Sunday Street' the low-key tale of a capital Sabbath. 'Gone to the Dogs' describes a night at Walthamstow, amid the tic-tac men, the greyhound owners in overcoats and trilby hats.

Like most of the music in this book the songs of Squeeze are inspired by London, but in Chris Difford's case it's often a single square-inch of the *A–Z*. 'King George Street' is a domestic drama in SE10; 'Cigarette of a Single Man' was born in the Rose & Crown in

Croom's Hill; 'Elephant Girl' concerns inter-racial love in Charlton. 'F-Hole' was set in Thames Street, by the Cutty Sark while, amazingly, even the song called 'Peyton Place' relates to an actual street in Greenwich. But we must travel west to Battersea and Clapham for 'Up the Junction', whose radiant riff and tuneful tale of ordinary urban lives will always make it the best-loved of their songs. It was written on a US tour with a Dylanesque narrative in mind, culturally transplanted. And it has two remarkable pub-quiz qualities – firstly it is a hit without a chorus, and secondly (in common with Roxy Music's 'Virginia Plain') its title does not appear until the very last line.

The group have split, re-formed and split again. One of their incarnations coincided with Britpop, when Blur and Elastica were among the bands to acknowledge their influence. Meanwhile their old pianist Jools Holland would make his name as a TV presenter. His showmanship was already evident from a penchant for fulsome stage announcements. Now he commanded the nation's attention through *The Tube* and his own show *Later ... With Jools Holland*. An offshoot of the latter, his annual New Year's *Hootenanny*, became a TV institution. As a master of ceremonies he is unrivalled. It is perfectly possible to imagine him in charge of a music hall – 'And now! Ladies and gentleman! For your delectation and delight!' – with gavel in hand, heaping grandiloquent praise and urging the crowd to new heights of enthusiasm and liquid consumption. Music hall is truly the core of English pop, and in Jools Holland we find its twenty-first-century chairman.

Madness: Welcome to the House of Fun

In the early days of the motor car an observer of London saw something new. Londoners, he said, had learned to swivel their heads left and right before stepping off the pavement. Often to their cost, visitors from the country did not. Probably, the Londoners' habit was not entirely new, for the city streets were mayhem as far back as Roman times – the coming of the internal combustion engine merely raised the stakes. When you watch Suggs, of Madness, moving on a stage you seem to see the instinctive personal ballet of a Londoner, clocking the ever-changing scene, weighing the dangers, looking for an opening.

In their pop prime Madness had seven members. Their group photos and renowned videos displayed an uncanny gift for making collective shapes and moving in unison, like the well-oiled parts of a single machine. For a band so obviously rooted in North London their appeal was nationwide. From beginnings in slapstick reggae they moved to cheery pop and bittersweet ballads, and became enduring entertainers with the common touch. It's interesting that 'North London' is sometimes used as a shorthand for the liberal bourgeoisie – a long-running *Private Eye* cartoon, It's Grim Up North London, mocks a clique of self-obsessed trendies – but of course the city patchwork can never be so simple. Madness are pure North London, but not of the so-called chattering classes. It makes more sense to think of them as counterparts to the Southside's Squeeze. But they're not exactly that, either. Madness stand for a working-class manor that's as universal as *The Beano*'s Bash Street.

They were formed from a loose confederation of friends who mostly lived between Camden and Kentish Town. Early gigs were often in the former: 'There were no women about,' Suggs recalled for *The Word*. 'It was just hordes of Irishmen pouring out of pubs and taking wild swings at fresh air. The bonding in the band took place in Hampstead because that's where the girls and the parties were.' Several members, including the keyboard-player Mike Barson, were enormous fans of Ian Dury's Kilburn & the High Roads: 'They were all characters,' he said, 'all individuals. If you watched just one of them all night, it would be a complete show.' The Kilburns' influence on the Madness stage act is clear. But the key to Madness's breakthrough came with 2-Tone, the ska-punk fusion led by Midlands band the Specials. The brittle reggae rhythm of ska was important to the Madness mix, and several of the band had personal memories of the skinhead era, ten years previously, to which such music had been the soundtrack. Its attendant fashions, especially the

West Indian-inspired pork-pie hats, the mod-derived suits and Crombie overcoats, were likewise incorporated, giving a unified look to an otherwise motley bunch. They made their 1979 debut, 'The Prince', on the 2-Tone label before moving to Stiff Records.

More than any other act of that time Madness had the attitude of natural showmen, and were a 'people's band' in ways their more political peers could never be. But at first their very authenticity could be a liability. Skinheads were enjoying a full-scale revival in the early years of Madness's career, and this time around the political boot-boy element was more organised. The group's ska connection and robust London following made for a combustible mix. Like Sham 69, Madness found it tough to be a street-level band when the London street felt entitled to a place on the stage.

In the end it was the band's irresistible hit singles and collective good humour that overcame all doubts. 'My Girl' with its catalogue of domestic tribulations ('My girl's mad at me') could be straight from the mouth of Gus Elen. 'Night Boat to Cairo' evokes the comedy sand-dancing turns like Wilson, Keppel and Betty. In 'House of Fun', 'Baggy Trousers' and a dozen others they were the cheeky scamps of a Saturday morning matinee. The music hall heritage was everywhere in their act, with Suggs's loud check suits and Barson's jangling pub piano helping to prod the tribal memory. And yet they proved as rounded as the life of their city. 'One Better Day' was a poignant vignette of Camden's Arlington House (the same hostel featured in the film *The London Nobody Knows*; it was also known to George Orwell in his *Down and Out* days). There was even a little number called 'In the City', no relation to the Jam's song of the same name, as frantic as traffic at Hyde Park Corner, done for a Honda car ad in Japan.

Early success can bring its own penalties to a young band, though. They must grow up in public, saddled by the image they first became known for. There was a touch of the teenage gang about Madness, as there is in nearly all groups, which starts to feel uncomfortable as the members approach their thirties. Restyled, for a while as 'The Madness', the group shrugged off their carefree 'nutty boy' act in favour of something a little heavier. It was not their finest hour, musically, and the group's survival looked in doubt. In 1992, however, a rather triumphant open-air show at Finsbury Park – the event dubbed 'Madstock' – restored morale. From that point on their appeal proved far wider than their North London powerbase, and Madness have steadily ascended to the status of national treasures. Even up in the grittier parts of Northern England, they are looked upon with affection – the cockneys you can take to your heart.

It was nearly inevitable, therefore, that there would one day be a Madness musical, reminding us that London music is only inches away from theatre. Set in Camden, with the wide-boy scion of a close-knit Irish family for its subject, *Our House* was chirpy and a little bit rude, but fundamentally warm and even sentimental. In among the re-purposed Madness songs are playful nods to the London tradition. In its Camden Market sequence a troupe of coster cockneys do their dance and hawk their modern wares: 'Who will buy my Indian joss sticks?'

More impressively, in the band's thirtieth anniversary year of 2009 they had a new collection of songs, *The Liberty of Norton Folgate*. At a point in their lives when dutiful canters around the back catalogue were all that anyone expected, they produced something that was daringly fresh. Premiered in rousing music hall style at the Hackney Empire in 2008 ('All the gentlemen in the house say "Ugh!"'), the set takes its name from a road between Bishopsgate and Shoreditch that was in past times a hub of London lawlessness. (Though microscopically small it's still in the A–Z.) From its Overture ('We are London') to 'NW5' and 'Clerkenwell Polka' *The Liberty of Norton Folgate* presents a teeming, kaleidoscopic portrait of the city, past and present, travelling whole centuries at a leap. It might seem an ambitious idea for the cartoon 'Nutty Boys' of Camden Town. But the rich history of this city was in them all along.

Spandau Ballet: 'In a City Like This You Have to Stand Out'

Gary Kemp was born in Smithfield, at Bart's Hospital, not only in earshot of Bow Bells but on the site of London's medieval revels. The first music he remembers is a little less ancient: Billy Cotton singing 'I've Got a Lovely Bunch of Coconuts'. He grew up near the Essex Road in Islington, where the social divide becomes noticeable:

> On the one side was Canonbury, Barnesbury, where middle-class people owned their own homes. But on our side no one owned their own homes. Until I was fifteen we lived in a house with three other families on different floors. Then the council put us into a renovated house with a little garden and a bathroom. Before that my dad took us down to a local baths to wash, where you'd get in a cubicle and shout for more hot water.
>
> So there was definitely a sense in London in the sixties of a real class divide and it was difficult to make the leap across. It was only through pop music and film and photography, and the whole Swinging London thing that the working class began to make that leap. I grew up with that in mind. And being in a band was an aspirational attempt to break out. I went to a grammar school in Islington, so I got to see the middle-class kids and I went to their houses and saw they had books. It gave me a glimpse of something beyond, that I wanted.

Kemp, the future new romantic, was already absorbing an old London tradition – the way of the dandy apprentice. You might lack money or status, you might be an East End guttersnipe, but with the right clothes, and the right attitude, you were as good as any man in this town.

> In a city like this you have to stand out. I grew up with very strong images of mods. There was a pub next door and once a week the scooters would all arrive – I'd see these almost silent, gliding machines with beautifully coutured blokes and girls on them. My dad always wore a tie, working-class people in those days didn't wear jeans. We were poor but what we did take seriously was our toiletry, and I think punk got it wrong in the end, it was a middle-class view of the working class. Soul boys

were connected to the mods and before the mods it was the Edwardian coat, and after soul boys came the new romantics. It's that aspiration to rise above the situation you're in. I remember my dad getting clothes tailored down in the East End. He took me to this Jewish tailor in Brick Lane where I got these two-tone strides made for myself. And then *Budgie* came on in 1971 [Adam Faith's TV series], and he represented everything we wanted to be in London: he had his clothes made by Mr Freedom. I remember getting my fake Budgie jacket in Brick Lane and wearing it proudly.

From the daily street promenade it's not a big leap into London's other passion: acting. Kemp was lucky in that a woman named Anna Scher had set up her Children's Theatre in his neighbourhood. From the age of nine he was attending her lessons – ten pence a session – with his brother Martin.

It was all improvised work, acting out scenes from home or school life. My parents didn't know I was going until I was offered my first part in a film . . . So that gave me and my brother confidence. If you live in London you have to have confidence, because there are so many people to compete with. It's so easy to get swallowed up that an element of bravado is necessary.

But it was music that would make the Kemp brothers famous. Years before, their father had been a keen show-goer at Collins's Music Hall on Islington Green. (To earn a little money, he and his parents made sweets and toffee apples and bags of peanuts, to sell outside.) In 1976, just a few yards away from the old hall, Gary went to see the Sex Pistols and the Clash performing at the Screen on the Green:

It felt like familiar territory for me because the Bromley Contingent were all dressed up in Bowie-type clothes, and I recognised it. My seminal moment had been Bowie doing 'Starman' on *Top of the Pops*, which set my benchmark for how pop music should look. It had to be visual, something I couldn't see on my street. But within a few months we lost interest in punk, it burned out very quickly. I didn't go for the Clash, I liked Mick but I didn't believe in Strummer – for me, as a boy who *did* have a real cockney accent, he didn't convince me. What I wanted from music went back to that first vision of 'Starman', and the Clash never fulfilled that for me. So a lot of us moved back into clubs and dancing to imported soul music. You'd go to a little record shop in Hanway Street, just off Oxford Street, and buy your twelve-inch records.

The thing about dancing in a club was it was all about *you*. There was no audience watching a band, it wasn't about someone else. You were the star and we tried to promote that idea when we formed a band.

For the next few years Gary Kemp explored the West End clubs with his older friend Steve Dagger, an LSE student who had organised the Sex Pistols outing. In a Soho dive called Billy's downstairs in Meard Street, he met Steve Strange and Rusty Egan, who worked the door and the DJ decks respectively. Tuesdays at Billy's were given over to Bowie, with a side-order of Roxy Music, plus the emerging overlap of European electronica with black-inspired dance: Kraftwerk, Gina X, Telex. It's fair to say there was a great deal of dressing-up involved, as well:

I'd never seen anything more wonderfully exotic, it looked like *Cabaret*, a mixture of working-class flash, ex-soul boys and art students, a mixture of sexual preferences. Those movements have always been arty middle-class kids embracing arty working-class kids, and coming up with something edgy. Everyone was either wearing clothes they made themselves or they'd got from a dressing-up box in Oxfam.

In 1979 the Billy's crowd moved to Blitz, a wine bar at 4 Great Queen Street on the edge of Covent Garden. Here and in Soho venues like

St Moritz and Le Kilt, an underground cult was taking shape. Its extravagant dress codes, with a hint of Regency fop or Ruritanian corporal, were eventually called 'new romantic'. It was easier to wear such things in central London – as opposed to, say, Steve Strange's native South Wales – and, as Kemp recalls, they spent more time running away from Japanese film crews than from boot-boys. But violence was not unknown:

> There was a big fight one night in the Blitz. This other group had gone off at a tangent and created what they called 'the futurists' – they all came down to the Blitz to fight. It was the most bizarre sight. All these people came through the door with hair hanging over one eye, wearing sort of *Star Trek* costumes, then us lot, all manner of dressed-up characters and this big fight.

Rather like mod before the Who, all the scene lacked was a band to represent it. Enter Spandau Ballet, the new incarnation of Kemp's school group. Managed by Steve Dagger, they brought in Martin Kemp on bass because he attracted the girls. They avoided the grubbier end of the rock circuit, playing instead to invited audiences of Blitz friends, including a show at the Scala by Tottenham Court Road, where the Beatles had once appeared in *A Hard Day's Night*. Within their coterie were future fashion stars like John Galliano and the film-maker John Maybury, both at Central St Martins, and media interest was aroused.

From the start, Spandau Ballet considered themselves the band of a new Soho. Kemp recalls:

> I remember Soho changing at the time, it was coming out of the depressed seventies into the more affluent side of the eighties. When we started going to Billy's, Soho was a dark place of porn shops and strip joints. I remember the opening of the Soho Brasserie – it was the first place where I'd seen anyone drinking a bottle of beer with a piece of lemon sticking out. And tables outside! Punk had said, 'We're working-class.' But it also said,

'We don't care about making money.' And we knew the way to wind everyone up was to say, 'We *want* to sell millions of records.' It was almost subversive. It became something people talked about.

We had a pride in coming from an important place, we took confidence from that. We laughed at Paul Weller because he was a Woking boy and didn't have what we saw as the credibility . . . I think you have to cling to your raft in London. You start to become your own island. You have to really hold on to who you are to survive here.

I also like the ghosts, the fact there is a history and you have a responsibility to that history. If you are going to do something as a band in London you can really hear the other elements of music behind you, all calling out, 'You've got us to compete with, too.' You're fully aware of Ronnie Scott's and Tin Pan Alley and the Marquee Club.

Kemp's band hit big in the new decade, when pop was being revolutionised by video and glossy magazines displaced the weekly music papers. Spandau Ballet are best remembered for 'True', a chart-topper in 1983. But their perfect London moment came a little earlier, in a song called 'Chant No. 1' – a record propelled by the rhythms of London club culture. Cruising past the Talk of the Town (alias that Edwardian palace of varieties the Hippodrome), 'down Greek Street', Friday nights at the Beat Route – it's a terrific piece of work, one that shudders with all the hectic vibrancy of a Soho night. Kemp smiles at the memory: 'I could be on a box, selling the place, couldn't I?'

New Romantic London: Cocktail Hour Again

We first spot the young Boy George – still, at this point, George O'Dowd – pining outside the rambling home of his hero. Throughout his teens, he has written, his fantasy was to become David Bowie's friend and hang out with him at Haddon Hall in Beckenham. A schoolboy of Irish family living in nearby Eltham, George stood vigil outside the Bowies' residence – and was invited, he says, to 'fuck off' by the star's wife Angie. On other days he would play truant from school to get a bus in to the West End, where he could browse the boutique branches of Chelsea Girl.

Already a promising self-stylist, George perfected his look in the photo booths at Lewisham and Charing Cross stations. In the late seventies he met another flamboyant future pop star, called Marilyn, when both were extras on the set of Hazel O'Connor's rock-biz movie *Breaking Glass*. There are teenage dreamers in every town, but only in London are the worlds of media and show business so readily accessible. George worked in fashion shops around Carnaby Street and was pretty quickly noticed. I encountered him hanging around the *NME* office, making contacts, offering to fetch us sandwiches. He teamed up with Malcolm McLaren, who was experimenting with new line-ups for Bow Wow Wow. When George finally became famous, in a new band called Culture Club, it seemed somehow pre-destined.

He had a fine, light soul voice, and a series of hits put him at the forefront of the new romantics (the small clique of London clubbers was growing, assisted by cheap mail-order clothing, into a national youth tribe). He tripped from *Smash Hits* photo-shoots to *Top of the Pops* appearances, dressed in *Mikado*-like robes and rabbinical hats, decked in floral symbols and heavily made-up. London allowed the freedom he needed. Even before he became famous there was safety in West End clubs like Blitz, though his prettiness concealed a city-boy toughness. As time passed his porcelain delicacy gave way to the London-Irish heaviness of his genes, and though he made a successful second career as a club DJ, his life became a succession of unwelcome headlines. But he had the London instinct for theatre and his story became a stage musical, *Taboo*.

Bigger than Boy George, however, were Wham! They were George Michael, the son of a Greek Cypriot restaurateur, and his school-friend Andrew Ridgley. Though Michael spent his childhood in Finchley, the family moved in his teens to a prosperous corner of

Hertfordshire, where he teamed up with Ridgley and formed a group. And Wham!, in their own way, were absolutely the real thing. Their biggest rivals of the time – Culture Club, Duran Duran, and Frankie Goes To Hollywood – all had roots in rebel sub-cultures, whether gay or punk. But George Michael and Andrew Ridgeley were authentic children of the kingdom they came to rule. Their roots lay in the suburban disco boom of the late seventies, a world of glitterballs, Outer London soul boys and *Saturday Night Fever*. For all that we talk of punk rock as a mighty revolution, there were vast swathes of English life that punk rock left untouched. Here there lived a tribe of people who turned on *Top of the Pops* to discover Morrissey singing 'Hang the DJ' and hadn't the faintest idea what he was on about.

Wham! were quite unlike the Smiths or Joy Division or any of that ilk. They were suntanned and upbeat. If they were not exactly London, they were definitely Home Counties. The early 1980s were a time when Britain's Northern cities and urban ghettoes seemed locked in a long, resentful decline, but the south-east of England had actually never had it so good. Instead of dressing for winter all year round, like Lancashire indie bands, the Carnabetian Army now opted for a permanent summer of Ray-Ban shades and no socks. Their number 'Club Tropicana' (where membership was simply 'a smiling face!') was so attuned to a new cocktail culture that it for ever fixed Wham!'s image as spoiled sons of Thatcherism. (Cocktails were enjoying a new vogue, nearly on a par with the 1920s. In a club like the Embassy, in Mayfair, it seemed as if time were going backwards. Stories from the distant North, of hunger marches and miners' strikes, only added the perfect period touch.)

You hear the Wham! manifesto set out in their early singles. 'Young Guns (Go For It)' and 'Wham Rap!' exude a swaggering hedonism. Both are invigorating blasts of hard-edged pop-funk, pulling in the rap influence that had begun to reach the white mainstream. Neither was conceived as a work of social commentary but they caught the ideas of their day in a cute, perceptive manner. 'Wham Rap!' was praised for articulating Malcolm McLaren's new gospel – already advanced through Adam Ant and Bow Wow Wow – that youth could defy hard times by reinventing itself as something golden and fabulous. For their fans, George and Andrew made a world where Every Day Was Like Friday. In the giddy rush of hits they released between 1982 and '86 there was the trembling heartbeat of a teenage generation, sitting in bedrooms that were littered with chain-store make-up and new clothes. Wham!'s music was bought up in truck-loads by young girls, who comprise the infantry of pop.

Fashionable London was once more celebrating itself. Whatever the bad news from elsewhere, Soho and the recently prettified Covent Garden were of a mind to party. Julien Temple's 1986 movie of *Absolute Beginners* was set in dream-like Soho streets, peopled by the new style-setters. These included Patsy Kensit, a former child-actress and friend of Gary Kemp, who now had a band called Eighth Wonder, and the elegant Sade Adu, a St Martins' graduate with a glamorous line in soulful poise. Also in the film were elder statesmen David Bowie and Ray Davies, with their memories of the real Tin Pan Alley.

Like that of Boy George, Wham!'s rise coincided with the tabloids' colonisation of pop music. As Michael remarked, ruefully, his duo 'would be on the front page whenever Princess Di wasn't having her hair done'. If sceptics wondered what, exactly, Andrew Ridgley brought to the Wham! equation, their manager Simon Napier-Bell had no doubt – he was there to be the perfect teen dream that George could not and did not want to be. But the Finchley son of energetic immigrants was still ambitious for more. In the week they topped the charts with their final single, 'The Edge of Heaven', Wham! played a grand farewell performance at Wembley Stadium. It all went out in fine 1980s style. Elton John installed a swimming pool backstage for the beautiful people. There were boys from Spandau Ballet there, and Patsy Kensit, and afterwards they all went on to another party, at the Hippodrome. Ridgeley and Michael were both just twenty-three. This was Wham!'s crowning achievement. They didn't outstay their welcome and they never lost their exclamation mark.

There came a rash of new acts in that decade, typically London in their well-stocked contact books, and often with a weakness for high concept. Tony James, who had been big on the West London punk scene and Billy Idol's partner in Generation X, re-emerged with an achingly futuristic conceit named Sigue Sigue Sputnik, who aimed to fuse the dystopian dread of *A Clockwork Orange* with hi-tech visions of a neon-lit Piccadilly. James had studied his cultural history and the band were children of Larry Parnes and Malcolm McLaren – especially keen on beating the businessmen at their own game – with a touch of Dickensian street gang and Ziggy Stardust. But their music could never live up to the legend that Sigue Sigue Sputnik had created for themselves, not even with their abundant media connections. They were, unluckily, just a couple of years too early for the actual revolution-in-waiting, namely the Internet.

Big Audio Dynamite comprised the Clash's Mick Jones, the punk DJ Don Letts and Kensit's future husband Dan Donovan (himself the son of the sixties cockney photographer Terence Donovan). Haysi Fantayzee were a McLarenesque duo, whose Jeremy Healy became a clubland fixture (and, for a while, the beau of Patsy Kensit). Transvision Vamp were fronted by the former drama student Wendy James. The three girls of Bananarama, all familiar faces from punk times, led the revels in the WAG club, formerly the Whiskey-A-Go-Go, over the old Flamingo in Wardour Street.

From a different world came the West Ham-loving Iron Maiden, an East End heavy metal group whose popularity has been enduring. Heavy metal, in general, is more often associated with the old industrial heartlands of the North and Midlands, but it thrived in a pub annexe in Kingsbury, North London, where the DJ Neal Kay ran his Soundhouse club in defiance of hipper tastes. 'The reason I don't like the term heavy metal any more,' he told me at the time, 'is that people are trying to turn it into a fashion.'

> I will not have hard rock as a fashion. It's not a five-minute thing. It's a way of life ... This is not the sort of music where people come to shake their bums and pick up chicks. People into

rock are sincere music people. I used to work in clubs in the West End – the disco syndrome – and I just had to get out because it was destroying my head. I can't relate to people like that. I've starved for my beliefs, man. I've driven furniture vans and fuck knows what, rather than play things I didn't believe in.

George Michael, too, was grappling with questions of integrity. The new romantic age was over by the late 1980s, and his solo career led him far from Wham!'s happy simplicity. He was not the only idol of the era to find adult life a challenge: Marilyn and Steve Strange, Boy George and Adam Ant all encountered widely reported personal problems, while Michael's tribulations ranged from litigation with his record company to his involuntary 'outing' by the Los Angeles police in a public toilet. More than any of his contemporaries, though, he remained a commercial force. So confident, or stubborn, was he that albums followed with uncompromising titles like *Listen Without Prejudice Vol 1* and *Older*. 'Golden lads and girls all must,' as Shakespeare wrote, 'as chimney-sweepers, come to dust.' In a particularly wistful number, 'Waiting For That Day', Michael ends on a mantra borrowed from the Rolling Stones' elegy for an earlier London scene: 'You can't always get what you want . . .'

A13, Trunk Road to the Sea: Billy Bragg and Essex

Travel away from London, to the north, south or west, and its character starts to fade. But if you go east, to Essex, an imprint of London stays strong. There is a theory that the cockney accent was itself created in Essex – the kingdom of the East Saxons – and persisted down the centuries, even as the capital was absorbing elements from elsewhere. It's possible that the more educated classes of London adopted Wessex (or West Saxon) speech, back in the times when England was ruled from Winchester. Cockney survived as a street language, fast and gutteral, part of an oral culture and not a written one.

More recently Essex earned national notoriety as the spiritual home of 'white van man' – the aspirational working-class voter who abandoned Labour for Margaret Thatcher – and the *nouveau riche* City dealer. Each was a modern update on the old coster image. The *Spectator*, in 2008, described 'Marauding barrow boys' in the financial markets, 'who shouted and swore from 7 a.m. until 5 p.m., who only broke for football discussions, the odd read of the tabloids and lunch (pie and mash, fish and chips and pickled onions).' Their female counterpart, the Essex girl, was herself a stock figure of fun, supposedly silly and vulgar in her white stilettos and fake tan. These were stereotypes of the cockney diaspora – you could take an East Ender out of the slums, they seemed to say, but don't expect the results to be entirely civilised.

Musically, Essex went its own way. Just as pockets of R&B loyalists kept the flame alive in Canvey and Southend, so there thrived a soul music underground to rival the northern clubs of Wigan and Blackpool, themselves the last bastions of mod values. By the 1980s the latter taste was ridiculed as part of yet another Essex image – the jazz-funk soul boy in white socks and loafers, casual knitwear and gold jewellery, driving a car with furry dice, his Sharon or Tracey by his side. But the real picture was of course more mixed. This, after all, was the land of Ian Dury, of Crass and Viv Stanshall . . . and Billy Bragg.

My first trip to Essex was with Billy Bragg, and he was an excellent guide. 'The Big-Nosed Bard of Barking', as one of his early self-descriptions put it, Bragg built a national following from 1983. His plain, utility-store clothes and bloke-ish manner were a world away from the new romantics, while his openly political material made him a dissident voice in the midst of Margaret Thatcher's social revolution. With a doleful cockney voice he would thrash away at his electric guitar, like the one-man punk band he was. He'd once been in a real punk band, Riff Raff, and afterwards joined the Army for a spell – probably, he told me, because he missed the stimulating fear of being onstage. 'So, the most scary way of doing gigs was to do 'em solo. I thought, Fuck it, it's gonna come from *me*.'

One night I drove with him through Essex to Southend, where he was playing a gig in support of the Labour Party. By coincidence, his debut appearance on *Top of the Pops* was being screened that same evening – he was singing a post-Falklands number called 'Between the Wars' – which meant he would end the night a hundred times more famous than he had begun it. (A man from his record company said to me, 'I'd better wear shades so people don't see the pound signs in my eyes.') Present backstage were some Labour MPs, including Robin Cook, who seemed self-conscious in their suits and ties. 'We're going for a drink at the bar,' said Cook. 'Is that OK for our image, Billy?'

'Only if you don't spill it down your shirt fronts,' he replied.

I seemed to cover a lot of Billy Bragg tours, including a few visits to America, where the socialist message sounded as alien as his Estuary accent. At a show in Washington DC he said a few words about Britain's embattled Labour Party, to ragged cheers from the student audience, who seemed to think Neil Kinnock led a distant liberation army, holed up in some jungle clearing.

Bragg has always been unusual in rock, in that his radicalism is not dramatic and posturing, but takes the stance of a patient pragmatist. He was first made conscious of politics by seeing the far-right National Front recruiting outside his school, the Barking Abbey Comprehensive. In time he joined the mainstream of London Labourism, though he admits he faced some sceptics: 'Everybody else in the Labour movement has an electorate behind them, a union or something. But who do I represent? The Billy Bragg Fan Club of Great Britain? No wonder they're sceptical.' Twenty-five-years later, however, he moves with ease from BBC panel discussions to festival stages, ever articulate but never lost for populist charm. He told me that he wanted a new national anthem, but could not decide between William Blake's 'Jerusalem' and West Ham United's 'I'm Forever Blowing Bubbles'.

He has been fortunate in his manager, Peter Jenner, who has steered his career since the beginning. Jenner was a left-wing teacher at the London School of Economics in its insurrectionary period of the 1960s, who went on to join the music business. As well as organising the famous Hyde Park concerts, his clients included Pink Floyd, Marc Bolan, Ian Dury and the Clash; he combines a practical mind with a talent for theoretical overview. He's hardly the Tin Pan Alley type, therefore, but he offered Bragg the same depth of experience that Larry Parnes could show to his own wide-eyed tyros.

Bragg has steadily moved beyond London punk into a wider idea of English, or even global, folk music. He's more reminiscent now of Woody Guthrie than of Joe Strummer – when he wears jeans you're suddenly reminded they were first designed as work clothes. And yet his love songs, especially the early essays in youthful awkwardness, are at least as powerful as the polemical numbers. I tend to remember 'The Milkman of Human Kindness' ('I will leave an extra pint') better than, say, 'Help Save the Youth of America'. The truth may be that Bragg is at heart an East End music hall turn. It's evident in a few of his songs (like 'Honey I'm a Big Boy Now') and more generally in the way he engages crowds of all ages and outlooks. He casts his mind back to the family gatherings of his East London childhood, when his granny or Uncle Stan would take to the piano for 'Lily of Laguna', 'Daisy Bell' and 'Knees Up Mother Brown'. His mum, he told me, was named after Marie Lloyd. There were also sing-songs at the working-men's club in Dagenham, summer jaunts to Southend and hop-picking in Kent.

Of all the London vocalists he remains the most unvarnished. The longer vowels can cause problems. As he confessed to *Time Out*:

You can't sing something like 'Tracks Of Your Tears' in a London accent. The cadences are all wrong. It's also difficult to sing harmonies in a London accent. And you can't sustain syllables for long: 'Greetings to the New Brunette' starts with that sustained 'Shirrrr-LEY!' when I sound like a fucking foghorn. You end up with a higher density of words in a song, which betokens a certain urgency. It's like those early Jam gigs, where Weller seemed like he could hardly get his words out quick enough, as if he was just bursting with the energy of youth.

After our Labour Party trip to Southend we returned along the Essex route he has immortalised in one of his funniest songs. Adapted from the old American classic 'Route 66', his 'A13, Trunk Road to the Sea', is a recitation of not-so-exotic place names. Instead of St Louis, Missouri and Oklahoma City we get Shoeburyness, Leigh-on-Sea, Grays Thurrock and so on. 'I was sick of hearing people sing songs about America,' he told *Time Out*:

> How did we know that Amarillo, New Mexico wasn't as dreary as Dagenham? There was a punk perversity about it, but also a pride in singing about my manor. And the dual carriageway to Southend does have a mythic weight for boy racers that's part of that rock 'n' roll dream. If Springsteen could romanticise New Jersey, I didn't see why I couldn't do the same for estuarine Essex.

At one point we temporarily left the A13 to call in at his mum's house. He wanted to check she had seen that evening's *Top of the Pops*. 'Marvellous, innit?' he said on the way out. 'They'll be asking her in work tomorrow, "'Ere, wasn't that your son on telly, singing about international socialism?" And she'll say, "Didn't he have a nice shirt on?"'

'The Fake Cosmetic Glamour of it All'

Among Billy Bragg's peer group in the 1980s was Croydon's Kirsty MacColl, daughter of the Ewan MacColl who had once ruled London folk music. She was a different sort of artist to her father, being raised on rock and country and punk, with a highly developed sense of irony. An early signing to Stiff Records, her first Top 10 single was a cover of Bragg's song 'A New England', and she later scored with a version of 'Days' by the Kinks, but MacColl soon proved a fine songsmith in her own right. Of her London songs, 'Autumngirlsoup' is the most beautiful, opening on a sublime image of herself in flight above the city rooftops in search of love.

Given the tragic fact of her untimely death in 2000, though, there is a fresh poignancy to her 1993 song 'Soho Square', nowadays marked by an annual ceremony, held next to an engraved bench of the sort the song describes (the site for two lovers' reunion). Unfairly, I think, MacColl is best remembered for another song she did not write, this time a vocal contribution to the Pogues' perennial Christmas hit 'A Fairy Tale of New York'.

The Pogues themselves have been rejuvenated by that song, becoming a seasonal fixture on the December live circuit. But they have made an even more important contribution, as the unlikely conduit that brought the London-Irish tradition – a vibrant part of the capital's life for centuries – into the mainstream of popular acceptance. It was never hard to find jigs or reels or rebel songs in a Camden pub or Hibernian social club, but the Pogues breathed new life into the old forms by shackling Irish folk idioms to London punk rock. It's a blend that seems quite natural now that we're used to it, but it was far from obvious in the early 1980s.

Their frontman Shane MacGowan had arrived from Ireland as a child, and was never entirely assimilated. Not even his time as a scholarship boy at Westminster School, at the heart of the British establishment, could wean him from an emotional allegiance to the Auld Country. But he took to London's music scene with gusto, working at Rock On's record stall, mingling with the first punks at Louise's lesbian club in Soho, drinking with Sid Vicious and producing a fanzine called *Bondage*. One sees him in old footage of the Roxy, pogo-ing in a Union Jack coat. I first came across him at an *NME* Christmas party, where he was blamed (fairly or not) for the vomit on the narrow staircase, over which the fashionable revellers were all obliged to step.

The Pogues were among the hundreds who took advantage of the freedom that punk encouraged, attempting a brazen hybrid of rockabilly and folk, delivered with MacGowan's inimitable rasp. If there were stirring echoes of traditional Irish styles, the band were plainly branded by the city that gave them birth. 'The Dark Streets of London' (with its 'dear dirty delightful old drunken old days' at Hammersmith Broadway) and 'Lullaby of London' meet 'NW3' and an elegy for the greyhound track that closed in 1984, 'White City'.

Most famously, there is 'Rainy Night in Soho', one of those songs that hymns the city as the scene of a million chance encounters, a place that churns indifferently onwards while lives are changed for ever in unremarked doorways.

Like Elvis Costello (who was the Pogues' mid-eighties producer and later married their bassist Cait O'Riordan), Boy George and Johnny Rotten, MacGowan belongs to the vast tribe of Irish descendants who have populated London. Another such, though he's more associated with his native Manchester, is Morrissey. With the Smiths he wrote a song, 'London', addressing the experience of all provincial youths who have steamed down to Euston station, remembering those tearful goodbyes back home, but also noting the jealousy that he senses in those who had to remain on the platform. For a sense of the Smiths' internal hierarchy, we see that when they first moved south in 1983, Morrissey came to Kensington, his guitarist Johnny Marr chose Earls Court, while the rhythm section of Andy Rourke and Mike Joyce settled for humble Willesden. A little while later, or so the self-mythologising singer assured me, he had taken a flat in Chelsea: 'Quite dark, no natural daylight, which I insisted upon, *obviously*. They've bricked up the windows! No, but it's a very dark place, and ghostly.'

In his career as a solo artist, London became part of the fabric of Morrissey's writing, evidenced by album titles such as *Your Arsenal* and *Vauxhall and I*. The charm of a song like 'You're the One for Me, Fatty' is in its very particularity – few are the love songs located in Battersea. 'Piccadilly Palare' looks at a rent boy's life in Earls Court and the West End, and *palare* itself, the time-honoured slang of theatrical folk, homosexuals and street traders, gets a second acknowledgment in *Bona Drag*. 'Hairdresser on Fire' is yet another London story, specifically recounting a salon mishap in Sloane Square. And Morrissey's interest in the rougher legends of the city informs his Kray Twins ditty, 'Last of the Famous International Playboys'. (On the album sleeve of *Under the Influence* we find him outside the Grave Maurice, a favoured pub of Ron and Reggie's, just along the Whitechapel Road from the Blind Beggar.)

'I've grown attached to London now,' he told me. 'The experience I have of it is quite cushioned – I imagine if I lived in a squat in Shoreditch I wouldn't have such a romantic view of London. But I have. I like just walking around, inhaling the cosmetic fake glamour of the whole thing.'

Back to Life: London Soul and Dance

Meanwhile a glossy kind of anglo-soul remained the most popular music of the day, led by acts we've already met, like George Michael, Boy George and Sade, and others including Paul Young, Eurythmics and Basildon's Alison Moyet (who would one day name an album *Essex*). In West London, the Ladbroke Grove district continued to be a melting pot of white bohemia and Caribbean influence, inspiring acts including Neneh Cherry, Rip Rig & Panic and the Pop Group, though reggae's centrality would steadily give way to hip hop. London more generally was still in thrall to imported black American music – it was common to see the Hammersmith Odeon hosting sell-out nights by Philadelphians Frankie Beverly & Maze – and the veteran DJ Tony Blackburn won new respect through his championing of English soul acts on the BBC's Radio London (no relation, alas, to the pirate station of that name where Blackburn started out).

Eddy Grant, as we saw earlier, returned to the charts in his distinctively London way, but black British stars were still a rarity. One exception was the Trinidad-born Billy Ocean, formerly a night-shift worker at Ford's in Dagenham, whose enduring career began with hits like 'Get Out of My Dreams, Get Into My Car'. The south-east of England proved the biggest market for a home-grown upsurge, nicknamed Brit-funk, led by Londoners like Hi-Tension, Light of the World, Freeez, Central Line and Incognito. Before the decade was over there emerged a collective named Soul II Soul, with a sound more rooted in black London than in the US imports rack. Their leader, from Hornsey Rise, was a sound system DJ called Jazzie B, born Trevor Beresford Romeo (and since 2008 the owner of an OBE to boot). The Soul II Soul collective would feature a wide cast of players, including Nellee Hooper and Caron Wheeler (who sang on their definitive 'Back to Life'), and maintained London's dominance in dance music as the nineties began.

Soul, jazz, funk and hip hop are all detectible in London tastes, which at their more esoteric gave rise to 'rare groove'. Then came acid jazz, a club scene that fused those genres in a new style informed by electronic dance music. Its early leaders included the DJ Gilles Peterson (a co-founder of the Acid Jazz label) and Ealing's Brand New Heavies; its star graduate was Jamiroquai. As the 'Balearic' styles of dance music were brought back from Ibiza, London contended with a vogue for Mancunian groups like Happy Mondays. But the capital quickly embraced acid house, Ecstasy and rave culture with its customary appetite, and a couple of local bands sprang up, notably East 17 from Walthamstow and Flowered Up from Camden. It's in the nature of modern dance music, as opposed to more traditional songwriting, that its appeal is less rooted in a sense of place or local culture. It's hard to claim, therefore, that there was any distinctly London stamp on much of rave music. But the capital helped define the age through its new generation of clubs like Shoom, Trip and Ministry of Sound. And the M25, the little-loved motorway that girdles London, became proverbial for the out-of-town events that occurred within its rural orbit – the Kentish duo Orbital taking their name from that very phenomenon.

The eighties and nineties saw various English attempts to emulate hip hop. Derek B and Monie Love, both Londoners, were inevitably under the US influence (and Love was eventually to settle in America), but there was a Battersea flavour to Rodney P of the London Posse; it's nice to recall, also, that one of the earliest 'Brithop' singles was 1983's 'London Bridge is Falling Down' by Ladbroke Grove act Newtrament. Even so, hopes of a fully formed UK movement were disappointed – at least until the next century, whose heroes we shall meet a little later. For the time being, people forgot about Brithop – in fact the term has never caught on – and turned their ears to something else . . .

Who Invented Fish 'n' Chips? Britpop and New Labour

The big white noise of the 1990s was Britpop. Its leading players were conscious of their lineage, from the Beatles, the Who and the Kinks, through the Sex Pistols and the Jam, to Madness and the Smiths. All of these acts were identifiably British – or more exactly, English – and most were shaped by London. In any event, Britpop was swiftly linked with a certain London scene. While some of the movement's stars, such as Oasis and Pulp, were avowedly Northern, London became their headquarters and their playground. There was a rejection of recent Americana, especially the 'grunge' school of Nirvana. Britpop's dress style vaguely evoked the 1960s mods, though without the fastidious neatness; and it was often laddish in the beer-and-football sense. But there were art school influences in there, too, and even a trace of androgynous glamour – especially in the band who really got the whole show rolling, namely Suede.

Suede's leader Brett Anderson grew up in Haywards Heath, a south-east satellite town midway between the capital and Brighton. It was, he told me, 'this grotty little place. As a kid, walking past the station you knew that each train was going up to London and you'd think, I wish I was on that.' With his friend Matt Osman he moved to London as soon as he could, acquiring a girlfriend (and temporary member of Suede) in Justine Frischmann, and a guitarist in North Londoner Bernard Butler. Anderson sang with a dramatised south-eastern accent, recalling Bowie's camper moments, with a dogged insistence on English reference points ('Picnic by the Motorway' is an emblematic Suede title). Their thrilling 1993 debut, *Suede*, suggested it was time for the musical baton to pass back over the Atlantic. (Indeed, due to a name-clash in America, they were billed over there as the London Suede.)

Frischmann left Anderson to form her own band, Elastica, who forsook theatrical swagger for a clipped, angular style. Meanwhile, another band was taking shape, one whose success would take this small London phenomenon to a new level. The whole creative impetus of the 1990s, wrote Alex James, the bassist of Blur, can be traced to one corner of the bar of Goldsmiths College in 1988. Blur's guitarist Graham Coxon, from Colchester, was an art student at the same creative hothouse, which had already nurtured Mary Quant, Bridget Riley, Lucien Freud, Malcolm McLaren, John Cale, the Bonzo Dog Band, Linton Kwesi Johnson, Damien Hirst, Sarah Lucas and Sam Taylor-Wood. Here he met James, a language student, and the band was born. With their drummer Dave Rowntree, the trio were now joined by Coxon's boyhood friend from Colchester, Damon Albarn.

They were called Seymour at first and unglamorous New Cross was their base. Alex James recalls of his twenty-first birthday party, that Albarn climbed on the roof of Deptford Town Hall and changed the time on its clock, which remained wrong for years. Another haunt of those days was the Syndrome Club in Oxford Street, where jealous eyes might glance towards the scene's first stars, Suede. (When Justine Frischmann left Brett Anderson and took up with Damon, the bands' rivalry acquired a more personal edge.) The cluster of acts who came to be called 'Britpop', however, had their chief HQ at a Camden pub, the Good Mixer in Inverness Street.

With Morrissey and members of Madness to lend old-school status, the Good Mixer was now home to Blur, Pulp and more. Menswear formed here, and Elastica signed their deal at its bar. Having joined Food, the new label of a Merseyside musician Dave Balfe, Blur were fusing their identity with London, and with Camden in particular. Sitting in the garden of his very big house in the country (later immortalised in a Blur hit), Balfe describes the early days of Britpop:

> After Food's initial success we needed bigger offices and converted a light industrial unit in Camden on Arlington Road. The pub on the corner was literally next to a homeless hostel [Arlington House, in fact]. It was certainly not up to much. But we started going there with the bands, and journalists came to interview the bands. So the place got mentions in the *NME* and then there was this phenomenon of kids who started going [he mimes a wide-eyed gawper]; they'd taken their trip to London hoping to see one of Blur, and sure enough there was Graham playing pool! It became like Carnaby Street or something.

But Damon Albarn, the voice of Blur, had an ambiguous background. He'd lived as a child in Leytonstone, East London, of middle-class parents – his father worked in TV and once managed Soft Machine – attending the same school as Jonathan Ross. The family then moved out to Colchester in Essex, which seems to have bred in Albarn a cockney nostalgia. He spoke of being exiled to a rootless white suburbia, adrift from London's proletarian, multi-racial vitality. According to Balfe, 'He had this "Mockney" accent when he sang, though he was a nice middle-class lad in conversation. He dropped a few points on the social scale when he sang.'

London, as a concept, soon informed Damon's song-writing. 'For Tomorrow' descends the Westway to Primrose Hill, via Emperor's Gate where Lennon once lived. ('When my parents first moved to London,' Albarn told *Time Out*, 'they had a flat in Emperor's Gate, right next to the Beatles. For the whole of my life I had this image of my parents living next to the Beatles.') The band took to performing the old music hall numbers 'Daisy Bell' and 'Let's All Go Down the Strand'. By 1994 and their breakthrough album *Parklife*, Blur were nationally understood to be 'geezers', with Walthamstow greyhounds on the record sleeve, the actor Phil Daniels supplying a cockney voiceover, and red Routemaster buses winding through the videos.

The greyhounds, says Balfe, 'were a conscious aesthetic from Damon ...'

What really kicked it off was touring America for the first time. They came away thinking, 'This is all that we are not.' It defined him as a Londoner, in antipathy to America. We might have been *Nevermind* fans [Nirvana's most acclaimed album] but we hated grunge and wanted to define ourselves in opposition to it.

And Albarn has spoken of 'all these American things we'd embraced' which in his view included plastic decor, obesity and a culture of greed. In parallel to the creeping corruption of England by American values, he saw the British as keen to vandalise themselves, the 'fun pub' being one especially vivid innovation that bothered him: 'I saw it coming over here and I started to write songs about it.'

A reaction to Americana, Britpop was also a rejection of the rave-inflected rock, or 'baggy' style that was mostly associated with Manchester. Yet the biggest band of the new era would themselves be Mancunians. Oasis appeared as oik-ish interlopers on the London scene and their image of coarse Northern proles was pitched, by some, as a piquant contrast to Blur. A feud duly arose, in which the 'Mockney' (mock-cockney) epithet was daily levelled at Albarn. 'Blur are the Chas and Dave of pop,' sneered an Oasis employee. Partisans of the Gallagher camp found Blur too middle-class, too suburban, to pass the rock authenticity test. The southern boys' East End affectations were dismissed as mere Dick Van Dykery.

The whole spat coincided with a new Blur album, 1995's *The Great Escape*, which indeed took the London school of storytelling to new lengths. But after this point, in part responding to the backlash, Blur would lead their music in a darker, less explicit direction (influenced, ironically, by some US music, such as Pavement). Oasis themselves were soon deemed guilty of self-parody, yet the Britpop 'brand' was now obsessing mainstream media. It was interpreted as evidence of a new Swinging London. The incoming Labour government of Tony Blair allowed itself to be linked to the phenomenon. In Westminster, pop stars and politicians met and fed one another's yearnings.

The irony was that pop was now quite traditionalist, but politics was truly post-modern. Musicians revered their influences with a respect that verged upon ancestor-worship; politicians embraced a new world of 'perceptions' over truth, and of history rewritten as self-serving 'narrative'. In their haste to create a Year Zero sense of national renewal, New Labour were courting some deeply nostalgic performers.

London itself was enjoying a new prestige, fuelled by its economic success and a celebrity-driven taste for hedonism. In 1997 the glossy journal *Vanity Fair* featured Liam Gallagher of Oasis and his girlfriend Patsy Kensit, swathed in a Union Jack with a cover line proclaiming,

'London Swings Again!' The motto of the hour was 'Cool Britannia' (which few would have recognised as a Bonzo Dog Band title). And, rather as Julien Temple's film of *Absolute Beginners* had recast Soho of the 1950s for the style-conscious 1980s, so Mike Myers's comic pastiche, *Austin Powers: International Man Of Mystery*, offered a 1997 parody of 1967, where dolly birds danced with Beefeaters in Carnaby Street delirium.

In the same year came *Spice World*, a larky movie vehicle for the Spice Girls. If the band had been artfully constructed as a cross section of contemporary Britain, their movie was really an engaging tribute to London of the 1990s, seen through that same 1960s prism.

But others took the parallel further, took it, perhaps, to the palace of excess. Alex James, Blur's resident *boulevardier*, asserts the sixties were soon surpassed in the quest for pleasure. The London of 1998, he says, rivalled the old Hogarthian days of gin houses and aristocratic debauchees. While green waves of absinthe washed upon Soho's shores, Alex romped around the Groucho Club with his Goldsmiths ally Damien Hirst (now a famous lion of Britpop's counterpart, Britart) and the actor Keith Allen. 'I occasionally had very debauched evenings out with Damien Hirst, Keith Allen and Alex,' says Dave Balfe. 'But even at that point I didn't have the stamina for what they did. It was a convocation of forces, very similar to that convocation in the mid-sixties, with the photographers and fashion designers and so on. This time it was certainly happening with the new artists and the bands.'

Under the name Fat Les, the trio of James, Allen and Hirst made a thumping anthem for the England football team's 1998 campaign. 'Vindaloo' was inspired by the drumming of fans at a Fulham game, and in its vulgar communal jollity there lives the spirit of London music hall – the video featured scores of extras and celebrities dressed as Max Wall, together with Rasta pearly royals. Fat Les played their new creation at a party, in a line-up including Joe Strummer and Keith Allen's young daughter Lily – of whom we shall hear more soon. Flushed by their success they followed on with a record of

William Blake's 'Jerusalem', for the Euro 2000 competition, and a single called 'Who Invented Fish 'n' Chips?' Fat Les, I believe, would have warmed Harry Champion's heart.

Chapter Eleven

Innit?

The modern mosaic: London music in the twenty-first century.

For all its rough charm, something about London can rub people up the wrong way. Britain's greatest media controversy of 2008 concerned two BBC celebrities, the DJ Jonathan Ross and the comedian Russell Brand, who had broadcast comments deemed offensive and obscene. Objections were raised to their vulgarity and enormous salaries, and questions asked about the role of the BBC. But there was something else, I think, that fuelled the nation's ire. Ross and Brand are utterly and irredeemably London. It's an aspect you are more likely to notice if you live a long way from the capital. They sounded coarse, cocky and 'too clever by half'.

As an interviewer, Ross has traded well on his barrow boy sharpness. He has a Londoner's easy familiarity with the high and mighty, and an urchin's irreverence. (The fault, in 2008, was that his victim seemed unequal to him, a harmless and fondly regarded elderly actor.) Brand is a drama school brat who made a drama of his everyday life. He became a kind of rock star without putting himself to the inconvenience of making music, and has the classic London talent for self-styling. Interviewed in Los Angeles for the *Sunday Times*, he wore a West Ham shirt with a pearl necklace and purple knickers. 'I like being famous. I did it on purpose . . . Obscurity does not suit me. You can't have this haircut and not be famous. It's unbecoming.' There speaks the ghost of Marc Bolan. Or Macheath, the highwayman of *The Beggar's Opera*.

When a provincial looks at London ('*that* London', as they sometimes say), it can seem a glittering place, especially to the young. Or it appears intimidating – what anarchy and din. Or it may look annoyingly smug. After the 'Big Bang' of 1986 (the deregulation of the City's financial markets), its image was of a crass, 'loadsamoney' boomtown, a privileged place of rocketing property prices, where fortunes were brokered from Mayfair to Canary Wharf. But the real London was mixed, as it always has been. The clash of wealth and want has forged its very personality. *The Economist*, in 2007, reported of London: 'It has come to seem, for many people, a sort of laboratory in which a rawer, less-cohesive Britain is emerging; a crowded, hustling place of vaulting earnings for the rich and of widening income disparities, which drains talent and wealth from the rest of the country.' Within a year there came the first signs of 'Bad Times Just Around the Corner', as Noël Coward once sang. Few, I imagine, have wept for London's chastised financiers.

Within the shifting patterns of a restless metropolis, the early years of the twenty-first century saw an opening up of East London. Low-rent areas of Shoreditch and Hoxton had already attracted pioneer artists; now there followed high-end galleries, restaurants and private clubs. The rising generation of London's glitterati, many of whom bore very familiar surnames – Jade Jagger, Peaches Geldof, Stella McCartney – bestowed their patronage. Back west, the formerly hippified Notting Hill became political shorthand for an ambitious faction of the Tory Party. Conversely, the district's venerable indie trading post, Rough Trade, opened a second shop, Rough Trade East, in Whitechapel's now trendy Brick Lane.

Where Londoners might once have travelled west for big shows at the Hammersmith Odeon (latterly the Apollo), they're now as likely to visit Greenwich, where the huge O2 inhabits the blob created for the unlamented Millennium Dome. Hammersmith's Palais de Danse, unfortunately, has closed, though ghosts will always glide, cheek-to-cheek, across its spectral floor. More happily, the stately yard of Somerset House, a Thameside palace since Tudor times, has been thrown open to concert-goers and winter skaters.

Actually, London's very accent seemed to move east. 'Mockney' was only a new name for a trend that was evident since the sixties, when middle-class bohemians started trading down. To appear less uptight or elitist they would modify their speech with glottal stops and beatnik vagueness: 'I'm, like, not 'avin' tha', yeah? It's to'ally *weird*.' This was not the rich, throaty dialect of Gus Elen or Marie Lloyd, nor was there the elegance and clarity of standard, educated English, only a noise both lazy and affected. 'Estuarial' English was another term coined, describing London's cultural colonisation of the whole south-eastern region, ironing out both local and class variety. Politicians and media people adopted it wholesale.

But at the street level, London talk may still snap and crackle. Among the young was a clear influence from US hip hop and, regardless of ethnic category, from Jamaican patois. (The comic creation Ali G, with his 'Staines massive', was a clever satire of the trend's less authentic side.) In 2004 the comedian Catherine Tate alerted the rest of Britain to London's new teen argot: 'Mate! Innit though, izzit that ... well-'arsh. Ax me a question: Is this face bovvered? Wot-evah.' At its best the new speech was energetic, inventive and almost poetic. The most exciting new London music was not from orthodox rock bands; it was the work of a newer breed, spitting rhymes of guttersnipe eloquence.

More Geezer Than Gangsta: London Hip Hop

A glance today at London's pirate radio listings reveals these genres, among others: African, bashment, breakbeat, conscious, drum & bass, dub, dubstep, eski, funky house, Greek, grime, hardcore, hip hop, house, jungle, lovers, old skool, R&B, ragga, raggae, reggae, revival, soca, soul beats, sublow, trance, Turkish, UK garage.

The names of the stations are equally mesmeric: Beat, Bounce, Chillin, Eruption, Freeze, Hav It, Hot, Ice Cold, Klash, Klimaxx, Laylow, Mystic, Passion, Rude, Shine, Surprise, Wax, Woah. It could nearly be a Biblical reverie by William Blake.

Of the multifarious dance music genres, which are apt to spawn, mutate and diversify like microbes under a scientist's glass, the most pertinent here is UK garage. At London clubs and parties of the nineties, often at after-hours affairs for people who had been to Ministry of Sound or similar, the American soundtrack received a novel British spin. While the DJs took US 'garage' tracks (essentially electronic dance music) and sped them up, local MCs rhymed over the dub versions in place of the original vocals. The pirate stations, proliferating from their high-rise perches across the capital, took the UK garage sound to a wider, younger audience. (Like their offshore sixties forerunners, Radio London, Caroline *et al*, these unlicensed operators were a vital conduit for music underserved by mainstream media.) From this style, and its next refinement, 2-step, arose a host of new acts including So Solid Crew, Ms Dynamite, the Streets, Wiley and Dizzee Rascal.

So Solid Crew grew up on the Battersea estates that Surrey commuters gaze down upon as their trains rattle along towards Waterloo. It's a world quite separate from the expensive neighbouring terraces, housing Wandsworth's prosperous people in the once plebeian streets that *Up the Junction* described all those years before. So Solid Crew were reared on the music of black London, from reggae sound systems to hip hop to UK garage and 2-step's variant dubstep, over which they would perform on stations like Delight FM. As a collective of MCs, DJs, vocalists and producers, they numbered up to thirty members and came to the world's attention with a big hit in 2001, '21 Seconds'. They've been a training ground for talents including Lisa Maffia and MC Romeo, but violence at shows, and in the private lives of some associates, was a problem. (Their producer Carl Morgan, for example, received a thirty-year murder sentence in 2005.)

One of their early collaborators was Ms Dynamite, a girl of Scottish–Jamaican parentage from Archway on the other side of London. Too smart for the bad-girl-with-attitude trap, she has often condemned young Londoners' 'gangsta culture' (as thuggery is known when there are hip hop overtones). But her targets have ranged up the scale, as well, even unto Westminster. In 2003 New Labour's spin-doctor Alastair Campbell learned the perils of endorsing music stars, no matter how hip, black or female. Having cited Ms Dynamite as his favourite act she took the most outspoken opposition to the Iraq War and blasted Campbell's masters from the stages of Hyde Park rallies and on record. 'Mr Prime Minister' lambasted Tony Blair as a broadsheet balladeer would once have pilloried Pitt or Walpole.

The most interesting British hip hop is that which speaks the language of its own streets, not of Compton or the Bronx. There have been startling tracks by Blak Twang, a rapper raised in Deptford, known for his waspish way with localised rhymes: the title of one track, 'Queen's Head', plays on 'dead presidents', the US slang for dollars. Even better known is his sometime collaborator, Stockwell's Roots Manuva. His style bears a reggae imprint of his Jamaican heritage, but a song like 'Witness (1 Hope)' can celebrate cheese on toast and pints of bitter. (Its video finds him back at his old primary school in Streatham, reliving his humiliations in the egg-and-spoon race.) Another contender is the Ghanaian-descended Sway, a North Londoner who claims Madness for a major influence. In his rhyme of childhood 'Little Derek' he describes life 'on the north side of the city where it's gritty like pie'. And he thanks a musical career for ensuring that he 'ended up in HMV not HMP'.

In the urban storytelling of Mike Skinner, alias the Streets, we hear a graduate of UK garage embracing the London lineage of Ray Davies and Ian Dury. 'What I've been successful at is characters and stories and drama,' he told *The Word*. 'That's always been what's got me through – I know I can tell a good story.' Though he spent most of his childhood in Birmingham, and some of its accent clings to him, London is where he was born and blossomed as a writer. Skinner is especially good at switching a smooth rapper's flow for awkward, lurching lines whose cockney-Brum syllables crash memorably into the garage/R&B scenery. His earliest efforts were imitation US rap, until he found a voice more geezer than gangsta – a world where girls are 'birds not bitches', as he once sang – more ordinary than angry.

He broke through in 2001 with a hit called 'Has it Come to This', which brought to the beats of garage an unpretentious urchin who measured his life in Tube stops, from Mile End to Bounds Green. The songs of his debut, *Original Pirate Material*, were documents of his listeners' lives, so deadpan-vivid that he was given an Ivor Novello Award (and what, one always wonders, would Ivor make of those so honoured in his name?). In decades past a long white limousine would have been a stupefying sight on British streets, as extraordinary as a flying saucer. But now, every Saturday night the town centres are full of them, hauling cargoes of puking kids re-enacting the bling scenarios of hip hop videos. Mike Skinner, the cheeky chavvie, looked set to become those teenagers' Poet Laureate.

Instead, like a true London writer, he kept his eyes open and reported on what he saw now that he was famous; dispatches, really, from the other side of the VIPs' red rope. His reference points had formerly included an overdue rental DVD, beer mats, his mobile phone menu and watching *The Bill* on TV. Now they took in Ferraris, promotional marketing budgets and the perils of celebrity drug consumption. (The advent of camera phones, he says at one point, makes every passer-by into a potential papparazi.) Very bright and always self-questioning, Skinner has recently declared he is sick of the Streets. Wherever he develops, the records he made will stand as true testaments of their time.

Grime Time: Hold Ya Mouf

Like Burlington Bertie, Dizzee Rascal comes from Bow. So does his fellow grime star Wiley. Two performers from the same neighbourhoods that gave us Vera Lynn and the Small Faces, they were the first to represent this East End movement. The names of grime acts present another picturesque litany, and slightly Dickensian: Crazy Titch, Lady Sovereign, Scratchy, Tinchy Stryder. One could imagine them on a yellowing playbill outside Wilton's Music Hall.

The style we call grime grew up in the area's UK garage clubs, where MCs would add their own touches of hip hop, of dancehall (the hedonistic, DJ-heavy school of reggae) and some old-fashioned cockney cheek. Soon it could be heard in Peckham as well as Bow, in

Tottenham as well as Hackney. Exposure on pirate radio was once again crucial, the stations including Freeze and Rinse. Like Roots Manuva and Blak Twang, the grime acts sang of London – a real and often very bleak London, but not a received image of some US ghetto. Grime was not really hip hop, and its beats were often too irregular to even be dance music. Grime was angular, tense and fractured, full of unexpected gaps and abrupt terminations. Within its minimalist sound there was actually a lot happening, and the noise of modern London was captured in ringtones and car alarms, bleeps and crashes. Often there hung, above it all, a claustrophobic cloud of dread.

Wiley's signature track was 'Eskimo' which gave its name to his style of grime, called 'eski'. But he really hit big in 2008 with a hit called 'Wearing My Rolex', a night-life tale of living it large, wherein the bling ethos of hip hop merges with London wide-boy flash. Dizzee Rascal, who had earlier been in Wiley's crew Roll Deep, struck out in 2003 with a rather bitter thing called 'I Luv U', about a teenage pregnancy. He credits the Streets' Mike Skinner for steering him towards a London style of lyric; he has called 'I Luv U', 'a soap opera, the kind of conversation that's going on all over London at the moment.' He also recalled looking out of his window in Bow and seeing the towers of Canary Wharf, flaunting their wealth and power in his face.

Harsh as grime can sometimes be, Dizzee Rascal quickly found a wider public for his music, and critical recognition came with a 2003 Mercury Prize for his first album, *Boy in da Corner*. He sings of places a lot of his new audience will never want to visit, but the human dimension to his storytelling is always vivid. 'Hold Ya Mouf' is dark with threat. 'Graftin', from 2004, offers a desolate manifesto for the young hustlers of London. From the later album *Maths + English*, released in 2007, 'Sirens' is a youth days confessional (Limehouse police knocking at his door) and Dizzee himself compares another track, 'Suk My Dick', to his London forerunners the Sex Pistols.

From Waltham Forest, in the east, came More Fire Crew, who in turn gave us Lethal Bizzie; before he left they had a hit called 'Oi!', a title that echoes both 'The Lambeth Walk' and the Cockney Rejects. Perhaps some aspects of the London language are historically indestructible. Another star, Kano, came from East Ham and developed on the same scene as Wiley and Dizzee. As he sings on his *London Town* album (which features Damon Albarn), this is a city where you either toughen up or disappear. And from a council estate up in Wembley there was a young white girl called Lady Sovereign – she quickly made some inroads in the USA where she signed to Jay-Z's label, yet her chirpy, Madness-like videos and a cover of the Sex Pistols' 'Pretty Vacant' indicate an artist whose London roots will never be eradicated.

Without acts like Lady Sovereign or Dizzee Rascal to represent it, an entire slice of the city's life would go unnoticed, except for those headline moments of tragedy that occur with a schoolyard knifing or a gang-inspired shooting. For a more rounded portrait of real human existence, in places that are under most Londoners' radar, grime and hip hop have been important – the broadsides of our time. The paradox, of course, as Mike Skinner has acknowledged, is that fame and success will separate these artists from the life they have portrayed. Cries of sell-out or commercial compromise are common. But then, the scene's internal tensions are themselves a kind of entertainment. The rap tradition of one-to-one rhyming contests is taken up by rival MCs; at their best these widely promoted 'battles' are dazzling shows of verbal expertise and pointed wit. But the 'beef' can sometimes be too real. At the Old Bailey in 2006, on the site of Newgate Gaol, Dizzee Rascal's former adversary Crazy Titch received a thirty-year prison sentence for a murder in Chingford – the argument arose, the court was told, over a lyric deemed 'disrespectful'.

Written descriptions of London's dance music culture are doomed to swift obsolescence. In recent years the noise has been of Croydon's dubstep scene or the 'funky house' genre played in venues like Casa Funk at Mile End's Club E3. Both have overlapped with grime, though dubstep is on the whole a slower affair, bass-heavy and suffused with atmosphere. The sometimes mournful music of a Putney-raised producer, William Bevan, has been widely praised.

Under the name of Burial, he's made music that I've seen described as 'the secret sound that the Victoria Line makes in the middle of the night'. This may well be true: 'I spend a lot of time wandering around London,' he told the *Wire*. 'I always have ... Being on your own listening to headphones is not a million miles away from being in a club surrounded by people, you let it in, you're more open to it. Sometimes you get that feeling like a ghost touched your heart, like someone walks with you.'

London Undersound: The World in a Microcosm

In the early 1980s I realised the video age had reached my corner of London when the local convenience store began filling its shelves with Asian VHS tapes. Bollywood was pushing out the Hovis and the Weetabix. 'It's not the young people,' our shopkeeper explained. 'It's the old ones. The TV's no good to them if they've never learned to speak English.' Perhaps the tapes have gone now that we have satellite TVs that can beam the evening's news from Delhi or anywhere else. But it reminded me how insular the lives of first-generation immigrants may be. In Monica Ali's novel *Brick Lane*, it is the girl back in Bangladesh who keeps her sister in Tower Hamlets informed about Britney Spears.

The districts around Brick Lane, such as Spitalfields and Whitechapel, have hosted incomers since at least the time of the Huguenot French, and figure in the family histories of numerous London Jewish musicians, from Bud Flanagan to Lionel Bart. The heartland of music hall was among the least uniformly English places in England. In our own time it's the Bangladeshis who have given Brick Lane its special flavour, though even this will probably change one day. Everything in the city is a balance of alterations and secret continuities. The music of any immigrant community works two ways – enriching the adopted country while also being shaped by it, absorbing its particular essence.

The flavours of southern Asian music, if not the complete substance, were introduced to pop by the Beatles and others of that time, when sitars seemed both psychedelic and vaguely indicative of spiritual wisdom. Since then the mainstream has sporadically received contributions from artists of Asian background like Shelia Chandra's Monsoon, the polemical Asian Dub Foundation or the Midlands act Cornershop. Meanwhile, within its own ethnic base and largely unknown to the wider market, there developed new forms of the classic Punjabi form, bhangra. By tradition, bhangra would be a celebration of the harvest, highly rhythmic, to be sung and danced to. Among the first generation immigrants therefore, its role was a nostalgic one, a tribute to the homeland. Weddings were (and still remain) the great occasions for bhangra performance – but over time the live players made room for DJs and their records.

From the seventies on, bhangra was being heard in pubs and clubs, and began to get mixed with genres unknown to the older generation. In London the DJ San-J Sanj would emulate the sound systems of reggae, but also introduced bhangra to hip hop, rave or techno. By 1988 it was possible to find Leicester Square littered with flyers of a turbaned smiley face, advertising nights of acid bhangra. Out west, the Hammersmith Palais played one more historic role as a gathering point for bhangra shows – no longer a nostalgic folk form but a driving, urgent and distinctively British Asian music. Figurehead performers emerged (usually from bhangra's stronghold in the West Midlands), like Panjabi MC, Apache Indian and Bally Sagoo. Their work was often strong on reggae's influence. But, from Hounslow, the singer Jay Sean found stardom with a very modern blend of R&B and hip hop.

Boundaries were shifting, barriers collapsing. Back in *Brick Lane*, one of Monica Ali's characters is Karim, complaining about the lack of Bengali music in his youth: pop was white, hip hop was black and bhangra was Punjabi. Another young man, a musician, rejects the bhangra tag – he prefers the reggaefied 'bhangramuffin' or 'bitta raga infusion'. By the same token you might hear bhangra crossed with jungle, producing 'bhangle'. In the twenty-first century, no young Londoner of any race can go for long without exposure to other traditions – to more variety than was dreamed of by previous generations.

For illustration look to M.I.A., alias the Hounslow-born Mathangi Arulpragasam. As a child her parents took her back to their native Sri Lanka, where her father was active in the Tamil political resistance. In her teens, she and her mother returned to London where they were housed as refugees – her stage name M.I.A. stands not only for Missing in Action but also Missing in Acton. In turn, M.I.A. went to Central St Martins, and she's led a parallel career in visual art (an early commission being for an Elastica record sleeve). Her albums to date, *Arular* in 2005 and *Kala* in 2007, are hugely enjoyable distillations of all she has heard growing up in London and abroad, including dancehall, hip hop and electro. She loves the Clash and, interestingly, cites the inspiration of Malcolm McLaren. (Her beats, chants and war-whoops can, at times, resemble Bow Wow Wow – they're like the electro-primitive anthems of some future global tribe.) Like Neneh Cherry she has the enviable knack of turning her varied background into something entirely personal and natural-sounding. 'You get exposed to everything,' she has explained. 'I'm kind of like a walking mixtape.'

In the work of a very different British Asian artist, Nitin Sawhney, we hear the elegance of music that has been nourished by different traditions. Sawhney grew up in Kent, the son of middle-class Indian parents, and absorbed everything from Western classical to modern club, as well as Eastern forms. He prefers to see his music not as a 'fusion' of different things, but simply as part of one thing – just as a painting is not a fusion of paints, but simply a painting. As a child, raised near to London, he fell under the city's spell as so many others have done. But for him, it had a special resonance:

Growing up in Rochester in the hey-day of the National Front, I was the only Asian in my whole area. I'd get an NF van following me back from school, shouting 'Paki'. I liked to get away to London because it seemed more accepting. But then I did see skinheads marching through London too. It was a strange time, but London was a lot more exciting, especially when we had the Anti-Nazi League and Rock Against Racism. I found it had a less parochial attitude.

London to me represents diversity. London is now more diverse than it's ever been, and as a result has an even stronger identity. Somebody once asked me, 'If London were a book, which would it be?' And I said an encyclopedia. It actually is the world in a microcosm.

In his 2008 album *London Undersound*, Sawhney portrayed the capital as it felt to him and his collaborators. Its keynote track, perhaps, is 'Days of Fire' featuring the singer Natty, who saw at close hand two landmark events: the London bombings of 7 July 2005, and the killing of Jean Charles de Menezes, mistaken for a terrorist at Stockwell station. Its vividly topical narrative recalls the old broadside approach, presenting a story of its time, but here with an extra tang of first-hand experience. (Sawhney admires the calypso form for that same reason.) Another track finds Paul McCartney – vastly famous, but still surprisingly given to wandering London's streets and Tube system – with a celebrity's-eye view of media intrusion. 'McCartney's experience was as valid as anyone else's,' says Sawhney:

It's his take on things, feeling invaded by the paparazzi. When a photograph is taken of him he feels like they're stealing his soul. He's still a human being, no matter how celebrated he is or how much money he makes, we are all human beings. It's humanity that I'm interested in. And not nationalism.

Musicians don't have the problem. Music is a universal language, the language of emotions. It's the cathartic language that helps us to relate to each other. I can tell more about a person when they pick up a guitar or start singing than if we spend all day waffling. You can't bullshit with music, it cuts across barriers, it's *automatically* multicultural.

Elsewhere on *London Undersound* are artists sharing their sense of isolation. There is a locked-in aspect to Londoners in the street, each within the protective shell that helps us move about the city more easily, yet separates us from the greater human organism that gives our lives its meaning.

Amy Winehouse: 'You Know What? It's Gotta Be Done'

The great revelation of recent British pop has been Amy Winehouse. The daughter of a cockney cab driver, she is the classic London deal, writing of the city she sees. I met her in the winter of 2005, during the last weeks she could move about the capital unrecognised. Sitting in a Camden Town tapas bar, she was a young star-in-waiting with a debut CD (*Frank*) that everyone loved. But Amy did not look as happy as one might expect. Only when our small talk turned to London did her mood magically brighten. 'Oh, I *love* this city! I love it. Wherever I go in the world, to land back in London is the best feeling. I get to see so many amazing places when I'm working, and I think, I could live here. But then I go, Yeah, but I wouldn't be in London . . .'

Frank was her diary of a torrid adolescence – she was just nineteen when it was recorded – sung with all the funky poise of a jazz veteran and the glottal stops of a mouthy schoolgirl on the Piccadilly Line. It was a fine piece of modern British R&B. For all its retro US stylings, *Frank* could not have been made anywhere but in London, in the twenty-first century. When I said that, she beamed.

> That is the best compliment you could pay to me. The city is really important to me. I've always been a really independent girl. From the age of thirteen or so I've always found my own way in the city and there's nothing I like more than to find another part that I didn't already know. It really fascinates me.

Winehouse was raised in the North London suburb of Southgate. Her mother, who is from Brooklyn, and her East End father separated when Amy was nine. Winehouse came into pop after a spell as a singer with the National Youth Jazz Orchestra. But she was already a showbiz kid, whose turbulent education had taken in a few stage schools. One of these was the Sylvia Young Theatre School in Marylebone: it's almost the Eton of the *Pop Idol* generation, having educated sundry Spice Girls, All Saints and members of S Club 7. Winehouse, however, got expelled.

'Well,' she ponders, 'that is not a shit school, the Sylvia Young. They've got a reputation because they are the best. It's not a pop star factory, they channel your creativity and you learn to use it. That's what I did. For every precocious kid there were kids who really worked. They sent you out to work. Stage school is a job. You learn how to get the fuck on with it. I learned a lot of important things.'

But you didn't get along with it?

'No. But I've never been to a school that I came away happily from.'

Frank was a storyteller's album. There were graphic accounts of her sexual infatuations and star-crossed romances. But if she could seem self-absorbed, she was also observant. A track called 'Fuck Me Pumps' was a merciless portrait of women who prowl the clubs of London on their primal hunt for alpha males, like the girl whose dream is to become a footballer's wife. (In a certain light, she could pass for a hip hop Jane Austen.) Then came her *Back to Black* album (2006) with its extraordinary opener 'Rehab' which was only too revealing of a fraught existence. Her music had grown wonderfully and her popularity rocketed. But the corollary, in the new London of insatiable celebrity media and spiralling opportunities for self-indulgence, was more than Winehouse looked able to manage. She has rarely spent a single day out of the headlines since then, and seldom has the news been edifying.

Back in the Camden tapas restaurant, before all this happened, her steely resolve seemed to be winning. If Winehouse looks Amazonian in some photographs, she is quite petite in person. Yet she has a cold stare that you guess she can deploy to deadly effect. In 2005 I found her very bright, though not in a systematic way, as if she had learned so much so quickly that the patterns had not yet come together in her head. She was a forthright young woman, and her manner was direct. By our interview's end, however, she appeared preoccupied by private anxieties. 'You learn as you go along,' she sighed, to no one in particular.

It's true she was a nervous interviewee, but tense and self-critical rather than hostile. I'm glad we met before the smoking ban came into force, for much of her conversational drama was signalled by urgent searches in her bag, the pause for a nicotine hit, the fierce exhalations afterward.

If you had to give up either singing or songwriting, I asked her, which would it be?

She picked up her fork and impaled a meatball.

I'd cut my throat out. Singing is singing. If I couldn't sing a song, and express it, I'd be fucked. I've always sung. I always assumed that everyone could sing, that that's what they do when they're happy or sad. And when I was growing up and having the pain and suffering that teenagers do, I could sing like a little bird. I can't sing like that no more. I'm too complacent. They gave me too much free shit . . .

She sighed even more deeply and stared at the table. What do you mean, they gave you too much free shit?

'They put it all on a plate. I feel like I've got nothing to work for sometimes, even though I've got lots to work for.'

But of course you have, surely?

She lights another cigarette. 'Yeah. Anyway . . . Amy, chill the fuck out. I'm sorry.'

Do you feel pressurised by all the weight of expectation around you?

'A little bit. But that's *myself*. No one could be a harsher critic than myself. I am feeling that pressure. There are days when I wish I could just take a break from my own head.'

We talk about the London music business. She blows out hard, hot cigarette smoke. She suddenly seems sixty-five years old. 'There's nothing real in it, nothing real. Which really drains me. But you know what? It's gotta be done.'

She gave me a tired, trouper's smile and walked back out into Parkway, where that big old-fashioned pet shop advertised its parrots, monkeys and other exotic but imprisoned creatures.

Twelve Glottal Stops and Home: Lily and Her Peers

We had entered in a new age of unashamed show business. It was rather like the world that Larry Parnes and his type had ruled in the 1950s, before rock culture (and its cult of 'authentic' artists) had made mainstream entertainment look uncool. In the twenty-first century there was a pop chart filled with winners of TV talent contests, or former cruise-ship singers. Cover versions, even of very old songs, were no longer looked down upon. A big proportion of new acts had specialist career training, whether at traditional stage schools or the BRIT School for performing arts at Croydon. And thanks to a realignment of the media, via digital TV and celebrity-driven print, there was coverage for all – far broader than ever before and correspondingly more shallow.

Going out in London had always involved a slight element of theatre, of putting oneself on display, but this was pushed to new extremes. Even a minor and transient face in the public eye could expect unlimited attention from the free papers that now lay deep like dirty snow in homebound train carriages. Hardly any were well equipped to deal with such attention. And the drunker or brawlier they became in public, the more attention they received. Like unlucky gladiators, few enjoyed more than a season in this arena before oblivion came to claim them. When even a real and potentially enduring talent like Amy Winehouse could nearly be destroyed, what were the odds for anyone else?

One survivor may be Lily Allen. We caught our last glimpse of this Mockney gamine at a performance by Fat Les, of which her father Keith was an instigator. Also there was Joe Strummer, who was Lily's godfather. She has other entertainment connections. Her mother (who raised her largely without Keith Allen) is the film producer Alison Owen; for some of Lily's childhood her mother's partner was the comedian Harry Enfield. She seemed pre-destined, then, for some degree of celebrity. 'I get slagged off for going to premieres and showbiz parties,' she protested to *The Word*, 'but my mum's a film producer and my dad's an actor!'

It was said that she became a star through MySpace – in other words, not by hype but through the democratic power of the Internet. This was not entirely true, as she was already signed to an EMI label. But her early online tracks were so fresh and appealing that the word-of-mouth was genuine. Her first CD (*All Right, Still*, in 2006) confirmed her way with sharp, sardonic London pop. As *Time Out* said, 'She is a post-punk Marie Lloyd; she is Irene Handl reinvented as a calypsonian; she is the urchin flower-seller in Lionel Bart's *Oliver!* transplanted into latterday Dalston Market.' When you hear her duet with Dizzee Rascal on his 'Wanna Be', you hear a slice of real London life – in this case a self-deluding youth with gangsta pretensions – whipped into a little comic gem.

'I was never into American pop music, ever,' she told the *Spectator*. 'I never really got Michael Jackson.' Her roots, she says, were in bands like Pulp and Blur; from there she delved back into Squeeze and the Kinks. Humour, wordplay and a feeling for her native city were the key to her songs, delivered in the everyday speech of a young Londoner, not quite posh and not quite street. Admirers have likened her to Mike Skinner; I think at her best she has a touch of Kirsty MacColl, especially in her female way with a withering dismissal ('Friday Night', Knock 'Em Out'). She can also do Ian Dury oompah ('Alfie') and streetwise calypso ('LDN') and clinches it all with a number rhyming 'Kate Moss' with 'weight loss'.

Three years and a thousand tabloid stories later, she made her return to music (which now seemed less and less central to the mere media fact of Allen's existence). If she was warier, and perhaps more glamorous than the breezy young woman she had formerly appeared, it was only natural – nobody stays the ingénue for ever. She talks of her disillusionment with celebrity culture and her yearning for something more serious. We'll see. For the moment, she's a resident of those over-photographed few yards of London pavement, outside the Groucho and the Ivy and the unblinking eye of the modern media.

It was a fertile period for London female singers, whether of the waif-like indie persuasion like Kate Nash, or with the fuller-lunged soul power of Leona Lewis or Estelle. Nash, who is from Harrow, went to the BRIT school (like Amy Winehouse) and developed a glottal-stop vocal that went quite naturally with her plain vignettes of student life. Adele was also from the BRIT school, but was rather more a voice of London's white working class: *The Times* pronounced of one show that 'ordinariness is part of her appeal, and she played on it relentlessly, chatting nineteen-to-the-dozen between tracks in an ear-grating accent that was part *EastEnders* barmaid, part till-girl at Lidl.' North Londoner Leona Lewis, a graduate of the BRIT and other schools, came to fame by winning the *The X Factor* TV talent show, the same vehicle that launched Alexandra Burke, another North London girl whose mother, Melissa Bell, once sang with Soul II Soul. Less identifiably of London, perhaps, though certainly a star, was the South Londoner Estelle, who has gone from early collaborations with Blak Twang to hits with Kanye West and a career relocation to America.

Pete Doherty, of the bands the Libertines and Babyshambles, has become one of London's rock 'n' roll legends, though on the musical level he remains a case of promise unfulfilled. Instead he embodies the drive and the inspiration that the city can give to a newcomer, but also the snares and temptations that await the unwary. When he and his musical partner Carl Barât began their careers they were of the indie school that is still defined by my old paper the *NME* – fittingly, the Libertines' first album was produced by Mick Jones of the Clash – and by 2002 the tall, poetic Doherty was the decadent figurehead of a druggy Whitechapel rock scene. The Libertines could easily be seen as inheritors of a distinctly English tradition, from the Beatles to the punkier edge of Britpop, with a romantically Dickensian taste for London town, so deep that they bestowed their hip approval on dear old Chas & Dave. Even Pete's side project, Babyshambles, was shrewdly named with an eye for cute English *kitsch* and up-to-the-minute nihilism.

Things got messy very soon for Doherty. He had regular fallings-out with Barât, whose flat he was convicted of burgling; as a result he spent a portion of 2003 in Wandsworth Prison. It was the first in a series of highly publicised arrests, normally drug-related, made all the more headline-worthy by his romance with Kate Moss. Fans of the rock 'n' roll myth that Doherty seems to represent will speak approvingly of Keith Richards or Iggy Pop. But you have to wonder if their respective musical legacies are on course to compare. Though the career of Coldplay (who, like Doherty, came to London as university students) has much less of an outlaw swagger, its material advantages are obvious.

The Feeling made an impressive debut in 2006 with a London-flavoured CD, *Twelve Stops and Home*, whose artwork and 'Blue Piccadilly' evoke the Tube and the hidden heartbreak of a star-crossed lover. Their singer, Ben Gillespie Sells, had the definitive London voice of his time, a softened, classless cockney, but he was yet another BRIT school boy, where Estuarial English is probably on the curriculum. Jack Peñate and Wimbledon's Jamie T were other singer/songwriters of the same wave (the latter's hit, 'Sheila', samples John Betjeman in mid-meditation on London's 'vast suburban churches'). Meanwhile there were bands like Razorlight, Bloc Party, Hard-Fi and McFly, at work with varying degrees of originality in the rock or rock/pop forms that now look as familiar as Trafalgar Square.

The record industry was quite unlike its earlier self. Most of its familiar labels – Island, Virgin, Stiff, A&M and so on – had been swallowed up by corporate owners. Even CBS joined the Japanese firm Sony. And the really big companies, including Sony, Warners and RCA (now part of the German BMG), had merged into new Goliaths like Universal. Behind the consolidation lurked a fear of the unknown future. The rise of the Internet, of MP3s and file-sharing, were changing life for ever and London acts were enveloped in the same uncertainty as everybody else. As revenues crashed, only the live circuit seemed in rude health – even if a few revered venues, such as the Marquee and the Astoria, succumbed to market forces. (Studios, too, including Olympic and Whitfield Street, where much of the music in this book originated, faced closure.)

Should all else fail, musicians could return to the streets as buskers. (Since 2003, it's been possible for licence holders to perform legally at designated spots in London Underground stations, too.) The streets, of course, were the place where London's popular music started.

Conventional careers are being rethought. From Tommy Steele to Ray Davies to Lady Sovereign, London musicians have shown their openness to the city's history, and to the creative stimulus it supplies. An especially interesting venture has been Damon Albarn's 2007 project, The Good, The Bad & The Queen. With his West London neighbour Paul Simonon, and other collaborators, the Blur and Clash men made what Albarn called 'a song cycle that's also a mystery play about London'. It was only one more stage in a busy career for him: since Blur's last record he'd had the virtual band Gorillaz with artist Jamie Hewlett, investigated the music of Mali and staged an 'opera-circus' called *Monkey: Journey to the West*. (His old Blur colleague Dave Rowntree, meanwhile, entered politics, becoming Labour's prospective candidate for the Cities of London & Westminster. Their bassist, Alex James, was now a gentleman farmer.)

The resulting album, *The Good, the Bad & the Queen*, was scarcely a frolic in the park. Though tuneful, it was overall a mournful, ominous affair with nothing of Dick Van Dyke – Albarn could at last sing openly of London without invoking *Parklife*. In fact its discordant pub pianos and heavy washes of abstract sound were more akin to an old-time London fog. The news of a Middle Eastern war lay heavily on its making; numbers such as 'History Song' spoke of melancholy Sundays and ships on the Estuary. They unveiled the music at Christmas 2006, in the brave, scarred setting of Wilton's Music Hall.

Afterword
Last orders: a London particular

London is 'a roost for every bird' said Benjamin Disraeli. Long may it be so, and long may music ease the roosting. Our much-maligned London pigeons (who are not without a music of their own) colonised the great city buildings, such as St Paul's, where the nooks and perches were like the habitats of their rock-dove ancestors. During the Great Fire of London, among the most affecting sights recorded by Pepys were the pigeons. So attached were they to their urban homes that they delayed their escape until too late, and with burning wings fell to the ground.

'Millions of people' swarm towards Ray Davies's 'Waterloo Sunset'. In T. S. Eliot's *The Wasteland* a similar swarm is overwhelming London Bridge. But each solitary soul, alive and dead, had some tale of its own and, probably, a song to match to its private sorrows and joys. In our own time, on those bridges, fully half the crowd might be wearing earphones to consolidate their privacy. We now deploy music as a barricade, where it used to be communal.

Millions of Londoners live side by side, but their lives are largely unshareable. The poignancy of Patrick Hamilton's novel, *20,000 Streets Under the Sky*, is underlined by its protagonists, Bob and Ella, lying in their adjacent attic rooms above the pub; two close friends, separated by mere inches of plaster-board, yet they're sublimely unaware of one another's emotional turmoil. In his biography of Shakespeare, Peter Ackroyd describes the young playwright adjusting to life in rented city rooms – he's experiencing a privacy unknowable in Stratford, a new kind of urban existence that helped to shape a new literature of the self, of the individual in a crowd.

. London music is a projection of the self against a constantly shifting canvas of other people's bodies. We thread our separate lives through the city's collective fabric. Commerce, satire, the companionship of a pub, the news of the day … these are the recurring themes we find in a city that can drive people deep into themselves, but never lets them forget its existence. Loneliness seems part and parcel of London life, but every song is an act of reaching out. Occasionally a special individual takes shape for us emerging from the fog – the 'London Particular' as those famous pea-soupers were known – and the romance will inspire another song.

Maybe it's because I'm *not* a Londoner that I have the outsider's sense of wonder at finding myself in the middle of all this. Some music in this book helped me find my way in the city – to its well-hidden but hospitable heart – and for that I will always be grateful.

London's Brilliant Parade: 140 Recommendations

Here is some suggested listening. The tracks are all personal favourites with some bearing on the book. Most are by London acts; the rest are by outsiders under the city's influence. Not every song here is 'about' London. But each of them, in its own way, carries something of the city's essence.

Obviously, no list of London music can ever be complete, or final. And no list that lurches from Madness to *Mary Poppins*, from 'Brompton Oratory' to 'Any Old Iron', needs to be taken entirely seriously. It is what it is.

For the sake of breadth I've limited the entries to one per artist. In this age of streaming and downloads you can sample nearly any artist and decide if you'd like to hear more. Occasionally I've indicated whole CDs that are worth acquiring. A predilection of mine is second-hand vinyl. Show tunes, soundtracks and vintage pop still show up in charity shops, where browsing is half the pleasure.

The dates I've quoted are those appearing on the discs I have and may not always be the exact year of recording. I've concentrated on the popular music of the last hundred years; for earlier pieces I've tried to quote the year of composition or first public performance. But enough. With luck you'll find some friends for life here . . .

Adele: 'Hometown Glory', 2007

Soul-inflected singer-songwriter ponders her London, from the streets to the government, concluding that it's the people she has met who are the 'wonders' of her world.

The African Messengers: 'Highlife Piccadilly', 1958

Invigorating instance of the immigrant sounds that were, post-war, now seeping into the wider city's consciousness. A multi-album series, *London Is the Place For Me*, is the ideal guide to Afro-Caribbean music of fifties Britain.

Lily Allen: 'LDN', 2006

From old Londinium to text-message LDN the city presents its contradictory faces. Lily is caught between a sunny calypso mood and darker visions of pimps, crack whores and cut-throats. Hogarth, Blake and Dickens would all have empathised.

Chris Barber: 'Petite Fleur', 1959

A delicate Top 3 hit which brought some mainstream recognition for the presiding guru of post-war jazz and blues scenes.

The Beatles: 'Norwegian Wood (This Bird Has Flown)', 1965

Session players were rare on Beatle records, though George Harrison would soon be hiring the tabla player Anil Bhagwat, and the Asian Music Circle (of Finchley), for Indian-influenced tracks like 'Love You To' and 'Within You, Without You'. For the moment, though, Harrison gamely attempts the double-tracked sitar himself, on Lennon's brilliant song of surreptitious liaisons with a downstairs neighbour at Emperor's Gate in Kensington.

The Beggar's opera: 'If Love the Virgin's Heart Invade', 1728

From John Gay's sprawling tale of London's rottenest scoundrels. Mrs Peachum, the thief-taker's wife, ponders her daughter's marriage to a highwayman. This version is sung by Anne Collins, from Benjamin Britten's arrangement of what has been called the first true musical.

BLAK TWANG: 'CHAMPAGNE LIFESTYLE', 2008

Anyone familiar with West End clubs will recognise the champagne-ordering protagonist with his forlorn pretensions to a Premiership footballer's lifestyle. Sardonic observations of the high-spending ladies' man who is actually on a 'Coca-Cola budget'. Twang is the Arsenal-loving Sex Pistols fan who has given hip hop a convincing London accent.

BLUR: 'PARKLIFE', 1994

Song that marked the commercial high-point of Britpop's bloke-ish phase. The actor Phil Daniels's voiceover lends a cockney authenticity that Damon Albarn himself might have struggled with.

JON BON JOVI: 'MIDNIGHT IN CHELSEA', 1997

Odd to note, the US overlord of stadium rock once recorded a solo album in London, living for three months in Wandsworth. 'I never understood why people thought that was funny,' he told me. 'I coulda lived in Holland Park. But I like Wandsworth.' Quite. (He drank at the old Surrey Tavern, by the Common.) Skinny goths, a red bus and a Sloane Ranger all catch his fish-out-of-water eye in this rather nice, understated song.

BONZO DOG BAND: 'I'M GONNA BRING A WATERMELON TO MY GIRL TONIGHT', 1966

A trad jazz joke, delightfully told. Stanshall plays the ardent swain whose lady responds with ever-growing gratitude to his ever-enlarging gifts of fruit. You see where he's going with this . . .

BOW WOW WOW: 'C30 C60 C90 GO', 1981

'Home taping is killing music,' said the record companies. BWW's creator Malcolm McLaren thought otherwise. A celebration of the cassette when it was still seen as guerrilla technology.

DAVID BOWIE: 'THE LONDON BOYS', 1966

Bow Bell sounds a mournful note across the London rooftops, and life for the runaway mod is far from sweet. A fine little Soho melodrama from Bowie's Anthony Newley period. His early years are much-anthologised and should not be overlooked.

BOY GEORGE: 'EVERYTHING I OWN', 1987

Graceful interpretation of the Ken Boothe reggae number that gave BG a post-Culture Club Number 1.

JOE BROWN & THE BRUVVERS: 'A PICTURE OF YOU', 1962

A cut above the larkier numbers he was also known for, this one's wearing well.

BURIAL: 'GHOST HARDWARE', 2007

William Bevan's atmospheric mutation of dancefloor dubstep, sounding like the music of an abandoned city.

KATE BUSH: 'MOMENTS OF PLEASURE', 1993

Dreamy recollections of nights passed in Abbey Road. Given the time musicians spend in studios it's surprising how few songs ever mention them. A reluctance, maybe, to let light in on the magic? Or an acknowledgement of how boring the process can often be?

THE BYRDS: 'EIGHT MILES HIGH', 1966

Borne aloft to London Airport, Californian boys reach the Beatles' London with a pang of cultural and psychedelic dislocation: the swinging city they heard so much about is rainy-grey and fundamentally foreign. Their public relations man for this trip was the Beatles ex-press man Derek Taylor, who indulged their dreams by taking them on a compartment-carriage British Railways train like the one they'd seen in A Hard Day's Night.

WALTER CARLOS: 'TITLE MUSIC FROM *A CLOCKWORK ORANGE*', 1972

The awful pageantry of death, now with added synthesisers. This was Purcell's music for a solemn state occasion, the funeral of Queen Mary in 1695. Three centuries later the piece was electronically revamped to set the nightmare tone for director Stanley Kubrick's vision of future Thamesmead. And Walter, incidentally, changed his name to Wendy.

CATATONIA: 'LONDINIUM', 1999

When bands arrive from elsewhere – in Catatonia's case, from Wales – to crack the music business, London is a kind of entrance exam they have to take. The need to escape may never leave them: Cerys is urging her taxi-driver to speed her station-wards, to Paddington and the journey home.

NICK CAVE: 'BROMPTON ORATORY', 1997

Erotic obsession meets religious majesty in the beautiful interior of a Kensington church.

HARRY CHAMPION: 'ANY OLD IRON', 1911

The rag-and-bone man's plaintive call is comically deployed as Harry inherits his uncle's watch-chain. Cue a barrage of disrespectful catcalls from street urchins and the Mayor of London himself. The best available collection of Champion, Marie Lloyd and co is a CD box set called *Night at the Music Hall*. There again, you can now download individual Harry Champion tracks on MP3. Rather incredible, when you consider he recorded with the musical equivalent of tin cans linked with string.

CHAS & DAVE: 'GERTCHA', 1979

The Gilbert and Sullivan of 'Rockney' address the inscrutable meaning of 'gertcha', a word so commonly uttered by irate fathers, yet mysteriously absent from the dictionary.

CHILLI WILLI & THE RED HOT PEPPERS: 'GOODBYE NASHVILLE HELLO CAMDEN TOWN', 1975

Heroes of the pub rock wars, captured in the last months of that genre's pre-punk hey-day. Available on a fine pub rock compilation of the same name.

THE DAVE CLARK FIVE: 'GLAD ALL OVER', 1963

Tottenham's response to the Merseybeat takeover. Quite impossible to dislike.

THE CLASH: 'POLICE ON MY BACK', 1980

Plenty of splendid Clash songs celebrate London, if 'celebrate' is quite the word for righteous condemnations of Babylon, etc. Which to pick? The clarion call of 'London Calling'? I have a fondness for the endearingly gawky 'Guns of Brixton'. 'London's Burning' is incandescent. But their version of Eddy Grant's 'Police On My Back' is fiercer yet.

COCKNEY REBEL: 'SEBASTIAN', 1973

Phantasmagorical example of Biba-pop, delivered in the most mannered London accent ever. Absurdly overwrought, but lovable.

RY COODER: 'POWIS SQUARE', 1970

An aptly chilly (not 'chilled') guitar instrumental by the Californian maestro Cooder, lending menace to the soundtrack of Jagger's Notting Hill film *Performance*. By the late 1960s, London seemed as natural a setting for these primeval blues riffs as anywhere in America.

ELVIS COSTELLO: 'LONDON'S BRILLIANT PARADE', 1994

A fuller portrait of his home town – both emotionally and geographically – than the better-known '(I Don't Want to Go to) Chelsea'.

288

Noël Coward: 'London Pride', 1941

A little urban flower, growing by the 'crrr-evices' and 'rrr-ailings'. Rolled 'R's and city flora are enlisted to fight the Nazi war machine in Britain's Darkest Hour. And they win.

Tony Crombie: 'Teach You to Rock', 1956

Stiff attempt to replicate the natural funkiness of roots American rock, but a likeable glimpse of Soho in the dawn of its cappuccino age.

Smiley Culture: 'Cockney Translation', 1984

A service to Rastafarian travellers in the East End: Smiley lists the linguistic differences that 'Terry, Arthur and Del-Boy' may have with 'Winston, Lloyd and Leroy'. For example, where the former call a thief a tea-leaf, Smiley and his boys say 'sticksman'. And do take special care with 'Old Bill' and 'Babylon'.

The Damned: 'New Rose', 1976

The official first blast of UK punk, reverberating down the ages.

Billie Davis: 'I Want You to Be My Baby', 1968

The US soul influence, smuggled in via clubs like the Flamingo, was now resurfacing in blue-eyed form, and seldom better than this.

Dave Dee, Dozy, Beaky, Mick & Titch: 'Last Night in Soho', 1968

Exactly *what* did our narrator get up to 'last night in Soho'? We are not told. This morning, however, a prison cell awaits. And, rather ominously, he can never face his sweetheart again . . .

Damien Dempsey: 'Kilburn Stroll', 2007

Like many another exile, the Dubliner Dempsey walks the North London pavements with another place on his mind.

DEPARTMENT S: 'IS VIC THERE?', 1981

A tough little post-punk classic by one of the era's great 'nearly' bands.

THE DEVIANTS: 'PAPA-OO-MAO-MAO', 1968

Mick Farren's hippy guerilla band take on Western society. And lose.

DIRE STRAITS: 'SULTANS OF SWING', 1979

A song about a struggling Dixieland jazz band on a drizzly night in South London. How could it fail?

DIZZEE RASCAL: 'STAND UP TALL', (2004)

Alphabetically, should he be filed under 'D'? Interviewed on the BBC about his political ambitions, he was addressed by Jeremy Paxman as 'Mr Rascal', so perhaps not. Anyway, this is a defiant East-side brag by a compulsive celebrant of the city's harshest streets.

DOLL BY DOLL: 'STRIP SHOW', 1979

Late one night, as its 'neon universe' blinks out and yawning cab-men dawdle in the streets, an exiled Scot finds London's sleaze a mirror for his soul. A great song by Jackie Leven, the barrel-chested bard of Fife.

DONOVAN: 'SUNNY GOODGE STREET', 1965

The gentle beatnik guitar-picker, a pop star graduate from London's folk circles, sings of a hash-smoker's altercation with a vending machine. Thus he nails a once-typical sound of London's Tube stations: the futile rattling of a jammed drawer, the inchoate fury and despairing curses, echoing down the tunnels . . .

DIANA DORS: 'THE HOKEY-POKEY POLKA', 1955

From the film *As Long as They're Happy*, the former Miss Fluck of Swindon breathes invitingly over this brief party-piece. She'd earlier appeared in *Oliver Twist* with Anthony Newley and the two became teenage sweethearts. By the 1950s she was a brassy sex symbol of resurgent Soho. When she was fifty, with two years left to live, she made a video with Adam Ant and the *NME* sent me to her splendidly vulgar house in the stockbroker belt, where she beguiled me with stories. What would she say to a present-day Miss Fluck, hopeful of showbiz fame? 'I would say, Be prepared for a lot of hard work, and a lot of disappointments, and a lot of sadness. But then, that's what everyone told *me*. And I wasn't the slightest bit interested.'

JOHN DOWLAND: 'WEEP YOU NO MORE, SAD FOUNTAINS', 1600

Among the earliest of London's formal songwriters and surely unsurpassed for sombre beauty.

NICK DRAKE: 'SUNDAY', 1970

Forever at odds with London's unmerciful tumult, Drake may have written this peaceful instrumental in tribute to the one day when life slowed to a tolerable pace.

DUFFY: 'WARWICK AVENUE', 2008

A London station fulfils its secondary function as venue for lovers' meetings and farewells. In this case it's the latter. Dreading the encounter, she asks him to promise that he won't stand by the light.

STEPHEN DUFFY: 'LONDON GIRLS', 1995

A wry snapshot of Camden pub life in the Britpop years.

IAN DURY & THE BLOCKHEADS: 'MY OLD MAN', 1977

The tenderest of his London numbers, many of which were not tender at all. This was a tribute to his bus-driver dad.

MS DYNAMITE: 'IT TAKES MORE', 2002

In what amounts to a dissident voice in hip hop, the London girl repudiates the flash lifestyle and gangster bragging: she is the sort of girl, she says, who needs more than that.

EAST 17: 'HOUSE OF LOVE', 1992

From *Walthamstow*, the debut album by the rave-inclined urchin boy-band. Among its hits was this – as yet unheeded – demand for an immediate end to war.

GUS ELEN: 'IF IT WASN'T FOR THE 'OUSES IN BETWEEN', 1899

He has 'a werry pretty garden' and a view that stretches all the way to 'Ackney Marshes – or it would, if it wasn't for the houses in between. There is some precious footage of Elen in a documentary DVD called *Music Hall Days*.

DAVID ESSEX: 'GONNA MAKE YOU A STAR', 1974

A dogged survivor shares some thoughts about the machinations of Tin Pan Alley.

THE FACES: 'DEBRIS', 1971

The first generation of London rockers grew up in a bombed city. East Ender Ronnie Lane locates his saddest love song by the rubble that hosts the Sunday morning market.

FAIRPORT CONVENTION: 'MEET ON THE LEDGE', 1969

Neither a London song nor something of the countryside, but really transcending both. Universal and quite sublime.

ADAM FAITH: 'WHAT DO YOU WANT?', 1959

. . . if you don't want money? A classic London sentiment, somehow.

THE FEELING: 'WITHOUT YOU', 2008

American tour blues, homesick yearning worsened by the West Virginian rain, so like London.

FLANAGAN & ALLEN: 'HOMETOWN', 1937

The rustic nostalgia sounds a little implausible, but charming just the same.

FLEETWOOD MAC: 'MAN OF THE WORLD', 1969

Peter Green's Fleetwood Mac were never more poignant than here, the song of a haunted man surveying his life and rather wishing he hadn't.

FREEEZ: 'SOUTHERN FREEEZ', 1981

The finest London Brit-funk.

EDWARD GERMAN: 'NELL GWYN, MERRYMAKERS' DANCE', 1900

A composer so highly regarded he was Gilbert's choice of partner when Sullivan died, though without spectacular results. His English historical pieces have been called 'musical mock Tudor' but they were staples of light orchestral radio for decades.

GILBERT AND SULLIVAN: 'MY GALLANT CREW, GOOD MORNING!', 1878

From *HMS Pinafore*, their first big success. Introduced the phrase 'What, never? Hardly ever' to Victorian London, ensuring instant merriment.

NAT GONELLA: 'STARDUST', 1935

A soft-shoe shuffler, as they used to say, led by the Armstrong-influenced trumpeter and vocalist. I relish the nearly extinct cockney softness of his letter 'R' – lost in his 'wevewie', each kiss an 'inspiwation'.

DAVY GRAHAM: 'ANGI', 1962

Completely perfect guitar piece that inspired many to learn the instrument – and perhaps persuaded more that there was no point trying.

EDDY GRANT: 'ELECTRIC AVENUE', 1983

The Brixton market street was apparently London's first electrified shopping arcade. With such a name it was bound to inspire a song eventually.

HAMMERSMITH GORILLAS: 'YOU REALLY GOT ME', 1974

If ever a band has slipped between the cracks of history it's Jesse Hector's power trio; this raging Kinks cover indicates why some tipped them to be the Next Big Thing.

HARD-FI: 'TIED UP TOO TIGHT', 2005

Discontented Staines gang (*Stars of CCTV*, as their debut album had it) resolve to hit the Great West Road in a bid for the bright lights of town.

THE JAM: 'IN THE CITY', 1977

All the pent-up sense of possibility that London can present to the energetic incomer, compressed inside of two minutes twenty seconds.

BERT JANSCH AND JOHN RENBOURN: 'SOHO', 1966

The crime, the market cries, the naked dancers and the helplessly drunk . . . It could be a song of Sodom or Gomorrah, except that your nearest Tube stop is Leicester Square.

JOHN'S CHILDREN: 'DESDEMONA', 1967

The psychedelic power-pop band that harboured Marc Bolan for a while – hear his winsome bleat in the background of this slightly saucy flower-child freak-out.

LINTON KWESI JOHNSON: 'DI BLACK PETTY BOOSHWAH', 1980

The poet laureate of reggae turns his baleful gaze towards some Afro-Caribbean high achievers and questions their motives. As ever with LKJ the interest is partly in the lyrical idea but also in the melodious rendition of raw Jamaican patois.

KILBURN & THE HIGH ROADS: 'BILLY BENTLEY (PROMENADES HIMSELF IN LONDON)', 1974

A prime Ian Dury romp across town. Nowadays available as a bonus track with the *Handsome* album.

B. B. KING: 'BETTER NOT LOOK DOWN', 1979

Mississippi blues giant takes the air in London, England. Bumps into the Queen of England – as you do – and offers her sage advice in matters of the heart. She is duly honoured.

THE KINKS: 'WATERLOO SUNSET', 1967

Perverse not to nominate this song, though it's certainly worth investigating the band's lesser-known London numbers like 'Berkeley Mews', 'Denmark Street', 'Shangri La', 'Big Black Smoke' *et al.*

THE KURSAAL FLYERS: 'DRINKING SOCIALLY', 1976

The wittiest of the pub-rock mafia align themselves with London's immemorial tavern tradition.

RONNIE LANE: 'KUSCHTY RYE', 1979

The Romany-cockney overlap is interesting, from the hop-fields of Kent to the arcane coster slang with its *bona palare* undertones. A cultural coalition is sweetly depicted here, Ronnie romancing his blinged-up gypsy princess.

THE LEYTON BUZZARDS: 'SATURDAY NIGHT (BENEATH THE PLASTIC PALM TREES)', 1979

Very engaging memoir of youthful escapades among the skinheads of Tottenham Hale in 1969 – keeping a wary eye out for the crews from Balham and Golders Green.

THE LIBERTINES: 'UP THE BRACKET', 2002

Garage-punk story of dark dealings in Bethnal Green and Penton-ville, with a sinister cast from London's criminal netherworld. Darkly thrilling.

LIGHT OF THE WORLD: 'LONDON TOWN', 1980

Summery celebration of the city in its sunniest aspect, by loyalist London funketeers.

MARIE LLOYD: 'THE COSTER GIRL IN PARIS', 1912

In which she recounts her honeymoon trip across the Channel. Paris is not so bad, she allows – if only they could plant the Hackney Road there. So much for the fancy boulevards of Baron Haussmann.

LORD KITCHENER: 'UNDERGROUND TRAIN', 1950

Two years after his arrival from Trinidad, the great calypsonian enters EMI Studios in Abbey Road to chronicle his perplexing first encounter with the Tube system. Misunderstandings, mostly involv-ing young ladies, ensue from Piccadilly to Lancaster Gate.

VERA LYNN: 'THE LONDON I LOVE', 1941

Through the black-out and carnage, Londoners lived the Blitz in a form of exile from normality. Vera shares their longing for the city's restoration – even if, as they probably sensed, things could never be the same.

KIRSTY MACCOLL: 'AUTUMNGIRLSOUP', 2001

Dreamlike song beginning with an out-of-body experience above the city, gently descending into the earthier realms of physical love and longing. Spellbinding.

MADNESS: 'IN THE CITY', 1982

Began life as a ten-second TV jingle selling Honda 'City' cars to the people of Tokyo. The session was unexpectedly gruelling: 'How do you say, "Can I have some more treble on the bass drum?" in Japanese?' But even expanded to song-length it's a great distillation of the band's essence.

BRAM MARTIN: 'SHE'S MY LOVELY', 1937

In 1916 he was playing cello at the Woolwich Music Hall, went on to cinema work for silent movies, then an inter-war residency at the Holborn Restaurant. After that came panto, a spell in Mantovani's band and finally session jobs for everyone from Max Bygraves to the Beatles. Had he lived, you imagine he would have gone on to acid house, Britpop and grime.

MARY POPPINS: 'STEP IN TIME', 1964

Dick Van Dyke leads full complement of sooty chums in rooftop extravaganza. Try to forget the vowels that are dying in agony. Admire, instead, the sheer vitality of its Hollywood coster conceit.

RALPH MCTELL: 'THE STREETS OF LONDON', 1974

The song began as 'The Streets of Paris', but was later switched. Its central character, McTell explains, is the friend to whom he is singing – a self-pitying heroin addict who needed reminding of others less fortunate.

M.I.A.: 'XR2', 2007

Brick Lane and Ladbroke Grove feature in this energetically nostalgic hymn to the early London rave scene.

MAX MILLER: 'MARY FROM THE DAIRY', 1935

The Cheeky Chappie's signature song. For the full experience, though, find a recording of his whole stage act. You then realise how he became such a staple of British life – even pictured on the *Sgt. Pepper* sleeve.

MILLIE: 'MY BOY LOLLIPOP', 1964

She was a young Jamaican singer, brought to London by Island's Chris Blackwell; the song reached Number 2 at the peak of the Beatles' supremacy and must, I'm sure, have planted a love for reggae-pop in the British heart. Its jollity still sounds indestructible.

MATT MONRO: 'WALK AWAY', 1964

One of the great break-up songs, lyrics by Don Black. Monro's performance is an epic of self-renunciation – beneath the tuxedo there trembles a noble, manly heart.

VAN MORRISON: 'SLIM SLOW SLIDER', 1968

Some would say his *Astral Weeks* is the best album ever made. I certainly know of no starker song than its desolate finale. Here is Morrison, re-enacting some mysterious scene of grief descending, sure as death, on a pavement in Ladbroke Grove.

MOTT THE HOOPLE: '(DO YOU REMEMBER) THE SATURDAY GIGS?', 1974

A grand, self-mythologising ballad of one band's history, from youthful dalliance with Chelsea girls, to some Damascus-like moment at a gig in Croydon, via Bowie's gift of a career-rescuing hit, 'All the Young Dudes'.

MY FAIR LADY: 'WOULDN'T IT BE LOVERLY?', 1956

The timeless pining of a lonely and homeless Londoner. Julie Andrews sings this version, from the original Broadway cast recording. Or you might try the 1964 movie soundtrack – be aware, though, that contrary to appearances, Audrey Hepburn does not sing (her vocals were dubbed by the perennially un-credited Marni Nixon).

ANTHONY NEWLEY: 'DO YOU MIND', 1960

Hip, finger-snapping slickness, written by Lionel Bart.

Nick Nicely: 'Hilly Fields (1892)', 1981

An eerie piece of neo-psychedelia that seems to describe some strange Victorian timeslip in a small South London park. Nicely's obscure but haunting single is one of the great lost oddities of English pop. It finally re-emerged on a 2004 CD of his work, *Psychotropia*.

Ray Noble featuring Al Bowlly: 'Love is the Sweetest Thing', 1932

Lovely. The fuller version (including its delicate prelude, usually skipped) was on the soundtrack of Bob Hoskins's BBC series *Pennies From Heaven*.

Nolay: 'Unorthodox Daughter', 2004

By a young female MC, this was one of the outstanding tracks on a 2004 grime sampler called *Run the Road* – itself a key document of the genre.

Oliver!: 'Who Will Buy?', 1968

From the 1968 film of Lionel Bart's greatest work. The number builds from a solitary street-seller's song to an ensemble round of sweetly competing calls, thence to Bart's exquisite tune itself, topped off with a big gor-blimey singalong. Dickens would have loved it.

Jack Peñate: 'Torn on the Platform', 2007

Platform 3 of Waterloo Station is the arena for this little tale of London chauvinism. Why would anyone leave this city? Jack is 'torn' by indecision as the carriage doors close.

Pet Shop Boys: 'West End Girls', 1985

Tennant and Lowe return obsessively to themes of London, usually from a slightly detached viewpoint ('London', 'Sexy Northerner', 'Dreaming of the Queen', 'King's Cross'). This was the first and most famous example.

THE POGUES: 'A RAINY NIGHT IN SOHO', 1985

The most affecting of several London numbers in MacGowan's catalogue.

THE PRETENDERS: 'TALK OF THE TOWN', 1980

Among the great US imports into London's music scene, Chrissie Hynde went from a spell at the *NME* to working for McLaren and Westwood in the King's Road, to fronting one of the sleeker chart acts to emerge from punk. The single's artwork showed the West End club, formerly a grand Edwardian music hall, at the peak of its neon glory.

THE PRETTY THINGS: '13 CHESTER STREET', 1965

Shuddering Brit-blues from the shaggy band who somehow blagged a pad in Belgravia. Here the shade of Slim Harpo walks the leafy squares; the spirit of Bo Diddley moves imperiously through the mews; harmonicas wail the ancient pains of injustice within a short, agreeable stroll from Buckingham Palace.

PULP: 'COMMON PEOPLE', 1995

The Northerner Jarvis Cocker kept a nicely sardonic eye on his adopted city; this tale of recreational slumming comes from his time at Central St Martins. Bizarrely, there is also a good version of it by the *Star Trek* actor William Shatner.

GERRY RAFFERTY: 'BAKER STREET', 1978

It's by no means a bad song on its own. But Raphael Ravenscroft's saxophone riff remains indomitable.

CLIFF RICHARD: 'MOVE IT', 1958

An urgently libidinous debut disc, Presley-esque and panting, twangsome to the max. Had he never recorded another note, Cliff would be a sort of legend for 'Move It', worshipped by every obsessive who salivates over rock 'n' roll footnotes. But the Lord had other plans.

The Rolling Stones: 'Play With Fire', 1965

The social highs and lows of London, surveyed with level contempt. There's something of *The Beggar's Opera* in that approach.

The Ruts: 'West One (Shine On Me)', 1980

The West London punks' posthumous hit, darkly angst-ridden, released just after Malcolm Owen's death.

Saint Etienne: 'London Belongs to Me', 1991

The Croydon band have always been loving observers of London. Bob Stanley ascribes this song (whose title invokes a 1945 novel by Norman Collins) to the joyful liberation of first living in London. From under a willow tree at Regent's Park, from Camden Tube via Parkway, it's a shimmering recollection of one romantic day when peace reclaimed the heart.

Nitin Sawhney featuring Natty: 'Days of Fire', 2008

Dramatic events from London's recent history are recalled by an eyewitness, with dispassionate calm. Bombs and gunfire bring a portion of foreign wars to London's very innards, the Tube system.

Alexei Sayle: ''Ullo John! Gotta New Motor?', 1982

This is how a Northerner hears the cockney voice. The drink of choice? A light and bitter. The Thames 'Barria'.

Sex Pistols: 'God Save the Queen', 1977

It was the Queen's Jubilee Year, but there was 'no future', said the Pistols, in 'England's dreaming'. Happily, however, both the Pistols and their monarch had many more anniversaries to come.

Helen Shapiro: 'Walkin' Back to Happiness', 1961

The first female voice of British suburban teen-pop.

Ella Shields: 'Burlington Bertie from Bow', 1916

The pride of the poor is a perennial element in music hall. The phoney 'swell' is meant to be comical, yet not to be despised.

Frank Sinatra: 'A Foggy Day', 1953

The Gershwins' show tune given a swingin' update. Despondent Frank is kicking his heels in glum old Bloomsbury. All of a sudden, though, that nasty pea-souper is banished by the radiant arrival of love.

The Small Faces: 'Itchycoo Park', 1967

Wherein Ilford explodes into a million colours and floats in crystalline particles to a land beyond the stars.

So Solid Crew: 'Way Back When', 2001

Her man's just bought a flash new car, innit? Won't the other girls be jealous! Conspicuous consumption as advanced mating technique, celebrated – in a satirical way – by the first family of South London hip hop.

Soul II Soul: 'Back to Life (However Do You Want Me)', 1992

Mesmeric hit single (sung by Caron Wheeler) that became a landmark of British soul and dance.

Spandau Ballet: 'Chant No. 1', 1981

All the vitality of the Soho night, perfectly captured.

Spectrum: 'Nodnol', 1969

A woozy curio from the last days of sixties psychedelia. Involves a place called 'Nodnol' (try it backwards), where ethereal pearly queens float by. Available on the box set *Real Life Permanent Dreams*.

DUSTY SPRINGFIELD: 'NOTHING HAS BEEN PROVED', 1989

From her late-career revival with the Pet Shop Boys, a number featured in the Keeler/Profumo movie *Scandal*.

SQUEEZE: 'UP THE JUNCTION', 1979

An evergreen contender for the title of All-Time London Favourite, though 'Waterloo Sunset' still looks unassailable. But then, who needs to choose?

TOMMY STEELE: 'ROCK WITH THE CAVEMAN', 1956

Stalagmites and stalactites are rhymed with holding one's cave-girl 'very tight!' Admittedly, it's not Lionel Bart's greatest lyric, and the ensemble-playing is second-hand Bill Haley, but British rock had to start somewhere and this was it.

CAT STEVENS: 'MATTHEW AND SON', 1967

Growing up in Shaftesbury Avenue the former Steven Demetre Georgiou was a true child of the city: he would climb on theatre rooftops to hear the musicals playing below. And from his room above his parents' restaurant, he must have gazed daily at the mad commuter rush that informs this early hit.

THE STREETS: 'DRY YOUR EYES', 2004

The weeping strings subside to a slow, loping beat; Mike Skinner steps up to announce how suddenly, and sadly, a life can turn around. And so the old language of anguish finds a new translator, expressing it for the girl on the top deck of the bus, teardrops falling on her MP3 phone.

Suede featuring Raissa: 'Poor Little Rich Girl', 1998

Spacey re-imagining of Noël Coward from a fascinating tribute CD, *Twentieth Century Blues*, that also features Damon Albarn ('London Pride'), Paul McCartney ('Room With a View') and many others.

Sway: 'Products', 2006

He loves his city, sings the London rapper Sway: but it's a hard catalogue of hustle that he records, in a town where children give birth to children and stumble blindly into crime.

Thomas Tallis: 'Spem in Alium', 1573

The supreme masterpiece of London's early church music.

Tangerine Dream: 'London', 1987

The German prog-rockers asked a New York singer, Jocelyn Bernadette Smith, to recite the London poetry of William Blake: 'the hapless soldier's sigh/Runs in blood down Palace walls ... how the youthful harlot's curse/Blasts the new-born infant's tear' and what have you. She hated it. 'I'm an R&B singer,' she said, dashing the book to the floor, 'and I don't do this schoolkid bullshit!'

Television Personalities: 'Velvet Underground', 2006

Dan Treacy grew up in the King's Road, where his mum ran a laundromat; in the street he would see Bryan Ferry and David Bowie the way the rest of us saw postmen. For three decades the TVPs have kept up a cultural commentary from the margins ('Where's Bill Grundy Now?', 'I Was a Mod Before You Were a Mod') and there's characteristic wit in this shambling, jangly tribute to Lou Reed's band. But its parent CD, *My Dark Places*, is a harrowing dispatch from some bleak zone of London, more the backside of King's Cross than the high street of Chelsea.

THEATRE OF HATE: 'DO YOU BELIEVE IN THE WESTWORLD', 1981

Kirk Brandon's thundering post-punk dramatics, produced by Mick Jones. The meaning remains as impenetrable as ever.

T. REX: 'LONDON BOYS', 1976

Marc Bolan, near the end of his days, returns to the verities of his boyhood, when he could be the boss mod of Petticoat Lane.

MAX WALL: 'DREAM TOBACCO', 1977

A 'child in the wings', he said of his music hall upbringing. Wall took to the stage as 'The Boy With the Obedient Feet', survived the death of variety to play in straight theatre and then signed to Stiff, where he made some gems like this.

GENO WASHINGTON: 'QUE SERA SERA', 1966

Being a US soulman exiled to England Washington was cut off from the greatest material, but he's never lacked for a devoted live crowd. He probably did the right thing.

ELISABETH WELCH: 'SOLOMON', 1933

A Biblical Cole Porter song gets suitably blood-curdling treatment from the transplanted US diva. The king's thousand wives start giving him grief, so he ordains they be sliced up into 'jigsaw puzzles'. Harsh but fair.

WHISTLING JACK SMITH: 'I WAS KAISER BILL'S BATMAN', 1967

Not an 'authentic' record of Swinging London, simply a cheerful cash-in. But then, what was ever authentic in Swinging London? Lovely 'Oi!' at the end.

THE WHO: 'REAL GOOD-LOOKING BOY', 2004

Their hits are pretty familiar but this sad tale of a West London childhood is a late addition to Pete Townshend's great achievements.

How many rock stars have written about their sense of physical ugliness? And made it sound so touching?

WILEY: 'SLIPPIN', 2007

The boy from Grimesville E3, finds himself stranded in south-west London. Being in the wrong place at the wrong time, he resolves to 'splurt'.

AMY WINEHOUSE: 'TAKE THE BOX', 2003

Wonderful storytelling. Break-up numbers lend themselves to wide-screen performances. But it's the sordid trivia of separation that's dwelt upon here – the division of worldly goods into cardboard boxes: the Moschino bra that he gave her; the Frank Sinatra disc that doubtless soundtracked their romantic evenings. As a blameless symbol of the psycho-drama raging around the room, the box is poignantly perfect.

HAYDN WOOD: 'SKETCH OF A DANDY', (1950)

The light-music composer, known for his *London Landmarks Suite*, wrote many such pieces, broadcast by the BBC to listeners grateful for quaint vignettes of an elegant city lost to redevelopment.

WARREN ZEVON: 'WEREWOLVES OF LONDON', 1978

A jangling comic-rock delight, classically Yank in its Hollywood vision of Soho's ill-lit alleyways, and a fearsome hirsute character who has lately wrought terror in Mayfair.

Sources and Acknowledgements

My thanks are due to many people I have interviewed down the years. Each of them, in different ways, deepened my appreciation of London's music. Among them are Brett Anderson, Adam Ant, David Balfe, Allan Bernard, Jon Bon Jovi, Bow Wow Wow, David Bowie, Billy Bragg, Kirk Brandon, Lee Brilleaux, Joe Brown, Jack Bruce, Geoff Bullen at RADA, Bernard Butler, Miles Copeland, Hugh Cornwell, Elvis Costello, Ray Davies, Chris Difford, Diana Dors, Ian Dury, Kathy Etchingham, Mickey Finn, Eddy Grant, Steve Harris, Jools Holland, Chrissie Hynde, Neil Innes, Mick Jagger, Bert Jansch, Peter Jenner, Wilko Johnson, Kenney Jones, Neal Kay, Gary Kemp, Lemmy, Nick Lowe, Phil May, Paul McCartney, Malcolm McLaren, Tony 'TS' McPhee, Spike Milligan, Morrissey, Van Morrison, Simon Napier-Bell, Nick Nicely, Andrew Loog Oldham, Malcolm Owen, Jimmy Page, Michael Palin, Larry Parnes, Andy Partridge, John Peel, Marco Pirroni, Noel Redding, Penny Rimbaud, Dave Robinson, Nitin Sawhney, Rat Scabies, Siouxsie Sioux, Dusty Springfield, Joe Strummer, Screaming Lord Sutch, Derek Taylor, Dick Taylor, Glenn Tilbrook, Vaughan Toulouse, Pete Townshend, Edward Tudorpole, Tony Visconti, Tom Watkins, Paul Weller, Helen Wellington-Lloyd, Amy Winehouse and Steve Winwood.

Some were interviewed especially for this book; I talked to others in the course of my work for *NME*, *Q*, *Mojo* and *The Word*. To the various editors who gave me those opportunities, and to all the colleagues who have helped me along the way, I owe a great debt of gratitude. The same magazines have been invaluable to me in my research; among the other journals consulted, I might mention the *Evening Standard* and *Time Out*.

For the picture research I thank Kevin Hayes. For making me the London compilation tape which helped inspire this book: Jon Savage. And for their kind assistance in miscellaneous ways: Will Birch, Joolz Bosson, David Buckley, Arwa Haider, Andrew Harrison, Liz Lacey, Doll Makin, Jude Rogers, Robert Sandall and Colin Shearman.

Above all, my thanks are due to Ros Edwards, my agent at Edwards-Fuglewicz; to my editors Ed Faulkner and Davina Russell and all their colleagues at Virgin Books; and to my wife Una Du Noyer.

Bibliography

Ackroyd, Peter, *London the Biography*, Chatto & Windus, 2000.

Ackroyd, Peter, *Thames: Sacred River*, Chatto & Windus, 2007.

Adams, Tim (Ed.), *City Secrets: London*, Little Bookworm, 2001.

Ali, Monica, *Brick Lane*, Doubleday, 2003.

Altham, Keith, *No More Mr Nice Guy*, Blake, 1999.

Barnes, Richard, *The Who: Maximum R&B*, Eel Pie, 1982.

Bernard, Jeffrey, *Reach for the Ground*, Gerald Duckworth, 1996.

Birch, Will, *No Sleep till Hammersmith: the Great Pub Rock Revolution*, Virgin, 2000.

Bowie, Angie, *Backstage Passes*, Orion, 1993.

Boy George (with Paul Gorman), *Straight*, Arrow, 2005.

Bramwell, Tony, *Magical Mystery Tours: My Life with the Beatles*, Robson, 2005.

Buckley, David, *Strange Fascination: David Bowie the Definitive Story*, Virgin, 1999.

Buckley, David, *The Thrill of it All: Bryan Ferry and Roxy Music*, André Deutsch, 2004.

Bushell, Peter, *London's Secret History*, Constable, 1983.

Cann, Kevin, *David Bowie: a Chronology*, Hutchinson, 1983.

Charlesworth, Chris, *The Complete Guide to the Music of the Who*, Omnibus, 1995.

Chesterton, G. K., *The Napoleon of Notting Hill*, The Bodley Head, 1904.

Chesterton, G. K., *Selected Essays*, Collins, 1936.

Citron, Stephen, *Noël & Cole: the Sophisticates*, Sinclair Stephenson, 1992.

Clapton, Eric, *The Autobiography*, Century, 2007.

Clarke, Victoria Mary & MacGowan, Shane, *A Drink with Shane MacGowan*, Sidgwick & Jackson, 2001.

Cohn, Nik, *AwopBopaLooBop AlopBamBoom*, Weidenfeld & Nicolson, 1969.

Cohn, Nik, *Today There are No Gentlemen*, Weidenfeld & Nicolson, 1971.

Coward, Noël, *Present Indicative/Future Indefinite*, William Heinemann, 1937.

Davies, Ray, *X-Ray*, Viking, 1994.

De Koningh, Michael & Griffiths, Marc, *Tighten Up! The History of Reggae in the UK*, Sanctuary, 2003.

Diamond, Michael, *Victorian Sensation*, Anthem, 2003.

Difford, Chris & Tilbrook, Glenn with Drury, Jim, *Squeeze: Song by Song*, Sanctuary, 2004.

Dors, Diana, *Dors by Diana*, Futura, 1981

Drury, Jim, *Ian Dury & the Blockheads: Song by Song*, Sanctuary, 2003.

Dudrah, Rajinder, *Bhangra*, Birmingham City Council, 2007.

Dunn, Nell, *Up the Junction*, MacGibbon & Kee, 1963.

Du Noyer, Paul (Ed.), *The Illustrated Encyclopedia of Music*, Flame Tree, 2003.

Earle, John, *Micro-Cosmographie*, Robert Allot, 1628.

Egan, Sean, *Jimi Hendrix: Not Necessarily Stoned, but Beautiful*, Unanimous, 2002.

Essex, David, *A Charmed Life*, Orion, 2002.

Faithfull, Marianne, *Faithfull*, Michael Joseph, 1994.

Farren, Mick, *Give the Anarchist a Cigarette*, Pimlico, 2001.

Fitter, R. S. R., *London's Natural History*, Collins, 1945.

Frame, Pete, *Rock Family Trees*, Omnibus, 1979.

Frame, Pete, *The Beatles and Some Other Guys*, Omnibus, 1997.

Gaunt, William, *The Aesthetic Adventure*, Jonathan Cape, 1945.

Grossmith, George and Weedon, *The Diary of a Nobody*, Arrowsmith, 1892.

Hackwood, Frederick W., *Inns, Ales & Drinking Customs of Old England*, Unwin, 1909.

Hamilton, Patrick, *Slaves of Solitude*, Constable, 1947.

Hardy, Phil & Laing, Dave, *The Faber Companion to 20th-Century Popular Music*, Faber and Faber, 1990.

Harper, Colin, *Dazzling Stranger: Bert Jansch and the British Folk and Blues Revival*, Bloomsbury, 2000.

Harris, John, *The Last Party*, 4th Estate, 2003.

Heckstall-Smith, Dick and Grant, Pete, *Blowin' the Blues*, Clear Books, 2004.

Hewitt, Paolo, *Small Faces: The Young Mods' Forgotten Story*, Acid Jazz, 1995.

Hibbert, Christopher, *Cities and Civilisations*, Weidenfeld & Nicolson, 1986.

Honri, Peter, *Working the Halls*, Saxon House, 1973.

Humphries, Patrick, *Nick Drake: the Biography*, Bloomsbury, 1997.

James, Alex, *Bit of a Blur*, Little, Brown, 2007.

Lee, Edward, *Folksong & Music Hall*, Routledge & Kegan Paul, 1982.

Leigh, Spencer and Firminger, John, *Halfway to Paradise: Britpop 1955–62*, Finbarr, 1996.

Leigh, Spencer, *Brother, Can You Spare a Rhyme?*, Spencer Leigh, 2000.

Levy, Shawn, *Ready Steady, Go!*, Fourth Estate, 2002.

Lewisohn, Mark, *The Complete Beatles Recording Sessions*, EMI/Hamlyn, 1988.

Lightwood, James T., *Charles Dickens and Music*, Charles H. Kelly, 1912.

Longmate, Norman, *How We Lived Then*, Hutchinson, 1971.

Lucas, E. V., *A Wanderer in London*, Methuen, 1906.

MacInnes, Colin, *Absolute Beginners*, Alison & Busby, 1959.

May, Chris and Phillips, Tim, *British Beat*, Socion, 1974.

Mayhew, Henry, *London Labour and the London Poor*, Kimber, 1851.

Melly, George, *Owning Up*, Weidenfeld & Nicolson, 1965.

Melly, George, *Revolt into Style*, Penguin, 1972.

Miles, Barry, *In the Sixties*, Pimlico, 2003.

Morton, H. V., *The Heart of London*, Methuen, 1925.

Morton, H. V., *The Spell of London*, Methuen, 1926.

Morton, H. V., *In Search of England*, Methuen, 1927.

Muggeridge, Malcolm and Hogarth, Paul, *London à la Mode*, Studio Vista, 1966.

Napier-Bell, Simon, *You Don't Have to Say You Love Me*, New English Library, 1982.

Napier-Bell, Simon, *Black Vinyl White Powder*, Ebury, 2002.

Nicholson, Dorothy, *The Londoner*, Collins, 1944.

Norman, Philip, *John Lennon: the Life*, HarperCollins, 2008.

Nuttall, Jeff and Carmichael, Rodick, *Common Factors/Vulgar Factions*, Routledge & Kegan Paul, 1977.

Oldham, Andrew Loog, *Stoned*, Secker & Warburg, 2000.

O'Neill, Alastair, *London – After a Fashion*, Reaktion, 2007.

Owens, Judith, *Commerce and Cadiz in Spenser's Prothalamion*, Thomson Gale, 2007.

Palmer, Roy, *The Sound of History*, Pimlico, 1988.

Paytress, Mark, *Twentieth Century Boy: the Marc Bolan Story*, Sidgwick & Jackson, 1992.

Paytress, Mark and Pafford, Steve, *Bowiestyle*, Omnibus, 2000.

Pearson, Hesketh, *Gilbert and Sullivan*, Harper & Brothers, 1935.

Peel, John and Ravenscroft, Sheila, *Margrave of the Marshes*, Bantam, 2005.

Picard, Liza, *Victorian London*, Weidenfeld & Nicolson, 2005.

Randall, Lucien & Welch, Chris, *Ginger Geezer: the Life of Vivian Stanshall*, Fourth Estate, 2001.

Read, Mike, *The Cliff Richard File*, Roger Houghton, 1986.

Reed, John, *Paul Weller: My Ever Changing Moods*, Omnibus, 1996.

Rogan, Johnny, *Starmakers & Svengalis*, Queen Anne Press, 1988.

Rossi, Francis, Parfitt, Rick, Young, Bob (Eds), *Status Quo*, Cassell, 2006

Saunders, Nicholas, *Alternative London Survival Guide for Strangers*, Nicholas Saunders, 1972.

Savage, Jon, *The Kinks*, Faber and Faber, 1984.

Schreuders, Piet, Lewisohn, Mark and Smith, Adam, *The Beatles' London*, Hamlyn, 1994.

Scott, Rebecca with Scott, Mary, *A Fine Kind of Madness: Ronnie Scott Remembered*, Headline, 1999.

Secrest, Meryle, *Somewhere for Me: a Biography of Richard Rodgers*, Bloomsbury, 2001.

Spark, Muriel, *The Ballad of Peckham Rye*, Macmillan, 1960.

Steele, Tommy, *Bermondsey Boy*, Michael Joseph, 2006.

Stewart, Tony (Ed.), *Cool Cats*, Eel Pie, 1981.

Thomas, Steven & Turner, Alwyn W., *Welcome to Big Biba*, Antique Collectors Club, 2006.

Thomson, Graeme, *Complicated Shadows: the Life and Music of Elvis Costello*, Canongate, 2004.

Time Out editors, *50 Best London Songs*, 25 September 2006.

Tomalin, Claire, *Samuel Pepys: the Unequalled Self*, Viking, 2002.

Tuer, Andrew W., *Old London Cries*, Leadenhall Press/Pryor Publications, 1885.

Turner, Steve, *A Hard Day's Write*, Carlton, 1994.

Various authors, *The English Broadside Ballad Archive*, University of California-Santa Barbara.

Widgery, David, *Beating Time*, Chatto & Windus, 1986.

Wilkins, Nigel, *Chaucer and Music*, Goldberg Magazine 22, 2003.

Wooldridge, Max, *Rock'n'Roll London*, New Holland, 2002.

Wyman, Bill, *Rolling with the Stones*, Dorling Kindersley, 2002.

York, Peter, *Modern Times*, William Heinemann, 1984.

Videos & DVDs

Music Hall Days, Green Umbrella, 2003.

Live Forever: The Rise and Fall of Brit Pop, Helkon Films, 2003.

Punk In London 77, Studio K7, 1991.

The Clash: Westway to the World, Sony, 1999.

Sex Pistols: There'll Always Be an England, Fremantle, 2008

Websites

www.arthurlloyd.co.uk
www.pauldunoyer.com
www.recordoftheday.com

Index

Abbey Road studios, 55, 96, 99, 106–7, 146, 225
Absolute Beginners (Colin MacInnes), 87–8, 90, 117, 154, 161, 167, 219
film of, 189, 244, 259
Ackroyd, Peter, 190, 282
Ad Lib club, 100–1, 103, 107, 145
Adam Ant, 6, 226, 244, 246
Addinsell, Richard, 62
Addison, Joseph, 9, 18
Adele, 278
Adu, Sade, 244, 253
African-American music, 18, 46, 56, 75–6
see also blues
Aitken, Laurel, 162
Alabama 3, 230
Albarn, Damon, 227, 256–8, 268, 280
Ali, Monica, 269–70
Ali G, 263
All Saints, 274
Allen, Chesney, 60
Allen, Daevid, 183
Allen, Keith, 259–60, 276–7
Allen, Lily, 259, 276–8
Allen, Woody, 134
Altham, Keith, 112, 159
Ambrose, Bert, 47–8, 56–7
Anderson, Brett, 227, 255–6
Andrews, Julie, 51, 54, 64–5
Angry Brigade, 178, 190
Apache Indian, 270
Arden, Don, 131–2
Armstrong, Louis, 55, 75, 181
Arulpragasam, Mathangi, 271
Asher, Jane, 96, 105

Asher, Peter, 105, 176
Asian Dub Foundation, 270
Asian music, 269–73
Astaire, Fred, 51, 63, 148
Aswad, 162
Auger, Brian, 152
Austen, Jane, 175
Ayers, Kevin, 183

Babyshambles, 278–9
Bacharach, Burt, 110
Bacon, Francis, 70
Bailey, David, 105
Baker, Danny, 225
Baker, Ginger, 141, 147–9, 159
Baldry, Long John, 141, 152
Baldwin, James, 102
Balfe, Dave, 256–7
Ball, Kenny, 90
ballads, 4, 43
broadside ballads, 11–14, 91, 268, 272
Ballard, J. G., 208
Bally Sagoo, 270
Bananarama, 245
Band, 198
Banister, John, 16
Barât, Carl, 278–9
Barber, Chris, 72, 75–6, 90, 141–2
barrel organs, 14–15, 29, 34, 48
Barrett, Syd, 182, 217
Barson, Mike, 234
Bart, Lionel, 39, 63, 81, 86, 89, 97, 102, 125, 194, 269
and David Bowie, 183–4
and *Oliver!*, 66–8, 131, 277

and Rolling Stones, 67, 105
and Tommy Steele, 78–80
Basse, William, 21
Baverstock, Jack, 144
Bayliss, Lily, 128
Beatles, 6–8, 55, 67, 74, 79, 81, 84–6, 90,
     95–7, 145, 167, 174, 228, 255, 257
   and Ad Lib club, 100–1
   and Asian music, 269
   and Bonzos, 163–4
   and Englishness, 105, 207, 278
   and Epstein's death, 102–3
   films, 16, 35, 102, 107, 109, 132, 164,
     240
   and Joe Brown, 83
   and psychedelia, 133, 133
   and Rolling Stones, 45, 97, 99–100, 109,
     111, 197
   rooftop concert, 108–9, 185
   and Sgt. Pepper, 103–4, 106, 146, 148, 182
   and song writing, 106–8, 132, 161
   and soul music, 152
   and Tara Browne, 107, 146
   and USA, 66, 111
   and Who, 127–8
Bechet, Sidney, 90
Beerbohm, Max, 31, 51
Bees Make Honey, 198
Beggar's Opera, The, 6, 18–20, 36, 64, 128,
     130, 261
Behan, Dominic, 154
Bell, Melissa, 278
Bellwood, Bessie, 25–7
Bennett, Cliff, 152
Bennett, Tony, 63
Berlin, Irving, 56
Bernard, Jeffrey, 70
Berry, Chuck, 98, 142–3, 225
Betjeman, John, 202, 279
Bevan, William, 268–9
Beverly, Frankie, 253
Biba, 190–2, 196, 214
Big Audio Dynamite, 245
Bilk, Acker, 90
Binge, Ronald, 62
Birch, William, 12
Black, Don, and John Barry, 63
Black & White Minstrels, 18

Blackburn, Tony, 115, 253
Blackwell, Chris, 161–2
Blair, Tony, 164, 258, 265
Blak Twang, 265, 267, 278
Blake, Peter, 200, 202
Blake, William, 18, 124, 138, 168, 211, 228,
     229, 248, 260, 263
Blind Faith, 149
Bloc Party, 279
Blockheads, 200–1
Blondie, 215
Blowup, 114, 220
blue beat, 161
blues, 57, 75–8, 90, 98, 114, 139–51, 153,
     159
   see also R&B
Blur, 26, 138, 233, 255–9, 277, 280
Bob and Marcia, 162
Bogart, Humphrey, 192–3
Bolan, Marc, 81, 117, 166–74, 176–8,
     180–3, 194, 249, 261
   and David Bowie, 131, 169, 172–3, 181,
     183, 186, 197
Bollywood, 269
Bond, Graham, 141, 147, 152, 176
Bonzo Dog Doo Dah Band, 163–4, 256, 259
boutiques, 104
Bovell, Dennis, 162
Bow Wow Wow, 226, 242, 244, 271
Bowie, Angie, 184, 188, 242
Bowie, David, 48, 55, 70, 107, 121, 179–94,
     205, 217–18, 255
   and Absolute Beginners film, 189, 244
   and Anthony Newley, 89, 182–3
   and blues boom, 143–4
   and Jubilee film, 226
   and London, 227–8
   and Marc Bolan, 131, 169, 172–3, 181,
     183, 186, 197
   and new romantics, 238–9, 242
Bowlly, Al, 55
Bowman, Derek, 194
Boy George, 138, 197, 227, 241–2, 246,
     252–3
Boyd, Joe, 157, 175
Bragg, Billy, 11, 154, 246–50
Brand, Russell, 261
'Brand New Cadillac', 84, 89

Brand New Heavies, 254
Branson, Richard, 176, 191, 204
Brecht, Bertolt, 20
Brel, Jacques, 183
Breslaw, Bernard, 88
Brilleaux, Lee, 202–3
Brinsley Schwarz, 198, 203, 220
Brithop, 254
Britpop, 116, 121, 135, 164, 233, 255–60, 278
Britton, Thomas, 16
Brooks, Louise, 213
Broonzy, Big Bill, 155
Bros, 138
Brown, Joe, 82–3, 228
Browne, Sam, 56
Browne, Tara, 107, 146
Bruce, Jack, 141, 147, 149, 158–9
Bruvvers, 83
Buckley, David, 192
Budgie, 84, 238
Burial, 269
Burke, Alexandra, 278
Burke, Solomon, 152
Burns, Tito, 86
Burroughs, William, 174
Burton, Tim, 66
Bush, Kate, 227–8
Bushell, Garry, 225
buskers, 226, 280
Butler, Bernard, 255
Bygraves, Max, 88, 181
Bynge, Ronald, 55, 162
Byrd, William, 7
Byron, Lord, 14

cabaret, 54, 188
Cabaret, 195, 205, 213, 239
Café de Paris, 54, 56, 59–60, 80
Caine, Michael, 114
Cale, John, 256
calypso, 90–2, 160–1, 163
Campbell, Alastair, 264–5
Campbell, Judy, 53
can-can, 35
Carbon/Silicon, 214
Carlos, Walter, 8
Carthy, Martin, 155–6

Catnach, Jeremy, 12
Cavemen, 79
Central Line, 253
Champagne Charlie, 26–7
'Champagne Charlie', 26–7, 43, 225
Champion, Harry, 25, 29, 65, 80, 83, 90, 129, 260
Chandler, Chas, 158
Chandra, Sheila, 270
Chaplin, Charlie, 31, 41, 56
Chapman, Michael, 155
Charles I, King, 228
Charles II, King, 4, 8, 16
Charles, Prince of Wales, 207
Charles, Ray, 152
Chas & Dave, 225, 258, 279
Chaucer, Geoffrey, 5, 20, 228
Cherry, Neneh, 253, 271
Chesterton, G. K., 37, 46, 55
Chevalier, Albert, 28–9
Chicken Shack, 150
Child, June, 170, 172
Chirgwin, George H., 32
Christie, Julie, 114, 122
Christy, Edward, 17
Churchill, Winston, 53, 56
cinema, 41, 88
Clapton, Eric, 110, 136, 140, 146–51, 155, 165, 195
    and Jimi Hendrix, 159
    and Marc Bolan, 170–1
Clark, Dave, 96–7
Clash, 2, 113, 163, 197, 207–13, 217, 218, 221, 225, 238–9, 249, 271
Cleave, Maureen, 100
Cleese, John, 42
Cliff, Jimmy, 162
Clockwork Orange, A, 8, 187–8, 195, 211, 245
Coates, Eric, 62
Coborn, Charles, 31–2
Cochran, Eddie, 83, 168, 199
Cockney Rebel, 184, 191, 194
Cockney Rejects, 224, 268
cockneys, 2, 24, 27–30, 58, 60, 88, 125, 227, 236
    cockney diaspora, 247
    dandies, 116, 237–8
cocktails, 46–7, 243

coffee bars, 77, 87, 163, 180
Cogan, Alma, 102
Cohn, Nik, 86, 100, 111
Coldplay, 279
Collins, Dave and Ansell, 162
Collins, Grenville, 120
Collins, Joan, 89
Collins, Phil, 67
Colyer, Ken, 72, 75, 99, 153
Commedia dell'Arte, 88
Como, Perry, 63
Conn, Leslie, 169, 181
Cook, Paul, 130, 204, 207
Cook, Robin, 248
Cooper, Lady Diana, 56
Copeland, Miles, 231
Cornershop, 270
Cornwell, Hugh, 156, 215
Costello, Elvis, 7, 198–9, 203, 215, 219–21,
    232, 252
costermongers, 27–8, 33, 49, 60, 89, 130,
    177, 236
Cotton, Billy, 61, 78, 88, 237
Count Suckle, 161
country music, 77–8
Coward, Noël, 6, 47, 49–54, 59–60, 67, 80,
    89, 114, 123, 158, 164, 199, 211, 262
  and Bryan Ferry, 192–3
  and Ian Dury, 42, 199
Cowell, Sam, 24
Coxon, Graham, 256–7
Coxson, Lloyd, 163
Crass, 222–3, 225, 247
Crazy Titch, 266, 268
Cream, 141, 147–8, 158
Crisp, Quentin, 70
Crombie, Tony, 77
Cromwell, Thomas, 12
Crosby, Bing, 159
Crowley, Aleister, 152
Crown, Don, 226
Culture, 210
Culture Club, 242–3
Cure, 227

Dagenham Dave, 216
Dagger, Steve, 239
Daltrey, Roger, 20, 84, 126–7, 130, 145

Damned, 173, 203, 208, 210, 213
dance orchestras, 55–7
d'Ancona, Matthew, 207
Daniels, Phil, 257
Dankworth, Johnny, 73–4, 77
Darwin, Charles, 202
Davies, Cyril, 57, 120, 141, 147
Davies, Dave, 119–20, 125
Davies, Ray, 42, 114, 118–26, 132, 134, 156,
    207, 244, 265, 280, 281
Davis, Billie, 152
Davis, Miles, 72, 117
Davis, Sammy, Jr, 89
Dawson, Les, 42
de Menezes, Jean Charles, 272
de Quincey, Thomas, 3
Dee Johnny, 144
Deep Purple, 205
Dekker, Thomas, 6
Delfont, Bernard, 102
Dene, Terry, 83
Denny, Sandy, 156
Depeche Mode, 227
Depp, Johnny, 66
Derek & the Dominoes, 149
Derek B, 254
Deviants, 176–7
Dexys Midnight Runners, 152, 215
Diana, Princess of Wales, 8, 244
Dickens, Charles, 14, 22, 24, 33, 36, 114,
    177, 222, 278
  and Barnaby Rudge, 204, 222
  and Oliver Twist, 66–8
  and Tommy Steele, 78, 80
Diddley, Bo, 142
Dietrich, Marlene, 60, 192
Difford, Chris, 230–3
Dire Straits, 230
Disney, Walt, 65
Disraeli, Benjamin, 37, 281
Dizzee Rascal, 12, 264, 266–8, 277
Do Not Adjust Your Set, 164
Dr Feelgood, 199, 202–4, 210, 217
Doherty, Pete, 278–9
Donegan, Lonnie, 75–6
Donovan, 155
Donovan, Dan, 245
Donovan, Terence, 245

Doonican, Val, 82
Dors, Diana, 145
Dowland, John, 7
D'Oyly Carte, Richard, 36–9
Drake, Charlie, 88
Drake, Nick, 155, 157–8, 161, 219
Driscoll, Julie, 152
drums, 2, 5–6
Ducks Deluxe, 198
Dunbar, John, 105–6, 176
Duncan, Jimmy, 144
Duran Duran, 8, 243
Dury, Ian, 13, 42, 198–204, 216, 221–2,
     231, 247, 249, 277
   and Kilburn & the High Roads, 191, 200,
     204, 234
   and Ray Davies, 124–5, 265
Dylan, Bob, 37, 101, 105, 145, 155–6, 165,
     174–5, 183, 190

Eagles, 214
East 17, 254
EastEnders, 88–9, 124
Eddie & the Hot Rods, 202
Edison, Thomas Alva, 38
Eel Pie Island, 2, 72, 141, 147, 188, 194
Egan, Rusty, 239
Eggs Over Easy, 198
Eighth Wonder, 244
Elastica, 233, 256, 271
Elen, Gus, 29–30, 88–9, 235, 263
Eliot, T. S., 40, 281
Elizabeth I, Queen, 7, 13, 222
Elizabeth II, Queen, 91, 94, 110, 144, 206
'Elizabethan Serenade', 62, 162
Enfield, Harry, 277
Eno, Brian, 192–3
Entertainer, The, 41
Entwistle, John, 126, 130
Epstein, Brian, 39, 81, 95–8, 100, 102–3,
     114, 127, 132
Equals, 112–13, 202
Ertegun, Ahmet, 148
Essex, David, 84, 194–5
Essex, 246–7
Estelle, 278
Etchingham, Kathy, 160
Eurythmics, 253

Everett, Kenny, 115
Evita, 195

Faces, 135–6
Fairport Convention, 156, 161
Faith, Adam, 77, 84–5, 96, 110, 168, 238
Faithfull, Marianne, 105–6
Falklands War, 248
Fame, Georgie, 152, 158
Farlowe, Chris, 152
Farren, Mick, 176–7, 209
Farthingale, Hermione, 184
Fat Les, 42, 259–60, 276
Feeling, 279
Fenton, Lavinia, 20
Ferry, Bryan, 54, 191–2
Festival of Britain, 122
fiddles and fiddlers, 2, 5, 21, 28
Fields, Gracie, 183
Finn, Mickey, 171, 174, 188
First World War, 15, 34, 40, 46, 48, 61, 222
Fitzgerald, Ella, 63
Fitzgerald, F. Scott, 46
Flack, Roberta, 154
Flanagan, Bud, 60, 269
Flanders and Swann, 62
Fleetwood Mac, 132, 141, 150
Fleming, Ian, 161
Flowered Up, 254
folk music, 114, 139, 153–6, 249, 251
   folk-rock, 136, 156–8, 219
Folly, The, 22
Formby, George, 183
Formby, George, Snr, 14
Four Tops, 102
Four Weddings and a Funeral, 4
Foxton, Bruce, 218
Frankie Goes To Hollywood, 243
Franz, Johnny, 110–11
Fraser, Robert, 106
Freeez, 253
Freud, Lucien, 256
Frischmann, Justine, 255–6
Frost, David, 86
funk, 209, 254
Fury, Billy, 81, 195

Galliano, John, 240

Gallimore, Florrie, 33
garage, 264–5
Gardiner, Boris, 162
Garfunkel, Art, 155, 225
Garland, Judy, 145
Gay, John, 18–20
Gay, Noel, 60, 70
Gee, Cecil, 71
Geldof, Peaches, 262
Generation X, 208, 214, 231, 245
Genet, Jean, 112
George I, King, 8
George III, King, 16
Geraldo, 61, 73
German bands, 14–15
Gershwin, George and Ira, 63
Gilbert and Sullivan, 20, 29, 36–9, 50, 65,
    78, 87, 102, 165
Gillespie Sells, Ben, 279
Gillett, Charlie, 198
Gina X, 239
Ginsberg, Allen, 174–5
Gish, Lilian, 128
glam rock, 151, 183, 190–8
Gonella, Nat, 55
Gong, 183
Good, Jack, 82–4, 86, 111
Good Old Days, The, 43, 207
Gordon Riots, 203–4, 222
Gosling, Ray, 87
Gosson, Stephen, 21
Grade, Lew, 102
Graham, Davy, 154–5
Grant, Eddy, 112–14, 202, 212, 253
Gray, Maisie, 51
Green, Benny, 74, 79
Green, Bill, 117
Green, Peter, 140, 150
Greene, Graham, 122
'Greensleeves', 6, 8, 19, 21, 65, 105, 107
Greer, Germaine, 148
Gregg, Brian, 83
Gregg, Hubert, 59
Greyhound, 162
Grimaldi, Joseph, 17
grime, 266–9
Grossmith, George and Weedon, 25
Groundhogs, 150–1

Gulf War, 212
Guthrie, Woody, 249
Gwynn, Nell, 8

Haley, Bill, 76, 199
Half a Sixpence, 80
Hall, Henry, 61
Hall, Jack, 13
Hamilton, Lady, 108
Hamilton, Patrick, 41, 70, 281
Hamilton, Richard, 106
Handel, George Frideric, 8–9, 19, 22, 146,
    158, 160
Handl, Irene, 277
Happy Mondays, 254
Hard-Fi, 279
Hardy, Thomas, 104
Harley, Steve, 184, 194
Harper, Roy, 155
Harrison, George, 83, 96, 101, 107, 148–9
Harrison, Pattie, 149
Harrison, Rex, 64
Harvey, Laurence, 87, 97
Hawkins, Coleman, 74
Hawkins, Sir John, 21
Hawkwind, 178, 209
Hayes, Tubby, 74
Haysi Fantayzee, 245
Healy, Jeremy, 245
Heath, Edward, 107
Heath, Ted, 57, 63, 74
heavy metal, 245–6
Heckstall-Smith, Dick, 195
Heinz, 86
Hemmings, David, 114, 220
Hendrix, Jimi, 9, 102, 110, 112, 145, 148,
    158–60, 175, 186, 195
Henry I, King, 3–4
Henry VIII, King, 8, 221
Henry, John, 125
Hepburn, Audrey, 64
Hewlett, Jamie, 280
hip hop, 28, 253–4, 263–5, 268
Hirst, Damien, 256, 259–60
Hitchcock, Alfred, 78
Hi-Tension, 253
Hitler, Adolf, 57, 60–1
Hogarth, William, 11, 259

Holiday, Billie, 63
Holland, Julian 'Jools', 230-3
Hollies, 112
Holloway, Stanley, 20, 26, 64, 89
Holly, Buddy, 78, 84, 168
Honri, Percy, 40
Hooker, John Lee, 145, 151
Hooper, Nellee, 254
Hopkins, John 'Hoppy', 175-6
Hopkins, Nicky, 141
Hoskins, Bob, 20, 124
Howard, Trevor, 165
Howlin' Wolf, 151
Humble Pie, 134
Hurley, Alec, 30
Hutchings, Ashley, 156-7
Hutchinson, Leslie 'Hutch', 56
Hynde, Chrissie, 124
Hype, 184

Idle, Eric, 164
Idol, Billy, 189, 214, 245
Ignorant, Steve, 222
'I'm Burlington Bertie from Bow', 31, 266
'I'm Henry the Eighth I Am', 8, 29, 83
Incognito, 253
Industrial Revolution, 40
Innes, Neil, 163-4
Internet, 245, 279
Iraq War, 265
Iron Maiden, 245
Italian Job, The, 54
'I've Got a Lovely Bunch of Coconuts', 61, 237

Jackley, Nat, 183
Jackson, Jack, 61
Jackson, Michael, 277
Jagger, Bianca, 188
Jagger, Jade, 262
Jagger, Mick, 77, 98-100, 105-9, 114, 159, 175, 182, 188, 215
  and blues boom, 140-3
  and song writing, 99-100, 132
Jam, 14, 50, 137, 210, 214-19, 235, 249, 255
James, Alex, 255-6, 259-60, 280
James, Jimmy, 152

James, Tony, 208, 214, 231, 245
James, Wendy, 245
Jamie T, 279
Jamiroquai, 254
Jankel, Chaz, 200
Jansch, Bert, 154-7, 159-60
Jarman, Derek, 56, 226
jazz, 32, 46-7, 50, 71-7, 87-8, 90, 98, 116, 153, 174
  acid-jazz, 219, 254
  and blues boom, 140-2
  and Bonzos, 163-4
Jazzie B, 253
Jenner, Peter, 170, 248
Jerome, Jerome K., 134
jigs, 6, 28
jingoism, 33-4, 52
Jobson, Eddie, 193-4
John, Elton, 107, 152, 227, 244
John's Children, 169
Johns, Glyn, 133
Johnson, Gary, 225
Johnson, Ken 'Snakehips', 60
Johnson, Robert, 146
Johnson, Wilko, 202, 217
Johnstone, Clarence, 56
Jolson, Al, 18
Jones, Brian, 98, 109, 114, 141, 144-5
Jones, Davy, 67
Jones, Gloria, 172-4
Jones, Kenney, 131, 135
Jones, Mick, 208-9, 214, 239, 245, 278
Jones, Peter, 97
Jones, Steve, 130, 204, 208
Joy Division, 243
Joyce, Mike, 252
Joyce, William (Lord Haw-Haw), 60
Jubilee, 226-7
Jukebox Jury, 48
Jupp, Mickey, 202

Kajanus, Georg, 194
Kano, 268
Kay, Neal, 245-6
Kemp, Gary, 236-41, 244
Kemp, Lindsay, 183, 226
Kemp, Martin, 238, 240
Kennedy, John, 79, 81, 100

Kensit, Patsy, 244, 258
Ketelbey, Albert, 62
Khayyam, Omar, 201
Kidd, Johnny, & the Pirates, 84, 226
Kilburn & The High Roads, 191, 200, 204, 234
Killjoys, 215
King Bees, 48, 181
Kinks, 90, 110, 116, 118–27, 129–30, 133, 140, 188, 216, 230, 250, 255, 277
    and song writing, 119–25
    'Waterloo Sunset', 2, 119, 122, 281
Kinnock, Neil, 248
Kirk, Roland, 74
'Knees Up Mother Brown', 65, 207, 223, 249
Kon-rads, 180
Korner, Alexis, 57, 120, 141, 147, 151, 176
Kraftwerk, 239
Krautrock, 204
Kray twins, 111, 145, 195, 211, 252
Kubrick, Stanley, 187–8
Kureishi, Hanif, 189
Kwesi-Johnson, Linton, 256

Labour Party, 247–8, 250
    New Labour, 258, 264–5
Lady Sovereign, 266, 268, 280
Lambert, Constant, 127–8
Lambert, Kit, 127–9, 158
'Lambeth Walk, The', 60–1, 268
Lane, Ronnie, 131–4, 136–7, 149
Langtry, Lily, 128
Laurie, Cy, 72
Lawrence, Gertrude, 50–2, 54
Layton, Turner, 56
Leadbelly, 76, 155
Lean, David, 89
Led Zeppelin, 148, 153, 156, 159, 196
Leigh Hunt, James Henry, 17
Lemmy, 160
Lennon, Cynthia, 96
Lennon, John, 45, 74, 76, 85, 96, 99–100, 102, 109, 133, 148–9, 183, 257
    and song writing, 38, 106–8, 132
    and Yoko Ono, 108, 176
Lennon, Julian, 96
Léotard, Monsieur, 33, 35

Lethal Bizzie, 267
Letts, Don, 21446
Lewis, Harry, 57
Lewis, Leona, 278
Leybourne, George, 26–7, 31, 33, 43
Leyton, John, 86
Liberace, 191
Libertine, Eve, 223
Libertines, 225, 278
Light of the World, 253
Limelight, 41
Little Richard, 76, 164
Livingstone, Dandy, 162
Lloyd, Bert, 154
Lloyd, Marie, 12, 30–1, 34, 40, 43, 54, 249, 263, 277
Loach, Ken, 228
Lockwood, Sir Joe, 102
Logan, Andrew, 191
London Calling, 50–1
London Nobody Knows, The, 31, 114, 235
London Posse, 254
'London Pride', 49, 53, 59
London SS, 208, 214
Lord Kitchener, 91, 160
Loss, Joe, 57, 61, 220
Love, Monie, 254
lover's rock, 162
Lowe, Nick, 203, 220
LSD, 107, 132, 148, 152
Lucas, Sarah, 256
Lulu, 148
Lwin, Annabella, 226
Lynch, Kenny, 85
Lynn, Vera, 12, 42, 57–8, 207, 225–6, 266
Lyttelton, Humphrey, 55, 72, 74

McCartney, Linda, 74, 101
McCartney, Paul, 74, 76, 85, 95–6, 101, 105, 159, 164–5, 175, 272
    and song writing, 6, 38, 54, 99, 106–8, 132, 161
McCartney, Stella, 262
MacColl, Ewan, 154–5, 250
MacColl, Kirsty, 154, 250–1, 277
Macdermott, G. H., 33
McFly, 279
McGowan, Cathy, 103

MacGowan, Shane, 251–3
Mackay, Andy, 192
McLagan, Ian, 131
McLaren, Malcolm, 81, 180, 191, 197,
    203–6, 218, 222, 226, 242, 245, 256,
    271
Maclaren-Ross, Julian, 70
McNair, Archie, 94
McPhee, Tony, 150–1
McTell, Ralph, 155, 157
McVie, John, 150
Madness, 12, 30, 42, 121, 124–5, 137, 200,
    228, 233–6, 255–6, 265, 268
Mael, Ron and Russell, 195
Maffia, Lisa, 264
Magoo, Johnny, OMB, 226
Manhattan Transfer, 191
Mankowitz, Gered, 218
Mantovani, 55, 58, 60
Margaret, Princess, 54, 63, 67
Marilyn, 242, 246
Marks, Louisa, 163
Marley, Bob, 162, 210
Marmalade, 134
Marr, Johnny, 252
Marriott, Steve, 67, 131–6
Martin, Bram, 55
Martin, George, 63, 86, 88
Marvin, Hank, 86
Mary II, Queen, 8
Mary Poppins, 64–6, 105, 183
Mason, James, 31, 114
Matlock, Glen, 204, 208
Matthews, Jessie, 48
Matumbi, 162
May, Phil, 142–6, 151
Mayall, John, 57, 141, 147, 150–1
Maybury, John, 240
Mayhew, Henry, 14–16, 28, 33, 130
Maytals, 210
Maze, 253
MC Romeo, 264
MC5, 143
Me and My Girl, 60–1
Meaden, Pete, 126–7, 129
Meek, Joe, 86, 97
Melanie, 205
Melly, George, 77, 79, 100–1, 114, 140, 229

melodrama, 32–3
Menswear, 256
Mercury, Freddie, 191, 196
Merton Parkas, 137
M.I.A., 271
Michael, George, 227, 242–6, 253
microphones, 41, 47
Miles, Barry, 176
Miller, Glenn, 74, 230
Miller, Max, 41–2, 76, 123, 125, 179, 199
Miller, Roger, 104
Millie, 161
Milligan, Spike, 74–5, 88
Milton, John, 228
Minogue, Kylie, 138
minstrel acts, 17–18, 32
Misty In Roots, 162, 224
Mitchell, George, 18
Mitchell, Guy, 80
Modley, Albert, 183
mods, 116–18, 120, 126–7, 129–31, 137–8,
    184, 216, 228, 240, 247, 255
  and Marc Bolan, 167–8, 183
  mods and rockers, 87–8, 118
  and reggae, 161–2
Money, Zoot, 152
Monkees, 67, 148
Monro, Matt, 63, 67, 89
Monty Python, 164
Moon, Keith, 126, 129–30, 135, 142, 164,
    195
More Fire Crew, 267
Morgan, Carl, 264
Morgan, Laurie, 71–2
Morrison, Bryan, 144
Morrison, Van, 75, 150, 165
Morrissey, 121, 243, 252–3, 256
Morton, Charles, 35, 39
Morton, H. V., 11, 222
Moss, Kate, 277, 279
Move, 134
Moyet, Alison, 253
Ms Dynamite, 264–5
Muddy Waters, 142
Murphy, Kieron, 171
Murvin, Junior, 210
music hall, 12, 17, 20, 24–36, 46, 50, 62,
    111, 215

and audience misbehaviour, 34–5
decline of, 40–4, 54
legacy of, 76, 83, 89, 109, 124–5, 133,
    148, 163, 165, 183, 207, 233, 249
and Oliver!, 67–8
and topical songs, 33–4
musical comedy, 36
musicals, 60, 63–8
David Bowie and, 187–8
Mustard, Earl of, 226
My Fair Lady, 64
Myers, Mike, 259

Napier-Bell, Simon, 81, 102–3, 129, 168–9,
    244
Nash, Kate, 278
National Front, 210–11, 248, 271
National Youth Jazz Orchestra, 274
Nelson, Lord, 108
Neville, Richard, 178
new romantics, 237–44
New Vaudeville Band, 164
New York Dolls, 191, 204
Newgate Gaol, 7, 13, 20, 91
Newley, Anthony, 67, 88–90, 129
and David Bowie, 182–3
Newtrament, 254
Nicol, Simon, 156
'Nightingale Sang in Berkeley Square', A,
    53, 56, 58
Nirvana, 143, 255, 257
Noble, Ray, 55
Norman, Philip, 106
Northern Soul, 137
Notting Hill Carnival, 92, 209–10
Notting Hill race riots, 87, 161
Novello, Ivor, 48, 51, 56, 158, 164, 266
Numan, Gary, 189, 227
Nureyev, Rudolph, 145
Nuttall, Jeff, 42

Oasis, 26, 137, 255, 258–9
O'Brien, Richard, 196
Ocean, Billy, 253
O'Connor, Hazel, 242
Oh Boy!, 82
Oklahoma!, 63–4
Oldfield, Mike, 176

Oldham, Andrew Loog, 81, 94–5, 97–9,
    105, 126–7, 131–4
and Rolling Stones, 94, 97–9, 103, 131
Oliver!, 66–8, 131, 183, 277
Olivier, Laurence, 20, 41, 52
Only Ones, 231
Ono, Yoko, 45, 108, 176
operas, 16, 36
rock operas, 128–9, 134, 146
operettas, 36–9
Orbital, 254
Original Dixieland Jazz Band, 46, 72
O'Riordan, Cait, 252
Ormsby-Gore, Alice, 170
Orwell, George, 15, 188, 235
Osborne, John, 41
Osman, Matt, 255
Owen, Alison, 277
Owen, Malcolm, 224

Page, Jimmy, 140
Page, Larry, 120
Panjabi MC, 270
pantomime, 17, 32, 41, 84, 86
Paramor, Norrie, 86
Parker, Charlie, 72, 74, 180
Parnes, Larry, 79–83, 88, 97, 102–3, 152,
    168, 180, 183, 205, 214, 245, 249, 276
Partridge, Andy, 215
Pearson, Hesketh, 38
Peel, John, 24, 115, 171, 176–7
Peellaert, Guy, 191
Peñate, Jack, 279
'penny gaffs', 32
Pepys, Samuel, 8, 10–11, 22, 78, 281
Peregrine Took, Steve, 170–1
Perfect, Christine, 150
Performance, 109
Perrett, Peter, 232
Pet Shop Boys, 110
Peterson, Gilles, 254
phonographs, 38
Pickett, Wilson, 148
Pilcher, Sergeant, 149
Pink Fairies, 178, 209
Pink Floyd, 146, 157, 175–6, 196, 213, 249
Pioneers, 162
Pitt, Ken, 181, 183

Pitt, William, 13, 265
Playford, William, 18
pleasure gardens, 21–2
Plunkett Greene, Alexander, 94
Pogues, 251–2
Police, 215, 231
Poly Styrene, 215–16
Pop, Iggy, 185–7, 279
'Pop Goes the Weasel', 25, 38, 89
Pop Group, 253
pop music, 134, 139–40, 244, 258, 276
Pope, Alexander, 19
Porter, Cole, 56, 59
Potier, Suki, 107
Powell, Enoch, 113
Presley, Elvis, 8, 76, 78, 80, 90, 167, 179,
    186, 204
Pretty Things, 133, 140, 142–6, 151, 176,
    188
Price, Antony, 192
Prince, Viv, 142
Prince, 60
Prince of Wales, 26, 56, 59
Printemps, Yvonne, 49
Private Eye, 234
Proby, P. J., 111, 145
Profumo affair, 110
pub rock, 198–9, 202, 214, 220
public houses, 20–2, 41, 43, 47
Puff Daddy, 60
Pulp, 255–6, 277
Punch and Judy, 15
punk rock, 42, 93, 138, 143, 151, 163, 173,
    189, 191, 196–9, 202–27, 231
    and new romantics, 238–9, 240, 243
    Oi! (skinhead-punk), 225–6
    and Pogues, 251–2
Purcell, Henry, 8, 128
Pursey, Jimmy, 223, 227

Q Magazine, 74
Quaglino's, 56
Quant, Mary, 93–5, 97, 104, 194, 256
Queen, 107, 196
Queen Elizabeth, the Queen Mother, 80, 127

R&B, 90, 98–9, 131–2, 141, 151–2, 161,
    181–2, 247, 273

R&B All-Stars, 141
radio (wireless), 41, 47, 62, 114–15
    and wartime, 57–8, 61, 78
ragtime, 32, 46
Rahere, Brother, 3–4, 7, 67, 80
Ramones, 143, 203
Rampling, Danny, 229
'Rat Catcher's Daughter, The', 24, 68
rave culture, 254
Razorlight, 279
Ready Steady Go!, 97, 103
Redding, Otis, 152
Reed, Lou, 107, 191, 230
reggae, 161–3, 204, 209, 214, 253
Reid, Jamie, 203, 206
Renbourn, John, 154–7
revues, 50–1
Rice-Davies, Mandy, 145
Rich, John, 17–20
Richard, Cliff, 67, 77, 86–7, 89
Richard, Wendy, 88
Richards, Keith, 98–100, 105, 114, 132,
    142, 279
Ridgley, Andrew, 242–4
Riff Raff, 247
Rigg, Diana, 188
Riley, Bridget, 256
Rimbaud, Penny, 222
Rip Rig & Panic, 253
Riviera, Jake, 220
Robey, George, 29, 42
Robinson, Dave, 220
rock 'n' roll, 54, 76–90, 111, 154, 163, 171,
    199
    and *Absolute Beginners*, 87–8
    and managers, 81–4
'rock culture', 139
rock operas, 128–9, 134, 146
rockabilly, 209
Rocky Horror Show, The, 196–7, 226
Rodgers and Hammerstein, 63–4
Rodgers and Hart, 39, 47–8
Rodney P, 254
Rogers, Bill, 91
Roll Deep, 267
Rolling Stones, 95, 97–101, 103–5, 108–9,
    113, 134, 159, 174, 207, 218, 246
    and Andrew Oldham, 94, 97–9, 103, 131

and Beatles, 45, 97, 99–100, 109, 111, 197
and blues boom, 140, 142
and Eric Clapton, 147
Hyde Park concert, 109, 177
and Kinks, 120, 123
and Lionel Bart, 67, 105
and Marianne Faithfull, 105–6
and R&B, 98–9, 181
Rock and Roll Circus film, 109
and song writing, 99–100, 132, 144
and tax exile, 165
and Who, 126–7, 129
Roosevelt, Franklin D., 53
Roots Manuva, 265, 267
Ross, Jonathan, 257, 261
Ross, Ronnie, 226
Rossi, Francis, 229
Rotten, Johnny (John Lydon), 81, 89, 204–8, 215, 222, 252
Rourke, Andy, 252
Rowland, Kevin, 215
Rowntree, Dave, 256, 280
Roxy Music, 191–4, 205, 233, 239
Royal Albert Hall, 83, 91, 149, 156, 174
Rutles, 164
Ruts, 224

S Club 7, 274
Sailor, 194
St Bartholomew's Fair, 3–5, 92
San-J Sanj, 270
Sarne, Mike, 88
Sassoon, Vidal, 94–5
Saturday Night Fever, 243
Sawhney, Nitin, 271–3
Sayer, Leo, 84
Scher, Anna, 238
Scorsese, Martin, 109
Scott, Jimmy, 108
Scott, Ronnie, 73–4, 79, 97
Scratchy, 266
Scrooge, 80
Sean, Jay, 270
Second World War, 43, 48, 52, 57–9, 74, 78
Secret Affair, 137
Seeger, Peggy, 154–5
Seeger, Pete, 155

Sellers, Peter, 88
Severin, Steve, 213
Sex Pistols, 2, 70, 130, 191, 197, 200, 202–8, 210, 213–16, 217, 224, 255
and grime, 267
Islington Green show, 43, 238–9
and Small Faces, 135, 204–5
and Vera Lynn, 57, 207
Shadows, 77, 86
Shakespeare, William, 2, 6, 12, 19, 33–4, 88, 97, 168, 282
Sham 69, 223, 235
Shapiro, Helen, 85, 167
Sharp, Cecil, 153
Sharp, Martin, 148
Shaw, George Bernard, 64
Shaw, Sandie, 84, 110, 112
Shelley, Percy, 228
Sherman, Richard and Robert, 65
Shields, Ella, 31
Shrimpton, Chrissie, 132
Shrimpton, Jean, 105
Sickert, Walter, 31
Sigue Sigue Sputnik, 245
Simon, Paul, 155–6, 225
Simone, Nina, 89
Simonon, Paul, 208, 280
Sinatra, Frank, 20, 60, 62–3, 159, 181
Siouxsie & the Banshees, 191, 213, 227
Sir Henry at Rawlinson End, 164–5
6.5 Special, 82
ska, 138, 161, 235
skiffle, 75–6, 78–9, 141–2, 153, 167
skinheads, 162, 177, 223–4, 235, 272
Skinner, Mike, 265–7, 277
Slim Chance, 136
Slits, 208, 226
Small Faces, 2, 43, 57, 67, 85, 116, 130–7, 216, 230, 232, 266
'Itchycoo Park', 66, 133
and Sex Pistols, 135, 204–5
Smith, W. H., 37
Smiths, 243, 252, 255
So Solid Crew, 264
Soft Machine, 175–6, 183, 257
Sondheim, Stephen, 66
Sopranos, The, 230
Soul II Soul collective, 254, 278

soul music, 114, 139–40, 151–2, 159, 247, 254
  see also R&B
Spandau Ballet, 188, 228, 240–1, 244
Sparks, 195–6
Spears, Britney, 269
Specials, 234
Spectator, The, 9
Spector, Phil, 97, 111
Spencer Davis Group, 152
Spice Girls, 60, 259, 274
spivs, 70–1
Springfield, Dusty, 110, 112, 219
Springsteen, Bruce, 250
Squadronaires, 126
Squeeze, 30, 125, 221, 228–33, 277
SS *Empire Windrush*, 90–1
Stamp, Chris, 127, 130, 158
Stamp, Terence, 104–5, 122
Stanshall, Vivian, 163–5, 195, 247
Star!, 51
Stardust, 85, 195
Starr, Ringo, 96, 99, 159, 172, 195
Status Quo, 217, 229–30
Steele, Tommy, 43, 67, 77–83, 86, 100, 111, 167, 180, 195, 280
Stephen, John, 117–18, 132
Stevens, Cat, 155
Stevens, Guy, 211
Stewart, Al, 155
Stewart, Rod, 132, 134–7, 140, 152, 194, 213
Stigwood, Robert, 102, 147–8
Sting, 7
Stone, Lew, 47
Strange, Steve, 239–40, 246
Stranglers, 156, 215
Stratton, Eugene, 32
street performers, 14–16, 24, 280
  see also buskers
street traders, 9–11, 53, 65, 78, 85, 89, 182, 201
Streets, 89, 264–6
Strummer, Joe, 199, 202, 208–9, 211–13, 215, 239, 249, 259, 276
Style Council, 219
Suede, 51, 255–6
Suggs, 200, 234

Sway, 265
Sweeney Todd, 66
swells, 26, 31, 35
Swift, Jonathan, 19
Sylvester, Victor, 61
Symarip, 162

Tallis, Thomas, 7, 223
Talmy, Shel, 127
Tate, Catherine, 263
Taylor, Derek, 100
Taylor, Dick, 142–6
Taylor, Roger, 196
Taylor, Vince, 84, 89, 186
Taylor-Wood, Sam, 256
Teddy boys, 88, 167, 199–200, 203, 206, 229
television, 18, 41, 61–2, 82, 88
Telex, 239
Temperance Seven, 164
Temple, Julien, 207, 244, 259
Tennyson, Alfred Lord, 30
Thackeray, William Makepeace, 24
That'll be the Day, 195
Thatcher, Margaret, 225, 243, 247
Theatres Act (1843), 24
Them, 150
This is Spinal Tap, 66
Thomas, Dylan, 70
Thompson, Richard, 55, 156–7
Tiddy Doll, 11
Tilbrook, Glenn, 230–2
Tilley, Vesta, 31, 34
Tin Pan Alley (Denmark Street), 67, 69–70, 76–7
Tinchy Stryder, 266
Tipica Orchestra, 55
Top of the Pops, 212, 222, 242, 248, 250
Tornados, 86
Townshend, Pete, 114, 125–30, 132, 137, 159, 175, 181, 184, 195–6, 228
Traffic, 153, 161, 219
Transvision Vamp, 245
Travers, Pamela, 65
Tremeloes, 134
Trinder, Tommy, 26, 43, 207
Turner, Tina, 142
Tyburn, 7, 11, 91–2, 205

Tyrannosaurus Rex (T. Rex), 169–73, 176–7, 186

underground, 174–8
Up the Junction (Nell Dunn), 228–9, 264

Valentine, Dickie, 63
Van Dyke, Dick, 64, 66, 258, 280
Vance, Alfred, 26–7, 33
Vanian, Dave, 213
Variety Bandbox, 78
vaudeville, 25, 40, 65, 183
Velvet Underground, 143, 177, 184, 191, 214
Vicious, Sid, 81, 208, 251
Vincent, Gene, 83, 186
Vipers, 77
Virgil, 18
Visconti, Tony, 170, 172–3, 196

Wace, Robert, 120
Wailers, 162, 210
Walker, Johnnie, 115
Walker, Scott, 111–12, 195
Walker Brothers, 111–12, 219
Wall, Max, 41–2, 199, 259
Walpole, Robert, 19, 265
Warhol, Andy, 185
Warren, Betty, 27
Washington, Geno, 152
Waterhouse, Keith, 125
Watts, Charlie, 98, 141
Waugh, Evelyn, 46
Wayne, Jeff, 195
Weill, Kurt, 20
Welch, Bruce, 86
Welch, Elisabeth, 56
Weller, Paul, 50, 116, 131, 135, 203, 216–19, 221, 223, 227, 240, 249
West, Kanye, 278
Westwood, Vivienne, 197, 203–5, 214, 226
Wham!, 81, 169, 243–6
Wheeler, Caron, 254

Whistling Jack Smith, 104
Whiteman, Paul, 46
Whittington, Dick, 1, 119
Who, 20, 109, 116, 125–30, 134–5, 137, 140, 212, 216, 240, 255
    and David Bowie, 181, 188
    and rock operas, 128–9, 146
Whyton, Wally, 77
Wilcox, Toyah, 226
Wilde, Marty, 81–2
Wiley, 264, 266–8
Williams, Robbie, 54, 67
Williamson, Sonny Boy, 140, 142
Willingale, Thomas, 222
Wilson, Harold, 107
Wilson, Keppel and Betty, 235
Winehouse, Amy, 20, 273–6, 278
Winston, Jimmy, 131
Winters, Mike and Bernie, 79
Winters, Tiny, 47
Winwood, Muff, 196
Winwood, Steve, 152–3, 164–5
Wodehouse, P. G., 46, 63
Wood, Peggy, 50
Wood, Ronnie, 134, 137
Wordsworth, William, 5, 228
Worried Men, 77
Wyatt, Robert, 183
Wyman, Bill, 98

X Factor, The, 279
X-Ray Spex, 215
XTC, 214

Yardbirds, 81–2, 140, 147, 169, 181, 188
York, Peter, 193
Young, Arthur, 58
Young, Lester, 74
Young, Mary, 19
Young, Paul, 253
Young Growler, 91
Young Tiger, 91